The 1970s

AMERICA IN THE WORLD

The 1970s

A NEW GLOBAL HISTORY

FROM CIVIL RIGHTS

TO ECONOMIC INEQUALITY

Thomas Borstelmann

PRINCETON UNIVERSITY PRESS
PRINCETON AND OXFORD

Published by Princeton University Press, 41 William Street,
Princeton, New Jersey 08540
In the United Kingdom: Princeton University Press,
6 Oxford Street, Woodstock, Oxfordshire OX20 1TW
press.princeton.edu
All Rights Reserved

Library of Congress Cataloging-in-Publication Data

Borstelmann, Thomas.
The 1970s : a new global history from civil rights to
economic inequality / Thomas Borstelmann.
p. cm. — (America in the world)
Includes bibliographical references and index.
ISBN 978-0-691-14156-5 (hardcover : alk. paper)
1. United States—History—1969– 2. United States—Social
conditions—1960–1980. 3. United States—Politics and
government—1969–1974. 4. United States—Politics and
government—1974–1977. 5. United States—Politics and
government—1977–1981. 6. United States—Economic
conditions—1971–1981. 7. United States—Foreign
relations—1945–1989. 8. United States—Commerce—
History—20th century. 9. Equality—United States—History—
20th century. 10. Nineteen seventies. I. Title.
II. Title: Nineteen seventies.
E839.B59 2012
909.82'7—dc22   2011007790

British Library Cataloging-in-Publication Data is available
This book has been composed in Sabon

Printed on acid-free paper. ∞

Printed in the United States of America

10 9 8 7 6 5 4 3 2 1

For my brother John,

foundation and best friend of my 1970s

This is the growing complication of the modern condition, the expanding circle of moral sympathy. Not only distant peoples are our brothers and sisters, but foxes too, and laboratory mice, and now the fish.

—Ian McEwan, *Saturday*

The market gives people what the people want instead of what other people think they ought to want. At the bottom of many criticisms of the market economy is really lack of belief in freedom itself.

—Milton Friedman, "The New Liberal's Creed"

Here's where the concept of neoliberalism—the idea of the free market as the essential mechanism of social justice—is genuinely clarifying. A society free not only of racism but of sexism and of heterosexism is a neoliberal utopia where all the irrelevant grounds for inequality (your identity) have been eliminated and whatever inequalities are left are therefore legitimated.

—Walter Benn Michaels, *The Trouble with Diversity*

CONTENTS

ILLUSTRATIONS

PREFACE AND ACKNOWLEDGMENTS

WE ALL HAVE OUR HISTORIES. Most of mine was shaped in the 1970s. I turned twelve years old in 1970 and twenty-two in 1980. In between, I played a lot of basketball, fell in love with literature, left home, had my first jobs and girlfriends, spent time hitchhiking, and graduated from high school and college. I grew up. And coming of age in the 1970s did not mean just surviving orange shag rugs, polyester clothing, inflation, and national uncertainty. For me, it also included watching powerful people have their corruption exposed, learning to love the outdoors, taking spiritual searching seriously, and imbibing the struggle of half the people I knew—women—for equality and respect. This was liberating and exhilarating, and I learned to be political: to try to keep my eye on power, to see who had it and how they used it, who benefited and who did not. While some people in the "Me Decade" turned away from the sphere of public life and politics, I was fascinated by it.

We all have geographies, too. Mine was fairly expansive in this decade, split roughly in thirds between the South, New England, and the West. An extended stay in Italy and visits to Mexico, Greece, the United Kingdom, and, a few years later, China widened my perspective. Along the way, I was blessed with enduring friendships that inevitably colored the 1970s with a positive hue. I was fortunate to live in two of the most beautiful places on earth—Florence, Italy, and Fallen Leaf Lake, California. I was, in the words of Canadian songwriter Bruce Cockburn, "cut by the beauty of jagged mountains" and have never completely recovered from the wound.[1] My Seventies involved a lot of extremely good fortune and stumbling into majesty and love and grace. It made me grateful.

I have been thinking about this era for thirty years, and I have had a lot of help along the way, from family in particular.

My oldest brother, John "JB" Borstelmann, taught me the most at the time and has laughed with me the most ever since, as we have examined and reexamined our intersecting paths through that decade. My older brother, Michael Borstelmann, was, as our father put it, "countercultural before the counterculture," modeling a gentler and kinder manner than almost anyone I knew. He helped me more than he may ever imagine. My older sister, Nancy Chandler, provided encouragement and a robust example of independent, back-to-the-land living. My parents, Jane and Lloyd Borstelmann, gone on now and much missed, gave us a home that was lively, literate, tolerant, and generous. They were the ground of my 1970s and my work as a historian. My wife, Lynn Borstelmann, is my same age, and though we did not meet until 1986, she took a roughly parallel path through the Seventies and we have compared notes now for twenty-five years. Indeed, we may even have crossed paths, unawares, somewhere in the second half of the decade, along the campuses or byways of Durham, North Carolina, my hometown and her college town.

Several readers made this a better book, rescuing me from a slew of embarrassing errors and forcing me to reconsider several issues. They will recognize their handiwork in the best parts that follow. For any faults in the book they bear no responsibility, since those faults mark precisely where I bullheadedly chose not to follow their advice. JB Borstelmann and Elaine Tyler May combed the manuscript with a degree of care that was extraordinarily generous, and each nurtured the project with enthusiasm and penetrating intelligence. Tom Bender and an anonymous reader for Princeton University Press provided unusually helpful and insightful feedback. Suzanne Mettler cheered for the book from the beginning and shared the wisdom of a political scientist in improving it. Andrew Preston offered a kindly endorsement and detailed suggestions, as did Steve Willborn. David Painter threw me a life ring on oil. Daniel Sargent, Jeffrey Engel, Ken Osgood, and Lew Erenberg invited me to present aspects of the book to audiences at, respectively, Harvard University, Texas A&M University, Florida Atlantic University, and

Loyola University of Chicago, where I received thoughtful and challenging responses. My able agent, Lisa Adams of the Garamond Agency, helped place the book at Princeton University Press, where Brigitta van Rheinberg, Sarah Wolf, and the rest of the staff upheld their reputation for professionalism and efficiency. Copyeditor Karen Verde rescued me from several mistakes. The University of Nebraska provided crucial financial support. For their concern for the author and the completion of the book, I am grateful to Suzanne Mettler, Daniel and Elizabeth Nelson, and those with whom I live, my wife Lynn and our sons Danny and John.

For a historian, working on the recent past has peculiar challenges. Our perspective is still necessarily limited. If journalism is the first draft of history, contemporary history is merely the second draft. The past changes as our perspective changes, and the passage of time is crucial for deepening our understanding. Unavoidably, our views of the era of the 1970s will continue to evolve as the future unfolds. But thirty years after the decade ended, enough time has passed to begin to open up new perspectives on the significance of what happened then in the United States and the world.

What I found after I began the research for this book was not fully what I had expected. The usual version of U.S. history in the 1970s offered a tale of decline, uncertainty, and self-centeredness. I knew there was plenty of truth in that story, but it also seemed inadequate—and it certainly did not match the lively, exciting, and contentious era that I remembered living through. So I went looking for the optimistic reformers I had known: the feminists, environmentalists, evangelicals, new immigrants, and others. I found them, and they are an important part of this book. But I also found a story of citizens' faith being transferred from the public sector to the private sector, from government to business, and of public policy shifting in the same direction. And I encountered an international story with a similar trajectory that provided crucial context for developments in the United States. These discoveries allowed the project to become not a comprehensive history of the world in the 1970s, but an interpretation of the American past in its global context.

The result is a book shaped by the evidence found, rather than one limited to the concerns with which the research began. I have aimed at honest history, a history in which all who appear here may read it and be able to recognize themselves and their perspectives, proffered in good faith. I have my own views about the developments at the center of this story, of course, and they inevitably shape this presentation of the years from 1973 to 1979. But this book is not a work of polemic or policy recommendation. It is an effort to explain a crucially important shift in the recent past about which my own feelings are mixed. Making sense of the present, and deciding what to do about it, require understanding the past rather than trying to reshape it to fit our liking.

T. B.
Lincoln, Nebraska

THE 1970S ARE A DECADE of ill repute. "A kidney stone of a decade," one character in the popular cartoon strip *Doonesbury* called it. The nation's core institutions seemed to be breaking down as the United States, in most tellings of the story, sank into a mire of economic decline, political corruption, and military retrenchment. The last U.S. combat troops left Vietnam in defeat and demoralization, a new outcome for armed forces that, despite something closer to draws in the War of 1812 and the Korean War, had little experience with outcomes other than victory. The United States withdrew from, or scaled down, much of its presence in international affairs, from Southeast Asia to Panama to Iran. Public confidence in the nation's leadership withered. Richard Nixon disgraced the office of the presidency in the Watergate scandal and became the nation's first chief executive to resign. Gerald Ford could not overcome his status as an appointed president to get elected in his own right, while Jimmy Carter failed to win reelection.

None of the three presidents brightened the country's dimming economic prospects. An eightfold increase in the price of oil stemming from Middle Eastern turmoil exacerbated inflation from Vietnam War spending, which combined with a slowing economy to create the new dilemma of "stagflation." Americans' confidence in the economic future of their families sank. The nation's largest city, New York, came within a whisker of declaring bankruptcy in 1975. Neither major political party offered compelling solutions to the country's serious problems. Ford, a longtime U.S. congressman from Michigan, recalled how as a freshman in the House of Representatives he had listened to President Harry Truman describe the state of the union as "good." When Ford's own chance came to make the annual presidential address, on January 15, 1975, he was blunt: "I must say to you that the state of our Union is not good."[1]

If the nation's military, political, and economic institutions sputtered in the 1970s, the private lives and culture of its citizens seemed equally wracked by confusion and failure. Families, the traditional foundation of American society, unraveled amid soaring divorce rates. This change brought liberation and relief to millions of people, but also psychological distress and considerable downward mobility for many women and children. Another measure of dissatisfaction was the widespread use of addictive drugs, ranging from legal versions such as alcohol and prescription medications, to recreational ones such as marijuana and cocaine, to unforgivingly destructive ones such as heroin. One nonpartisan critic suggested wryly that the fact that Ford and Carter had actually lived in the White House was "a possible explanation for the rampant substance abuse at the time." Another measure of uncertainty was a distinct decline in the percentage of collegians who agreed that "students are morally obligated not to cheat" on exams. Basic matters of cultural taste also seemed out of whack, particularly in retrospect. The appeal of orange shag carpets, polyester pantsuits, wide ties, the "happy face" logo, and disco music was mysterious to many Americans at the time and to more ever since. Only films seemed to improve, artistic creativity being often associated with periods of turmoil and uncertainty. Recalling the decade as a time of "bad hair, bad clothes, bad music, bad design, bad books, bad economics, bad carpeting, bad fabrics, and a lot of bad ideas," writer Joe Queenan noted "the widespread feeling that America had taken a totally wrong turn in the '70s."[2]

Historians and other analysts have described the 1970s in a similar vein. The decade served as a "virtual synonym for weakness, confusion, and malaise," historian Andreas Killen declared in his revealingly titled book, *1973 Nervous Breakdown*. Pulitzer Prize–winning historian David Kennedy lamented "the odd blend of political disillusionment and pop-culture daffiness that gave the 1970s their distinctive flavor." Two of the best historians of these years, Beth Bailey and David Farber, found them to be perhaps "our strangest decade," a period of "incoherent impulses, contradictory desires, and even a fair amount of self-flagellation." Observers such as Philip Jenkins and David Frum portrayed a nation in the throes of cultural anxiety and moral decline, while others emphasized the origins of the modern conservative movement that arose partially in response to the sense of disorientation that was so pervasive at the time. The familiar narrative of the 1970s offers a largely depressing and forgettable decade, one most Americans were happy to see end.[3]

The decade's neighbors, chronologically speaking, are part of the problem. Both the 1960s and the 1980s have clear story lines of strong reforming forces, exciting social and political conflicts, and significant international engagements. Both decades also experienced considerable economic growth and much less inflation, allowing most Americans a good deal more confidence about their future prospects. Each of these other decades has developed a substantial literature of memoir and historical analysis. For the 1970s, this is somewhat akin to the old problem faced by historically minded residents of North Carolina who referred to their state as "a valley of humility between two mountains of conceit," South Carolina and Virginia. The 1970s has a similar status, falling between two "real" decades, when important movements and great events happened, for better or worse.[4]

Upon closer examination, however, the decade turns out to be a crucial period of change and adjustment that reshaped the contours of American history and indeed global history ever since. Beneath the surface waves of economic, political, and cultural challenges that have captured the most attention flowed two powerful undercurrents. One was a spirit of egalitarianism and inclusiveness that rejected traditional hierarchies and lines of authority, asserting instead the equality of all people, particularly women, gays and lesbians, people of color, and the disabled—that is, the majority of people. For most Americans, "the 1960s" really happened in the 1970s. Even animals found a place in this inclusive vision through the Endangered Species Act of 1973.

The second powerful undercurrent was a decisive turn toward free-market economics as the preferred means for resolving political and social problems. Well before the election of Ronald Reagan to the presidency in 1980, Americans across the political spectrum had shifted from a faith in the benefits of some collective action through government intervention, represented by the New Deal order that culminated in the Great Society programs of the 1960s, to a new commitment to purer market values instead as the key to an efficient economy and a fair society. These same two undercurrents of egalitarianism and market values gained significant traction in the 1970s throughout the world, as empires declined and capitalism spread. The United States was thus quintessentially a part of, rather than an exception to, the broader world around it in this decade. While sometimes at odds with each other, egalitarian values and market values converged to form a purified version of individualism and consumer capitalism, one in which all were welcome as buyers and sellers, but the devil might take the hindmost.[5]

These years marked a transformation in American society that has gone largely unnoticed, even though its reverberations are still being felt decades later. It was the moment when the United States fully embraced two profound yet in some ways antagonistic values: formal equality and complete faith in the marketplace. Together, these prototypical American beliefs created a society committed to treating everyone equally, while simultaneously becoming increasingly unequal. Hyper-individualism has been the result: everyone can and should compete, in the pursuit of individual advantage and happiness. Americans have, by example and by influence, promoted this combination of equality in word and inequality in deed around the world.

In the decades after 1970, life in the United States, particularly in its public sphere, became strikingly diverse and inclusive. No other great power—and certainly no dominant world power—had been so shaped by people with ancestors from all over the world. And Americans became accustomed to a culture of formal equality. Women, men, gays and lesbians, heterosexuals, whites, nonwhites, able-bodied and disabled: all were to be officially treated equally. Overt discrimination was illegal and widely reviled. "Racist" became one of the worst epithets. Women now ran large corporations, sat on the Supreme Court, and filled half of graduate and professional schools and more than half of undergraduate colleges. Black and female politicians served as leading contenders for the highest offices in the land. Of course, private prejudice and its very real negative impacts still endured— a powerful legacy of a bitter history. But the public expression of prejudice in the United States by the new millennium was furtive and usually costly. An American from as late as the 1960s, brought forward in a time capsule, would have been startled by the egalitarian, inclusive flavor of contemporary America.

Side by side with the commitment to equality was an American culture of faith in the market. Confidence in the mechanisms of supply and demand had replaced confidence in government management. The military filled its ranks with volunteers, not with a draft of all eligible citizens. Deregulation of business—airlines, banks, credit card companies—had the support of both major political parties. Welfare provision had the support of neither: people should be on their own, to rise and fall as they deserved, according to mainstream political thinking. Taxes and social spending remained distinctly lower than in other industrialized nations. Americans generally believed the marketplace solved problems by providing profit incentives for efficient production of whatever was needed. Across the political spectrum from Republicans to Democrats, the private sector was associated primarily with virtue and efficiency while the public sector of government continually had to defend itself and its budgets. Long gone were the New Deal order of the 1930s to the 1960s and its confident use of an activist federal government.

The consequences of this market faith, however, were complicated. The logic of the market was to give people whatever they wanted, whether inexpensive toys at Wal-Mart or the online pornography and gambling that had metastasized into vast industries. The increasing coarseness of American culture in the twenty-first century, measurable in public profanity, sexuality, and violence, as a visit to any movie multiplex confirmed, fed on the celebration of individual consumer choice. The only morality of the market was efficiency. Free markets were certainly not "conservative" in any meaningful sense of the word. Rather than conserving anything, the unconstrained pursuit of profit through economic exchange brought constant and often relentless change, as the American Rust Belt demonstrated by the loss of its manufacturing base and jobs to the Sun Belt and to overseas places with lower costs of production. Small business owners knew too well the radical changes brought by large corporate chain stores. The economist Joseph Schumpeter had famously called this dynamic the "creative destruction" of capitalism. Indeed, capitalism had been perhaps the greatest force for change, for better and worse, in the modern world. For social and religious conservatives concerned about the preservation of a particular kind of social order and the shaping of a moral citizenry, the unrestrained indulgence of individual consumers should have been anathema. For a generation after the 1970s, the Republican Party reigned in American politics by holding together its two primary wings, social conservatives and free marketers, but the inherent tension between these two constituencies reemerged in the 2008 presidential primary and seemed unlikely to disappear completely. The conservatism that pervaded American politics after the 1970s was considerably more libertarian than puritanical.[6]

Whatever its other benefits or drawbacks, the process of unleashing market forces deepened economic inequality in the United States for the generation after the 1970s. A society increasingly committed to treating everyone equally was, in practice, increasingly unequal. Indeed, this very inclusiveness actually provided a kind of cover for economic inequality; declining discrimination seemed to mean that remaining differences among individuals' circumstances were their own responsibility. Identity politics wound up bolstering class differences. Our task is to examine this paradox of growing equality and growing inequality, and to explain how it reshaped America and the world in the 1970s.

Chronology, the old saying goes, is the historian's best friend. The past unfolds across time, and change over time is the historian's primary quarry. But isolating the time frame for any particular story is fraught with challenges. In the present case, the logic of focusing on the decade of the 1970s seems clear enough, yet, on careful inspection, that logic can become elusive. No magical powers adhere to numbers that end with 0; people's lives and important trends unfold with little regard for the beginnings and ends of decades. Other ways of organizing these years abound, using different criteria: 1965–73 as the period of full-fledged U.S. combat in Vietnam, 1969–77 as the years of Republican control of the White House, or 1979–85 as the era of the renewed Cold War. Each of these periodizations can be compelling for different reasons. "In trying to make sense of American politics and attitudes," writer Louis Menand has argued, "the decade business is a complete distraction."[7]

In fact, the years at the center of this particular story are those from 1973 to 1979. Like a line of thunderstorms rolling across the prairie, a series of jolts hit Americans in 1973, leaving them uncertain of what new weather would come along behind this powerful storm front. U.S. troops withdrew from Vietnam; the cover-up of the Watergate scandal unraveled amid calls for the president's impeachment; the oil embargo by Arab members of the Organization of the Petroleum Exporting Countries (OPEC) began, while Nixon unplugged the dollar from the gold standard and average real wages (adjusted for inflation) declined for the first time in forty years. "Any one of these events would have challenged America's image of itself," Andreas Killen wrote, and together they provided a roundhouse punch to the national psyche. Some visceral shocks had hit earlier, such as the assassinations and war protests of 1968, amid much talk of revolution among young radicals, and those blows had loosened the sense of national cohesion and a predictable narrative of where the world was headed. But the heavy weather of 1973 was clearly coming in to stay longer, and everyone was going to get at least a little wet. Across the next six years squalls continued to blow in, down to the nuclear near-disaster at Three Mile Island in 1979 and the seizure of American hostages later that year in Tehran. The early 1970s marked the time when, in the most important regards, Americans crossed a divide into a new watershed of what Beth Bailey and David Farber have astutely called "productive uncertainty."[8]

It was not immediately clear how productive the new uncertainty would be. Mostly, it made people poorer, an inevitable result of inflation, though many families held their own by sending more members, teenagers and especially women, out into the paid workforce. Few were inclined to look to their government for solutions, for the share of Americans with a "great deal" of confidence in the president and the Congress plunged from more than 40 percent in 1966 to 13 percent by 1975. Broader personal freedoms from traditional constraints—of dress, hair, language, sexual behavior, gender roles—contributed to this uncertainty and, for many, an increased sense of vulnerability and even crisis. "America is moving out of Vietnam after the longest and most divisive conflict" since the Civil War, renowned journalist James Reston wrote in the *New York Times* on January 24, 1973. "There has been a sharp decline in respect for authority in the United States as a result of the war—a decline in respect not only for the civil authority of government but also for the moral authority of the schools, the universities, the press, the church and even the family." Many of the most creative historians were turning away from grand political narratives to focus instead on social histories of narrower and less familiar, less elite subjects. Because the engine of U.S. history seemed somehow to have jumped the tracks, derailing after a generation of affluent confidence, citizens and historians alike found their old certainty about the country's unique place in world history slipping away. "It is our Bicentennial Year, and we don't seem to know how to celebrate it," prominent Washington journalist Elizabeth Drew wrote in 1976. "Our history began so grandly, and it doesn't seem so grand anymore." Many bicentennial celebrations around the country took a local approach, avoiding contentious national issues by focusing instead on folk culture, such as genealogy, quilting, bluegrass music, and local history. Reston concluded, "Something has happened to American life, something not yet understood or agreed upon, something that is different, important and probably enduring."[9]

In the mid-1970s, Americans tended to think of themselves no longer as a chosen people, but more often as survivors: of the Vietnam War, of cancer, "of the sinking ships, burning buildings, shark attacks, zombie invasions, and other disasters and trage- dies that reflected the siege mentality and were staples of Hol- lywood in the era," as historian William Graebner put it. Presi- dent Ford, the most amiable national leader of the era, survived two separate assassination attempts in November 1975. Ameri- cans were dismayed at hostage crises in which no one was res- cued, such as the eleven Israeli athletes and coaches seized and executed by Palestinian terrorists at the Munich Olympic Games in 1972, and they increasingly identified with Israel as the ulti- mate survivor nation due to the Holocaust of European Jews in World War II. Survivor stories were popular. In 1974, Piers Paul Read published a best-selling paperback, *Alive*, that recounted the extraordinary tale of sixteen young men from the Uruguayan national rugby team whose plane crashed into the snowy side of an Andes mountain peak near the Chilean-Argentine border. They survived for ten weeks in the freezing, high-altitude cold before rescuers finally located them, and it soon became clear that their feat hinged upon eating the well-preserved bodies of some of the other twenty-nine passengers who had died in the crash. Reviewers and readers applauded the young men's deter- mination to make it out of the mountains alive. In 1980, the American Psychiatric Association's *Diagnostic and Statistical Manual of Mental Disorders* added post-traumatic stress disor- der (PTSD) to its roster, an explicit recognition of the ongoing experiences of Vietnam War veterans but also a metaphor for American society as a whole by the end of the 1970s.[10]

When the familiar world begins to disintegrate, when the center seems no longer to hold, when authorities are revealed as corrupt, when things turn out to be quite different from what one has long believed, the crucial question becomes: How does one respond? This is the moment where uncertainty becomes productive—or not. Will it be liberating, a breaking free of old, unexamined assumptions to new wisdom and new action? Or will it be enervating, sapping one's faith in other people and in the possibilities for social reform and improvement? Does knowledge empower or dismay, when the emperor turns out to have no clothes? On the answers to these questions hinged the course of the 1970s and the path of American history and much of world history ever since.

One option in response was rage. Simmering anger pervaded many American lives in the 1970s. The sense of national failure in Southeast Asia and the revelation of corruption in the White House created frustration, which declining real wages and rising unemployment exacerbated. Because women and people of color in these same years were shedding much of their traditional deference and workplace segregation, many white men's unhappiness at least temporarily focused on women and blacks, something visible in the white backlash against school busing and some men's resentment of what they disparagingly called "women's libbers." But the rage that bubbled underneath the surface was not limited to any particular group of Americans. Hollywood captured it best in dark vigilante films such as *Dirty Harry* (1971) ("Go ahead, make my day," the eponymous, trigger-happy detective played by Clint Eastwood instructs the bad guys, hoping they'll give him a reason to shoot them) and *Taxi Driver* (1976) (the paranoid Vietnam veteran portrayed by Robert DeNiro promises to "wash all this scum off the streets"), as well as with a lighter touch in *Network* (1976), in which a likeable but disaffected television news anchorman embodied his viewers' frustrations by denouncing social chaos, consumerism, economic decline, and the media itself in a broadcast tirade. The anchorman commanded his audience to "get up right now and go to the window, open it, and stick your head out, and yell, 'I'm as mad as hell, and I'm not going to take it any more!'" This line became a common, only partly parodic slogan in the year of the Bicentennial.[11]

Another response to the perfect storm of public and private trauma rolling through American society was to ratchet up a sense of irony and skepticism. Things were not as they seemed on the surface—presidents lied, U.S. soldiers committed war crimes against civilians, the Communist Chinese were no longer enemies but potential allies—so keep your guard up, don't take things at face value, and assume ulterior motives on the part of people in charge. Above all, don't be a sucker, and keep your distance. The 1970s did not create irony, but they gave it a mighty boost as a default setting, partly in reaction against the now naïve-seeming quest of so many young people in the previous decade for authenticity and sincerity.[12] One of the most popular films of the era, *Blazing Saddles* (1974), sparkled with irony as it maniacally satirized the most heroic genre of moviemaking, the Western. A witty, worldly black sheriff rides to the rescue of a small desert town's dully racist citizens, aided by a washed-up, alcoholic white gunman he finds in the town jail. As the two unlikely heroes, in this early version of a biracial buddy film, ride off at the end into the sunset to the swelling strains of classic Western movie music, the camera lingers, and lingers, until the duo dismount, hand their horses to assistants, slap hands, climb laughing into a waiting limousine, and head off the set bound for the bright lights of town. The tough, honorable, lonely protectors of society were no more.[13]

The turn to irony and the disinclination to take things at face value fed the growth of postmodernism in the realms of philosophy and literary criticism. Postmodernism emerged in the 1970s as a mood and a sensibility, a stance against the certainties of modern life, whether of the Left or Right, of religion or socialism, of progress or reason, of any coherent narrative of history leading anywhere foreseeable. Postmodernists understood reality as socially constructed—that is, as only perceivable through the particular interests represented by particular language or discourse, and not as something eternal and objectively knowable. Viewing any permanent truth as a kind of hoax and therefore all cultures as having equal claims to truth, postmodernist thought was fundamentally relativist and bolstered the idea of multiculturalism. A central text for postmodernism was Edward Said's *Orientalism* (1978), which offered a powerful critique of how Westerners had long dominated but little understood the Middle East and Asia. Said himself, however, had little tolerance for the more extreme versions of postmodernism that considered language all-important, as he observed that human rights, for example, "are not cultural or grammatical things, and when violated are as real as anything we can encounter." At its best, postmodernism challenged people to examine the assumptions embedded in the language they used, and the power relations implicit in those assumptions.[14]

Beyond resentment and ironic detachment was a broader tendency to turn inward from public to private life, to focus on one's self rather than the corrupt or unknowable larger world. This is the version of the 1970s most frequently cited, the "Me Decade" famously labeled by journalist Tom Wolfe, though that label would prove to be an even more apt description of the following ten years. A new emphasis on self-improvement, self-expression, self-gratification, and self-indulgence moved to the center of American culture, to the detriment of more community-oriented values. For novelist Dana Spiotta, life in Los Angeles in 1974 seemed "as if someone had taken the aura of the counterculture and extracted every decent aspiration. What was left was the easy liberation of sex and drugs." The knowing slogan, "Better living through chemistry" (originally a DuPont advertisement), referred primarily to illegal drugs, but legal ones were even more prevalent. The anti-depressant Valium reigned as the largest-selling drug of the decade, peaking in 1978 with nearly 90 million bottles prescribed annually—the same year former First Lady Betty Ford admitted her addiction to it. Personal freedoms pushed ahead of long-term commitments; marriage rates declined, divorce increased, fewer children were born.[15]

The engagement of Americans with community activities dropped off. Political scientists have measured the beginning of the decline of political participation and "social capital"—the sinews of shared civic life and social engagement—in the contemporary United States from the 1970s, when citizens became decreasingly likely to vote, join civic organizations, trust the government and each other, or even have company over for dinner. In a famously insightful but politically maladroit speech on July 15, 1979, President Carter observed that "in a nation that was proud of hard work, strong families, close-knit communities and our faith in God, too many of us now tend to worship self-indulgence and consumption." One of the scholars Carter consulted in the weeks leading up to that address was historian Christopher Lasch of the University of Rochester, whose best-selling book, *The Culture of Narcissism*, had just been published. Lasch wrote regretfully that "to live for the moment is the prevailing passion—to live for yourself, not for your predecessors or posterity."[16]

Yet another response to the traumas and changes of the 1970s was to reject them and call for a return to an earlier era, one of remembered national strength abroad and a home front not yet struggling with rising crime and divorce rates, legal abortion, court-ordered school busing, and expensive energy. The new conservative movement that would reshape contemporary American politics is most frequently dated to Ronald Reagan's election as president in 1980. Yet Reagan's ruggedly handsome visage as the symbol of conservatism might be better understood by analogy to Yosemite's El Capitan, the most famous mountain in his home state of California for rock climbing, a sport that boomed in the 1970s. El Capitan appears a smooth, monolithic face from afar, but turns out, when viewed up close as climbers do in ascending a rock face, to contain all kinds of cracks, ledges, corners, and overhangs. Similarly, the conservative movement was not a monolithic team but an amalgam of at least three major wings: those concerned primarily with social issues such as crime, drug abuse, abortion, gender roles, and sexual preferences; those focused on liberating the economy from government regulation and management; and those determined to reassert U.S. political and military hegemony in international affairs.

These social, libertarian, and neoconservative elements of modern conservatism did not mesh easily. After all, it was not easy to make a government both stronger (for moral and military purposes) and weaker (for economic purposes) at the same time. Reagan helped the movement coalesce and hold together with an optimistic style and likable manner that made all three wings feel he belonged to them, along with his "Eleventh Commandment" to "speak no ill of another Republican." All of these elements of the Republican Party found their first mainstream political traction in the turmoil of the 1970s, including Reagan's own nearly successful campaign for the party's presidential nomination in 1976, and they shared a common desire to rebuild a more unified and more powerful nation.[17]

For many more Americans than has generally been recognized, the years of uncertainty and disillusionment in the mid- to late 1970s turned out to be something different: an unprecedented opportunity to press for reform and improvement of American society. Environmentalists, political reformers, human rights activists, and evangelical Christians all sought enthusiastically to reshape American life along what they saw as healthier lines. Egalitarian reformers were most important of all, led by women who in the 1970s surged past the old barriers that had constrained them in education, work, public life, and personal relationships. This feminism directly affected more American lives, female and male, than any previous reform effort, as it challenged people to reconsider assumptions and behaviors regarding what it meant to be—and to act on a daily basis as—a male human being or a female human being. Some women challenged the very meaning of gender, revealing how it varied in different times and places, rather than being *the* eternal, essential form of human identity. The intimacy of women and men, of girls and boys, in each others' lives meant that few families were untouched by this rising wind of change. Between 1973 and 1979, the United States developed a more egalitarian culture.[18]

The new inclusiveness in the United States reflected a worldwide trend in the same direction. As Americans moved to eliminate the remnants of discrimination from public life—against women but also against the disabled, non-European immigrants, and homosexuals—so, too, did the world make a major turn in the 1970s away from formal inequality, colonialism, and empire. In the European sphere, the last great overseas empire, Portugal, caved in with the liberation of Angola and Mozambique. The penultimate racist state, minority white-ruled Rhodesia, gave up the ghost and was transformed into Zimbabwe, while the final wave that would soon wash minority rule out of neighboring South Africa, the last redoubt of legal white supremacy, began to build in the black township of Soweto. In the less formal U.S. sphere of empire, Vietnam fought its way free of American occupation, Panama negotiated a return of its control of the Canal Zone, Nicaragua overthrew the brutal pro-American dictatorship of the Somoza family, and Iran did the same by driving Shah Reza Pahlavi into exile. In the Soviet sphere, empire entered its terminal stage when Red Army troops marched across the Amu Darya River into Afghanistan and into eventual disaster. Dissident movements in Russia and Eastern Europe gained traction, leading to the creation in Poland of Solidarity, the first labor union in a Communist state—an extraordinary admission of the failure of Communism to achieve its supposed highest priority, the well-being of the working class. Across the globe, human rights organizations such as Amnesty International became an important force in international affairs in the 1970s, and old hierarchies of race and sex lost much of their power to be understood as natural and right.[19]

Replacing the now clearly artificial hierarchies of race and sex in the 1970s was a new hierarchy considered more natural: the sorting out of people in what were seen as their natural socioeconomic levels by the operation of the free market. With unnatural barriers based on irrelevant group identities eliminated from public life, free marketers—sometimes known as neoliberals or libertarians—could more readily claim that the inequalities remaining were the just and reasonable result of letting the natural laws of supply and demand operate and letting people rise and fall on the basis of their abilities and how hard they worked. People were both more equal and less equal than they used to be. What was understood to be "natural" in social relations had changed. Historian George Fredrickson called this "a global capitalism that draws no color line, because it seeks customers and collaborators from every race." William Weidner, the president of Las Vegas's huge Venetian gambling resort, explained this dynamic in regard to the recent rapid increase in the number of Asian gamblers in the southern Nevada city: "This is a merit system here. The highest quality players will get whatever they want. The Chinese are the highest and best quality players in the world, so they'll have preference. We don't care how tall you are, how short you are, how fat you are, what color you are. Green is the most important color."[20]

The turn toward free markets in the 1970s was a global rather than just an American story, in the same way that the shift toward greater formal equality and inclusiveness in this decade was a worldwide rather than a national process. In the Southern Cone of Latin America, in western Europe and particularly in the United Kingdom with the 1979 election of Conservative Margaret Thatcher as prime minister, and in Eastern Europe in its early anti-Communist organizing, people across the globe were losing faith in the welfare states and socialist states that had emerged from World War II. They were turning instead to the mechanism of the market as a way to stimulate economic growth after the worldwide recession of the early 1970s. The vast scale and diversity of human societies assured that such a trend was not uniform and did not happen everywhere at the same time. Vietnam and Nicaragua, for example, spent the 1970s building revolutionary socialist states of their own kind. But even those exceptional boats paddling upstream would soon, within ten years, be turned around and swept along with the rising current of the capitalist river. The most dramatic evidence came in the largest country, the one that had also long had the most fervidly anti-capitalist government: China. Following the death of Mao Zedong in 1976 and a brief interlude of intra-governmental struggle in Beijing, a new regime under Deng Xiaoping moved forcefully by 1978 to introduce market reforms in order to speed its economic growth. World economic history has not been the same since.

The expanding formal recognition of the dignity and equal worth of all people, both in the United States and around the world, arrived, then, not at a time of socialist or even liberal hopes, but at a moment of capitalist resurgence. The confluence of a new commitment to legal and cultural equality with an equally strong drive toward free markets produced a version of capitalism increasingly purified of the inefficiencies of artificial discrimination. The feminism that filtered throughout mainstream American life was not, for the most part, the more radical 1960s dream of making new women and men or creating a more caring and compassionate society. It was instead a feminism narrowed mostly to the channel of individual rights and equal opportunity for competition as individuals. All would be included—on juries, on playing fields, in corporations, everywhere—but only as individuals. Ever since, women have been increasingly able to choose a lifestyle of whatever mix of family life and work life that they can put together, mostly on their own. The new egalitarianism did not change the system, but included all within the system, one marked by individual choice, the logic of consumer capitalism. A de facto agreement had emerged that seemed to say: all are welcome to join the game now, but we're dropping our gloves and playing for keeps, with no more state regulation to act as referee. Welcome, and you're on your own.

An unexpected and little noticed result of this peculiar confluence of egalitarianism and market values in the 1970s was a striking reversal in the contents of the public and private spheres of American society. What had long been considered essential elements of public life, such matters as taxation, military service, welfare provision, and economic regulation, began to shift out of the realm of government responsibility and into the private sphere where markets ruled. The market rather than a draft created soldiers; taxes were sharply cut back; airlines and other industries were freed from regulation. And what had long been considered concerns of the private sphere, such as religious faith, family life, and sexual behavior, moved instead into the mainstream of public life. Politicians began to assert their personal relationships with God; divorce shed its aura of shame and became commonplace; contraception, abortion, and homosexuality seized public attention. Discretion and restraint started to seem quaint in a culture increasingly monopolized by explicit sexuality. A 2006 headline in the nation's leading conservative newspaper captured a bluntness that would have been unimaginable in that venue a few decades earlier: "New Network Will Showcase Greed, Lust, Sex." Suggestions to limit the sharply widening gap between the wealthiest Americans and their fellow citizens, by contrast, were a touchier subject, one regularly denounced by affluent political leaders as a form of unpatriotic "class warfare" that could weaken the social cohesion of the country. The reversal of public and private spheres stemmed directly from the changes of the 1970s.[21]

Crucial political and cultural developments often stand out more vividly in retrospect than at the time. This is part of the attraction of doing history. Amidst the confusing crosscurrents of the 1970s, it was not clear that the United States would emerge both more committed to formal equality in the public sphere and less actually equal in measurable economic terms, due to the shift toward deregulation and freer markets. Nor was it obvious that this would be part of a global trend. There was always contention over these developments as the era unfolded. But hindsight, while not perfect, does reveal that the years between 1973 and 1979 witnessed a critical transition that made American society simultaneously more equal and less equal, and American culture still more individualistic, than they had been before.

Chapter 1

CROSSCURRENTS OF CRISIS IN 1970S AMERICA

BIG TROUBLE splashed into most Americans' lives in the 1970s. Few symbols embodied this as fully as the 25-foot great white shark that rose from the murky depths to devour swimmers and terrorize a Long Island beach town in the blockbuster movie, *Jaws.* The film opened on June 20, 1975, after an unprecedented television advertising campaign, and quickly became the first movie to earn over $100 million, the model for future summer blockbusters, and one of the two most popular films of the decade (along with 1977's *Star Wars*). *Jaws* spawned a series of spoofs and parodies, including a towering hit man in a subsequent James Bond film with sharpened metal teeth who was nicknamed "Jaws." But the film's extraordinary success stemmed from its ability to tap into a range of popular fears. One was the common anxiety about deep water and what might lurk below the visible surface, especially beyond the artificial clarity of chlorinated swimming pools. Another was the memory of the last great threat to cruise just beneath the waters of the nation's Atlantic coast, killing unsuspecting Americans on the surface: the German U-boats of the early months of World War II in 1942. Most obviously, the efforts of the town's leaders in the film to cover up the shark attacks in order to preserve the tourist trade evoked for Americans in 1975 pervasive concerns that authorities, for their own interests, might be keeping some hidden evil from public view. In the era of investigations of the My Lai massacre in Vietnam, the Watergate scandal, and CIA efforts to assassinate foreign leaders, such concerns were more realistic than paranoid.

Three years earlier, another very popular film had used different dangers of the deep to examine growing anxieties about

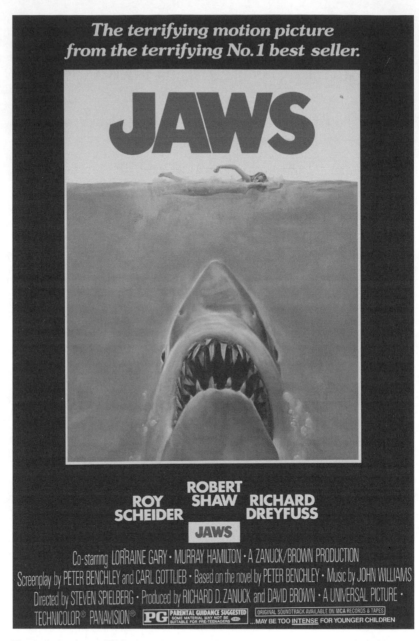

FIGURE 1.1.
Americans by the 1970s learned to worry about unknown dangers hidden beneath the surface. Released in 1975, *Jaws* was the first big summer blockbuster film. Courtesy Universal Studios.

where American society and perhaps all of Western culture were headed. In *The Poseidon Adventure* (1972), a tidal wave—improbably in the Mediterranean Sea—capsized a cruise ship bound for Greece, leaving the boat upside down and requiring the passengers to escape up through the bottom or hull. At one level a simple escapist adventure tale, the film also raised larger questions. With ancient Greece, the cradle of Western civilization, lost as a compass and everything turned literally upside down— by the civil rights struggle, by antiwar protests, by the counterculture and the movement for women's liberation—how were people to survive and go forward in this new era? A charismatic Roman Catholic priest, played by Gene Hackman, provided guidance to the other passengers for an escape from disaster. He was bound for work in Africa, "the future" as he called it, a multicultural, inclusive view of the world beyond just Europe and of the United States beyond just European Americans. While *Jaws* reflected the shift in the second half of the 1970s toward sheer entertainment and profit-making, *The Poseidon Adventure* also imagined disaster but captured some of the optimism of egalitarian reform that still motivated many American citizens in the first half of the decade.[1]

Events of the previous decade of the 1960s had knocked loose certain longstanding foundations of American society and thought. Traditional hierarchies of whites over nonwhites, men over women, and adults over youth no longer seemed commonsensical or even acceptable. Popular attitudes, particularly among younger Americans, toward sexuality, dress, and language were more tolerant and less judgmental, the standards of acceptable behavior less clear. This less confident culture was then buffeted by powerful crosscurrents in the 1970s that reshaped both the nation and the world beyond it. Military, political, economic, and environmental crises unfolded rapidly on top of each other, leaving many citizens uncertain of which to address first and how to do so. In the backwash of defeat in Vietnam and humiliation from the Watergate scandal, and in the midst of inflation and an oil crisis, distrust of government pervaded American society. The loss of confidence in public authority laid the foundation for deregulation and a turn toward the free market, a path that led to growing disparities between rich and poor. At the same time, the more tolerant and individualistic mainstream American culture increasingly rejected old forms of group discrimination and inequality.[2]

Challenges to the economy affected Americans most immediately throughout the 1970s. Rising unemployment, persistent high inflation, and the loss of manufacturing jobs through deindustrialization made the future uncertain. One of the people at mid-decade who best articulated the fears and hopes of working-class and middle-class citizens came out of a humble background in the small New Jersey town of Freehold. Singer and guitarist Bruce Springsteen recorded four albums in the 1970s, vaulting to fame and the covers of both *Time* and *Newsweek* in October 1975 with his third album, *Born To Run*, as he gave eloquent voice to quiet desperation and hopes for personal transcendence, if only in the private sphere of a speeding car at night. These were smaller, narrower dreams, framed more individually, than the great public causes of the 1960s. The United States was in for a rougher ride now, and comfort would be found in small doses. Springsteen's popular vision was deeply egalitarian and inclusive—the iconic cover of *Born To Run* showed the white musician leaning fondly on his bandmate, black saxophonist Clarence Clemons—but was also imbued with a sorrowful sense of the slipping economic prospects of so many citizens. The America Springsteen evoked in the mid-1970s was both more equal and less equal than it had been.[3]

TROUBLE ABROAD

More than 200 million people lived in the United States in the 1970s. Widely diverse in age, income, personality, ethnicity, family circumstances, life experiences, and a host of other characteristics, Americans recognized their common ground most clearly in national crises, events that visibly shaped the entire country. The foremost issue that had loomed over American life since 1965 was the U.S. war in Southeast Asia, and it brought little comfort. From the first combat troops wading ashore in South Vietnam that spring, the U.S. military commitment escalated steeply, reaching an apex of more than 500,000 American soldiers in the country in 1968 and 1969. Victory in the political struggle for the loyalties of the South Vietnamese remained elusive, however, even as superior firepower enabled U.S. forces to inflict enormous damage on their mostly Communist enemies and on the millions of civilians caught up in the fighting. Stalemate on the battlefield, rising American casualties, and declining support at home for the war encouraged the Nixon administration to begin bringing U.S. troops home, as did Nixon's recognition of the futility of the war and his plan to refocus U.S. foreign policy toward balancing China and the Soviet Union. The steady process of withdrawal from 1969 onward, accompanied by further buildup of South Vietnam's own military forces, led to the last U.S. combat troops leaving Vietnam in March 1973. The United States had clearly not won this war, and how and why the war had been lost remained the subject of contentious debate for decades to come.[4]

Nixon and his chief foreign policy adviser, national security adviser and later Secretary of State Henry Kissinger, understood that withdrawing U.S. forces from Vietnam meant an implicit admission of defeat. Ideally, the South Vietnamese government that the United States had created in 1954 and sustained ever since would survive on its own. But Nixon and Kissinger were far too clear-eyed in their view of Southeast Asia to expect that the corrupt, unpopular regime in Saigon would be any match for the coalition of disciplined North Vietnamese regular army forces and their insurgent Communist allies in the South, the National Liberation Front (disparaged by Saigon and Washington as the "Vietcong," a pejorative term meaning roughly "Vietnamese Commies"). Nixon and Kissinger instead hoped merely for what became known as a "decent interval" between the departure of the last U.S. troops and the triumphant arrival of Communist forces in Saigon. The longer that interval lasted, the less obvious might be the link between these two events, and the less attention that might be paid internationally to an apparent U.S. defeat. To Nixon's assertion that "South Vietnam probably is never gonna survive anyway," Kissinger agreed: "So we've got to find some formula that holds the thing together a year or two, after which—after a year, Mr. President . . . no one will give a damn." Nixon and Kissinger were keenly sensitive to the perceptions of others, both enemies and friends, and sought to extract the United States from a lost war while preserving as much of its reputation for toughness and military competence as possible.[5]

The corrosive effect of a long, slow withdrawal over four years, even if intended to bolster an ally, spread unease among Americans abroad and at home. Most dramatically, four more years of war resulted in the deaths of 21,000 more U.S. soldiers as well as over half a million Vietnamese, both combatants and civilians. Inevitably, a policy of slow, steady troop withdrawals made clear that the United States was no longer in the war to win it, and military morale plummeted. Official U.S. Army figures for these years listed nearly eight hundred fraggings—attempts by military personnel to murder a superior officer—while the real number may have been much higher. Drug use metastasized throughout the ranks, reaching well beyond just marijuana. By 1973, the Pentagon admitted that a third of all army enlisted men had tried heroin. The goal of eighteen-year-old draftees was simply "to turn 19" and get back home again. Racial tensions, desertions, disrespect for officers, and antiwar organizing among GIs proliferated, piling on top of accusations of war crimes against Vietnamese civilians, most infamously the murder of hundreds of women, children, and old men at the village of My Lai in March 1968, a story covered up by the army until late 1969. In 1971, Marine Colonel Robert Heinl wrote in the *Armed Forces Journal* that the U.S. Army remaining in Vietnam "is in a state approaching collapse" and had reached "the lowest state of military morale in the history of the country." Decorated Vietnam veteran and future U.S. senator John Kerry famously asked an April 1971 hearing of the Senate Foreign Relations Committee, "How do you ask a man to be the last man to die for a mistake?" Being forced to continue fighting a war that clearly had been lost was a recipe for disaster, and the American military spent the rest of the decade trying to rebuild its morale.[6]

Vietnam veteran and memoirist Tobias Wolff recalled visiting a particularly edgy and unhappy U.S. base at Dong Tam in South Vietnam, where he saw "something that wasn't allowed for in the national myth—our capacity for collective despair." He drew a biblical analogy. "A sourness had settled over the base, spoiling and coarsening the men. The resolute imperial will was all played out here at empire's fringe," Wolff concluded, "lost in rancor and mud. Here were pharaoh's chariots engulfed; his horsemen confused; and all his magnificence dismayed." Before the Vietnam War, and across the sweep of U.S. history, such comparisons with ancient Egypt or any other great empire were rare among Americans, who long imagined themselves instead as the model of anticolonial self-government. "We Americans are the peculiar, chosen people, the Israel [not Egypt!] of our time; we bear the ark of liberties of the world," wrote novelist Herman Melville a century before. Even U.S. expansion seemed neither imperial nor self-interested to most of its citizens, who tended to see in American military success abroad a sign of divine approval. "We but pitch the tents of liberty farther westward, farther southward," Senator Albert Beveridge declared during the U.S. annexation of Hawaii and the Philippines in 1898. Such faith about the tents of liberty was hard to hold by the early 1970s. The publication of the Defense Department's previously classified official history of the war, known popularly as *The Pentagon Papers* (1971), and such journalistic accounts as David Halberstam's *The Best and the Brightest* (1972) revealed incompetence and extensive deception of the American public by its leaders, as well as something less than liberty in South Vietnam. By April 28, 1975, when helicopters began evacuating the last Americans from Saigon in a scene whose photographs became iconic symbols of U.S. defeat, most Americans wanted nothing more to do with Vietnam. Gallup polls showed public opinion running 54–36 against even granting refuge to America's allies, the anticommunist South Vietnamese, some of

FIGURE 1.2.
On April 29, 1975, anticommunist South Vietnamese try to scale the wall of
the U.S. Embassy in Saigon, hoping to reach evacuation helicopters, as the last
of the Americans depart from Vietnam. Courtesy AP Photo/Neal Ulevich.

them literally hanging from the skids of those helicopters in desperate flight from the victorious Communists. Close the door and put Indochina behind us, was the prevailing sentiment.[7]

The discovery that the United States was perhaps not the unique, special, ever-victorious nation its citizens had tended to assume marked a watershed in modern American history, a crisis of identity. Rather than being *the* exceptional nation, the United States now appeared to be much like other great nations across time, with some of the same strengths and some of the same challenges. In particular, it was an at least temporarily defeated imperial power in economic decline, marred by political corruption all the way to the top of its government. Freed from the burden of proving their nation's unique virtue in the face of growing evidence to the contrary, many politically engaged citizens found it refreshing to take a new, more skeptical, but also more realistic view of the United States. If knowing the truth could set one free, freedom might be coming on strong. Others, however, were not so happy. Conservatives and nationalists regretted what they called the "Vietnam Syndrome," in which uncertainty and self-doubt prevented the nation from acting effectively abroad, particularly in military fashion. Neither the Ford nor Carter administration was ultimately able to overcome this perception of military and political weakness. Ford did use naval force in response to the Communist Cambodian government's brief seizure of the U.S. container ship *Mayaguez* in May 1975, slaking a little of the considerable thirst on the Right for striking back vigorously at those disrespectful of the American flag. "It shows we've still got balls in this country," declared Senator Barry Goldwater (R-AZ). But the rescue operation cost forty-one American lives in order to free forty hostages, who turned out to have been already released before the U.S. naval operation began. The Vietnam Syndrome continued to haunt U.S. foreign policy decision-making well beyond the 1970s.[8]

For the United States, the war in Vietnam mattered most in what it meant for the larger Cold War. U.S. policymakers feared that the perception of American weakness in Indochina would embolden Soviet and Communist aggression elsewhere, the concern behind the "decent interval" strategy for withdrawal. For the most part, leaders of the newly independent nations believed in their self-designation as the "Third World," part of neither the capitalist First World nor the Communist Second World. Sometimes consciously, they followed the same path of the American revolutionaries of 1776 who took advantage of the Great Power struggle of that era between the British and the French in order to win their independence. Third World leaders tried to stay out of the Cold War while playing each side off against the other for various benefits. With the U.S. defeat in Vietnam still fresh, with the U.S. government in confusion over the Watergate scandal, and with the American public unhappy about overseas adventures and dogged by rising economic problems at home, the Soviets bid for fresh influence abroad, particularly among new, nominally socialist governments in Africa such as Angola and Ethiopia. It turned out that the Soviet Union was actually entering a period of profound economic stagnation and political sclerosis in the Kremlin, and in just a few years would invade Afghanistan, a decision that led directly to the collapse of the USSR. But for a few years in the mid-1970s, both Soviet leaders and American conservatives believed that the opposite was happening, that the United States was losing the Cold War competition for global influence.[9]

Angola became, briefly, a flash point of conflict in the post-Vietnam struggle over the U.S. role in world affairs. The last great overseas European empire dissolved in 1975 as Angolans and Mozambicans fought their way free of Portuguese control. Having won home rule, Angolan factions now began the fight over who would rule at home. The more pro-Western National Union for the Total Independence of Angola (UNITA), backed by the apartheid regime in South Africa that ruled neighboring Namibia, lost ground to the socialist Popular Movement for the Liberation of Angola (MPLA), which received some aid from the USSR but more important assistance from Cuban troops. Ford and Kissinger hoped to slow this advance by directing the U.S. Central Intelligence Agency (CIA) to provide large-scale support to the pro-Western forces, determined that the U.S. debacle in Vietnam not translate into other leftist advances around the world. Anti-imperialists in Congress hit the roof. Empowered by an infusion of liberal Democrats in the November 1974 elections in the wake of the Watergate scandal and Nixon's resignation, reformers in Congress refused to allow the United States to slide into another potential Vietnam-style commitment by engaging in a joint intervention with South Africa. Senator Dick Clark (D-IA), chair of the African Affairs Subcommittee, visited southern Africa, spoke in support of the end of white rule there, and held hearings in Washington to raise public awareness of a part of the world few Americans paid attention to, at least not since the slave trade of the 1700s. "Where the hell is Angola?" replied one U.S. senator to an invitation to the hearings.[10]

Angola almost seemed to be located right on Capitol Hill in the late fall of 1975, where the once obscure country received unprecedented attention. Congress had been reasserting its power on foreign affairs for two years, trying to correct an imbalance advertised by Vietnam and Watergate. Congressional demands for greater respect for human rights led one European diplomat to note: "It isn't just the State Department or the President anymore. It's Congress now." With the *Washington Post* and the *New York Times* investigating white supremacist South African aid to UNITA, and with the MPLA firmly in control of the capital city of Luanda and most of Angola, the House and Senate passed by a large margin Senator John Tunney's (D-CA) amendment to temporarily end U.S. aid to UNITA. The Clark Amendment then passed in January 1976 to make the Tunney Amendment permanent, and U.S. intervention in Angola halted. It was the most dramatic assertion of congressional control over the American intelligence community since the beginning of the Cold War, a watershed event in the brief anti-colonial heyday of the mid-1970s. Within a year, though, the tide began turning, conservatives gaining traction with the question, "Who lost Angola?" Tunney lost his reelection bid in November 1976, as did Clark two years later. The lines were drawn clearly between a

U.S. stance focused more on human rights and one committed more to reasserting American influence. Following the Vietnam debacle, most Americans were unsure which way to lean.[11]

The disorienting effect of the Vietnam War on the United States in the 1970s was sharply compounded by the opening of relations with the People's Republic of China. The Carter administration's formal exchange of ambassadors with Beijing in 1979 completed a thawing of perhaps the most frigid diplomatic relationship in the world, a process begun by Nixon's dramatic visit to Beijing in February 1972. For the previous generation, "Red China," as Americans called it, embodied the sheerest anti-Americanism, surpassing even that of the Soviets. The Chinese Communists had defeated the pro-American Guomindang government in 1949, ending the Chinese civil war and eliminating what Americans thought of as their special relationship with the Chinese people (even if that relationship had involved a condescension captured in Senator Kenneth Wherry's [R-NE] pledge to "lift up Shanghai, up and up, ever up, until it is just like Kansas City"). Within a year, Chinese and American soldiers were killing each other by the tens of thousands in Korea. While Soviet-American relations occasionally went through periods of relative thaw after 1953, ties to China remained nonexistent. Indeed, Mao Zedong's government positioned itself as the most exuberant, ideological promoter of socialist wars of national liberation throughout the Third World. Mao's instigation of the Cultural Revolution in China in 1966, which promoted Communist purity of thought and behavior and lasted until his death ten years later, only deepened the ideological chasm between the two countries. Into this icy non-relationship, Nixon's smiling visit to Beijing—the very symbol of evil to Americans for a quarter-century, on the first trip ever by a U.S. president to China—plunged like a torrent of warm water. Americans watched live television coverage of Nixon and Mao toasting each other and speaking warmly together, and a Chinese military band playing traditional American tunes such as "Home, Home on the Range." For many Americans and others, it was almost unbelievable, "one of the greatest diplomatic and political coups of the century," in the words of the Concord (NH) *Monitor*.[12]

The warming of Sino-American relations had enormous significance for world politics and confusing implications for Americans. First, the supposedly monolithic Communist bloc was no more. The Chinese and Soviet governments' wary alliance dating from 1950 had actually been deteriorating since the late 1950s, as the two neighbors' historic differences meshed with a growing competition for leadership of the anti-capitalist bloc. By 1969, Soviet and Chinese troops were engaging in firefights along their common border on the Ussuri River. It took Nixon, who built his early political career on denouncing Communism in China, to seize the opportunity to drive a deeper wedge between the two great Communist powers. The Soviets blamed Nixon for doing just that, but they also moved swiftly to warm relations with the United States rather than being left as the third wheel in the new "triangular diplomacy." Nixon and Kissinger visited Moscow three months after Beijing, and a new era of détente was born. After a generation of viewing the Soviet Union and China as a monolithic conspiracy straddling the Eurasian landmass, Americans were suddenly free to understand them instead as two complicated nations with often conflicting interests and priorities. The Cold War would never be the same.[13]

Second, the image of Nixon and Mao smiling and toasting each other, displayed around the world, instantly cast the U.S. war in Vietnam, just across China's southern border, in a different light. Americans were still fighting and dying in Vietnam in 1972, supposedly to prevent the spread of Communism and specifically the expansion of Mao's influence into Southeast Asia. After all, Nixon's predecessor in the White House, Lyndon Johnson, had pointed to "the deepening shadow of Communist China" as the real threat and the real answer to the question, "Why are we in Vietnam?" Nixon's presence in Beijing and his negotiations with Mao and Zhou Enlai made seven years of U.S. sacrifices in Vietnam suddenly seem unnecessary. Might all that death and destruction—more than 50,000 American lives and millions of Vietnamese lives, and all that rancor and national discord at home—simply have been avoided?[14]

Third, and perhaps most unsettling of all, official friendliness with China followed by détente with the USSR raised elemental questions about whether the nation's highest priority for the previous twenty-five years—opposing at great cost a monolith called "international Communism"—had been built on a myth. Throughout the Cold War, U.S. policymakers assumed that other nations' foreign policies were similar in dynamics to their internal politics, that they derived from the same political well-springs. Democracies were therefore responsible and restrained in international affairs, by this logic, while totalitarian states— Communists now, like fascists before World War II—were aggressive and hostile toward other countries. But now it seemed that U.S. policies in Vietnam had been less than responsible and that Communists in Beijing and Moscow could be reasoned and negotiated with. Indeed, it would even be possible that, seventeen years hence, the totalitarian Soviet Union in 1989 could peacefully allow its eastern European empire to go free. Returning to the United States from Beijing in 1972, Nixon declared, "What we have done is simply opened the door—opened the door for travel, opened the door for trade." But he and Kissinger had done more than that. They had opened the door to an entire reconsideration of America's purpose in the world and its manner of dealing with other nations. America's future "in a disordered world . . . seems uncertain," *U.S. News and World Report* concluded.[15]

The disorientation about world affairs that so many Americans experienced in the 1970s not only reflected events in Vietnam, Angola, and China. There was also a broader wave of private terrorism unleashed by radical leftists and state terrorism carried out by reactionary governments. Airplane hijackings, bombings, and hostage-taking became regular events as various revolutionary and nationalist groups sought publicity for their causes. The Irish Republican Army, the Japanese Red Army Faction, the West German Baader-Meinhoff Gang, and the Italian Red Brigades all attacked high-profile targets, failing in their larger goals of destabilizing governments but succeeding in sowing doubts across the industrialized world about personal safety and security. Leftist political organizing in this era met its fiercest response in the Southern Cone of South America. Right-wing officers in the Chilean military, aided by the U.S. CIA, overthrew the elected socialist government of Salvador Allende in 1973, "disappearing" thousands of political opponents and instituting a seventeen-year military dictatorship under General Augusto Pinochet. British poet Alastair Reid had close ties to Chile and remembered 1973 as the "lean, mean year, breeder of obituaries." The Pinochet regime even reached on to American soil to carry out its murderous purposes; in 1976, a car bomb in Washington killed Orlando Letelier, Chile's former foreign minister under Allende and an opponent of Pinochet, as well as Letelier's American assistant. In Argentina, another military coup in 1976 led to six years of an infamous "dirty war" that killed some 10,000 leftists and other dissidents. And farther north in the hemisphere, anticommunist Cuban exiles who had previously worked for the CIA blew up a Cubana Airlines flight in October 1976, killing all seventy-three people on board.[16]

The use of political violence to spread fear was not new in the 1970s, nor was it limited to any one continent, but during this decade terrorism came to be associated above all with the Middle East and opponents of Israel. Several major events shaped this development. First, the British in 1971 withdrew the military forces that had long dominated the Persian Gulf region, continuing their retreat from empire that included granting independence to India in 1947, pulling out of Egypt after the debacle of the Suez crisis in 1956, and acceding to independence for most of their African colonies between 1957 and 1964. Into the vacuum left by the British retreat flowed not only continuing U.S.-Soviet competition for influence, but also a growing clash between the ebbing forces of Arab nationalism and socialism, on one side, which had dominated the struggle for independence from the European imperial powers and ruled ever since, and the rising force of Islamism, on the other side, which sought to create new theocratic governments that looked backward to the seventh century rather than forward to a Western model of secular rule. Islamists gained traction first not among the majority Sunni in the Arab nations but among the less numerous Persian Shi'a of Iran. The 1979 overthrow of the pro-American Shah Reza Pahlavi created a Shi'ite Islamist regime under Ayatollah Ruhollah Khomeini, while Sunni Islamists unsuccessfully sought a similar outcome in Saudi Arabia and Egypt. When young Iranian revolutionaries stormed the U.S. embassy in Tehran in November 1979 and seized fifty-two hostages whom they held for over a year, the targeting of civilians struck Americans like a body blow.[17]

They might have seen it coming. Hostilities between Israel, America's closest ally in the region, and its Arab neighbors ratcheted up throughout the decade. The key event was the Six-Day War of 1967, a stunning victory for Israel that exacerbated simmering disputes from its 1948 war of independence by bringing vast new swaths of Arab-populated territories—the Sinai Peninsula, the Golan Heights, and the Palestinian lands of the West Bank, Gaza, and East Jerusalem—under Israeli control. Unwilling or unable to trade the occupied territories for secure borders, the government in Tel Aviv abetted the movement of Zionist settlers into those territories, a process condemned by most of the world and fiercely resented by the Palestinians whose lands and autonomy were at stake in the West Bank, Gaza, and East Jerusalem. Egypt and Syria attacked in October 1973 in an effort to retake the Sinai Peninsula and the Golan Heights, nearly overrunning Israel, but the Israelis fought back and reconquered the territories with a crucial resupply of equipment from the United States. The resulting oil embargo by the Arab members of OPEC highlighted U.S. links to Israel, ties that had grown since 1967. Anti-Semitism had declined sharply in the United States after World War II; gentile Americans had come to see Israelis since 1948 as sturdy European pioneer settlers building a democracy, a similar story to early U.S. history; and the United States and Israel shared equally a large majority of the world's Jewish population. By the 1970s, the United States had become identified with Israel in a way it had not been during the 1940s and 1950s.[18]

Assaults on Israelis resonated on American shores, as Palestinian frustration with the outcome of the 1967 war fueled a proliferation of attacks on Israeli targets, both military and civilian, in Israel itself, in the Occupied Territories, and further afield. Palestinians hoped for international publicity for their cause, which they believed received little sympathetic attention in the United States and Western Europe, publicity that might lead to pressure on Israel to agree to withdraw from Palestinian lands. But the impact of terrorist attacks on civilians was the opposite in the United States: most Americans tended to identify more with Israelis and to see Palestinian insurgents as similar to other anti-Western insurgents throughout the Third World, such as the guerilla fighters in South Vietnam whom most Americans viewed as the enemy. Events such as the simultaneous hijacking of four New York-bound commercial jets from Europe in 1970 by Palestinians bolstered American identification with Israel.[19]

Two spectacular attacks on Israelis defined the era. One was the seizure and execution of eleven Israeli athletes and coaches by Palestinian gunmen at the 1972 Munich Olympics, where images of Jews being led bound to their slaughter again on German soil resurrected terrible memories of the Nazi Holocaust only twenty-seven years earlier. Just days earlier the American swimming superstar Mark Spitz, a Jew, had won a record seven gold medals. The second attack was the 1976 hijacking of an Air France flight by armed Palestinians and two German sympathizers, who diverted the plane to Entebbe Airport outside Kampala, Uganda. There they released the gentiles and kept 105 Israelis and Jews of other nationalities—again echoing the Holocaust—for a week, until an Israeli military force landed at Entebbe, secured the airport, and rescued the hostages, losing three hostages in the crossfire. One Israeli commando died: the raid commander, American-born Jonathan "Yoni" Netanyahu, a symbol of the closeness of American and Israeli societies, whose brother Benjamin would later become prime minister of

Israel. The extraordinary operation unfolded on July 4, amid the U.S. Bicentennial celebrations, and Americans could not help comparing Israeli military success in Uganda with recent U.S. military failure in Vietnam. The story of the Entebbe raid was quickly made into two successful Hollywood films. Israel seemed to represent a toughness and competence against terrorists that Americans admired and wished to emulate in an era of declining American leadership in international affairs.[20]

To Americans in the 1970s, the world, in sum, appeared unstable and unpredictable. Their longstanding confidence in their nation's destiny was faltering. Withdrawal from Vietnam ended the widespread assumption that the United States was bound to win all its wars. Worse, an awful lot of Southeast Asians were happy to see the Americans leave. The United States had long been the admired, most popular destination for immigrants from Europe and around the globe, and Americans shared a powerful belief that most other peoples, in their hearts, really wanted to be like them. In Stanley Kubrick's film *Full Metal Jacket* (1987), an American colonel explains that U.S. troops are in Vietnam because "inside every gook [Asian] is an American trying to get out." Now, however, it turned out that most Vietnamese apparently were not really Americans at heart. Nor were most Cambodians, Angolans, Iranians, or, as the 1979 Sandinista revolution would show, Nicaraguans, all of whom created governments hostile to the United States during the 1970s. The political future of the United States in the world was unclear, at a time when the future of the American political system at home was also being shaken to its foundations.

CORRUPTION AT HOME

The United States was born of a struggle against corruption. The revolutionary generation of 1776 became convinced that the centralized power of the British Crown threatened their individual liberties as English citizens. Historian Bernard Bailyn wrote that in this era, "most commonly the discussion of power centered on its essential characteristic of aggressiveness: its endlessly propulsive tendency to expand itself beyond legitimate boundaries." The Founding Fathers spoke in vivid metaphors about power as "grasping" and being "like a cancer [that] eats faster and faster every hour." With an image easily accessible to a later, shark-conscious, popular culture, they spoke of the "jaws" of power as "always opened to devour." What power sought to destroy were liberty and law. The American revolutionaries followed established eighteenth-century Whig theory in noting that power had legitimate functions such as establishing social order and good government, but that power was also inherently corrupting for people in political office. The Declaration of Independence and the Constitution embodied the understanding that liberty's preservation hinged on establishing effective checks on power—the "checks and balances" Americans learn about in grade school. Unrestrained, the intoxicating temptation of power "converts a good man in private life to a tyrant in office." So citizens had to pay attention in order to defend their rights from the creeping hostility of centralized authority. In a 1765 sermon, colonial minister Andrew Eliot argued that when tyranny is abroad in the land, "submission is a crime."[21]

Precisely two centuries later, the Watergate scandal and investigation of 1972–74 reminded Americans of this heritage and of their need to resist the unjust behavior of corrupt power. References to "King Richard" abounded. Indeed, Nixon contributed as much as any one individual to the confusions of Americans in the 1970s. First, he undercut the nation's unifying ideology of anticommunism by warming relations with the Chinese and the Soviets; then his divisive actions at home eroded the national bipartisan consensus that had undergirded the Cold War for a generation. Abetted by his advisers, the president ignored legal constraints as he sought to consolidate power in the White House and assure an overwhelming reelection victory in 1972. Ironically, he need hardly have worried, given the Democratic Party's lack of cohesion and the weak campaign effort of presidential nominee, Senator George McGovern (SD). Nixon speechwriter Pat Buchanan effectively satirized McGovern's platform as "weakness abroad, permissiveness at home." But from Nixon's first months in office, he and Kissinger used wiretaps on their staffs and on reporters to identify the source of leaks about new U.S. bombing of neutral Cambodia, a violation of international law. They were determined to control the flow of information about the federal government and punish those on Nixon's "enemies list." The Committee to Reelect the President created a "Plumbers" unit to engage in a whole series of secretive "dirty tricks" against political opponents. Presidential assistant John Dean consulted with others in the administration about "how we can use the available federal machinery to screw our political enemies." Nixon agreed that "we have not used the Bureau [FBI] and we have not used the Justice Department but things are going to change now."[22]

On June 17, 1972, several Plumbers were arrested while trying to plant bugging equipment in the Democratic National Committee headquarters in Washington's Watergate office complex. "I'm not going to comment on a third-rate burglary attempt," Nixon's press secretary Ron Ziegler responded. But over the next two years, investigations by the press, the courts, and Congress slowly peeled back the layers of a full-blown cover-up of the Watergate break-in, orchestrated by the president and his closest advisers, who lied to the public by denying that they were doing precisely that. Several went to jail, including top aides Bob Haldeman and John Ehrlichman. Tapes of White House conversations revealed Nixon, in the words of the conservative *Chicago Tribune*, as a "devious" and "profane" man who had given "a shabby, disgusting, immoral performance." Under threat of impeachment, Nixon resigned on August 8, 1974, the only U.S. president ever to do so.[23]

His successor, Gerald Ford, a decent and likable person, aimed to move the nation forward. "Our long national nightmare is over," he declared. A month later, Ford granted Nixon "a full, free, and absolute pardon" for any crimes he might have committed, only to provoke widespread outrage. Ford's popularity plummeted. A large bipartisan majority of Americans be-

FIGURE 1.3.
Part of what comforted many Americans about President Gerald Ford was his large, likable family, gathered here at their house in Vail, Colorado, in December 1975. Courtesy Gerald R. Ford Presidential Library.

lieved Nixon should face justice for his actions. "There are only so many lies you can take," conservative Republican Senator Barry Goldwater declared. CBS News television anchor Walter Cronkite, a national icon of level-headedness, told friends, "I think we ought to take Lysol and scrub out the Oval Office." And corruption had spread further in the administration. The only person to enter the White House without having been elected either president or vice president, Ford had been chosen by Nixon to replace Vice President Spiro Agnew. Agnew had resigned after being found guilty of having accepted bribes while serving earlier as governor of Maryland, only the second vice president ever to leave the office voluntarily. During the Watergate cover-up, Nixon himself joked privately about Agnew's suitability for high office: "Then you think, well, Christ, this poor damn dumb President, why didn't he resign? Which might not be a bad idea, the only problem is, I mean, you get Agnew. You want Agnew?" And corruption in Washington was not restricted to the Executive branch or to the Republican Party. Powerful congressional committee chairmen embarrassed themselves and deepened public distrust of government. Two months after Nixon's resignation, police found Rep. Wilbur Mills (D-AR), chair of the House Ways and Means Committee, drunk in Washington's Tidal Basin with a buxom stripper nicknamed the "Argentine Firecracker." Rep. Wayne Hays (D-OH), chair of the Committee on House Administration, resigned after an investigation revealed in early 1976 the presence of an attractive young woman on his taxpayer-funded staff, Elizabeth Ray, whose sole duty was to serve as Hays's mistress. Ray confessed, "I can't type, I can't file, I can't even answer the phone."[24]

A major shift in American attitudes toward government and political leadership was under way. While the nation had originally emerged in the 1780s out of a struggle against centralized authority, and had fought the Civil War in the 1860s over the same issue, the United States in the twentieth century nonetheless developed an increasingly powerful federal government that most citizens came to trust and depend on. Amidst the industrialization of the final decades of the 1800s and the enormous wealth that it created, major corporations in industries such as steel and oil became so influential that Americans began to perceive them as the greatest threats to individual liberty. In the face of this danger, the only possible force to balance and restrain private economic might was the federal government. The Populists and Progressives at the turn of the century laid much of the groundwork for establishing a stronger national state. Then the crisis of the Great Depression in the 1930s opened the door to Franklin Roosevelt's New Deal and the creation of a more powerful U.S. government responsible for both managing the economy and assuring a minimal provision of material comfort—a safety net—for its citizens. The New Deal's modest welfare state set the pattern for national governance through the 1960s, primarily led by the Democratic Party and bolstered by the anxieties of the Cold War, and reached its apex in the further reforms of Lyndon Johnson's Great Society, particularly regarding racial equality, health care, and education. Citizens, until Vietnam and Watergate taught them otherwise, tended to assume their presidents were moral and competent men.[25]

Now, in the 1970s, public confidence in the decency and effectiveness of the federal government waned. Decency seemed to depart with Nixon. The Pulitzer Prize–winning reporters who tracked and broke most of the Watergate story, Bob Woodward and Carl Bernstein of the *Washington Post*, published their definitive account of those events in 1974. *All the President's Men* became a huge best seller. The popular film version of the book opened in April 1976, starring two of Hollywood's biggest names, Robert Redford and Dustin Hoffman, in time to consolidate a grim visual counterpoint of corruption and misdeeds to the nation's Bicentennial celebrations. The revelation of Nixon's deceptions created a thirst for honesty that resulted in the swift reassessment of another recent president, Harry Truman (1945–53). Truman had left the Oval Office with very low public approval ratings due to the stalemated war in Korea, accusations of graft among some low-level members of his administration, and condemnations by then-influential Senator Joseph McCarthy (R-WI). Twenty years later, Truman's Midwestern straightforwardness contrasted starkly with Nixon's Machiavellian style of secrecy, Truman's steady hand in the early Cold War looked admirable against failed U.S. policies in Southeast Asia, and Merle Miller's 1974 book, *Plain Speaking: An Oral Biography of Harry S. Truman*, became an immediate bestseller. "Plain speaking" seemed just what the country needed.[26]

In search of honest presidential leadership, citizens looked to Ford and then Carter, two men widely admired for their personal decency. "Lack of trust in government" and "corruption in government" together ranked second only to inflation as Americans' greatest concerns, according to polls. But the nation did not receive the kind of effective political management that it desired. Both men failed to consolidate their authority, Ford losing in his 1976 campaign to win election to the White House he had occupied only by appointment, Carter losing in his 1980 campaign for reelection. Along the way, Ford suffered from the appearance of a new, edgier generation of comedians who subjected him—and all other authority figures, including God—to unrelenting public satire. *Saturday Night Live* first aired live on national television on October 11, 1975, with Chevy Chase parodying Ford tripping and falling (as the president had done recently), a repeated routine that came to define Ford's public image, despite his status as probably the most accomplished athlete ever to serve in the Oval Office, having been the star center and linebacker on the University of Michigan football team. Then Ford raised questions about his intellectual competence as well when he declared during a debate with Carter on October 6, 1976: "There is no Soviet domination of Eastern Europe, and there never will be under a Ford administration." As Carter quickly suggested, Polish Americans and others of eastern European heritage could hardly believe the president's words. (After the election, Ford self-deprecatingly joked that he might accept a teaching position at the University of Michigan in a field other than European history.)[27]

Carter's own administration over the next four years, however, became almost a byword for limited success in governance at home and critical failures abroad. While that reputation belied several significant achievements of the Carter administration—particularly the 1977 treaties turning control of the Panama Canal over to Panama, the 1979 Camp David accords creating peace between Egypt and Israel, and the 1980 Alaska Lands Act doubling the size of the national park system—the evidence of the administration's failure to work effectively with the Democratic-controlled Congress is irrefutable. Carter proved to be a better prophet than administrator. He was the first president to identify "our serious energy problem" as crucial to resolve for the nation's future well-being, and he warned Americans that "too many of us now tend to worship self-indulgence and consumption" instead. "This is not a message of happiness or reassurance, but it is the truth and it is a warning."[28]

The element of paranoia evident in hit films such as *Chinatown* (1974) and *Three Days of the Condor* (1975) and other popular media of the mid-1970s reflected a growing public awareness that unethical and illegal behavior might be even more widespread in the government than was already known. It turned out that the people responsible for the nation's security during the ongoing crisis of the Cold War, housed in such agencies as the CIA and the FBI, had themselves been acting outside the laws and customs they were supposed to be enforcing. Revelations emerged that the FBI had for years been illegally harassing civil rights leaders such as Martin Luther King, Jr. *Three Days of the Condor*'s depiction of corruption within the CIA fed off the daily news. Readers of the nation's leading newspaper, the *New York Times*, woke on December 22, 1974, to this three-column headline on the first page: "Huge C.I.A. Operation Reported in U.S. Against Antiwar Forces, Other Dissidents in Nixon Years." Pulitzer Prize–winning reporter Seymour Hersh laid out in stark detail many of the misdeeds of the nation's security forces, opening a floodgate through which poured a year of further surprising revelations as other investigations followed. A Senate committee under Frank Church (D-ID) and a House committee under Otis Pike (D-NY) each spent most of 1975 on this, as did a commission under Vice President Nelson Rockefeller that Ford set up in an effort to head off less friendly congressional investigators. Disaffected former CIA agents Philip Agee and John Stockwell published revealing memoirs, *Inside The Company* (1975) and *In Search of Enemies* (1978), as other critics of American imperial behavior in the Third World weighed in. Evidence revealed deep U.S. involvement in the overthrow of foreign governments, most notably Chile in 1973, and even major CIA plots to assassinate at least five foreign heads of state. It was a sign of how new such an idea was that investigators and the public were shocked to make these discoveries, an era when the open discussions of thirty years later about the U.S. use of torture would have been unimaginable. Citizens were stunned and angry that the government acting in their name had been engaged in precisely the kind of actions abroad that the Soviets were supposed to engage in, and that were supposed to be the very reason for the United States having to stand up to the Soviets in the first place. Here was corruption indeed, a breaking of the trust of citizens in the democratic governance that they had long taken for granted.[29]

At one level, the idea that the U.S. government might act in some of the same ways that characterized the Soviet government was not far-fetched. From a cold-eyed, pragmatic perspective, the interests of large nations in international affairs have always been calculated and self-regarding. Altruism rarely determines state behavior. The hard world of global economic, political, and military competition and the enormous stakes involved invites "realistic" rather than idealistic actions. A dog-eat-dog world required tough behavior at times; the Soviet regime, with the blood of millions on its hands, was not a kindly adversary. The U.S. Congress had long understood and gone along with this. Before the mid-1970s, neither the Senate nor the House took an active interest in their official oversight responsibilities for intelligence agencies and activities. The intelligence agencies' share of the annual federal budget was highly classified information. Sen. John Stennis (D-MS), chair of the subcommittee with oversight responsibility for the CIA, put it bluntly in 1971: "You make up your mind that you are going to have an intelligence agency and protect it as such, and shut your eyes some and take what is coming." But Americans still wanted to believe that their nation was different, somehow less self-interested and more good-willed than other great powers, ultimately a promoter of liberty and justice abroad. So the news that U.S. taxpayers were footing the bill for official attempts at murder and mayhem was jarring, even to members of Congress doing the investigating.[30]

Congress's efforts to rein in the executive branch made 1973–78 a highly unusual period in recent U.S. political history. The War Powers Act of 1973 required the president to receive congressional approval within ninety days for any new posting of American troops overseas. While the law only came into effect once, during the 1975 *Mayaguez* incident in Cambodia, because presidents otherwise simply avoided reporting such actions directly to Congress, the War Powers Act nonetheless symbolized Congress's determination to reassert the influence in foreign policy that it had lost during the Cold War heyday of what had become known as the imperial presidency. The reports of the

Church Committee and Pike Committee about covert CIA operations caused President Ford on February 16, 1976, to issue an executive order banning U.S. government employees from involvement in political assassinations. Two years later, Congress passed the Foreign Intelligence Surveillance Act in an effort to prevent future widespread government monitoring of private electronic communications, in order to end abuses of wiretapping. Also enacted in 1978, the Presidential Records Act aimed to bolster the relationship between a republican government and its citizens by preserving public access to the paper trail left by a president. In response to Nixon's efforts to hide his administration's records by claiming them as his personal property, this legislation instead assigned clear ownership to the public, under the care of the National Archives, of the documentary materials generated during a presidency. The middle years of the 1970s, in sum, witnessed a brief flurry of congressional attempts to restrain the power of the Cold War presidency, a democratic strategy soon to be shunted aside during the crises of 1979–80 in Iran and Afghanistan, but an effort that showed vital American resistance to the corruptions of power.[31]

Conservatism and the Distrust of Government

Watergate was a Republican scandal. Just two years after Nixon's huge reelection victory, and three months after his resignation, the Democrats won a raft of new seats in Congress in 1974. Only 18 percent of Americans that year identified themselves as Republicans. It seemed, briefly, that the crosscurrents of American politics in this era might be shifting back to the more liberal party that had held the White House from 1961 to 1969. This was an illusion. The Democrats were divided, their old coalition fraying as much of the white working class distrusted the party's ongoing shift from economic liberalism to cultural liberalism and continued slipping into the Republican column.[32] The ultimate message embedded in Watergate and also in the deceptive Vietnam policies of the Johnson administration was simply not to trust government—ultimately a conservative attitude that rejected four decades of New Deal activist management from Washington. The public sector became associated with corruption, compromise, and self-dealing. Washington took on an aura of an "inside the Beltway" place, sealed off from the genuine concerns and interests of average citizens outside. "I'm mad as hell and I'm not going to take it anymore!" declared fictional TV news anchor Howard Beale in the 1976 hit film *Network*, as he urged citizens to yell the same from their windows across the nation. Carter's election that fall put the first person in the White House in more than half a century, since Woodrow Wilson, without previous experience in the federal government. Experience in Washington became a political burden rather than an asset, a remarkable measure of voter distrust in their government. Carter campaigned against Washington, touting his outsider status. Ronald Reagan, another governor, did the same in 1980. Bill Clinton in 1992 and George W. Bush in 2000 used similar strategies. Of the eight presidential elections following 1972, only one saw a non-incumbent victor—George H. W. Bush in 1988—with experience in Washington. The tide had changed in the mid-1970s.

Conservatives benefited most from the fraying of public connection to elected officials. While polls revealed that the portion of Americans who believed they could "trust the federal government" dropped from 75 percent in 1965 to 25 percent by the late 1970s, a still broader shift was taking place in which citizens became more skeptical of almost all major institutions in the country, including the medical profession, unions, educational systems, traditional churches, the military, banks, television, and the press. Civic engagement declined, whether measured in time spent volunteering or number of organizations being joined. Unlike Western Europe, where voting participation remained around 80 percent, the percentage of voting-age Americans who made the effort to cast a ballot during presidential elections dropped from 61 percent in 1968 to 53 percent in 1980, and dipped to just 38 percent in the 1974 congressional elections and 46 percent in 1978. By the end of the decade, in other words, not much more than half of the American electorate even bothered to vote, a portent in a nation long seen as a leader of the world's democratic countries. "Don't vote—it only encourages them," a popular bumper sticker advised. But a new generation of conservative activists saw in these developments an opportunity and a calling for rejuvenating American patriotism and what they considered traditional American values. One of the most influential of these new organizers, Jesse Helms of North Carolina, who would be elected to the Senate as a Republican in 1972 for the first of five terms, spent the preceding years warning that "the law-abiding citizens of this republic" would soon "push aside all the phony political doubletalk about 'movements' and 'marches' and 'non-violence' and 'civil rights.'" "These long-hairs keep talking about a revolution," he wrote to a friend in 1970. "One of these days they may get one—but not the kind they expect." It was a prescient view of a new conservative era about to dawn.[33]

What did it mean to be conservative in the 1970s and ever since? "Conserve" comes from the Latin for "to keep intact or unchanged," and the adjectival form implies carefulness. At least since the noted English philosopher Edmund Burke opposed the French Revolution in the 1790s, conservatism had stood for defending existing institutions—political, religious, and otherwise. By the 1970s, this was no longer the case. "I am a conservative because I am for change," declared recently elected Senator Roger Jepsen (R-IA) in 1980. After forty years of political dominance by the New Deal version of the Democratic Party, preserving the existing system was the exact opposite of what these new conservatives sought. They wanted to overthrow it. They aimed to take advantage of what pollster Lou Harris found in 1975: "People are disenchanted with liberalism because they feel it involves excessive federal spending that has not solved problems confronting the country." Bolstered by the conversion of a widening stream of white Southern Democrats, conservatives worked steadily in the 1970s to wrest control of the Republican Party from the shrinking liberal forces headed by Nelson Rockefeller and the besieged moderate forces coalesced around President Ford. Ronald Reagan became their hero, fresh off two terms as a popular California governor (1966–74). He nearly unseated Ford for the Republican presidential nomination in 1976 and rolled into the White House in 1980.[34]

Reagan's broad popularity among Republicans stemmed partly from his sunny personality and partly from his ability to hold together the three distinctive wings of the modern conservative movement that found its home in the Republican Party. The first wing consisted of the social conservatives, primarily self-identified religious voters who focused on what they considered to be moral issues, particularly opposing abortion rights, homosexuality, and feminism and promoting school prayer. Disturbed by recent changes in attitudes about sexuality, gender, religion, and—for many—race, they hoped to roll back the liberalizing social tendencies of the 1960s. The second wing of the conservative movement was nationalist, seeking to undo the outcome of the Vietnam War by resurrecting a powerful, self-confident U.S. presence around the world. These anticommunists, many of them neoconservatives who had previously been moderate or even liberal Democrats, feared the resurgence of Soviet influence abroad and bitterly opposed détente. The third wing of the conservative movement held the free-market forces, those sympathetic to business interests and eager to shrink government influence through deregulation and privatization. This commerce-oriented and libertarian-leaning group believed the mechanism of the market made the best social and economic decisions about allocating resources and produced the greatest freedom. The three wings of the movement overlapped in important ways, particularly on emphasizing national strength abroad, but they also differed rather sharply on the role of the government, with free marketers wanting to minimize it regarding the economy and religious voters seeking to increase it regarding people's sexual behavior. Social conservatives, ultimately, saw the intact family as the foundation of a healthy society, while free-market conservatives viewed the free individual as the essential building block. Social and religious conservatives gained considerable prominence from the 1970s onward, particularly in the media. But in terms of measurably changing the course of governance in the United States, free-market conservatives proved to be much more influential.[35]

Racial issues meant relatively little to libertarians but helped shape the essential contours of social conservatism. With economic challenges all around them in the stagflationary 1970s, many white working-class and middle-class Americans looked for explanations and were amenable to scapegoating. Leaders such as segregationist Alabama governor George Wallace and, more subtly, the once racially moderate Nixon offered up a traditional target for venting white frustrations: African Americans. Court-ordered school busing to achieve integration, from Charlotte to Boston, stimulated a backlash from whites whose motives ranged from simple racial prejudice to a desire to preserve neighborhood schools. Urban dwellers continued to move to the suburbs, extending a decades-long pattern that looked an awful lot like resegregation. Historian Kevin Kruse demonstrated that in cities such as Atlanta since the 1950s, as public spaces became desegregated, most whites who could afford to do so headed for the suburbs. They abandoned what became an increasingly black public sphere of the city for a mostly white private sphere of the suburbs, marked by private schools and health clubs and fewer public recreational amenities such as parks, municipal golf courses, and community swimming pools. More openly segregationist whites believed that they were fighting to preserve their traditional ability to associate only with whom they wanted to, and that blacks in league with a hostile federal government were trying to deprive them of that freedom. Nor was white resistance to black advancement merely a Southern story, as Thomas Sugrue and other historians have made clear. Boston, once the cradle of the abolition of slavery, experienced the worst school desegregation violence between 1973 and 1976. The title of John Egerton's 1974 book, *The Americanization of Dixie: The Southernization of America*, suggested the larger process under way, of the long distinctive and impoverished states of the former Confederacy breaking out of their isolation. Instead, as jobs and people moved into the Sun

Belt, symbols of Southern culture simultaneously spread north and west—evangelical Protestant Christianity, stock car racing, barbecue, country music, even the Confederate flag—and took hold in working-class and lower-middle-class communities across the nation.[36]

Jesse Helms emerged as the most influential new leader in the 1970s of the forces of racially tinged Southern social conservatism. Helms grew up in the small town of Monroe, North Carolina, and made his career in the state capital of Raleigh as a television news editorialist, defending segregation and opposing communism, two issues he saw as closely connected. He gained national attention first as a leader of the anti-busing campaign that followed the Supreme Court's 1971 decision in *Swann v. Mecklenburg*, which required Charlotte's public schools to be comprehensively desegregated rather than having just a token sprinkling of black students attending white schools. *Swann* forced Southern school districts to bus large numbers of black and white students, just as the Court's decision two years later in *Keyes v. Denver* (1973) did for schools outside of the South. Like most Southern segregationists in this era, Helms switched teams, leaving the now racially inclusive Democrats for Nixon's Republican Party with its coded appeals to white Southerners. Helms rode Nixon's coattails in 1972 to an unexpected victory in the Senate race over U.S. Rep. Nick Galifianakis by emphasizing his opponent's Greek ancestry as foreign, although Galifianakis was a former U.S. Marine and a lifelong resident of Durham. Helms matched his ideological fervor with a new organization called the Congressional Club, an enormously successful direct-mail fundraising effort that brought in millions of dollars from around the country for his campaigns. In 1978, he won reelection by outspending his opponent by a ratio of 32 to 1, burying him in an avalanche of negative television advertisements.[37]

Helms positioned himself as the most principled, uncompromising social conservative of the 1970s. Recognizing that explicit racism was increasingly unacceptable in an era of civil rights at home and decolonization abroad, he borrowed the rhetoric of anticolonialism and self-determination to defend white neighborhood schools from "cultural imperialism" and "contempt for the ordinary parent" by the federal courts. Helms was also the strongest voice in the U.S. Senate of the emerging Christian Right, whose concerns extended far beyond race. He supported the founding of the lobbying group Moral Majority in 1979 and was a featured speaker at its first major public event that spring, a 10,000-person "Decency Rally" in Washington. Particularly galling to Christian conservatives was the Internal Revenue Service's 1978 elimination of tax-exempt status for private schools that excluded students of color, primarily church-based "white-flight" academies that had sprung up in the South as an alternative to integrated public schools. President Carter's IRS refused to continue helping fund such practices with preferential tax status, but evangelicals were outraged by what they viewed instead as a "secular humanist" attack on religion. This was a key moment in energizing conservative Christians and bringing them into the political sphere that they had long avoided. Helms enthusiastically endorsed them: "We've had preachers in politics for 50 years, to my knowledge, but they've always been on the other side." Newly politicized conservative evangelicals and Roman Catholics focused on sexual and gender issues, particularly opposing the Equal Rights Amendment (ERA), abortion rights, homosexual rights, and sex education. They also disdained détente and demanded a stronger U.S. position in the world. Helms's vigorous stance in 1976 against negotiating a turnover of the Panama Canal to Panama helped push his ally Ronald Reagan to a crucial victory in the Republican presidential primary in North Carolina. Though Reagan ultimately lost the nomination that year to the incumbent Ford, the win in North Carolina stopped a downward skid in Reagan's campaign and renewed his legitimacy as a future candidate, setting him on the path to victory in 1980 and a conservative political ascendancy thereafter.[38]

For the nationalist wing of the conservative movement, particularly the neoconservatives moving into the Republican Party but also still grouped around Democratic Senator Henry Jack-

son of Washington, the middle years of the 1970s offered a challenge and an opportunity. These activists hated the perceived
loss of American power and prestige abroad resulting from the
outcome of the Vietnam War, the Watergate scandal, the congressional investigations of the CIA, and the Soviet buildup in
nuclear weaponry to parity with the United States. Ford's chief
of staff, Richard Cheney, feared the erosion of what he later
called "the authority I think the president needs to be effective,
especially in the national security area," an argument he would
later make with great effect as vice president from 2001 to 2009.
Helms declared that "the United States cannot afford to be a
second-rate power." Militant anticommunists saw détente as the
road to defeat. Reagan's 1976 primary victory in North Carolina stemmed from his labeling of Ford as weak and as allowing
the Soviets to overtake the United States in military prowess.
Ford told the press afterward that "we are going to forget about
the use of the word détente," to the surprise of his aides and of
Secretary of State Kissinger, détente's other architect along with
Nixon. Liberals, who might have been expected to stand up for
détente, had no interest in defending Kissinger or Nixon. Indeed, the coolheaded, realist calculations of détente tended naturally to alienate Americans on both the Right and the Left who
disliked authoritarian rule, whether (for the Right) in the Communist bloc or (for the Left) among right-wing non-European
dictators. Hawks inside and outside the government pressured
the CIA into a reassessment by a "Team B" of intelligence analysts of what they saw as the agency's underestimation of Soviet
military strength in 1975 and 1976. Détente of a sort lingered
under the Carter administration as the new president initially
oriented U.S. foreign policy away from concern with the USSR,
but died finally when the Soviets invaded Afghanistan in 1979.[39]

Part of the neoconservative task in the mid- to late 1970s
involved recasting the image of the United States. Rather than a
globe-straddling imperial hegemon inflicting massive damage
on small countries such as Vietnam while asserting control of
the non-Communist sphere, America was to be understood instead as a spunky underdog, the determined defender of free-

dom and individualism against the looming collectivist might of the totalitarian Soviet empire. This was roughly the script of the highest-grossing film of the decade, *Star Wars* (1977), and its sequel, *The Empire Strikes Back* (1980). After the loss in Southeast Asia and disturbing revelations of American war crimes such as the My Lai massacre and CIA corruption, these films helped Americans imagine themselves once again as warriors for justice and decency and helped them imagine war once again as a noble and even glorious undertaking, a view Reagan would promote vigorously from the Oval Office throughout the following decade. This cultural shift may have deepened the public disappointment with the Carter administration in April 1980 when the "Desert One" operation to rescue American captives in Iran failed. Rather than Luke Skywalker or Han Solo flying in to put things right, actual U.S. aircraft collided with each other, killing eight servicemen and rescuing no one. American strategists had hoped for another Entebbe rescue, four years after Israelis pulled off their stunning operation to liberate captives in Uganda, but it seemed that only Israel was capable of such a feat, something noted by the neoconservatives—and many evangelicals—who valued that country as one of the most important allies of the United States.

Economic Insecurity

The performance of the U.S. economy in the 1970s dismayed most Americans. Inflation, unemployment, and declining real wages pulled the prospects of American workers downward, and the gap between rich and poor began to grow quickly. But the economy of this decade only makes sense in the context of the extraordinary quarter-century that preceded it. The "long boom" of 1947–73 marked the most sustained period of rapid economic growth in world history. The combined gross domestic product (GDP) of all nations almost tripled in this period; world manufacturing output quadrupled; the world economy grew at an average annual rate of nearly 6 percent. The real median income of

American households shot up by nearly 50 percent just since 1960. The United States led the boom, but much of the rest of the world also benefited. Western Europeans experienced a "veritable golden age of economic growth," in the words of economic historian Barry Eichengreen, and largely caught up to American standards of income and lifestyle. Inexpensive oil underlay the boom. Petroleum remained at an average cost of just $2 per barrel during the post–World War II generation. The 1955 prediction by Admiral Lewis Strauss, chairman of the U.S. Atomic Energy Commission, that electricity would become so cheap by the 1970s that it would no longer need to be metered did not come to pass, but when adjusted for inflation, the real cost of energy in the United States actually did decline by an annual average of 5 percent from 1950 to 1973. Throughout these years, organized labor and U.S. corporations worked closely together to promote free trade and thus more exports. The steady expansion of comfortable and even affluent suburbs revealed a growing middle class. The vast majority of Americans arrived at the end of the 1960s wealthier than twenty years earlier and with considerable confidence about their economic futures. One of the most distinguished historians of the modern world, Eric Hobsbawm, called these "the golden years."[40]

It did not last. A slowing U.S. economy reached stagnation in 1973, dropping into recession for the next year and a half. The stock market lost nearly half its value. American productivity— the amount of value produced per worker—crossed a divide into a new watershed, plunging from 3 percent annual increases during 1947–73 to just 1 percent increases during 1973–80. The reputation of American goods for quality and innovation slid, inviting a flood of imported products. For the first time since the nineteenth century, the United States in 1971 became a net importer of goods from abroad. Pressed by international investors trading in dollars for gold, Nixon in 1971 detached the dollar from its guaranteed postwar price of $35 per ounce (part of the "Bretton Woods" system established in 1944), instead letting the dollar's value "float" against the value of other currencies. This introduced a new level of instability in the international economy—and a plummeting dollar, as gold quickly shot up to $800 per ounce by 1980. The early 1970s witnessed the end of thirty years of unparalleled prosperity in the United States and the end of the rapid growth of the American middle class. "We are aware, as never before, of distinct limits on our material resources," wrote historian Laurence Veysey in 1979. "'Abundance' no longer seems to be our special defining characteristic" as a nation.[41]

Abundance had underpinned the redistributive social policies of the 1960s Great Society. Money in people's pockets and confidence about their futures made enough voters sufficiently generous to support Lyndon Johnson's programs for poverty and education. When prices went up and jobs started to grow scarce, Democratic Party liberalism became defensive. The longer the 1970s experience of stagflation went on, the more it undercut the central theme of Keynesian economics at the heart of the New Deal order: that federal government management of the economy was effective. Economists and average citizens alike lost confidence in the political economy they had known and began to shift their allegiance to conservative doctrines they had found unconvincing since the end of the 1920s and the onset of the Great Depression. The established belief in a regulated American economy now lost ground to a growing sense that the market alone, with the least government input, could best allocate resources and stimulate growth. A similar if slower process unfolded in Western Europe, where declining economic growth, rising unemployment, and sharply higher energy costs began to weaken nations' abilities to provide the generous social benefits—unemployment, health care, pensions—available since the 1940s. Fiscal conservatism and cutbacks in social spending gained ground by the end of the decade in what historian Bruce Schulman called "a worldwide crisis of the welfare state."[42]

The oil embargo of 1973–74 by the Arab OPEC states pushed a slowing U.S. economy into its deepest recession since the 1930s. Even after the embargo ended, prices remained sky high. The price of oil soared from $3 per barrel in 1970 to $31 per barrel in 1980. Other oil-consuming nations suffered as well, including Japan and the countries of Western Europe, whose citizens were even more dependent than Americans on imported petroleum. In the previous twenty years, for example, the share of Europe's energy produced from oil had grown from 8.5 percent in 1950 (the rest being mostly from coal) to 60 percent in 1970. Africa's economic difficulties of the late twentieth century dated more from the 1973 spike in oil prices than they did from independence from Europe in the late 1950s and early 1960s, which had at first been followed by real economic growth. The impact on the Soviet bloc varied: most of Eastern Europe, which did not produce oil, suffered a declining standard of living, while the Soviet Union itself tapped dozens of new oil fields in Siberia to increase production and delay a little longer the country's gathering economic decline. But the United States used vastly more oil than any other nation, thanks to a fourfold increase since 1945 in the number of cars and trucks on the country's extensive highway network.[43]

The oil crisis caught most Americans by surprise. After all, the United States had dominated world oil production for the first half of the twentieth century, accounting for more than 50 percent of all oil pumped as late as 1950. But that figure dropped to 25 percent in 1965 and 20 percent in 1972 as the nation's postwar boom economy drained its proven oil reserves, which fell from nearly half of the world's reserves on the eve of World War II to just 6 percent in 1972. Domestic petroleum production peaked in 1970 and dropped off steadily thereafter, while U.S. consumption continued to climb. Here was the source of growing dependence. By contrast, oil production was shifting rapidly to the Persian Gulf region and North Africa, where the Libyan government led a concerted and successful movement in the 1970s to gain control of the process of production by nationalizing the international oil companies' holdings in OPEC nations. The United States imported five times as much oil in 1979 as it had in 1970, and imports doubled as a percentage of the nation's consumption to 43 percent.[44]

Americans faced a dawning realization that long lines and high prices at gas stations heralded a new era of energy dependence on other countries. On June 13, 1979, in the midst of the Iranian revolution that caused the decade's second spike in oil prices, more than half of American gas stations had their pumps turned off. Just a few years after the United States had put men on the moon, the nation was literally running out of gas. It seemed a lifetime since *Time* magazine had encouraged drivers in 1960 to drive four extra minutes each day to reduce the U.S. burden of glutted gasoline supplies. "The Saudis," President Ford admitted privately to a reporter with unusual bluntness, "have us by the balls." Popular anger throughout the decade targeted Arabs and Iranians, though Ford and others suggested a glance in the mirror would be appropriate. "We, the United States, are not blameless," the president announced in his 1975 state of the union address. "Our growing dependence upon foreign sources has been adding to our vulnerability for years and years, and we did nothing to prepare ourselves for such an event as the embargo of 1973." For two generations, Americans had considered easy access to inexpensive gasoline as almost a birthright, a defining feature of what it meant to be American. In the 1920s, advertising executive and best-selling author Bruce Barton called gasoline "the juice of the fountain of youth," a symbol of American freedom. Now in the 1970s the fountain was drying up, leaving the nation thirsty and vulnerable. Analogies to the decline of other great empires of the past seemed apt. A Gulf Oil executive recalled, "I could feel it everywhere; it was the ebbing of American power—the Romans retreating from Hadrian's Wall."[45]

How did the United States respond to the dramatic surge in energy prices? Innovative energy analysts Amory Lovins and L. Hunter Lovins called for a shift from the existing "hard energy path" of reliance on fossil fuels and nuclear power to a "soft energy path" of conservation and efficiency, including the development of renewable and nonpolluting sources such as solar energy. For about a decade, there was some movement in this direction. Petroleum imports dropped markedly through the early 1980s. Congress passed a national 55-mile per hour speed limit in 1974, a national "right-on-red" law that saved up to 12,000 barrels of oil per day, and the first set of fuel-efficiency standards for new vehicles in 1975. President Carter established a new Department of Energy in 1977. Between 1974 and 1989, the average miles per gallon of cars in the United States nearly doubled from 13.8 to 27.5. In the same period, the incentive of higher costs led to U.S. factories improving their energy efficiency by 30 percent and new homes and appliances being designed to be much less wasteful.[46]

Such advances stalled by the mid-1980s, however, as world oil prices declined once again, making waste less expensive. Americans increasingly bought larger, heavier, more powerful vehicles, particularly SUVs and vans, and by 2004 the size of the average new house had increased more than 50 percent from 1970, even as average family size shrank. Unlike Japan, which made permanent its own 1970s shift to greater energy efficiency, the United States retreated from its newly won green territory. The resistance Carter encountered to his efforts to make energy independence a permanent national priority caused him to note in his diary: "It was like pulling teeth to convince the people of America that we had a serious problem." One EPA automotive expert was blunter: "In this country, we don't sacrifice for anything."[47]

The most controversial alternative to fossil fuels was nuclear energy. Here the problem lay not just in the potentially real association with nuclear weapons, but also in the poisonous character of the radioactive waste left behind by the process of creating nuclear energy. Enthusiasts emphasized how nuclear power did not contribute directly to air pollution or global warming, while critics pointed to the half-life of tens of thousands of years, during which radioactive materials would remain potentially deadly for humans, and to the absence of any safe, permanent storage system. Commercial nuclear power reactors that had been under construction since the 1960s continued to come online. In 1976, fifty-five reactors produced 9 percent of total U.S. electricity. By 1998, 104 reactors were producing 23 percent.[48] ·

Despite federal subsidies, expense issues and safety concerns intervened to halt further new orders for such plants after 1973. Particularly critical for the turn away from this energy path was the partial meltdown of the nuclear core at the Three Mile Island reactor near Harrisburg, Pennsylvania, on March 28, 1979. The release of a plume of radioactivity caused an evacuation of the surrounding area, and sensitized the public to just how dangerous such a malfunction could be. An eerily similar version of a nuclear reactor accident had actually appeared, by chance, just ten days earlier with the opening of the Hollywood film, *The China Syndrome*, which provided publicity that fed anxieties when the near-disaster at Three Mile Island unfolded. Seven years later, an explosion at the Chernobyl nuclear reactor near Kiev in the Soviet Union caused the worst ever nuclear accident, killing at least dozens of people, poisoning the surrounding landscape, causing a permanent evacuation of more than 300,000 people within an 18-mile radius, and raising further questions about this form of alternative energy.[49]

Beyond raising prices and lowering standards of living, one of the greatest impacts of the 1970s energy crisis was the powerful stimulus it provided for new oil exploration and development, from the Gulf of Mexico to western Siberia and from Angola to the North Sea. Denver, the epicenter of Colorado's energy boom, leaped past Kansas City in this decade as the largest city between Chicago and San Francisco. Alaska was the biggest story of all for Americans. In 1968, the Atlantic Richfield Corporation announced the discovery of the largest oil field in North America in Prudhoe Bay on the remote northern slope of Alaska, which had only been a U.S. state for nine years. The frozen waters of the Beaufort Sea prevented tanker access for most of the year, so a pipeline four feet in diameter and 789 miles in length had to be built to carry the crude oil south to the ice-free port of Valdez on Prince William Sound, east of Anchorage. Concerns about the pipeline's impact on wildlife and about oil leakage and spills, along with memories of the 1964 earthquake that devastated Valdez, slowed the approval process until the embargo by the Arab OPEC states helped push it through Congress in November 1973. Skyrocketing oil prices created serious incentives for fast work. More than 21,000 workers operated out of thirty-one construction camps along the pipeline's route, and the first oil reached Valdez in the summer of 1977. Environmental questions took a back seat for twelve years, until the tanker *Exxon Valdez* hit a reef in Prince William Sound at midnight on March 24, 1989, just days before the twenty-fifth anniversary of the Valdez earthquake. Eleven million gallons of crude oil flooded the sound. By the next year, North Slope oil production peaked and began a steady decline.[50]

The economic problem of the 1970s that hit the largest number of average Americans the hardest was rising inflation. Inflation is often considered the "cruelest tax" because it hits the poor harder than anyone else, since they have the fewest alternative resources. After averaging 2.5 percent annual increases during the 1960s, prices soared 6.6 percent annually from 1973 to 1980. In Western Europe, inflation was even higher, including a 15.6 percent rate in the United Kingdom. In 1974, with U.S. prices running 11 percent higher for the year, Federal Reserve chairman Arthur Burns declared that "inflation at anything like the present rate would threaten the very foundations of our society." Inflation in the United States peaked at 13.5 percent in 1980. Besides the 1930s, the 1970s was the only other decade of the twentieth century that saw Americans poorer, on average, at the end than the beginning. The sense that inflation had become permanent undercut assumptions about the traditional virtue of saving money. If dollars lost value each year, it made more sense to spend them now than to save them up. Only a severe contraction of the money supply by new Federal Reserve chairman Paul Volcker beginning in 1979 was able to bring inflation back under 4 percent, but it took until 1983 to do so and led to a painful recession and sharp increase in unemployment along the way.[51]

The early 1970s marked a critical turning point in the real wages of the vast majority of American workers. The steady growth of real wages since World War II, the defining feature of the American economic landscape, came to a halt. Prices now rose faster than paychecks, and people's buying power began to decline. Average real wages drifted downward throughout the 1970s and 1980s and have never since returned to their 1973 peak. Of course, even lower real wages were better than no wages at all. As the national and world economies slowed in the early 1970s and slipped into recession in 1974, millions of workers lost their jobs. Unemployment nearly doubled from 1973 to 1975, reaching 8.3 percent, and it remained high through the 1970s, peaking again at 9.5 percent in 1982. The "Misery Index" told the tale: a combination of the rates of unemployment and inflation, the index passed 17 percent in 1975 and topped out at 21 percent in 1980. The decline in real wages was partially masked by the increase in total hours worked by all family members. Between 1979 and 2000, middle-income families worked an average of 12.5 more full-time weeks per year. Having all adults working for wages outside the home became the new family norm in the 1970s, as it has been ever since.[52]

Not surprisingly, the number of poor Americans spiked. Previously, the boom times of the 1950s and 1960s had brought prosperity that was widespread. During the Kennedy and Johnson administrations of the 1960s, federal programs for job training, education, child care, and welfare further reduced the number of indigent citizens. The percentage of Americans living below the official poverty rate dropped from 22.4 percent in 1959 to 11.1 percent in 1973, its lowest point ever. Then inflation, unemployment, and a reduction in government programs reversed this trend. By 1982, 15 percent were living in poverty, an increase of nearly one-third and a rate that would remain fairly steady for the rest of the century. Once again, 1973 proved to be a watershed year between a quarter-century of economic growth under an activist federal government, and the new era of economic retrenchment and disillusionment with the public sector.[53]

Structural shifts in the U.S. and world economies contributed to the decline of American manufacturing jobs and the shrinking of the ranks of organized labor. A service economy was gradually replacing an industrial economy in the United States, and the 1970s served as a critical transition period. Increasingly efficient flows of information and goods around the world encouraged "globalization," a new term for an accelerating version of an old reality. Trade increased. Tariffs plunged from the 1970s onward. Beginning in 1971, for the first time in the twentieth century, U.S. imports exceeded exports, beginning a trend that soon led to a huge U.S. trade deficit. By 1979, Japanese cars had captured 23 percent of the U.S. market, and former President Ford's daughter, Susan, could be seen dispensing this advice on a television ad: "Take it from a Ford. Drive Subaru." One consequence of twenty-five years of increasing wages was the incentive for U.S. factories to shift production to the American South and then abroad, wherever labor costs were lower. More than 30 million jobs disappeared from the United States in the 1970s, most of them in manufacturing. By 1981, Ford was producing more cars abroad than at home. Jobs evaporated disproportionately from the Rust Belt of the Great Lakes states and the Northeast, employment that had been heavily unionized and relatively high-paying. The percentage of civilian workers who were union members dropped from 25 percent at the start of the decade to 16 percent in 1981, and the percentage working in the service sector rose from 60 percent to 70 percent. Old notions of "workers" as the unionized white men of Michigan, Ohio, and Pennsylvania on assembly lines faded away. Indeed, references to "workers" as a class of people at all largely disappeared from mainstream discourse by the early 1980s, replaced by references to "Reagan Democrats" or victims of plant closings. In 1981, President Reagan put an exclamation point on this new reality by firing 11,000 striking air-traffic controllers, whose union had actually supported his election.[54]

Out of the inflation, stagnation, and structural economic changes emerged a new era of widening socioeconomic differences among Americans. By 1979, after four decades of relatively steady distribution of wealth and income in the United States, the wealthy began to pull away from the rest. "Fewer have more": Yale classicist Ramsey MacMullen's summation of five hundred years of social evolution in the Roman Empire fit the new American era. Workers' overall economic security deteriorated, not just because of shrinking real wages, but also because of declining availability of critical benefits such as employer-sponsored health insurance and defined-benefit pension plans. Consumer debt repayment began to fall. Technological innovations, particularly involving the increasing use of computers, raised the "college premium" for workers with post-secondary educations, whose wages rose while those of less educated workers stagnated. The biggest changes dating from 1979 came at the very top of the income pyramid. The top 1 percent of Americans hauled in 80 percent of the total gains in taxable income over the next three decades. But even within that tiny slice of the population, the distribution of gain was radically unequal; for the entire top 1 percent, average income doubled, but for the top 0.01 percent, income increased fivefold. In 1968, the CEO of the largest U.S. corporation, General Motors, took home in pay and benefits sixty-six times the amount of a typical worker in the company; in 2005, the comparable CEO of Wal-Mart earned nine hundred times what his average employee did. From the 1970s forward, as any chart of family income trends makes vividly clear with rising lines and falling lines, the United States became an even greater country in which to be rich, and a less secure one in which to be poor or working-class. Government policies since the late 1970s contributed crucially to this trend, disproportionately cutting taxes on the wealthiest citizens while reducing social spending on the poorest, a story to be examined more fully in chapter 6.[55]

TURNING INWARD

The most visible response to the cultural, political, and economic turmoil of the 1970s was for citizens to withdraw from the frustrations of the public realm and focus instead on im-

proving their private lives. The recent rise of the "hippie" counterculture, the women's liberation movement, and the sexual
revolution encouraged citizens of an already deeply individualistic culture to be even more expressive of their feelings and
needs. In the 1960s, the *New York Times* best-seller list rarely
had more than one self-help book on it; by May 1978, there
were seven. Eliminating feelings of inferiority and promoting
self-esteem became big business. Thomas A. Harris's *I'm OK,
You're OK*, originally published a few years earlier, soared in
popularity in the mid-1970s. Standards of civility shifted, with
previously obscene language now increasingly common in public discourse, films, and novels. The new frankness about sexuality troubled many but seemed liberating to others. A hugely
popular how-to book by British physician Alex Comfort, *The
Joy of Sex* (1972), framed intimacy in familiar terms by echoing
the most popular cookbook of the era, *The Joy of Cooking*, and
trying to help readers overcome anxiety and shame about their
sexual lives. Embarrassment and shame lost some of their power
to restrain individual behavior, including public disclosures of
one's own and one's own family's most intimate behaviors. Ten
million viewers watched a twelve-part PBS documentary in
1973 on the lives of the upper-middle-class Loud family of Santa
Barbara, revealing beneath a veneer of material comfort a caul-
dron of dysfunction that culminated in divorce. Divorce rates in
the United States doubled in the 1970s, part of a broader pattern in industrialized societies that also saw divorce legalized in
conservative Roman Catholic nations of southern Europe, Italy,
Portugal, and Spain. Rising divorce rates were closely connected
to women's empowerment through entering the paid workforce
and through easier access to birth control and declining fertility
rates. Divorce brought liberation from familial restraints and
limitations; among its other effects, divorce freed individuals to
"do their own thing." The title of Robert J. Ringer's *Looking
Out For #1*, a 1977 best seller, captured a growing trend in
American culture.[56]

One of the most striking aspects of the 1970s was the effort
of millions of Americans to change their personal lifestyles in

healthier directions, particularly in matters of diet and exercise. From eating organic and local foods to jogging, bicycling, and other forms of outdoor recreation, citizens tried to improve themselves. Such change was not easy, particularly during a decade when the percentage of calories being consumed from restaurant food—higher in fat and salt—was increasing measurably, due in large part to the prevalence of all adults in a household working outside the home and the time crunch this created for food preparation. Beginning in the 1970s, Americans over the next three decades increased their average salt intake by 50 percent, primarily from increased consumption of convenient prepared foods. By 2006, Americans were getting 33 percent of their calories from restaurant food, compared to 18 percent in the 1970s. The consumption of less expensive fast food accelerated, along with a dramatic jump in the percentage of calories Americans imbibed from sugary soft drinks. What would emerge by the end of the century as an epidemic of obesity had its origins in these years. By 2006, Americans ate 11 percent more food than in 1970, including 59 percent more fats. From 1960 to 2002, Americans gained one inch in average height but twenty-four pounds in average weight, and average body mass indices rose from 25 to 28. Concern about such emerging trends led to the coinage of the joking but pejorative term "couch potato" in 1976.[57]

Many Americans, however, resisted these developing trends and moved instead in the opposite direction. One healthier option was to use the same skills of the food science industry to develop new products with less negative impact on consumers, particularly sugars and fats. Sugar consumption by English speakers in North America, after all, had grown from just 4 pounds per year three hundred years earlier to 140 pounds in 2005 (50 percent more than in Germany or France). This was a sweet-loving culture. But in 1975, a young Indian scientist working in a London laboratory accidentally created sucralose, available ever since in small yellow packets under the name Splenda, the best-selling artificial sweetener in the United States. Six years later, the NutraSweet Corporation introduced Aspartame, which became the primary sweetener in the burgeoning diet soda industry. Like removing sugar from soda, reducing carbohydrates in beer held great promise. A biochemist doing postdoctoral work at Rheingold Breweries in Brooklyn developed a process to remove starch during the brewing process. Gablinger's Diet Beer was the result, first bottled in 1967. It flopped as a commercial product and Rheingold went out of business, but the diet formula passed on to Meister Brau Brewery in Chicago, which created Meister Brau Lite beer. When the giant Miller Brewing Company bought up Meister Brau in the early 1970s, a new marketing strategy boosted sales sharply by using professional football players and other rugged-looking men, arguing about the relative importance that "Lite Beer from Miller" "tastes great" or is "less filling." Competitor Anheuser-Busch responded with Bud Lite in 1982, and a vast new market for low-calorie beer opened up.[58]

The move to healthier lifestyles generally took a more natural and local bent in matters of food. The natural foods movement had older roots but became a national phenomenon in the 1970s, as food co-ops and health food restaurants proliferated. Moosewood, Inc., a collectively owned business in Ithaca, New York, opened a flagship institution, the Moosewood Restaurant, in 1973 and four years later published the *Moosewood Cookbook*, the most widely used alternative cookbook of the era. Whole Foods opened in 1978 as a single small vegetarian grocery in Austin, soon to grow into a vast international health food supermarket chain. Quaker Oats, the giant mainstream cereal company, began selling its own line of granola in 1972. Alice Waters represented the haute cuisine of this trend with the opening of her Chez Panisse restaurant in Berkeley in 1971. Waters married French cooking style with local, seasonal produce to create an extraordinarily successful high-end restaurant, one that embodied a vibrant "new American cuisine" that reveled in blending culinary traditions from around the world.[59]

The new American cuisine received a major boost in its wine sector in 1976 when French experts in a prominent blind tasting in Paris, for the first time ever, rated several Californian wines more highly than the top French wines. The emphasis on fresh, local American products also reshaped the contours of the beer industry. After decades of U.S. market domination by the homogenous giants Anheuser-Busch, Miller, and Coors, a revival of distinctive local craft brewing in the late 1970s initiated the growth of micro-breweries that spread throughout the country in subsequent decades. The new emphasis on quality and freshness swept into the coffee sector of the food industry as well. Starbucks opened its first small store in downtown Seattle in 1971, taking the first step toward the 15,000 stores it would operate around the world within a generation and stimulating the growth of a slew of successful independent coffee houses. Tom's of Maine created a successful new empire of all-natural personal care products, beginning with its first toothpaste and deodorant in 1975 and 1976.[60]

Smoking began to decline in the United States in the 1970s, both as a personal habit and as a culturally acceptable practice. Cigarette smoking reached its peak in the early 1960s, just before the first official warning by the Surgeon General in 1964 about its potential hazards to human health. After a small decline, smoking reached another, slightly lower peak in the early 1970s and then dropped steadily over the next three decades. In 1955, 59 percent of men and 31 percent of women smoked; in 1997, these numbers were 28 percent and 22 percent. A crucial step came with the 1972 Surgeon General's report about possible harm from simply being in the presence of other people smoking, "second-hand smoke." In 1978, the Roper polling organization did a survey for the Tobacco Institute and warned that for public opinion, "What the smoker does to himself may be his business, but what the smoker does to the non-smoker is quite a different matter." Pressed by flight attendants, United Airlines in 1971 became the first commercial airline to segregate smokers and nonsmokers, a practice soon followed by all airlines. But separate seating sections had limited impact in such a tightly enclosed space. One critic suggested that "a smoking section on an airplane . . . is like having a peeing section in a swimming pool." Smoking was soon banned on all U.S. flights. In 1973, Arizona became the first state to enact a law restricting smoking in public places, and within eight years, thirty-five other states had followed suit. The 1970s, in other words, saw American society reorient from a primarily smoking culture to a primarily nonsmoking culture. Audiences that had once watched film and television stars regularly light up now saw during the 2004 Super Bowl an anti-smoking advertisement satirizing sales pitches by offering "Shards o' Glass Freeze Pops" with the slogan, "Yes, it's gravely harmful, but you'll love it!" U.S. tobacco companies responded to a declining domestic market in 1974 by initiating huge advertising campaigns overseas. Cigarette sales may have dropped by more than 20 percent in the United States from 1975 to 1994, but U.S. cigarette exports more than tripled in the same years.[61]

Americans in large numbers began going outdoors for recreational exercise in the 1970s. In the 1960s, running was done on school track teams; by the 1980s, jogging and running had become normal parts of middle-class life for both men and women. Frank Shorter's gold medal in the 1972 Olympic marathon helped ignite the popularity of running in the United States. The first New York City Marathon counted 126 entrants in 1970. By 1978, it had 10,000. The Nike Corporation was created in Portland in 1972 to make running shoes, and cofounder Bill Bowerman, the University of Oregon track coach, developed the first waffle sole by pouring urethane rubber over a waffle iron. Lighter and giving better traction, waffle soles propelled Nike past German-based Adidas as the dominant manufacturer of running shoes. Seven years later another innovation—a bubble of air sealed in the polyurethane sole to cushion the foot— allowed Nike with its Air system to do the same with the basketball shoe market. In 1977, Jim Fixx published *The Complete Book of Running* and sold more than a million copies. By 1978, his second year in the White House, President Carter was running an average of 40 miles per week. Jogging and running pervaded the nation.[62]

Americans also found their way outdoors for other forms of human-powered recreation. As oil prices soared, the bicycle

Figure 1.4.
President Jimmy Carter embodied many of the central themes of 1970s
American culture. He takes a run around the White House grounds in
November 1978. Courtesy Jimmy Carter Presidential Library.

market boomed. Traditional European manufacturers such as Motobecane and Peugeot from France and Raleigh from the United Kingdom found new competition from the homegrown Trek company, founded in a barn in Waterloo, Wisconsin, in 1976. Trek handcrafted 805 bikes that year; in 2007, they manufactured 1.5 million. The first Ironman Triathlon debuted in 1978, combining three popular Hawaii races—a 2.4-mile ocean swim, a 112-mile bicycle ride, and a 26.2-mile marathon run— and spawning a new sporting culture of triathletes. Whitewater slalom kayaking became an Olympic sport in 1972, the same year that the Nantahala Outdoor Center opened as a small rafting company on the banks of the beautiful Nantahala River in western North Carolina, soon to become a mecca for whitewater canoeists and kayakers. Cross-country skiing took off in popularity in the same years, promoted in part by American Bill Koch's silver medal at the 1976 Winter Olympics in Innsbruck, Austria. Outdoor education expanded dramatically, led by the five Outward Bound Schools that had opened in the previous decade but whose enrollments more than doubled during the 1970s. *Outside* magazine first appeared in 1978 to further promote outdoor recreation as a lifestyle. Renowned rock climber and mountaineer Yvon Chouinard created Patagonia in 1973 as a comprehensive outdoor clothing maker and retailer to complement his earlier line of Chouinard climbing equipment. Patagonia developed innovative layering fabrics such as synthetic polyester pile jackets (1976) and polypropylene underwear (1980) for keeping warm and dry while exercising in severe weather. Hiking, backpacking, rock climbing, and mountaineering all grew sharply in popularity. Environmental consciousness spread as millions of American adults went out to play.[63]

In 1975, the United States launched two unmanned *Viking* spaceship probes that landed on the planet Mars. Two years later, *Voyager* was launched to get closer to the outer planets of the solar system. These extraordinary voyages brought back photographs of distant realms, but they found no signs of life elsewhere in the universe. The Earth, it turned out, appeared to be utterly unique and alone. Whatever humans would do with their planet, they would do it on their own. For Americans in this decade, the recognition of cosmic isolation—of no larger story beyond the Earth—seemed to fit with their experience of national and personal limitations, of a society hemmed in by international frustrations, political failure, and economic trauma. The blows just seemed to pile up: a lost war, a president removed, the nation's intelligence agencies humiliated, an economy in the worst condition in a generation, and an uncertain energy future.

Faced with so much damage in their country's public sphere, Americans turned increasingly to their personal lives to seek comfort and meaning. Distrusting government and less hopeful about the common ground of the public realm, they pursued different versions of self-fulfillment in the private realm. Some sought healthier diets and lifestyles, in closer touch with nature and the outdoors. Others engaged in what looked more like self-indulgence: the consumption of drugs, casual sex, frayed family relationships, and inattentive parenting. Singer Jimmy Buffett's Florida-based, party-oriented music embodied this spirit with a Sun Belt flavor, from his ironical "Why Don't We Get Drunk and Screw" (1973) to his mega-hit "(Wasting Away Again in) Margaritaville" (1978). While many Americans sought meaning in renewed spirituality, particularly in a new wave of fundamentalist Protestant Christianity, others inclined to a profound skepticism about all authorities and traditions. Irony and parody blossomed in popular culture, from *Saturday Night Live* to Hollywood films.[64] A group of ballet enthusiasts even banded together in 1974 to create Les Ballets Trockaderos De Monte Carlo, a vehicle for presenting a playful, amusing spoof of classical ballet that included men dancing en pointe to imitate female ballerinas. In the hugely popular film *Life of Brian* (1979), the British comedy troupe Monty Python parodied the Christian gospels' account of the life of Jesus, featuring a child born on the same night in a stable next door who spends his life being mistaken for a messiah. "He's not the Messiah, he's a very naughty boy!" declares his annoyed mother. Little was sacred in the 1970s, as traditional hierarchies weakened and the United States seemed to many of its citizens a nation adrift. Economic inequality increased, yet in other ways American society grew more inclusive and egalitarian, thanks to a more tolerant and inclusive culture and a new wave of reform, to which we now turn.

Chapter 2

THE RISING TIDE OF EQUALITY AND

DEMOCRATIC REFORM

"GOOD MORNING, BOYS AND GIRLS!" This greeting has rung out in elementary school classrooms throughout the United States for generations. Almost no one objects. After all, sex is a biological reality. The children are boys and girls. It seems natural to call them that. But is it really natural? Children can also be categorized in many other ways using different criteria. "Good morning, tall kids and short kids!" would surely raise some eyebrows. Why call attention to people's height, another clear biological difference? "Good morning, blacks and whites!" is unimaginable, a visible distinction freighted with an invidious past that few by the 1970s would have considered a positive way to distinguish children. Boys and girls, however, still worked. They just seemed to be naturally different, from their bodies to the clothes they wore, from the games they played to the bathrooms they used.

In the early 1970s, this began to change. Young activist women challenged traditional assumptions about the core human identity of being female or being male. Bathrooms did not change (despite anti-feminist warnings), sports teams remained primarily male or female, and women not only still gave birth to children but also continued to provide the vast majority of their care. But the old idea that the biology of one's sex determines one's fundamental identity no longer seemed so clear. Instead, for the first time, gender—the social and cultural roles associated with a particular sex—became a crucial and widely used term, as millions of women and men began to reconsider all sorts of previously unexamined assumptions about femaleness and maleness.

Part of what they realized was the inaccuracy of assuming that women and men were fundamentally different from each other—not just the other sex, but the *opposite* sex—and fundamentally similar to others of their same sex. Rather, male and female seemed to represent large circles that overlapped to a considerable extent, depending on the criteria being measured, instead of completely separate circles. On the wide range of human characteristics and behaviors, the biological category of sex appeared to be just one of several important variables.

The implications of this kind of rethinking were enormous. The segregation by sex that had pervaded American society no longer looked so natural. In the workplace, entire categories of employment were no longer restricted to men or to women. In the field of education, schools, colleges, and facilities eliminated whole frameworks of sex discrimination. In the eyes of the law, on issues from jury duty to abortion to marital rape, women gained a new empowerment and equality. And in their personal lives, women began to alter the contours of their most important relationships, with fathers, brothers, husbands, lovers, and sons, and renegotiate the personal politics of how households operated. Longstanding assumptions about women's roles and the meaning of femininity came under sustained assault, which necessarily raised elemental questions about men's roles and the meaning of masculinity. Very few American families navigated the 1970s untouched by these dramatic and intimate changes.

The weakening of traditional gender hierarchies marked the largest shift of the decade toward formal equality, since it encompassed slightly more than half of American citizens. But other old hierarchies also began to crumble in the 1970s as the reforming spirit of egalitarianism, spilling out from the black freedom struggle of the previous decade, seeped into almost all corners of American life. For the first time, homosexuals began to come out of the closet in large numbers. Freeing themselves from bonds of fear and loathing, they won the first scientific support for the psychiatric legitimacy of homosexuality and the first legal support for gay and lesbian civil rights. Physically and mentally disabled Americans also fought to ride the new wave

of inclusiveness as they gained federal support for fuller incor-
poration of disabled students into public school classrooms.
Young and old Americans pushed back against age discrimination. And a new cohort of immigrants, primarily from Asia and
Latin America rather than Europe, arrived in the United States
in growing numbers, ensuring that the nation would soon become an even less black-and-white society. Multiculturalism advanced. Rights were extended for the first time even to animal
species, as the enthusiasm for freedom and equality reached
flood tide.

Calling into question assumptions about gender on which
people had built their personal identities for generations was
not a recipe for immediate universal acceptance. Many Americans considered such questioning absurd—or dangerous. Defending traditional gender roles developed into a major thrust
of modern social conservatism, among some women as well as
men. Homophobia and anti-immigrant sentiment emerged as
other engines of conservatism. Timing mattered here. Women
and people of color had the bad luck to emerge from old restrictions in the public sphere—in education, politics, and especially
employment—during the 1970s, a time of economic downturn,
when white male workers and many women dependent on those
men's wages found their economic conditions declining and
resented the new competition in the workplace. In addition,
principled conservatives never viewed the relentless pursuit of
human equality as completely natural or healthy. For them, humans were inherently and obviously unequal, a fact to be acknowledged and respected rather than denied or reduced. They
tended to agree with the famous ancient Roman leader, Pliny
the Younger: "Nothing is more unfair than equality."[1]

In modern U.S. history, however, defending inequality of opportunity was rarely a winning position to take in the long run.
The dominant trend in legal, political, and cultural development
ran instead toward greater freedom and inclusion for a larger
and larger percentage of the population. Abraham Lincoln once
declared that "the leading object of government is, to elevate the
condition of men—to lift artificial weights from all shoulders—

to clear the paths of laudable pursuit for all—to afford all, an unfettered start, and a fair chance, in the race of life." American society became more formally committed to the inclusion of all individuals in that competitive race. In no decade was this more evident than the 1970s.[2]

WOMEN IN THE PUBLIC SPHERE

Women have struggled since the dawn of time against limitations placed on them by men and by other women. A fourteen-year-old girl named Hillary Rodham stood in a long line of American women when she wrote to NASA in 1961 asking what she needed to do to become an astronaut, only to receive a curt reply that the nation's new space program was not recruiting girls. Such a response was utterly typical on the cusp of the changes about to be initiated by the activism of the 1960s. The African American civil rights movement in the South not only changed black lives but also created a dynamic model of optimism about breaking through old barriers, particularly with the passage of the Civil Rights Act of 1964 and the Voting Rights Act of 1965. The Civil Rights Act banned discrimination not only on the grounds of race but also of sex, a key legal precedent even if it was not enforced for many years. A renewed movement for women's equality proceeded on two primary fronts in the 1960s. One was the pursuit of equality in the public sphere, such as equality of job opportunities, pay, jury duty, and legal status, a drive associated particularly with the National Organization for Women (NOW), founded in 1966. The other front included the push for equality in the more private sphere of family life, male-female relationships, and sexuality. These mostly younger proponents of "women's liberation" agreed with the need for equal opportunities in the public sphere but wanted also to reshape the politics of their private lives, as well as to help men find liberation from the limitations of traditional masculine roles. Visible nationally only after their protest at the 1968 Miss America contest in Atlantic City, New Jersey, these more radical feminists remained few in number at the end of the 1960s. It was only in the 1970s that most American women seriously challenged and rearranged the gender roles with which they had grown up.[3]

Most of the leading activists in the "second wave feminism" of this era (the first wave having won women the vote in 1920) came to their new political consciousness directly out of experiences in the civil rights movement and the movement against the Vietnam War. They were offended by blatant injustice and determined to help their country live up to its expressed ideals of equality and liberty for all. But they discovered that even liberal and radical men tended to treat them as inferiors; men committed to ending racial injustice and imperialism remained nearly blind to their own unequal treatment of women. In 1964, Mary King and Casey Hayden drafted a statement about the position of women in the Student Non-Violent Coordinating Committee, the most egalitarian of the civil rights organizations. "Assumptions of male superiority," they wrote, "are as widespread and deep-rooted and every much as crippling to woman as the assumptions of white supremacy are to the Negro." It seemed no coincidence that white men commonly referred to adult women as "girls," just as they referred to adult black men as "boys." By the end of the 1960s, African Americans increasingly took on the rhetorical mantle of Black Power as a rejection of older traditions of deference to whites. Feminists, in the same fashion, sought to "unlearn niceness," the tradition of female deference to male cultural authority.[4]

"Organize around your own oppression." This popular slogan emerged as a key concept in the late 1960s when Black Power began pushing whites out of leadership roles in the civil rights movement. For young women, their own oppression meant the restrictions of being female, and a strategic position to win early in this battle was the language used to describe women. They were to be "girls" no more, nor simple sex objects. The title of Gloria Steinem's new magazine, *Ms.*, first published in late 1971, went to the heart of the matter. If the proper title for a man, "Mr.," did not reveal any clue about his marital sta-

tus, why should the only two traditional titles for a woman—
"Miss" and "Mrs."—boldly advertise whether a woman was
already "taken" or potentially available? There seemed no clearer
indication from daily life of how women were traditionally seen
not as autonomous individuals, like men, but rather as identified
primarily by their relationship to men. "Ms." solved the problem,
just like "Mr." The first issue of *Ms*. magazine sold out in eight
days. For the next eighteen years, as the impact of the women's
movement spread out into every corner of American life, *Ms*.
served as the most popular mainstream feminist magazine.[5]

In October 1974, the *New York Times Magazine* published
excerpts from "Guidelines for Equal Treatment of the Sexes
in McGraw-Hill Book Company Publications." Gender-neutral
language was the goal. "Men and women should be treated primarily as people, and not primarily as members of opposite
sexes. Their shared humanity and common attributes should be
stressed, not their gender difference." The guidelines concluded
that both women and men should be "represented as whole
human beings with human strengths and weaknesses, not masculine or feminine ones." All were to be treated as distinctive
individuals, not primarily as members of a group. This marked
a watershed change in attitudes about gender, prominently pro-
nounced in the nation's leading newspaper and one of its most
influential sources of information. McGraw-Hill, for its part,
served as a major educational publisher and thus an important
voice through textbooks in the country's classrooms. In the middle years of the 1970s, people and institutions began to recalcu-
late stereotypically sexist language habits. What invidious differences were implied by such phrases as "man and wife," "the
men and the ladies," and "mankind"? While this proved to be a
complicated and enduring debate, and a term such as "mankind" certainly implied the inclusion of all women as well as all
men, the frivolous and casual use of male-coded language and
unnecessary male pronouns began to decline. In 1979, the National Weather Service first began naming hurricanes after men
as well as women, leaving behind the old chauvinistic assump-

tion that women were distinctively unstable, temperamental, and volatile.[6]

At stake, ultimately, was the nature of human beings. Were men and women two different poles of humanity, fundamentally different in essence? Or were they instead just two of many subsets of the human population, biologically different in such matters as genitalia, hormones, and reproductive organs, but fundamentally overlapping much more than not in regard to intelligence, character, size, and other physical, psychological, and moral characteristics? Most feminists emphasized men's and women's similarity, while their opponents defended the primacy of sex differences. But a minority of "women's culture" feminists also stood for difference, seeing women as essentially more nurturing, less competitive, and ultimately more virtuous. Some of these feminists drew an analogy of women with the independence-minded Third World, calling for equality for both sexes as for all peoples and nations while respecting their differences; equality, in other words, did not necessarily signify sameness. Feminism was complicated, a mansion of many rooms, and one shaped by ongoing psychological and neurological research into men's and women's differences and similarities.[7]

Not surprisingly, debates about gender in the 1970s were often emotionally charged, reflecting people's understanding of their own core identities and how they lived their daily lives. At a heated moment in a debate with anti-feminist Phyllis Schlafly at Illinois State University in 1973, feminist Betty Friedan blurted out, "I'd like to burn you at the stake!"—a particularly Freudian slip given the long history of dissenting women's persecution as witches. Similar sentiments often flowed in both directions, because the stakes were very high. And generalizing about a group of people as large as the category of women—more than 100 million Americans during that decade—was fraught with perils. Differences of class, race, religion, family situation, marital status, and other important criteria severely compromised the prospect of women identifying with all other women. This could happen on certain matters such as opposing sexual violence or promoting women's health care, but women as a group proved vastly more heterogeneous than homogenous.[8]

The gender issue of the 1970s with the highest profile was probably the Equal Rights Amendment (ERA). "Equality of rights under the law shall not be denied or abridged by the United States or by any state on account of sex," was the simple statement of the proposed constitutional amendment. First introduced in Congress in 1923, the ERA gained increasing political support through the 1960s. In October 1971, the U.S. House of Representatives approved it by an overwhelming vote of 354–23, and the Senate followed suit five months later by an 84–8 vote. President Nixon was a supporter, as were his White House successors Jerry Ford and Jimmy Carter and their wives, Betty Ford and Rosalynn Carter. Twenty-two of the necessary thirty-eight states approved the amendment within the first year of the seven-year (later extended to ten-year) period for approval mandated by Congress, and thirty-five eventually voted in favor of it. But opposition began to build, spearheaded by Phyllis Schlafly and her STOP-ERA campaign, as conservative women, particularly church women, organized to lobby against what they saw as an effort to force women to become like men—to work outside the home, to serve in the military, to not be financially supported by one's husband, even—supposedly— to use the same public restrooms. With the U.S. Supreme Court's January 1973 *Roe v. Wade* decision establishing women's right to abortion in the first six months of pregnancy, ERA opponents also argued that the amendment would bolster what they saw as an immoral decision by the Court. Momentum behind ERA ratification ground to a halt, giving anti-feminists a symbolic victory.[9]

The horse, however, was already out of the barn. Regardless of the fate of the ERA, women's growing insistence on equal treatment did not abate. In 1973, the Supreme Court overturned one of the most fundamental dividers of the sexes when it ruled that employment advertisements could no longer specify gender. Jobs were for people, not for women or men. In finance, women —whether married, separated, divorced or widowed—had long been frustrated by the resistance of financial institutions to allow them to establish credit in their own names. The NOW's Credit Task Force files were filled with thousands of letters from women angry about the discrimination they confronted in trying to secure bank accounts, credit cards, and mortgages—matters that men would consider a fundamental right. In 1974, Congress passed the Equal Credit Opportunity Act to remedy this inequality. A year later, the U.S. Supreme Court ruled for the first time that women and men were equally obligated to jury duty, another fundamental aspect of full citizenship. Airline stewardesses succeeded in having their title recategorized as "flight attendants." Gone were the days of sexist advertising, such as National Airlines' photos of alluring young women with captions such as, "Hi, I'm Linda, and I'm going to FLY you like you've never been flown before." One flight attendant organizer told *Ms.* magazine: "I don't think of myself as a sex symbol or a servant. I think of myself as somebody who knows how to open the door of a 747 in the dark, upside down and under water." As more and more women entered the professional workforce during the 1970s, the federal Equal Employment Opportunity Commission listened to complaints and in 1980 laid out guidelines for a new legal category of "sexual harassment" that was upheld six years later by the Supreme Court.[10]

Structural changes in the U.S. economy in the 1970s also encouraged women's growing participation in paid employment. Average real incomes for men peaked in 1973 and drifted steadily downward for the next two decades, as deindustrialization and the loss of manufacturing jobs mostly affected men. By 1976, according to one estimate, only 40 percent of American jobs paid enough to support an average family. The economic value of a blue-collar husband was declining. With men bringing home fewer dollars at the same time that rapid inflation (11 percent in 1974) was hollowing out families' purchasing power, millions of women went out to work simply to preserve their households' standard of living. In 1970, 43 percent of American women age sixteen or over were in the paid workforce; in 1980, this number increased to 52 percent. Of women with children

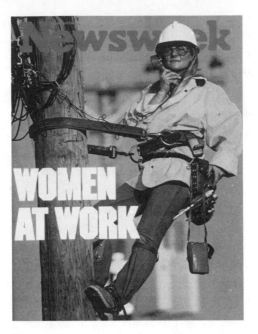

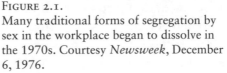

FIGURE 2.1.
Many traditional forms of segregation by
sex in the workplace began to dissolve in
the 1970s. Courtesy *Newsweek*, December
6, 1976.

under age six, 30 percent held paying jobs in 1970, and 50 percent did so by 1985. In industrialized nations around the world,
the shift to an economy based increasingly on services and information lowered barriers to female participation. Brains su-
perseded brawn. The transformation of the U.S. military to a
volunteer force in 1973 succeeded in part because of female re-
cruits; from 1.5 percent in 1973, they climbed to 7.5 percent in
1983 (a fivefold increase), and their inclusion kept test scores
and other qualifications higher. The broader pattern of increased
longevity in the twentieth century also pulled women into the
workforce. In 1900, the average American woman lived to age
fifty, often dying soon after raising a large family, whereas by the
1970s, she lived beyond age seventy-five, giving her more time
as well as the need for more money over time.[11]

The increased entry of women into the paid workforce produced ambivalent feelings on their part. Research suggests that most went to work in response to financial pressures rather than for personal fulfillment, though the satisfactions of paid employment were often considerable. Increased financial independence also inevitably reduced the willingness of women to remain in unhappy marriages. "Women don't have to put up with [men's] crap," one Indiana wife noted. "They can support themselves." But many women from the working class and lower middle class understood the work world through the often-difficult jobs their husbands held, and they were not always eager to give up the domestic sphere of children and housework in exchange for work that promised to be a far cry from a fascinating profession. They also knew that their increased hours outside the home were not, on average, close to being compensated for by husbands picking up half the share of housework and child-rearing duties. Indeed, working women in the 1970s averaged fifteen more hours per week of work at home and outside than their husbands. Greater financial independence and the other rewards of paid employment came at a cost of increased stress and less leisure. The perpetual popularity of the idea of early retirement suggests the complicated attitudes that most Americans had toward work.[12]

The most striking feature of the 1970s for women was their entry in large numbers for the first time into the professions. On the graph of women in these careers, 1970 is where the arrow begins to head up sharply. During this decade, the share of female lawyers rose from 4 percent to 15 percent, female physicians, 9 percent to 13 percent, and female engineers, 2 percent to 5 percent—all large jumps in terms of percentage change. The number of women in the U.S. House of Representatives increased from ten to sixteen. From 1972 to 1981, the number of women chemists rose from 10 percent to 22 percent and women pharmacists, from 13 percent to 26 percent. This was the turning point where a critical mass of women entered high-paying, high-status jobs previously reserved primarily for men.[13]

First-woman breakthroughs abounded. The first female Lutheran pastor was ordained in 1970, followed by the first female Jewish rabbi in 1972 and the first female Episcopal priest in 1974 (the latter officially recognized by the church two years later). In 1972, Sharon Goodyear became the first woman in upper-echelon management at the popular outdoor-education program Outward Bound. Women moved to the front of the plane, too. In 1973, Emily Howell Warner, age thirty-four, became the first woman pilot of a commercially scheduled airline when she took the controls for Frontier Airlines; three years later she was promoted to the first female captain. In politics, Connecticut voters elected Ella Grasso as governor in 1974, the first woman to win a governorship without being the wife or widow of a former governor. Chicago voters chose Jane Byrne as their first female mayor in 1979. Sandra Day O'Connor, who graduated third in her Stanford Law School class, was elected majority leader of the Arizona State Senate in 1973 and eight years later became the first woman appointed to the U.S. Supreme Court. The Bicentennial Year of 1976 brought other distinctive firsts: the first woman president of the *Harvard Law Review*, the first woman Rhodes scholarship winner, and the first women entering the NASA training program for astronauts. In one of the most traditionally masculine of arenas, Eva Shain became the first female referee of a heavyweight championship boxing match, the 1977 fight between Muhammad Ali and Ernie Shavers in New York City. After taking office that same year, President Carter appointed a record number of women to federal agencies and the White House staff and named forty women to federal judgeships (the previous highest number was three, by Lyndon Johnson), thereby quadrupling the number of women who had ever served on the federal bench.[14]

Just as women in large numbers entered the professions for the first time in the 1970s, so did women integrate the ranks of higher education and professional schools. In the early years after World War II, women had been disproportionately absent from colleges and universities, due in large part to most having not been veterans and thus unable to make use of the generous funding from the Servicemen's Readjustment Act, commonly known as the GI Bill. But the number of female students on campus soon began to rise. In 1950, women earned 25 percent of bachelor's degrees; by 2000, they earned 56 percent. Doctoral degrees followed a similar pattern, from 10 percent in 1950 to 41 percent in 2000, with a steep acceleration in the 1970s. During this decade, the share of female law students leapt from 10 percent to 36 percent and female medical students, from 9 percent to 25 percent. A similar pattern held for veterinary, pharmacy, and business schools. Almost all of the traditionally all-male elite colleges opened their doors to women for the first time in the 1970s, including Harvard and Johns Hopkins in 1970, Dartmouth and Notre Dame in 1972, and Amherst in 1975. Elite boarding schools did the same, such as Phillips Exeter Academy in 1970. The U.S. Congress required the nation's elite military academies—at West Point, Annapolis, and Colorado Springs—to accept female applicants in 1976. Most formerly all-female schools welcomed men, including Bennington, Vassar, and Skidmore between 1969 and 1971. Dormitories soon became coeducational, too, whether by room or by floor. The significance of this shift was enormous. For the first time, young women and men encountered each other continually as colleagues and friends, no longer kept in separate spheres and viewing each other primarily as potential mates. "It would be the first time many men dealt with women who were not relatives or girlfriends," recalled one of the Naval Academy's first female graduates. It is difficult to imagine a more momentous change in how men and women interacted with each other.[15]

The tide of women rolling into graduate programs and faculty positions in academia produced changes in the curriculum. Like young African American scholars beginning to uncover a mostly ignored black history, young female scholars began focusing research on the lives of women who had been little noticed before. This was not simple identity politics: studying one's own group because that is all one is interested in. It was much more urgent than that. The story of half of humanity had been mostly obscured, from history and political science to philosophy and literature. One of the first women's studies courses appeared at Cornell University in 1969. By 1975, 150 women's studies programs had been established around the country; by 1980, there were 300. The first annual Berkshire Conference on the History of Women met at Douglass College of Rutgers University in 1973, attracting three times the one hundred participants whom organizers had expected. Gerda Lerner, a pioneer in women's history, recalls only four other specialists in U.S. history in 1970 who identified themselves primarily as historians of women. One of her graduate students at the Graduate Center of the City University of New York, Renate Bridenthal, remembers: "Like so many others at the time, I suddenly wondered: Where have all the women been in history?" This burst of enthusiasm became a sustained line of inquiry, and over the next three decades the study of women emerged as one of the top areas of specialization within the field of history, an extraordinary reversal of status by the early 2000s.[16]

The changes in women's educational opportunities in the 1970s reshaped schools as well as universities. In 1972, Congress enacted Title IX (an amendment to the Higher Education Act), withholding critical federal funding from school districts and colleges that discriminated against students on the basis of sex. The new law meant little for physics laboratories or English classrooms, where girls and boys typically worked together. But it had enormous implications for school athletic programs and facilities. The chasm between spending on girls' sports and boys' sports was suddenly no longer merely "natural" or "a tradition." It could now mean a financial disaster for a school district. Athletic directors responded to the new incentive by putting institutional support behind equipment and facilities for girls' sports to an unprecedented extent. With new opportunities and encouragement, and with changing public attitudes about the capacities of females, girls took to playing fields and courts as never before. Girls' participation in high school athletics increased almost fivefold by the end of the decade. In similar fashion, the first girls began to play Little League baseball in the summer of 1974 in Hoboken, New Jersey, and the slower six-player version of girls' basketball (in which two players remained in the backcourt) was phased out in favor of the boys' five-player version. At the University of Tennessee in Knoxville in 1974, a young part-time coach named Pat Summitt was paid $250 a month to take the reins of the women's basketball team, the first step toward building a program of extraordinary popular and commercial success.[17]

The shift in institutional support for girls' participation in sports marked a major change in American life. Certainly, there had been star women athletes before, from Babe Didrickson to Althea Gibson. But they had been exceptions, just like mountaineer Arlene Blum who, on a climb of glaciated Mt. Waddington in British Columbia's remote Coast Mountains as late as 1969, had been informed by a climbing guide that "there are no good women climbers. Women climbers either aren't good climbers, or they aren't real women." Now this false dichotomy—of real athletes versus real women—was being unmasked as a fraud. No longer were girls and young women expected to be largely passive observers or sideline cheerleaders, to "glisten" rather than sweat. Instead, girls were to run, jump, kick, bang, hit, and sweat as hard as they could, and to be aggressive. "Playing like a girl" began to lose its very meaning, eventually to be made fun of in advertisements starring accomplished female athletes. The essential parameters of what it meant to be "feminine" in the United States were changing in a fundamental way. The Boston Marathon began openly accepting women runners in 1972, the same year *Sports Illustrated* put tennis star Billie Jean King on the cover as its first female athlete of the year. In 1978, Blum led the American Women's Himalayan Expedition that put the first two women on top of Annapurna, the tenth highest peak in the world at 26,504 feet and one only thrice climbed previously. Three years earlier, a Japanese climber had become the first woman to summit Mt. Everest. The all-female expedition of 1978 raised most of its $80,000 for trip expenses with sales of a T-shirt that read: "A Woman's Place Is On Top."[18]

WOMEN IN THE PRIVATE SPHERE

Just as American women shed old restrictions in the public realms of work and school, so, too, did they change the terms of their private lives in the 1970s. Above all, they moved to greater independence and individual freedom, nowhere more clearly than in marriage. The average age of an American woman at the altar dropped to a twentieth-century low of 20.5 (23 for men) in the 1960s and then headed up, increasing most sharply in the 1970s. By 1996, it reached twenty-five. Expectations of the quality of marriage changed. Older standards such as distinct, separate roles for husbands and wives and raising several children gave way to higher premiums on passion, intimacy, and friendship between spouses. Historian Stephanie Coontz pointed out that marriage became harder in this sense from the 1970s on, but also potentially more rewarding. Jimmy and Rosalynn Carter provided a model in the White House, openly affectionate with each other, frequently holding hands or kissing even in public, with Jimmy often consulting with Rosalynn on policy matters. Their friendship and intimacy were plain to see. The Carter family's younger generation also embodied the changing expectations of gender roles within marriage. At breakfast together in Georgia a week before Christmas in 1974, oldest son Jack, who had just gotten married, saw his wife walking through the dining room and called out, "Honey, get me some more grits!" She replied evenly, "Get them yourself," and disappeared through the doorway. "It was clear that the young generation had introduced the first stage of new rules to the Carter family," Jimmy recalled, "with more equal status among husbands and wives."[19]

Marriages also changed in the 1970s by ending much more frequently than ever before. The growing emphasis on individual rights came to include the option to divorce as one of the many rights available for pursuing greater happiness and per-

sonal growth. The rise in women's paid employment empowered women in large numbers to consider and often choose
being their own economic provider. Indeed, across all industrialized nations, there was a strong correlation between divorce and
the percentage of female participation in the paid workforce,
categories in which the United States ranked particularly high.
Marriage began to lose some of the considerable economic benefits that had long made it attractive. Legal changes followed to
grease the skids. Following California's lead in 1969, forty-six
other states in the next eight years enacted some form of no-
fault divorce laws, allowing incompatibility rather than specific
wrongdoing as satisfactory grounds for ending a marriage. "No-
fault" implied that divorce was a normal and natural development, a reasonable occurrence, rather than a result of someone's
particular actions. The results were dramatic. Divorce rates
nearly doubled in the 1970s, rising from twelve to twenty-three
break-ups per thousand married women per year. In 1975, for
example, more than a million couples divorced. Marriages con-
summated in the late 1970s stood only a 50 percent chance of
lasting a lifetime.[20]

The effects of an increased divorce rate and a changing landscape of American family structure were complicated and were
still being worked out a generation later. Certainly the impact of
divorce on children could be traumatic, though a reprieve from
continuous family tension may have compensated for much of
that negative impact. For people yoked together in unhappy
marriages, divorce, for all the sense of disappointment and failure it could bring, undoubtedly provided enormous relief and
liberation. One measurable outcome was the decline in income
for both women and men after divorce during the 1970s, averaging 20 percent for women and 7 percent for men, much of the
change because former spouses were no longer sharing household expenses. More doubtful of marriage's prospects, Americans sharply increased their rate of cohabitation during the decade. What had been commonly referred to as "living in sin" a
few years earlier now became widely visible for the first time,
though unmarried couples living together remained only 3 per-

cent of total households. Even churches adapted to the new realities. In 1973, the Episcopal Church first officially recognized civil divorce, and by 1981, the number of marriage annulments handed out by the Roman Catholic Church had soared to seventy-seven times the number handed out in 1968. Working more commonly outside the home and less confident about family stability, women also chose to have fewer children. The U.S. birthrate declined during the 1970s from 2.5 to 1.8 per woman of childbearing age. Ultimately, the rise in divorce embodied both of the primary themes of U.S. history in the 1970s: the greater equality and inclusion of all citizens, particularly women, as well as the increasing reliance on market mechanisms—supply and demand—rather than on government regulation to solve social problems and produce the greatest happiness for the most people. Together, these trends promoted individualism at the expense of communal connections, in this case family connections.[21]

Beth Bailey and other historians have pointed out that ideas of liberation for women were most complicated and contradictory in the realm of sex. Because they overlapped chronologically and because the loosening of gender roles meant greater personal freedom for women, the sexual revolution and women's liberation have often been confused. Some of this has been an honest confusion, since the two developments were related. But some of it was also promoted by a mass media eager to titillate audiences with stories of supposed bra-burning rather than of unequal wages, by anti-feminists trying to associate feminists with sexual irresponsibility, and by men anticipating the prospect of women's increasing sexual availability. The resulting minefield challenged women as they sought to partake in the culture-wide shift in sexual ethics and behavior that is commonly identified with the 1960s but that happened for most Americans in the 1970s.[22]

American sexual behavior and ideas had been evolving since the 1940s away from self-restraint and toward greater liberty. Important research about sexual practices in the United States was published by Alfred Kinsey in 1948 and 1953, and by

William Masters and Virginia Johnson in 1966. Sex before marriage and outside of marriage hardly began in the 1960s, though the availability of the birth control pill after 1960 did help sharply reduce the risk of pregnancy. What was different by the start of the 1970s was greater public acceptance of these realities, in part a rejection of the hypocritical gap between private behavior and public rhetoric. In 1979, 55 percent of Americans saw nothing inherently wrong with premarital sex, twice the percentage of ten years earlier. Television shows and films of the 1970s reflected a dramatic sexualization of American public culture, evident in dress, language, and attitudes. Among nineteen-year-old white women, 35 percent in 1970 had had sexual intercourse; in 1980 that figure was 50 percent, an increase of nearly half.[23]

In 1976, Shere Hite published the best-selling book, *The Hite Report*, detailing the results of hundreds of women's responses to surveys about the most intimate details of their sexual lives. While critics pointed out serious flaws in her research methodology, there was little debate about the book's central point: that women could have orgasms as commonly as men, even multiple orgasms, and that non-intercourse clitoral stimulation was the most likely method for doing so. *The Hite Report* spread more widely the profoundly feminist point of Anne Koedt's 1970 essay, "The Myth of the Vaginal Orgasm," that the male emphasis on intercourse as the center of sexual experience often tended not to treat women as equal partners in sexual relationships. Such public discussions of women's sexuality marked the beginning of American women's journey out of their old dead-end stereotypes as either virgins or "whores," toward a new era in which female and male sexuality might receive equal respect and understanding.[24]

Changing attitudes about female sexuality reflected a broader struggle to empower women in taking care of their bodies. Women's health care and health education constituted a major front for women organizers in the 1970s. In 1973, at a time when accurate, detailed information about female health and sexuality was not readily available to most women, the Boston Women's Health Book Collective published the self-help book,

Our Bodies, Ourselves, as a means to empower women to take care of themselves and to deal with their still mostly male primary physicians and gynecologists. In 1976, the American Library Association voted this best seller one of the ten all-time best books for young people. Weeks after her husband became president in 1974, Betty Ford underwent a radical mastectomy, an operation that in the past few women had wanted to speak about openly, due to concerns about disfigurement and femininity. The First Lady's refreshing directness in talking publicly about her surgery marked a highlight in a campaign for greater public awareness of breast cancer—one of the most common forms of cancer to strike women—and the need for early detection. Indeed, as critics of gender discrimination in medical research commonly noted, if breast cancer affected men as much as it did women, the disease would have been at the top of the list of research priorities.[25]

The most controversial women's health-care issue to emerge from the 1970s was abortion. Illegal in all U.S. states since the early twentieth century, abortion was still widely practiced in dangerous and sometimes deadly venues, a point made clear by Lawrence Lader in his carefully documented 1966 book, *Abortion*. Abortion reform efforts led to New York in 1970 being the first state to legalize abortion for more than just the existing exceptions in cases of rape, incest, and serious physical deformities. Hawaii, Alaska, and Washington quickly followed suit, repealing all criminal punishments for abortions performed by physicians up to a specified point in pregnancy. Thirteen other states expanded the circumstances in which abortions were allowed. In 1971, the U.S. Supreme Court heard its first case ever on abortion. Two years later, in a decision authored by Justice Harry Blackmun, the Court ruled by a 7–2 vote in *Roe v. Wade* that states could not restrict a woman's right to an abortion in the first two trimesters of pregnancy. The Court found that any such restrictive state laws were contrary to a constitutional right to privacy grounded in "the Fourteenth Amendment's concept of personal liberty and restrictions upon state action." "The Constitution does not explicitly mention any right of privacy,"

Blackmun wrote, but fourteen of the Court's precedent cases had recognized "a guarantee of certain areas or zones of privacy" that included "a woman's decision whether or not to terminate her pregnancy."[26]

The judges who decided *Roe v. Wade* did not at first tend to view the case in the context of other cases involving women's equality in the 1970s. The primary concern of Justice Blackmun, a former counsel for the Mayo Clinic, was for physicians' autonomy: allowing doctors to care for their patients to the best of their abilities without fear of criminal prosecution. Blackmun did, however, have some personal experience of the impact of unplanned pregnancies. In 1966, his daughter Sally, a nineteen-year-old sophomore, dropped out of Skidmore College after becoming pregnant, married her boyfriend, and then suffered a miscarriage three weeks later; the marriage did not last. Regarding privacy, key precedents for the Court were the birth control cases of *Griswold v. Connecticut* (1965) and *Eisenstadt v. Baird* (1972), which established respectively the rights of married women and single women to have unrestricted access to contraception. *Griswold* grounded that right in the concept of marital privacy, whereas *Eisenstadt* found that right in the broad principle of individual citizens being free from unwarranted governmental intrusion. An epic victory for its supporters, *Roe v. Wade* was a great blow for abortion-rights opponents, particularly Roman Catholics and a growing number of evangelical Protestants. An anti-abortion movement would soon develop and become a major political force by the mid-1980s. But during the 1970s, the political winds were blowing strongly in favor of women's rights on all matters of health and sexuality.[27]

While attitudes toward sexuality and abortion varied among the vast female population of the United States, women closed ranks in the struggle against male sexual violence. In the 1970s, feminists led the effort to eliminate the shame long associated with rape victims, to force police and prosecutors to take the crime seriously, and to roll back this enduring threat that narrowed women's sense of personal security and freedom. A group called Women's Advocates opened the first shelter for battered women in 1971 in St. Paul, Minnesota. The first rape crisis hot-line was established in Washington, DC, in 1972 to provide counseling for victims. In 1975, Susan Brownmiller published an acclaimed feminist study of the crime, *Against Our Will: Men, Women, and Rape*, emphasizing the impact of rape in in-timidating all women to various extents, for which Brownmiller was named one of the representatives of *Time* magazine's desig-nation of "American Women" as its annual "person of the year." "Take Back The Night" marches on college campuses and in cities across the country proclaimed the determination of women, along with supportive men, to denounce the evil of sex-ual violence and to organize and promote women's common struggle for the personal safety from sexual predation that most men took for granted. The case of Joan Little put a national spotlight on the issue. While in jail in the small town of Wash-ington, North Carolina, in 1974, Little, who was young and black, killed her jailer, who was white and twice her weight, in what she claimed was self-defense when he raped her. The evi-dence of rape was persuasive, and in less than ninety minutes of deliberation, a jury of six whites and six blacks found her not guilty, the first case in the United States of a woman being ac-quitted on the grounds of self-defense against sexual assault.[28]

If sexual assault was a uniquely personal form of violence and even torture, marital rape was the most intimate version of all. After rape by an unknown assailant, the victim lives with a harrowing memory, while after rape by a husband, the victim continues to live with the actual rapist. Yet before 1976, marital rape did not exist in the United States—legally. Following long-standing Anglo-American legal traditions in which a wife's body was viewed as the property of her husband, a man could not be accused of committing rape against his wife. She simply had no legal grounds to say no to his sexual advances. State legislators were not eager to intrude on what had traditionally been seen as a realm of family privacy. But as activists brought publicity to the issue of sexual violence, as divorce became more common, and as women moved to greater equality and independence on many other fronts, pressure continued to build. In 1976, Nebraska became the first state to eliminate the spousal exception from rape laws, and other states followed close behind. In 1978, Daniel Morrison of New Jersey was the first person found guilty of raping his wife and received a prison sentence of 4–12 years. A few years later, the New York Court of Appeals abolished that state's marital rape exemption, declaring that a marriage license was not "a license for a husband to forcibly rape his wife with impunity. . . . To ever imply consent to [rape] is irrational and absurd." The Georgia Supreme Court agreed in another case: "Certainly no normal woman who falls in love and wishes to marry . . . would knowingly include an irrevocable term to her revocable marriage contract that would allow her husband to rape her." A new common sense had taken hold regarding women's fundamental individuality and independence, even within the bonds of marriage.[29]

The story of women resisting discrimination and violence and moving forward into great equality was not a uniquely American tale in the 1970s. The British Parliament passed the Sex Discrimination Act in 1975 to eliminate unequal treatment of women and men in employment, education, and other areas of daily life. Abortion was decriminalized in 1967. British feminists tended to be more closely allied with labor unions and the traditional political Left than were their American counterparts, but women across the political spectrum in the United Kingdom were fast transcending traditional gender roles. In 1979, voters elected Conservative Party leader Margaret Thatcher the first female British Prime Minister. In France, feminist publications proliferated in the 1970s, and a 1972 law required equal pay for equal work. As part of a broad campaign for abortion rights, the magazine *Le Nouvel Observateur* published a "Manifesto of 343 Sluts," a public acknowledgment by hundreds of prominent women that they had broken the law by terminating a pregnancy. In 1974, abortion became legal on a trial basis, one made permanent in 1979. In 1975, a new French law allowed divorce by mutual consent. Outside Europe and North America, traditional gender roles were slower to change, as mountaineer Arlene Blum was reminded on a 1972 climbing expedition to the Kashmir region of India, where the men and women in her host family ate separately, though she was welcome in both companies. "They see you as a different sort of creature, neither man nor woman," her host explained. "You eat dinner, talk, and climb mountains with the men, but you look like a woman." Six years later, on the Annapurna expedition, Blum found her efforts to hire female as well as male Sherpas as porters derailed by fierce resistance from the Sherpa men.[30]

In the late 1970s, a fundamental conflict regarding gender equality began to emerge, one that would help shape world history thereafter. The rise of Islamism, or political Islam, and its decisive victory in 1979 in the Iranian revolution carried a very different vision of women's place in society than what was developing in the West. In Europe, North America, and other industrialized parts of the world, women were moving into traditionally male social and economic spheres. They were desegregating their public cultures by sex. But as American women filtered into formerly all-male workplaces and schools and thus into much greater equality and nonsexual intimacy with men, the new Islamist rulers of Iran were ushering women out of the public sphere—where the pro-Western Shah had previously been promoting their presence—and back into the home, into private space, and behind the veil. Political Islam would soon dominate Afghanistan and spread elsewhere as a powerful, backwards-looking influence in the Muslim world, contesting the American and European model of women's trajectory toward greater opportunities and self-determination.[31]

THE MANY FRONTIERS OF EQUALITY

Like a stone dropped into a pool, the force of the African American civil rights movement continued to spread outward in American life after the 1960s, inspiring others and reshaping the contours of political possibility. Women were the largest cohort affected, but the new tide of egalitarianism also lifted Native Americans, immigrants, homosexuals, and other groups that had been historically discriminated against, only half of whose members were female. It is not that such struggles as the gay rights movement were created in response to the black freedom struggle. Like women, they had their own histories and their own organizing efforts that long predated the 1970s. But, like women, these other communities did find considerable encouragement in the successes of racial desegregation and the growing willingness of the majority of Americans to see them as deserving of more equal treatment. It is also not the case that discrimination on grounds of sexual orientation, language, religion, and ability, as well as race, disappeared in this decade—hardly was this the situation. Indeed, elements of the new conservative coalition that emerged into political dominance in the 1980s found their purpose in the cause of resisting precisely this greater inclusiveness in American culture, a "backlash," as they were often called. But their anxieties were not grounded in mere fantasy. The worries of backlash conservatives reflected the very real growth of egalitarian, inclusive sentiment and practice in American life in the 1970s, a pattern that has continued shaping U.S. history ever since.

Most obvious to all was the continued racial desegregation of American public life in the 1970s. The protest marches, urban uprisings, and federal legislation of the previous decade gave way to the steady progress of African Americans into positions of prominence and influence, a process that would lead thirty years later to the election of the first black president, Barack Obama, who spent his teenage years in the formative 1970s. Breakthrough stories proliferated. In 1972, Barbara Jordan of Texas and Andrew Young of Georgia became the first black Southerners elected to the U.S. Congress since Reconstruction. Jordan soon emerged as a widely admired figure in the congressional investigations into the Watergate scandal, while Young was named the first black U.S. ambassador to the United Nations in 1977, a profoundly symbolic choice as the nation's chief representative to the world. In 1973, Los Angeles voters elected Tom Bradley, the son of sharecroppers and grandson of slaves, mayor of the second largest city in the nation. The nation's most elite sports followed. In 1975, the Masters golf tournament in Augusta, Georgia, welcomed its first black invitee, Lee Elder, and Arthur Ashe became the first black man to win the Wimbledon tennis championship in London. The first African American Cabinet secretaries, astronauts, and Episcopal bishops also appeared, and the Mormon Church in 1978 eliminated its ban on black men joining the lay priesthood. The most popular figures in music and sports were increasingly likely to be black, from Stevie Wonder and Michael Jackson to Ashe and Earvin "Magic" Johnson. The 1970s did not see an end to the enduring African American blend of integrationist and separatist tendencies regarding mainstream U.S. society, seeking to achieve more equal status within mainstream culture while still preserving traditionally black institutions such as churches and colleges as sources of community and inspiration, just as the decade did not see an end to white resistance to desegregation, particularly on issues of school busing. But the predominant trend was toward breaking down barriers in American public life.[32]

One of the best measures of this trend was the remarkable success of Alex Haley's book, *Roots*, published in 1976, and the television miniseries based upon it and broadcast in January 1977. Grounded in considerable research as well as stories from his elderly female relatives, Haley told the imagined narrative of his ancestors from West Africa, who were captured, transported across the Atlantic, and enslaved in the American South. *Roots* had "a catalytic effect on popular attitudes towards slavery," Southern historian W. Fitzhugh Brundage wrote. "His depiction of his slave ancestors' struggle to retain their dignity and to attain freedom removed the stigma from slavery for many African Americans, transforming their past into a saga of perseverance and quiet heroism." The book topped best-seller lists for six months and won the National Book Award and a special Pulitzer Prize. One hundred and thirty million Americans, over half of the nation's population and the largest audience in television history, viewed at least part of the eight-episode, twelve-hour television version. The phenomenon of so many citizens absorbing so much detail about the most oppressive labor system in the country's history was unprecedented. It marked a crucial shift away from the previously popular, "Gone With the Wind" view of American slavery as a benign piece of the national past, a view based on the wistful, pro-Confederacy blockbuster film of 1939. *Roots*, by contrast, established a new respect for the epic sweep of black history, one that affected both black and non-black Americans.[33]

Native Americans also swept back into public view in the early 1970s. For most white Americans, Indians had been gone a long time, decimated by wars in the nineteenth century and seen primarily on the losing end in Western movies ever since. However, the Indian population of the United States had, in fact, grown from its low point of a quarter million in 1900 to two million in 1970. Young Indian activists put an exclamation point on this revival with their 1969–70 occupation of the former federal prison island of Alcatraz in San Francisco Bay, which they reclaimed as Indian land. The occupiers and their supporters, like the new American Indian Movement (AIM) that engaged in a series of other symbolic land seizures, sought attention to, and funding for, the ongoing social and economic challenges facing mostly poor Native Americans, along with respect for Indian cultures and recognition of the long history of white violence and appropriation of Indian lands that underlay those problems. On Thanksgiving Day of 1970, AIM activists painted Plymouth Rock in Massachusetts red in protest against celebrating colonial expansion as a national holiday. Newly politicized Native Americans and others were determined to retell an American history that included a more accurate understanding of Indians' lives, just as African Americans were doing with slavery. Dee Brown published *Bury My Heart at Wounded Knee: An Indian History of the American West* (1970), a huge bestseller that reexamined the tragedy of Western history from the perspective of Native Americans. Francis Jennings's *The Invasion of America: Indians, Colonialism, and the Cant of Conquest* (1975) did the same with colonial American history by changing "discovery" to "invasion." In *Facing West: The Metaphysics of Indian-Hating and Empire Building* (1980), Richard Drinnon traced a direct line from Puritan wars against Native Americans in the 1630s to the U.S. war in Vietnam that had just ended.[34]

Native American activists shared with more radical women's

liberationists and Black Power advocates a sense of identification with Third World peoples seeking self-determination and an end to colonial rule. Many younger Indians considered this connection immediate and obvious. In 1973, two hundred Oglala Lakota and AIM activists occupied the village of Wounded Knee on the Pine Ridge Reservation in South Dakota, site of an infamous 1890 U.S. army massacre of unarmed Lakota. They held it for ten weeks as a protest against a long legacy of white actions against Indians and against what they saw as the corrupt rule of tribal leaders. Considerable gunfire and several killings ensued in a heavily armed standoff with federal government forces. Native American veterans of the U.S. military who had just returned home from fighting against the "Vietcong" or "VC" in Vietnam found these events disorienting. "Pine Ridge was more dangerous for me than Chu Lai," recalled Lakota veteran Guy Dull Knife, Jr. "We had become the VC in our own homeland."[35]

The Wounded Knee takeover marked the apex of Native American militancy and intergenerational Indian conflict, but the broader struggle for greater equality continued. The nature of reservations and the legacy of Indian autonomy—of peoples independent of the rest of the United States—meant that more equal treatment of Native Americans had as much to do with cultural respect and self-determination as it did with inclusion and integration (though more than half of Indians lived off the reservations and commonly had non-Indian spouses). In 1970, the Taos Pueblo won the return of 48,000 acres of mountain land including their sacred Blue Lake, and the Oneida filed suit for a similar return of land in upstate New York. A year later, the Alaska Native Claims Settlement Act allowed Native villages and regional corporations to select up to 44 million acres from the public domain, as a final settlement of conflicts about land ownership in the twelve-year-old state. In *United States v. Washington* (1974), U.S. District Court judge George Boldt, a jurist known as a law-and-order conservative on the bench, upheld the fiercely contested treaty rights of Indians in Washington and Oregon to fish off reservations regardless of state laws and to take 50 percent of the harvestable fish. This was a key deci-

sion in an area that had been a flashpoint of white-Indian conflict, one that recognized fishing for Indians as a cultural right as
well as a property right. In 1975, the U.S. Congress officially
replaced termination of reservations with self-determination as
the operating principle of national Indian policy in the Indian
Self-Determination and Education Assistance Act. In 1978, the
U.S. Supreme Court found in *United States v. Wheeler* that Indian sovereignty "is of a unique and limited character. . . . But
until Congress acts, the tribes retain their existing sovereign
powers."[36]

In a fashion parallel to women, blacks, and Indians, Jewish
Americans—half of them, of course, women—repositioned themselves in American life in the 1970s as less accepting of discrimination and more determined to have their distinctive history
respected. There had been Jews in North America from the early
days of colonial settlement, but their numbers became significant only in the mid-nineteenth century with settlers from Germany, and particularly at the turn of the twentieth century with
immigrants from the Russian and Austro-Hungarian empires.
Identified as members of "the Hebrew race" by U.S. immigration law from 1924 to 1965, and thus viewed by gentiles as
white but not quite fully white, Jews experienced considerable
success in the United States but also enduring prejudice. Then,
after World War II, open discrimination began to decline, including restrictions at universities and social clubs, because of
several factors. One was guilt and shame about the Holocaust.
Another was the establishment of the state of Israel, which altered the perceptions by many outsiders of Jews—in Israel but by
extension everywhere—as passive victims of the Nazis to instead
being tough, victorious pioneers carrying European civilization
to a foreign land, a tale familiar and comforting to Americans.
And the rhetoric of the Cold War about the evils of atheistic
Communism stimulated the widespread use of "Judeo-Christian
tradition" as a term emphasizing the common religious ground
of Christians and Jews. Most Jewish Americans spent the 1950s
and 1960s fitting into mainstream U.S. society.[37]

What changed in the 1970s for many Jews was a growing

sense of identification with the nation of Israel and more broadly
with a transnational Jewish identity. Events abroad were crucial. Israel's sweeping victory over its Arab neighbors in the Six-
Day War of 1967 revealed it as a regional military superpower,
leading to an increasingly close relationship with the U.S. government and stimulating considerable pride among Jewish
Americans. Then the close call of near-defeat for Israel in the
1973 Yom Kippur War, with its specter of wholesale destruction
of Jews just a generation after Auschwitz, sobered Israelis and
their supporters abroad, rendering Israel's status still more important. Terrorist attacks on Israelis and other Jews proliferated
in the 1970s, such as airplane hijackings and the slaughter at the
Munich Olympics in 1972, often linked to the defeats that Palestinians experienced. Both more secure in their complete assimilation as mainstream Americans and more attuned to the
vulnerability of the world's small Jewish population, American
Jews in the 1970s became more vocal in their support of Israel.
They also turned increasingly to the study of the Holocaust, an
unspeakably painful subject that had been largely downplayed
or avoided in the years since 1945. Now Jews in the United
States, supported by many Christians, became determined that
their history, like that of Native Americans and African Americans, would be known and appreciated for all its courage as
well as its tragedy. In this sense, Jewish Americans fit in with
other ethnic European American communities, particularly Irish
and Italians, who turned increasingly in the 1970s—partly in
response to Black Power—to celebrating a distinctive ethnic
heritage as part of their American identity. The common thread
was respect, equal treatment, and inclusion of all groups previously burdened by discrimination.[38]

Americans worked out their identities on many grounds, not
just ethnicity and race. Young people since World War II had
carved out a more distinctive niche than ever before. "Teenager"
emerged as a new category after 1945, reflecting the baby boom
emphasis on children and the new disposable wealth of postwar
middle-class youth who became formidable consumers. In the
1960s, the civil rights and antiwar movements and the counter-

culture were all distinctively youthful in profile. "Don't trust anyone over 30," young activists warned each other, and anger mounted at the seeming hypocrisy of drafting eighteen-year-old men to fight and perhaps die for their country while not allowing them to exercise the essential citizen's right to vote—and thus help decide whether to go to war in the first place. During the 1970s, young adults stepped on to firmer legal ground. The Twenty-Sixth Amendment lowered the national voting age to eighteen in 1971, with the overwhelming approval of Congress and the swiftest ratification by three-quarters of the states of any constitutional amendment. The U.S. Supreme Court moved in the same direction in *Carey v. Population Services International* (1977), a decision that found it unconstitutional to prohibit the sale or distribution of contraceptives to minors under the age of sixteen. Older Americans also found relief from unequal treatment with the passage of the Age Discrimination Act of 1975, which banned discrimination against seniors in programs and institutions receiving federal assistance. Most mandatory retirement ages were eliminated in the following decade. Disability, too, received new protections during the 1970s following the hard work of disabled activists in educating the public and Congress. The Individuals with Disabilities Education Act of 1975 required a "free appropriate" public education for children with disabilities. In particular, the act encouraged the mainstreaming of these children by requiring that they be taught, whenever possible, in the "least restrictive environment." Inclusion and equality remained crucial themes in reshaping American public life in this decade.[39]

One of the most striking demographic and cultural changes of the past forty years in the United States is what has sometimes been called the "browning" of American society. Americans in the decades before 1970 lived in a nation of primarily white people and black people (in a roughly 9 to 1 ratio), while in the twenty-first century the nation has become truly multiracial because of the significant increase of residents with roots in Latin America and Asia. Indeed, early in the new century, Latino Americans surpassed African Americans as the nation's largest minority, and California joined Hawaii as majority non-white states, symbols of the nation's demographic trajectory. The Immigration Act of 1965 provided the legal foundation for this shift by ending the old national origins system that had, since 1924, heavily favored immigration from northwestern Europe. This shift was momentous: no longer would the United States attempt to make or keep itself primarily a nation of European descent, a white country.

The egalitarian impact of the new immigration bill really began to appear in the 1970s. From its twentieth-century height of 14.7 percent in 1910, the percentage of foreign-born residents declined steadily to a nadir of 4.7 percent in 1970 (more than half of them European). This was America at its least diverse. From there, the numbers tilted upward. Foreign-born residents increased by 50 percent between 1970 and 1980, and for the first time fewer were from Europe than from Asia. "Asian American" emerged as a new category, combining peoples from such widely differing cultures as India, Korea, Taiwan, and the Philippines. Refugees from Vietnam, fleeing the new Communist regime after 1975, accounted for 120,000 of the new immigrants.[40]

In contrast with the influx of new people from Asia, the share of the new immigrants who came from Mexico remained steady at 14 percent from the 1960s through the 1970s. Some 750,000 people born south of the border lived in the United States during the 1970s. But these numbers began to increase sharply in the 1980s, as the U.S. economy righted itself and the Mexican economy slid into major difficulties. By the end of the twentieth century, Mexico became by far the largest single source of new Americans, with more than ten times as many of its natives living north of the border as in the 1970s. Mexico in 2000 was like Italy in 1900: the greatest giver of migrants to the United States, slightly darker-skinned than most white Americans, heavily Roman Catholic, non–English speaking, often returning home, and bearers of a cuisine at first alien to other Americans but soon to become practically their comfort food. This comparison also highlights one other major change from the turn of the twentieth to the turn of the twenty-first century: in 1900, 90 percent of the world's immigrants came from Europe, whereas in 2000, 90 percent came from elsewhere. One measure of Mexico's rising importance in American life was the mid-1970s moment when Spanish surpassed French, for the first time, as the most popular foreign language for study in American schools. No doubt to Madrid's chagrin, Spanish was viewed in the United States primarily as the language of Latin America. By 1990, twice as many college students were enrolled in Spanish as in French classes, and by 1998, three times as many high school students were doing the same. France remained the most popular international tourist destination in the world, but Americans were reorienting themselves culturally, at least to some extent, from Europe to Latin America.[41]

The rising tide of egalitarianism and inclusion that characterized the 1970s lifted homosexuals as well. In a crucial sense, the pursuit of full citizenship for gay and lesbian Americans had nothing to do with sex, but only with all individuals simply being treated respectfully. But the context of the emerging gay rights movement in this decade was the era of greater sexual freedom and experimentation—the sexual revolution—that spanned the 1960s and 1970s. An apt symbol of this era was the fad of streaking (running naked through public places) that spread through the country in 1974, striking major cultural, academic, and sports gatherings, including the Academy Awards. The University of Georgia set a record with a 1,500-person streak. Streaking inverted the traditional nightmare of being naked amid a crowd of people in clothes. Instead, everyone "let it all hang out" together. "Hang Up Your Hang Ups," sang jazz fusion pianist Herbie Hancock in a popular tune of the era. Gays and lesbians, like heterosexuals, ranged widely in their personal attitudes toward politics, culture, and even the increasing sexualization of public culture. There were no inherent connections between sexual orientation and greater public openness about one's sexuality. By rejecting the conservative view of sex as being healthy only within traditional marriage, however, homosexuals and their emergence into more public view were inevitably seen as part of the sexual revolution. They were also seen as different from other minorities because their distinguishing characteristic—whom they loved—was seen by many conservative Americans as a matter of choice rather than genetic predisposition, in contrast, say, to being black.[42]

The struggles of gays and lesbians in the United States and elsewhere for freedom from fear and violence had much older roots, but the cause entered a new era of "gay liberation" after the 1969 riot at the Stonewall Inn nightclub in New York City, where gay patrons fought back against brutal police harassment. The first gay rights marches took place in 1970. In perhaps the most momentous decision of a generation regarding sexual orientation, the American Psychiatric Association in December 1973 decided to remove homosexuality from the list of "mental disorders" in its authoritative *Diagnostic and Statistical Manual*. Gays and lesbians were, suddenly, no longer mentally ill but were instead just normal, from the perspective of the nation's highest medical authorities.

The struggle for mainstream acceptance would still not be easy. That same year, the popular film *Deliverance* included as its most famous scene a graphic incidence of homosexual rape ("Squeal like a pig!" commanded the Appalachian mountain man rapist), which contributed to an enduring popular association of homosexuality with sexual deviance and violence—no small irony in a society rife with heterosexual violence. But the gay rights movement soldiered on, convincing the U.S. Civil Service Commission in 1975 to lift its ban on the employment of homosexuals, persuading more than a dozen states to repeal their anti-sodomy statutes (finally catching up with most Western European nations), seeing several dozen cities add the category of sexual orientation to their civil rights laws, and convincing the Democratic Party in 1980 to include for the first time a gay rights plank. "I Am a Homosexual," declared Air Force officer Leonard Matlovich from the cover of *Time* in 1975, as the magazine noted the "public announcements of their homosexuality by a variety of people who could be anybody's neighbors." Actor Billy Crystal played television's first recurring gay character in the ABC sitcom

Discrimination by sexual orientation began to diminish in the 1970s. Harvey
Milk's successful campaign in 1977 for San Francisco city supervisor marked
the first election in the United States of an openly gay or lesbian public official. Courtesy Harvey Milk Archives-Scott Smith Collection, Gay & Lesbian
Center, San Francisco Public Library.

Soap that began airing in 1977. Two years later, more than 100,000 people gathered in the nation's capital for the first March on Washington for Lesbian and Gay Rights. There was plenty of anti-gay backlash still to come, but homosexuals were now visible and increasingly accepted in American public life in an unprecedented manner.[43]

Going beyond the realm of the merely human, the flood tide of equal rights and inclusion coursing through American society may have reached its high-water mark with the Endangered Species Act of 1973. For the first time, animals gained legal status as having the right to sustainable habitats, which humans were obliged to protect. This was not the same as an animal having distinct rights as an individual creature; the legislation concerned species, something closer to group rights. And the Endangered Species Act was not about inclusion in the sense of integration with humans, as these were wild animals, expected to remain wild. But the spirit of reform that underlay so much of the 1970s manifested itself in both ways: in greater social integration, and in greater respect for distinctive group histories and traditions. A broader animal rights movement, building on the century-old Society for the Prevention of Cruelty to Animals, emerged out of this era, stimulated particularly by the publication of moral philosopher Peter Singer's 1975 book, *Animal Liberation*. Singer called attention to the unnecessary suffering of animals in factory farming, scientific experiments, and the testing of commercial products such as cosmetics. His call for respectful treatment of other species helped persuade many readers to become vegetarians, further expanding the circle of human sympathy.[44]

POLITICAL REFORM

"Government reforms were a central part of the 1970s," wrote historian Julian Zelizer. The Executive branch of the federal government felt the powerful combined force of public opinion, the press, and Congress and the courts during the Watergate scandal of 1972–74. J. Edgar Hoover's nearly fifty-year reign at the Federal Bureau of Investigation ended with his death in 1972, finally freeing the FBI from a variety of scandals and corruption associated with his rule. Both the FBI and the CIA came under extensive public scrutiny and severe criticism for their Cold War–related excesses in targeting supposed enemies of the state. The consumer movement in the United States reached its apex in the early 1970s, with groups such as Ralph Nader's Public Citizen (founded in 1971) lobbying federal agencies and Congress to better protect American citizens; its four-year campaign to eliminate carcinogenic Red Dye #2, for example, succeeded in 1976 when the Food and Drug Administration banned the substance. Pressure for democratic reforms led to a weakening of political party elites' control of the presidential nominating process, readily visible in the Democrats' nomination of Senator George McGovern (SD) in 1972. Similar reform efforts combined with sex and corruption scandals to weaken the power of senior committee chairmen in Congress and open the legislative process to greater public input. The same spirit of egalitarianism and inclusiveness that was reshaping American public life in the 1970s also aimed to make the government more responsive to the needs of all its citizens.[45]

As the branch most directly responsible to its constituents, Congress was at the front end of the most important efforts to bring a greater degree of democratic practice into the federal government. Between 1970 and 1974, Congress enacted the most expansive campaign reforms in U.S. history. Stronger disclosure laws, public financing for presidential elections, and limits on contributions and spending brought greater public disclosure of information and ended the explicit domination of political campaigns by large individual investors. The new federal election laws aimed to democratize the landscape of political influence, an egalitarian effort that was only partially successful, as will become clear in the next chapter. Congress also passed the War Powers Act in 1973, in the wake of the withdrawal from Vietnam, to limit the president's ability to wage undeclared wars by ignoring the constitutional requirement for legislative approval. In 1974, Congress created the Congressional Budget Office, which quickly became a widely respected source of nonpartisan economic forecasting that allowed Congress the opportunity to no longer depend solely on an administration's own sometimes dubious numbers. That same year, Congress passed, over President Ford's veto, a set of amendments to strengthen the eight-year-old Freedom of Information Act in its purpose of providing citizens access to their government's records. In 1975, the Senate introduced a greater element of democracy into its own internal operations by decreasing the number of votes needed to end a filibuster from two-thirds to three-fifths.[46]

The reformist wave peaked at mid-decade. A month after Nixon resigned from the presidency in August 1974, pollster Lou Harris reported that all "establishment institutions in America are in deep trouble." When Ford pardoned the ex-president, Harris found that "anyone who tries to get out politically this fall and defend that pardon in any part of the country, North or South, is almost literally going to have his head handed to him." The Democrats swept the congressional elections that fall, gaining fifty-two seats in the House of Representatives and four in the Senate. Democrats now enjoyed majorities of 291–144 in the House and 60–37 in the Senate, as well as control of thirty-six governorships and thirty-seven state legislatures. The new U.S. Representatives were sworn in with reform on their minds; their resistance to the traditional seniority system caused House Speaker Tip O'Neill and President Carter, two years later, to commiserate about "the almost anarchic independence of the House." The House dismantled the House Un-American Activities Committee, long dormant but a preeminent symbol of Cold War excess in the hunt for subversives. The Tunney and Clark Amendments in the Senate ended U.S. assistance to Angolan insurgents backed by South Africa's apartheid government. The Pike Committee in the House and the Church Committee in the Senate spent most of 1975 investigating the nation's intelligence services, revealing a dark underside of anti-democratic behavior by the CIA and FBI. The Foreign Intelligence Surveillance Act of

1978 established a special foreign intelligence court to monitor domestic eavesdropping in order to prevent further illegal spying on U.S. citizens.[47]

"Let our recent mistakes bring a resurgent commitment to the basic principles of our nation," Jimmy Carter declared in his inaugural address on January 20, 1977, "for we know that if we despise our own government, we have no future." In the face of all the revelations of corruption in government, Carter had spent the previous year campaigning as a man of high personal standards and fundamental decency and honesty. He promised that he would "quit conducting the decision-making process in secret, as has been characteristic of Mr. Kissinger and Mr. Ford." National journalists, newly empowered by their role in Watergate and inclined to a skeptical and ironic view of officialdom, did not know what to make of the former Georgia governor—born-again Christian, Naval Academy graduate, nuclear engineer, Deep Southerner, environmentalist, supporter of civil rights, outsider to the Washington political establishment. "Once again, one wonders is Jimmy Carter not too good to be true," reporter Robert Scheer mused. "On one level, the man is simply preposterous. On another, he seems reasonable, sincere, and eminently sensible." One prominent Washington journalist had declared during the campaign that "Carter can't be President. He doesn't know his way around this city." Carter was apparently dead serious about his Christian faith and personal morality, yet he was "not self-righteous" but "very tolerant," according to Hamilton Jordan, one of several of his staffers whom Scheer referred to as being "as hard-drinking, fornicating, free-thinking a group as has been seen in higher politics." Carter's family confused them, too. His wife Rosalynn also grew up in the same small southwestern Georgia town of Plains. Ne'er-do-well brother Billy tapped into his brother's fame by endorsing a beer label, "Billy Beer." Sister Ruth was a Christian evangelist. Sister Gloria rode a motorcycle. His mother Lillian served in the Peace Corps in India at the age of sixty-eight. They seemed almost a real-life version of the *Beverly Hillbillies*, the top-rated television show that ran from 1962 to 1971, with funny characters from a rural family who were quite successful. Whatever people thought of the new president, he was clearly different from his predecessors and serious about trying to make the U.S. political system more responsive to its citizenry.[48]

In foreign policy as much as any other realm, Carter sought to make the United States hold to its ideals of human equality and individual freedom. In his commencement address at Notre Dame University on May 22, 1977, the new president placed the promotion of human rights at the top of his administration's agenda. Preceding Cold War presidents had all touted the need for human rights in the Soviet sphere, but Carter distinguished himself by emphasizing as well the need to stop repression of dissidents and the abuse of prisoners in non-communist countries, such as South Africa and Nicaragua. He also called for a halt to, and reversal of, the nuclear arms race, recognizing that nuclear war represented the greatest threat of all to the fundamental right of existence. In addition, he reoriented U.S. attention away from the old East-West conflict of the Cold War and toward issues between the global North and South, particularly poverty. "We know a peaceful world cannot long exist one-third rich and two-thirds hungry," he told the Notre Dame audience. Secretary of State Cyrus Vance rejected "a negative, reactive policy that seeks only to oppose Soviet or Cuban involvement in Africa" or elsewhere in the Third World. "The most effective policies," Vance argued, "are affirmative policies." Carter turned away from the often imperial behavior of his immediate predecessors, recently revealed in the congressional and press investigations of 1974–76: "We will not behave in foreign places so as to violate our rules and standards here at home." He reined in the CIA. Carter was the first U.S. president who immediately fired the existing director of central intelligence, George H. W. Bush. Carter instead created a new office of human rights within the State Department under the direction of Mississippi civil rights activist Patricia Derian, and appointed his friend Andrew Young, the Georgia congressman and former aide to Martin Luther King, Jr., as U.S. ambassador to the United Nations, a symbol of the administration's commitment to equal rights and inclusiveness at home and abroad.[49]

The Carter administration's mixed record in foreign policy included important early successes embodying the president's vision of greater respect for all peoples. Despite strong opposition from conservative nationalists, Carter expended considerable political capital in winning Senate approval in 1977 for the Panama Canal treaties, which arranged for the eventual return of the 10-mile-wide Canal Zone to Panamanian sovereignty and thus eliminated the most blatant remnant of U.S. imperialism toward Latin America. He continued his predecessors' policy of warming ties with China, reestablishing formal diplomatic relations in 1979 after a thirty-year hiatus. The administration supported the British-led process of negotiating a peaceful transition of white-ruled Rhodesia into majority-ruled Zimbabwe in 1980. Carter showed extraordinary tenacity in leading Egypt and Israel into the Camp David accords of 1979, establishing the first official recognition of Israel by an Arab nation. In each of these cases, Carter expanded the realm of egalitarianism and mutual respect among peoples.[50]

These successes were eventually undercut by events of 1979–80, particularly anti-American revolutions in Iran and Nicaragua and the Soviet invasion of Afghanistan, which stimulated old Cold War anxieties in the United States and helped clear the path to a resurgent, militant anticommunism and the election of Ronald Reagan. Neoconservatives denounced Carter's human rights policies as naïve and insufficiently focused on the dangers of communism. The Carter administration itself ultimately contributed significantly to the renewal of the Cold War, as the president and his advisers came to share the growing fear of the late 1970s that Soviet influence seemed to be on the rise once again and increased U.S. military spending accordingly. But the rekindled Cold War and Reagan's electoral defeat of Carter in 1980 could not hide the multiple ways in which the Carter administration embodied the previous decade's emphasis on multicultural respect and greater human equality.

RESISTANCE

Many citizens in the 1970s did not find the spread of egalitarian and inclusive practices in American public life to be completely inspiring. The rights revolution that began in the 1960s and expanded in the 1970s carried with it an obligation that others respect those rights, to tolerate people and behaviors that they had not had to tolerate in the past. Desegregation of the public sphere impacted everyone, and displeased some. Multiculturalism began to complicate and replace the traditional upbeat narrative of American history and culture. Relativism seemed to undercut older moral certainties about everything from sexual behavior to the purpose of the United States in the world. Defeat in Vietnam and anti-American revolutions elsewhere in the Third World contributed to the loss of a familiar story of national goodness and success. The economic downturn of the decade whittled away at Americans' sense of personal security, leaving them feeling anxious and even resentful. The context of rising unemployment and inflation meant that white heterosexual men, the heart of the old American working class, experienced the increased public presence of women, gays, and people of color as competitors at a moment when the long-robust U.S. economy had stopped growing for the first time in a generation. This was a recipe for backlash.[51]

The backlash had deep roots. Whites had resisted racial desegregation of neighborhoods, schools, and workplaces long before the major civil rights legislation of the mid-1960s, which is commonly credited with initiating the shift of white Southern voters from the Democratic Party to the Republican Party. "Law and order" conservatives had denounced antiwar protesters and black urban uprisings and crime in the late 1960s, helping put Richard Nixon in the White House in 1968. The backlash was also complicated. Class resentment colored working-class feelings about student protesters against the Vietnam War, who were often seen as arrogant children of the privileged middle and upper classes. Age resentment fed the "generation gap" of older Americans seeing younger Americans as disrespectful and self-indulgent. Gender resentment shaped the response of many men to newly empowered and less deferential women. Racial and cultural resentment spilled out against Arabs and Iranians after the oil crises and Tehran hostage crisis, and against Vietnamese refugees as reminders of American defeat. Immigrants felt the hostility summed up in the perhaps apocryphal story of the Nebraska legislator, during an earlier era of immigration restriction, who had spoken in favor of abolishing the teaching of foreign languages in the state's school systems (which happened, briefly, at the end of World War I): "The English language alone was good enough for Jesus Christ and it's good enough for the people of Nebraska." White anger over school busing for integration became a major issue in cities such as Boston in the mid-1970s, until eased by white flight to suburbs and private schools, by magnet schools, and by federal court decisions limiting the use of busing. In popular culture, the multifaceted backlash showed up in the lovable but bigoted character of Archie Bunker on the popular television show *All in the Family* that began in 1971; in Southern rock band Lynyrd Skynyrd's 1974 hit song, "Sweet Home Alabama" ("Watergate does not bother me, does your conscience bother you?"); and in the Academy Award Best Picture–winning *Rocky* (1976), which portrayed a tough white underdog boxer surprising everyone by going fifteen rounds with a Muhammad Ali-like dominant black world champion. No one navigated the current of resentment in the 1970s more successfully than Senator Jesse Helms of North Carolina, who denounced blacks, feminists, radicals, gays and lesbians, as well as Carter's pardon of Vietnam draft resisters "who cut and ran when their country needed them."[52]

Perhaps the strongest resistance to the new era of formal equality was evident regarding the issue of sexual orientation. Many of those citizens unhappy about recent changes in American society quietly admired the courage of peaceful civil rights protesters, recognized the injustice of paying a woman differently than a man for the same work, or at some level identified through their own family backgrounds with immigrants coming to the United States for greater opportunities. But very few of these resentful Americans had anything but scorn and disgust for gays and lesbians, with whom they rarely if ever had any contact—at least knowingly, since most homosexuals kept their orientation private. "Human garbage," Anita Bryant called them. The former Miss Oklahoma and popular singer organized the successful drive in Dade Country, Florida, in 1977 to repeal a new local ordinance banning discrimination on the basis of sexual orientation. Prominent Baptist minister Jerry Falwell flew into Miami to organize a large rally and announced that "so-called gay folks" would "kill you as quick as look at you." Tapping into growing concerns about child pornography and molestation, Falwell echoed Bryant's central argument that "homosexuals do not reproduce, they recruit." National newspaper columnist George Will identified homosexuality with national decline, calling the original Dade County ordinance another step in "the moral disarmament of society." Bryant's campaign spread to several other cities in 1977 and 1978, helping roll back some municipal ordinances protecting gays and lesbians from discrimination. What distinguished homosexuals from other groups trying to shed discrimination, for these opponents, was that they were seen as choosing immoral behavior rather than just suffering because of a genetic inheritance over which they had no control. They were, in this understanding, not victims but rather criminals and perverts, and granting them legitimacy would make it impossible to raise children in a morally healthy environment. This belief would endure long past the 1970s, leaving gays and lesbians as the last major group in American society against whom a substantial minority, mostly based in conservative evangelical Protestant churches, continued to believe it acceptable—and even morally mandatory—to discriminate.[53]

The largest impact of the new regime of formal equality came in the lives of women, by far the largest group surfacing against historic prejudice in the 1970s, so resistance to change was also particularly visible on issues of gender. Opposition to the Equal Rights Amendment crystallized the anxieties of gender traditionalists. "Women's lib is a total assault on the role of the American woman as wife and mother," Phyllis Schlafly argued, "and on the family as the basic unit of society." Here was the crucial point. For these mostly religious anti-feminists, American society was built not on a foundation of free individuals, but on a basis of families that "assures a woman the most precious and important right of all—the right to keep her own baby and to be supported and protected in the enjoyment of watching her baby grow and develop." Gender differences were not to be erased but cherished. ERA opponents believed women *were* different in essence than men: more nurturing, less selfish, less competitive. They believed in a gendered division of labor, with men earning income outside the home and women serving as homemakers in the best sense of the word. Indeed, they feared that the ERA might weaken men's commitment to provide financially for their families. They instead sought to strengthen that commitment. The intensity of those women who opposed the ERA reflected their determination not to be forced by law out of their normal, treasured lives and into something new and more vulnerable. They resented being made, as they saw it, more masculine. Social conservative Connie Marshner believed that "feminists praise self-centeredness and call it liberation." Anti-feminists viewed the legalization of abortion as part of the same threat to motherhood, child-rearing, and the traditional nuclear family, the foundations for the entire structure of a healthy society.[54]

Not surprisingly, the changes in women's lives in the 1970s made many men uncomfortable. They did not like being called "male chauvinists," and many did not want to reconsider how they spoke and acted toward the women in their lives. Even the most considerate men were newly unsure: Should they open doors for women? Should they avoid commenting at all on women's appearance? Should they not have full-time jobs if they wanted to be fathers? What, ultimately, did women really want and expect from them? Few people liked to be challenged about the most fundamental assumptions on which they had built their daily lives. Men had benefited for so long from women's inferior legal, economic, and social status that it would have been odd had they not resented, to some extent, the gendered desegregation of the workplace and of public leadership roles, as well as women's declining willingness to construct their lives around supporting men. More interesting was the fierce resistance of many women, mostly older and mostly religious, to altering the landscape of gender in American culture. Yes, they treasured the domestic sphere of the home and did not want to be forced out of it. But they also feared that changes such as the Equal Rights Amendment and abortion rights might actually liberate *men* more than women; "women's liberation" might prove to be a sham. They worried that men's sense of moral obligation was diminishing. In an era of deepening economic insecurity due to high inflation and high unemployment, working-class women in particular sought to bolster their increasingly precarious position by preventing women from losing traditional male protection and support.[55]

In a fundamental sense, feminists and anti-feminists shared the common ground of emphasizing women's economic vulnerability. Most women, they all believed, were just one man removed from impoverishment. Where they differed was on how to improve women's economic security. For feminists, the key was freeing women from dependence on men by making them equal and autonomous. For anti-feminists, the solution was tying men more firmly to their wives and children.

In other regards, the expected divisions between gender traditionalists and their feminist opponents were also not so clear. Pornography, a booming industry in the 1970s, was an example. Feminists divided on this issue. "Free-speech feminists" supported the rights of pornographers to make and dispense their graphic and titillating products; they believed in freedom of sexual expression and, regardless of whether they might dislike particular pornographic materials themselves, did not want the state limiting personal freedoms in this arena. Other feminists disagreed vigorously. They saw pornography above all as a way of demeaning women, and they associated it directly with such violence against women as rape, marital rape, wife battering, and sexual harassment. These feminists found considerable common ground with gender traditionalists, who opposed pornography for similar reasons.[56]

Religion was another example of a sphere where predictable differences about gender roles did not always pan out. The journal *Daughters of Sarah* began publication in November 1974, declaring: "We are Christians; we are also feminists. Some say we cannot be both, but Christianity and feminism for us are inseparable." Subsequent issues of the journal found an audience with a focus on sexist language in worship and hymns, the ordination of women, and egalitarian marriage. For these Christians, Jesus' life embodied not old hierarchies but radical new ideas of human equality. The very meaning of the word "liberation" remained contested for women on all sides of gender issues. Likewise, many devout Jews, particularly in the Reform movement, embraced feminism, revising the language of prayer books and rituals. For many women, both nominally feminist and anti-feminist, a major goal was avoiding being seen as sexual objects. A few years later, University of Richmond law professor Azizah Y. al-Hibri captured this purpose succinctly in a question: "Why is it oppressive to wear a head scarf but liberating to wear a miniskirt?" The pursuit of equality for women and others endured as a complicated, ongoing task, one that was not fully completed in the critical years of the 1970s.[57]

It is perhaps worth reiterating once again that prejudice and discrimination did not disappear in the 1970s. (They have hardly disappeared today.) Public schools proved a particular challenge to desegregate substantively, rather than just symbolically, due to decades and centuries of residential segregation by race. Eleven o'clock Sunday morning, as the phrase went, remained one of the most segregated hours of the week, with few churches multi-hued. A full range of words and actions in this decade reminded women, people of color, disabled folks, older and younger people, and gays and lesbians that they were not unanimously respected or appreciated. From locker room jokes to personal assaults, from all-white membership rosters of country clubs to glass ceilings in corporations, from sexist put-downs to racist insults, from police harassment to mostly black death rows, from decaying inner cities to expanding suburbs, American society remained littered with the debris of a history of enforced inequality. It was a vast clean-up project.

The sweeping, however, was vigorously under way. Prejudice and discrimination remained present but they moved increasingly into the realm of private life. In the public sphere, from classrooms to workplaces to television screens, American society shifted emphatically in this decade toward greater equality, fuller inclusion, and enlarged multicultural respect. Humor that had once been considered funny won fewer laughs. People who had once been shunned or ignored gained new status. Jimmy Carter, not George Wallace, was the Deep South governor who won the White House. "Racist" was fast becoming the term of greatest opprobrium in American public life. "Sexist" was not far behind. "Homophobe," still a decade or two off, was coming over the horizon. The ethics of daily life in the United States were changing in ways few could have imagined just a decade or two earlier—and sometimes just a few years earlier.

In 1969, American mountaineer Arlene Blum applied to join a climbing expedition to Afghanistan. "Dear Miss Blum," came the expedition leader's brief response, "Not too easy a letter to write as your prior work in Peru demonstrates your ability to go high, and a source I trust has furnished a glowing account of your pleasant nature in the mountains." But, he concluded, "one woman and nine men would seem to me to be unpleasant high on the open ice, not only in excretory situations, but in the easy masculine companionship which is so vital a part of the joy of an expedition. Sorry as hell." Six years later, the nation's most mainstream magazine acknowledged that an enormous change was under way. "They have arrived like a new immigrant wave in male America," *Time* announced in its cover story identifying "American Women" as its annual "Person of the Year" for 1975. "They may be cops, judges, military officers, telephone linemen, cab drivers, pipefitters, editors, business executives—or mothers and housewives, but not quite the same subordinate creatures they were before. Across the broad range of American life, from suburban tract houses to state legislatures, from church pulpits to Army barracks, women's lives are profoundly changing, and with them, the traditional relationships between the sexes." So, too, were the lives of people of color and other individuals from groups long excluded from the respectability of mainstream society. Americans had not reached the day of Jubilee, of forgiveness of past debts and renewed community, but they were on a road that was headed in that direction.[58]

Chapter 3

THE SPREAD OF MARKET VALUES

"THIS IS LIKE 1931," long-time socialist writer and activist Michael Harrington wrote in 1978. "Just as the conventional wisdom of the 1920s was totally shattered by the depression, the conventional wisdom of the 1960s has been shattered by inflation." Economic growth had defined human history for two hundred years, reaching a peak in the generation after 1945 when world economic growth averaged an extraordinary 5–7 percent per year. Americans rode that growth to a higher standard of living than anyone else. But in the 1970s it all seemed to be flowing away. Unemployment, oil shortages, a plunging stock market, recession, and, above all, inflation were apparently ending the golden years of unparalleled prosperity. Inflation hit everyone, and it hit the poor hardest of all. Persistent inflation undercut dreams and hopes for the future. Pan American Airlines' popular 1974 advertisement suggested how continuous high inflation might alter basic assumptions and behaviors: "Live today. Tomorrow will cost more." The economic trauma of the 1970s threatened to destabilize Americans' understanding of how the world worked.[1]

Recession and inflation together undermined the confidence of Americans in their government's management of the economy. Inflation tends to corrode citizens' faith in their government, which is seen as not keeping the promises it prints on the paper it issues. The money just is not worth what it says it is worth. For Americans in the 1970s, this brought into question the entire political economy built upon the New Deal of the 1930s and producing extraordinary economic growth and affluence ever since. If this system no longer worked, what was to be done? For the first time in more than a generation, a new cohort of economists began to look to the mechanism of the unrestricted market as a more efficient way of allocating resources, and they began to doubt the prominent role of the federal government in regulating the U.S. economy.

In the broadest sweep of world history, the 1970s can be seen as the most important turning point on the journey from 1945, a Left-leaning moment in world history when socialism and welfare states were newly ascendant as fascism and colonialism collapsed, to 1989, a Right-leaning moment around the globe when Communism collapsed and capitalism stood triumphant as the only credible economic system. In the United States, the political traumas of the Vietnam War and the Watergate scandal served as additional tributary streams into the rising river of disillusionment with government. This was not a total break with the past. The rhetoric of disillusionment—the "tax revolt" and the disdain for "big government" and "bureaucrats"—often masked enduring expectations of government entitlement programs such as Social Security and Medicare. Democrats in Congress vigorously defended such provisions. Indeed, a last salient of New Deal-style reform, focused on environmental and health issues, pushed well into the 1970s, like the final shot of a fireworks display going up while previous shots fall away. But the dominant trend of the decade was a separation of citizens from the national government that they had embraced for the preceding two generations, and therefore also from the political party that had most fully embodied that system of governance: the Democrats.[2]

Long-term structural changes in the U.S. economy accelerated in the 1970s, further weakening the old New Deal political and economic order. Labor organizing declined. The growth of the Sun Belt, made up of the non-union South and the less unionized West, shifted populations, jobs, and power away from the more unionized Rust Belt of the Northeast and Midwest. The nationalist and "Fordist" model of capitalism with its functional alliance of big business, big labor, and big government—and model cities like Detroit and Buffalo—increasingly gave way to an internationalized model of capitalism with emphasis on free trade, government deregulation, and entertainment and information industries—and model cities like Los Angeles and Orlando, where Disney World opened in 1971. Globalization encouraged technological innovation, including the personal computer industry of Microsoft (1975) and Apple (1977), as well as the biotechnology industry that appeared with Genentech's successful application of gene-splicing to the engineering of human insulin in 1978, key stimuli to the growth of Silicon Valley in California. Cheaper competition from abroad wooed manufacturing plants south of the border to Mexico and across the Pacific to Taiwan and Korea. Jobs in the growing service and information sectors, typically with lower wages and fewer benefits, replaced more remunerative jobs lost in the shrinking manufacturing sector. The gap between wealthy and working-class Americans, which had held fairly steady since World War II, began to widen.[3]

Economic changes and technological innovations helped reshape American culture in the 1970s. Entertainment shifted increasingly from the public sphere of the community to the private sphere of the home, just as city-dwellers continued to move to the larger homes of the suburbs. The spreading popularity of air-conditioning was crucial: instead of having open windows and going outside to be cooler, where interactions with neighbors and friends were almost unavoidable, Americans increasingly stayed indoors with the windows closed and the air conditioner humming. By 1980, Americans were consuming more man-made coolness than the entire rest of the planet put together. Rather than going out to the movies, people stayed inside to watch not just television but also now movies at home, thanks to the development of the videocassette recorder (VCR) in 1975, along with an expanding array of cable television options including ESPN (1979) and CNN (1980).

The premier symbol of the new era of individualized entertainment was the Sony Walkman, first marketed in 1979. This small radio and cassette player with headphones, a breakthrough of miniaturization and convenience, now allowed people to remain in their own isolated bubbles of entertainment, even when they were out in public. The Walkman presaged the later era of the iPod and cell phones with earpieces, of a public realm divided into atomized individual realities, a culture of entertainment and communication marketed to individuals with diminishing expectations of communal connections of even an incidental kind. Such pursuit of individual and individualized happiness was a central focus of the 1970s, the era of the aptly named *Self* magazine (begun in 1979) and a period in which the number of clinical psychologists in the United States tripled. Less trustful of their government and less interested in public life and civic activities, Americans instead turned inward to attend to their personal lives. The hugely successful *People* magazine, first published in 1974, the year of Nixon's resignation, epitomized this trend in its focus on the inconsequential but titillating private lives of entertainment celebrities.[4]

Above all, this decade was the seedbed for the growth of an extraordinary new confidence in market solutions to economic and political problems. Economists, political leaders, and average citizens all turned increasingly to the idea of the market—unregulated by government—as the most efficient way to produce and distribute goods and services, and thereby to free the U.S. economy from its slump. The logic of supply and demand took over, giving people whatever they wanted to buy. Increasingly liberated from traditional moral and legal restraints, a new, coarser, more profane, and more sexually explicit culture emerged in the 1970s, one in which pornography and gambling exploded into major industries. The individual consumer was the central figure. Nevada was the implicit model. Prostitution? It became legal there in 1971. Gambling? It had been central to the desert state's economy for decades. Instant marriages and quick divorces? Nevada was at the forefront. The old slogan of pleasure-seeking tourists that "what happens in Vegas stays in Vegas" now made less and less sense. Instead, the reverse was true. The culture and values of Las Vegas were spreading to everywhere else in what might be considered the "Nevada-ization" of the United States. The Left and the Right had found their common ground in a revitalized individualism, where the coun-

terculture's "do your own thing" met the libertarian desire to
remove governmental constraints on individual freedom. The
results of this shift were liberating to many but troubling to others. "The effect of liberty to individuals is that they do what they
please," British conservative Edmund Burke had warned two
centuries earlier. "We ought to see what it will please them to
do, before we risk congratulations."[5]

A Sea Change of Principles

The centrality of the profit motive and the ownership of private
property have made free-market capitalism a ready target for
critics. From Karl Marx to Pope John Paul II, they have denounced this global economic system for promoting greed and
exploiting humans and nature while diminishing community
and spirituality. But the incentive of working to improve the
economic circumstances of oneself and one's family is a powerful universal human motivation, regardless of whether it is
viewed as selfish. Indeed, those who have experienced the absence of that incentive, such as enslaved African Americans or
citizens of the Soviet Union, appreciated its importance more
than anyone else. The magnetic appeal of private property was
visible in the anti-slavery movement of the antebellum United
States, when enslaved workers yearned above all else to be able
to enjoy the fruits of their own labor.

The free-market proponents of the 1970s need to be understood in a similar light as true reformers, not merely as greedy
capitalists. To them, it was clear by this decade that capitalism
could produce fantastically greater wealth than socialism, and it
was equally evident that socialism was not distributing at all
equally what it did have. Sometimes called "neoliberals" for
their similarity to nineteenth-century liberals with their emphasis on individual freedom and property rights, and quite different from the regulated-economy New Deal–style liberals of the
twentieth century, these reformers sought to reenergize economies everywhere by unleashing individual entrepreneurship and

energy. They celebrated what Adam Smith had long before referred to as people's inherent "propensity to truck, barter, and exchange one thing for another," a positive tendency that was simply part of human nature, "of which no further account can be given." For them, old hierarchical bureaucrats in the Communist bloc represented the most corrupt, anti-idealistic view possible, but liberty was threatened by any form of state intervention in which collective judgment replaced individual freedom to choose. They considered markets, by contrast, to be decentralized and self-correcting, providing what people actually wanted, rather than what someone in government thought they should want, and providing it in the most efficient manner. Laissez-faire capitalism, for these neoliberals, established the foundation of human liberty and the most expedient route to prosperity.[6]

"The intellectual counterrevolution of the 1970s," as journalist Robert Kuttner has called it, brought back to influence enthusiasts for a pure free-market economy who had been marginal in American life since 1929. The stock market crash that year and the subsequent Great Depression thinned the ranks of such enthusiasts and isolated them from mainstream policy-making. The worshipful attitudes of the 1920s toward business and individualism came to be seen as fundamentally misguided. Economist John Maynard Keynes provided the most important road map for the New Deal of the 1930s, legitimating intensive government management of the economy and deficit spending when needed—a mixed economy ("Keynesian economics"), a regulated form of capitalism. By the end of World War II in 1945, depression and war had shaken the faith of people all over the world in the vitality of capitalism. Assistant Secretary of State Dean Acheson, a staunch defender of the interests of business, acknowledged as much in 1945 when he explained to a Senate committee the situation of afflicted peoples in Europe and Asia: "They have suffered so much, and they believe so deeply that governments can take some action which will alleviate their sufferings, that they will demand that the whole business of state control and state interference shall be pushed further and further." For the next generation, welfare states of various kinds flourished on both sides of the Iron Curtain, and government guidance of a modern economy came to seem like common sense.[7]

Then the inflation and recession of the 1970s staggered the U.S. and world economies, and popular ideas about political economy changed course again. In many ways, the 1970s reversed the 1930s. The earlier decade had shown that markets without restrictions could fail, but now the system of more active government management of the economy seemed also to be faltering at the tasks of producing growth and jobs and controlling inflation. The 1930s had greatly accelerated the building of an American welfare state that eventually provided crucial forms of social insurance for its citizens, including old-age pensions and medical insurance. The 1970s turned that tide back, reducing government revenues through tax cuts and beginning the privatization of retirement funding with the creation of 401(k) plans, a definitive move back in the direction of individualism rather than collectivism.[8]

A small handful of economists and writers had been working for years to provide the intellectual underpinning for a new embrace of the free market. Austrian economist Friedrich von Hayek published a crucial book in 1944 entitled *The Road to Serfdom*, condemning socialism as a path to slavery and promoting a libertarian vision of a very narrow government role in the economy. Over the next few decades, von Hayek taught at the London School of Economics and the University of Chicago, the latter a hotbed of free-market doctrine. In 1974, he became the first non-Keynesian economist to win the Nobel Prize in economics, a sea change in the intellectual center of gravity within the economics profession: away from government management, and toward the restoration of confidence in markets as the best way to organize economic activity, and in the price system as the most natural and effective mechanism for communicating information. Von Hayek's contemporary, writer Ayn Rand, gained a wide following with the novels *The Fountainhead* (1943) and *Atlas Shrugged* (1957), which promoted heroic individualism and rejected welfare states of any kind and sold briskly for decades—particularly during the 1970s. Fond of wearing a gold dollar-sign pin, this Russian refugee to the United States considered herself a "radical for capitalism." Her fervent, atheistic libertarianism lifted up self-interest as the highest good, denied all social obligations, and lauded capitalism as inherently self-regulating, rewarding virtue and penalizing vice through the infallible mechanisms of supply and demand.[9]

No one did more to legitimate and promote the return of unrestrained market principles in the 1970s than economist Milton Friedman. Like von Hayek, Friedman taught at the University of Chicago and also won the Nobel Prize in economics, awarded in 1976. With the rest of the so-called Chicago School, Friedman worried much more about the threat to liberty from government power rather than from monopoly corporate power. His book *Capitalism and Freedom* (1962) first won him a large audience. In it, Friedman argued that liberating markets from government interference would serve rather than undermine the public interest, and he dismissed inequality in capitalist societies as a necessary cost of efficiency and an impermanent result of a dynamic system. Among other reforms, Friedman called for the end of the military draft, the abolition of licensing physicians, and education vouchers to give parents the option to send their children to private schools. Private sector activity, he believed, was always better than public sector activity; it was more efficient and more liberating of human energy and potential.[10]

By the late 1970s, as a Nobel Prize winner and a columnist for *Newsweek* magazine, Friedman had become the most prominent and influential economist in the world. He served as an informal adviser to several governments, famously visiting Chile two years after the bloody 1973 coup there that replaced a socialist regime with a radically free-market economy, one actually managed by Chilean economists trained in Friedman's program at the University of Chicago. From 1977 to 1980, after his retirement from teaching, Friedman and his wife Rose, a fellow economist, worked on a ten-part PBS television series entitled *Free to Choose*, whose companion volume became one of the best-selling non-fiction books of 1980. With both erudition and flair, Friedman tilled the soil of the United States and much of the rest of the world in preparation for a new harvest of free enterprise enthusiasm.[11]

Pro-business conservatives spent the 1970s working to change the intellectual environment around issues of government regulation. They developed and articulated a view that the marketplace was the real locus of democracy, where consumers made individual free choices, without the constraints of labor unions or government bureaucracies, and where all those choices combined formed the most natural, democratic, and even populist form of governance. Yes, they believed, successful corporations might have great power, but it was always inherently constrained by the need to please customers. The National Association of Manufacturers, the U.S. Chamber of Commerce, and the new Business Roundtable (founded in 1972) promoted this vision. So did a series of new conservative think tanks, established in the 1970s to wrest the policy high ground from traditionally liberal institutions such as the Ford Foundation and Rockefeller Foundation. The Heritage Foundation (1973) with Colorado beer money from Joseph Coors, the Cato Institute (1977) with Wichita oil money from Charles Koch, the Manhattan Institute (1978), and the older but newly well-funded American Enterprise Institute helped to legitimate the ideas of conservative economics in mainstream Washington policy discussions.[12]

Free-market organizers renewed efforts to direct corporate funds to the lobbying process. In 1971, Virginia corporate lawyer Lewis Powell warned the U.S. Chamber of Commerce that criticism of the American free enterprise system had gone too far and it was time "—indeed it is long overdue—for the wisdom, ingenuity and resources of American business to be marshaled against those who would destroy it." Two months later, President Nixon's appointment of Powell to the U.S. Supreme Court bolstered a trend that led eventually to what journalist Jeffrey Rosen called "an ideological sea change on the Supreme Court," from the skepticism of corporations visible in the Earl

Warren years to the new millennium when even liberal Justices would be sympathetic to free markets. In 1977, the U.S. Chamber of Commerce established the National Chamber Litigation Center to file cases and briefs in state and federal courts on behalf of business interests. Meanwhile, the number of political action committees funded by corporations shot up, from 89 in 1974 to 1,467 in 1982. Business schools also flourished during this decade. In 1970, some 20,000 students received master's degrees in business administration; in 1980, the number was 55,000. Applications to undergraduate business programs doubled during the 1970s. By the end of the decade, business was the largest undergraduate major, almost twice as popular as its closest competitor, education.[13]

The Republican Party enthusiastically endorsed the new campaign for free enterprise. From the party's earliest years in the 1850s, the GOP had always supported the interests of business. After their heyday in the 1920s, Republicans had divided into those accommodating themselves to the regulatory state of the New Deal and those opposing it. The accommodators included Nixon's White House, often considered the last liberal administration, one that used government regulation such as wage and price controls to manage the economy in a proactive fashion. Nixon himself admitted in 1971 that "now, I am a Keynesian." As the decade progressed and the economy faltered, however, the opponents of the New Deal order seized the high ground. The course of environmental policy made this vividly clear. During the 1972 campaign, the Republican Party had celebrated and promoted Nixon's environmental achievements, including his signing of the bill creating the Environmental Protection Agency (EPA). But by 1975, as anti-regulatory forces gained ground, EPA administrator Russell Train lost influence with President Ford and his chief of staff, Richard Cheney. By 1980, the Republican Party had shed most of its remaining associations with environmentalism, a remarkable development for the party of conservationist Theodore Roosevelt, the original environmentalist party in the United States.[14]

Ronald Reagan emerged as the key figure in the Republican

shift to the right. Famous for his declaration that "government isn't the solution—government is the problem," the former California governor fell barely short in his effort to unseat the more moderate President Ford from the Republican presidential nomination in 1976. Four years later, he swept to victory in the primary and in the general election. Reagan's patriotic rhetoric assuaged the concerns of social conservatives, but his strongest commitment lay in reducing the role of government in the economy. In an interview with *Reason* magazine, he explained that "the very heart and soul of conservatism is libertarianism," the desire for "less government interference," "less centralized authority," and "more individual freedom." Reagan was a more genial version of Senator Barry Goldwater (R-AZ), who declared, "I fear Washington and centralized government more than I do Moscow." Reagan had a lighter touch, joking that "the best minds are not in government. If any were, business would steal them away." He would not have dissented from anti-tax crusader Grover Norquist's later assertion that the ultimate goal of the Republican Party was to return the country to the way it was "up until Teddy Roosevelt, when the socialists took over," and get rid of "the income tax, the death tax, regulation, all that."[15]

Most revealing of all was the path taken by the Democratic Party, the long-time party of working people, which began to shift away from its pro-labor stance and commitment to an activist federal government. Developing fissures in the unwieldy Democratic coalition bulged wider by the early 1970s. White Southerners and some of the white working class abandoned a party they saw as concerned primarily with cultural liberalism—minority and women's rights and environmentalism. Then in 1976, the party nominated and elected Jimmy Carter, a different kind of Democrat who favored deregulation and reliance on the market. A successful businessman from the Deep South, Carter with his fiscal conservatism and centrist style signaled that the Democrats were no longer the party of economic redistribution, no longer the party of Franklin Roosevelt and Lyndon

Johnson. Historian Steven Gillon called Carter "a Democrat who thought like a Republican," while Democratic activist Arthur Schlesinger, Jr., wrote in 1980 that "he is not a Democrat— at least in anything more recent than the Grover Cleveland sense of the word." In his second state of the union address, in January 1978, Carter declared, "We really need to realize that there is a limit to the role and the function of government. Government cannot solve our problems, it can't set our goals, it cannot define our vision. Government," the Democratic president concluded, "cannot eliminate poverty or provide a bountiful economy or reduce inflation or save our cities or cure illiteracy or provide energy." Well before Reagan's election and the famously pro-business era of the 1980s, the tide had already changed in the United States. Free-market ideas were in ascendance.[16]

THE ECONOMY GOES SOUTH

Structural changes in the U.S. economy helped loosen voters' loyalty to an engaged federal government and a welfare-state safety net. The long-term upward trajectory of American manufacturing, so instrumental in creating the wealth and power of the country, had begun to level off. After 1956, more Americans worked in the service sector, a proportion that increased further from 60 percent in 1970 to 70 percent in 1980. In the same ten years, more than 30 million jobs disappeared in the United States, most of them in manufacturing. International competition, particularly from West Germany and Japan, was one reason. Outsourcing was another: U.S. industrial companies began moving production to other countries, such as Mexico and Taiwan, where labor costs were dramatically lower and environmental and safety regulations less burdensome. This process of deindustrialization hollowed out old industrial cities of the Great Lakes region like Detroit and Cleveland. When wages are adjusted for inflation, the average American worker never earned as much again as in the peak year of 1973. Poverty rates also reached a historic low of 11 percent in 1973 and rose thereafter. Only the wealthiest fifth of American households saw their share of national income increase during the 1970s.[17]

The disappearance of industrial jobs gravely damaged the ranks of organized labor. Unions were most prominent on industrial shop floors and assembly lines, and their decline cut the legs out from under American working-class organization. Union members as a percentage of the civilian labor force dropped from 25 percent in 1970 to 16 percent in 1981, a loss of more than a third. Employment in the auto industry alone fell from 760,000 in 1978 to 490,000 in 1981. "The 1970s whimpered to a close," historian Jefferson Cowie concluded, "as the labor movement failed in its major initiatives, deindustrialization weakened the power of the old industrial heartland, market orthodoxy eclipsed all political alternatives, and promising organizing drives ended in failure." So at the same historical moment when women and men of color were gaining greater equality in the workplace, good jobs were in decline, heading south and west or overseas. Workers may have been increasingly diverse by sex and complexion, but they were ever more on their own as individuals in a difficult and increasingly global labor market where work, when it could be found, tended to not pay as well nor provide as many benefits. People were more equal, and less equal, than before.[18]

Closely related to deindustrialization was the growing sense of crisis by mid-decade in many of the nation's Northeastern and Midwestern cities. Higher-paying jobs were slipping away, leaving unemployment and impoverishment in their wake. Boston, Philadelphia, Pittsburgh, and Chicago lost over a third of their manufacturing between 1967 and 1977. Downtown retail sales declined by 48 percent in Baltimore, a pattern that was visible across other central business districts. Middle-class flight to the suburbs continued to weaken municipal revenue bases, particularly in Detroit and St. Louis. Racial tensions simmered in Boston's schools, while New York teetered on the verge of bankruptcy. Unionized public employees of New York and other cities—police, teachers, trash collectors—went out on strike in efforts to better their conditions, but wound up alienating the broader public and being blamed for budgetary nightmares that threatened the nation's municipalities, particularly their safety and cleanliness. Free-market conservatives found a ready national ear for denunciations of "union control of government" and the dire results. *U.S. News and World Report* called the problems of the increasingly impoverished urban cores "terminal." The New York serial killing spree known as the "Son of Sam" murders and the massive looting and arson that accompanied the electrical blackout of New York City on July 13, 1977, underlined the seeming helplessness and incompetence of city governments. The failure and corruption of government in the United States appeared to extend far beyond the national level of the Watergate scandal.[19]

Forecasters looked away to Dixie for signs of economic growth in the 1970s. A decade earlier, the states of the Old Confederacy had begun a successful campaign to lure Northern industry southward. A low wage scale, the absence of powerful labor unions, minimal environmental and safety regulations, and business-friendly state and local governments formed an attractive package. In the 1970s, for the first time in the twentieth century, more people moved into rather than out of the South, a quarter of them native Southerners returning home to work rather than to retire. By the end of the decade, the South and the Northeast had undergone an apparent role reversal, with the South—long oppressed and impoverished—now bursting with new growth and optimism, and the North—long dominant, wealthy, secure—now pessimistic about its economic future. The easing of the sense of racial crisis from the 1960s helped make the South more attractive, including to black former residents of the region who had been part of the outmigration of previous decades. By 1976, almost two thousand African American elected officials served in office across the region, including Maynard Jackson—the mayor of Atlanta, and three U.S. members of Congress—Barbara Jordan of Texas, Andrew Young of Georgia, and Harold Ford of Tennessee. "The region that had once been considered the least healthy section of

America," historian James Gregory has written, "—a land of boll weevils and pellagra, of enervating heat, deadly pests, and fevers—reemerged as the warm and attractive Sun Belt."[20]

Mitigating the heat and humidity was crucial. Air-conditioning penetrated deeply enough into the region in the 1970s to render livable and even enjoyable places once considered awful for at least several months of the year. The Sun Belt's boom hinged on the cooling systems that transformed cities such as Houston, Atlanta, Orlando, and Washington, as well as more westerly spots like Phoenix and Las Vegas. "The humble air-conditioner has been a powerful influence in circulating people as well as air in this country," the New York Times editorialized in 1970. "Its availability explains why increasing numbers of Americans find it comfortable to live year around in the semi-tropical heat." The problematic cold temperatures of the North could always be moderated by heating, but only with the spread of affordable air-conditioning could the same be said of the hot temperatures and humidity in the South. The proportion of Southern homes with AC, whether centralized or window-unit, expanded from 50 percent in 1970 to 73 percent in 1980. A similar increase cooled Southern automobiles. By the mid-1970s, 90 percent of Southern high-rise office buildings, banks, and apartments had air-conditioning.[21]

Not every native was pleased. One St. Petersburg, Florida, woman told an interviewer in 1982: "I hate air conditioning; it's a damnfool invention of the Yankees. If they don't like it hot, they can move back up North where they belong." But holdouts were few, and most of them simply lacked the money to pay for AC. Yankees kept coming to Florida. The increased availability of air-conditioning helped speed the decline of regional distinctiveness and the traditional sense of Southern community, as private television watching inside cool rooms behind closed windows replaced older habits of front porch sitting and neighborly visiting in warm weather.[22]

The expanding demographic and economic clout of the Sun Belt translated into political power and proved to be a crucial intermediate step on the path to a more globalized U.S. economy.

In the U.S. House of Representatives, Northeastern and Mid-western states in 1940 held a 251–184 seat advantage over Southern and Western states; by 2005, the Sun Belt states had reversed that ratio with a 252–183 advantage of their own. From 1964 to 2004, all elected presidents hailed from the South and the West, most of them former governors (of Georgia, California, Arkansas, and Texas). America's leadership in both political parties by the late 1970s, symbolized by Jimmy Carter and Ronald Reagan, was shifting to people with Sun Belt values, skeptical of government regulation, unsympathetic to labor unions, and admiring of entrepreneurship and business success.[23]

GLOBALIZATION'S GATHERING SPEED

"I have long dreamed," a former head of the Dow Chemical company said in 1972, "of buying an island owned by no nation and of putting the World Headquarters of the Dow Company on the truly neutral ground of such an island, beholden to no nation or society." One year later, Dow set up its own bank, Dow Banking Corporation, in the Cayman Islands of the Caribbean for just that purpose. A top Bank of America executive spoke of wanting to build "an international corporation that has shed all national identity." He was echoing Adam Smith's earlier contention that "the proprietor of stock is properly a citizen of the world, and is not necessarily attached to any particular country." In an effort to avoid regulation and particularly taxation by national governments, large multinational corporations moved parts or all of their business to offshore sanctuaries during the 1970s. Corporations were legally responsible to maximize their profits for shareholders, and the logic of minimizing taxation and regulation was unarguable. During this decade, international flows of information, goods, people, and capital increased, in part as a response to economic stagnation and as an effort to stimulate renewed economic growth. Liberalized currency exchange and capital markets were crucial: investment money, especially "petrodollars" from skyrocketing oil prices, flowed more readily across national borders to wherever opportunity beckoned, and governments lost some of their leverage in controlling their own national economies.[24]

American workers often lost out in an increasingly integrated and competitive world economy. Jobs disappeared, manufacturing moved overseas, and wages shrank. But American consumers—including those same workers when they went shopping—tended to benefit from the lower prices and greater choices that more competition could bring. The rising sales of Japanese cars in the 1970s provided one of the most visible examples. Overall, despite ambivalences, Americans generally began siding with globalization. Support for protectionist tariffs peaked in 1977 and declined steadily thereafter, replaced by popular support for free trade. No major party presidential candidate since then has supported protectionist policies.[25]

The process of rapid global economic integration was not new in the 1970s. The decades surrounding 1900, the apex of imperialism, had been an important era for building worldwide connections of trade and travel. Looking further back, Christopher Columbus's opening of links between the Eastern and Western Hemispheres around 1500 initiated what historians tend to identify as the rise of capitalism as a world economic system. Still further back, historian David Northrup argued, human history might be thought of in its broadest terms as first a period of *di*vergence—of peoples migrating out of Africa and around the globe, into smaller communities with diversifying languages and customs—followed later by a period of *conver*gence, beginning around AD 1000 with the Viking explorers' encounters with the people they called "Skraelings" in Newfoundland, a meeting of those who had earlier "turned left" out of Africa into Europe with those who had "turned right" into Asia and the Americas. Globalization has followed ever since, with the forces of convergence and divergence still in contention but the former winning out.[26]

Part of what the 1970s contributed to this longer history was a growing consciousness of the processes of global integration. As late as 1963, a distinguished American intellectual of liberal bent, Arthur Schlesinger, Jr., was still referring to the very use of the word "capitalism" as "demagoguery," his way of dismissing Marxist criticisms of, well, capitalism. But the economic crisis of the 1970s ended such willful aversion to the language of economics, and the shift to deregulation and privatization clarified anew that capitalism was the core determinant of American society. Rather than the Cold War defensiveness of Schlesinger a decade earlier, the 1970s would give rise to the breakthrough "modern world-system" theory of sociologist Immanuel Wallerstein that emphasized precisely global economic interconnections.[27]

A series of technological innovations shaped the process of globalization during this decade. U.S. Cold War spending on space travel and military projects underwrote many of these discoveries that stimulated global consciousness. The famous "Earthrise" photo taken by astronauts circling the moon on the *Apollo 8* expedition in December 1968 showed the Earth appearing alone in the darkened universe, a sublime visual demonstration of the Earth's unity and seeming vulnerability. "To see the earth as it truly is," wrote poet Archibald MacLeish, "small and blue and beautiful in that eternal silence where it floats, is to see ourselves as riders on the earth together, brothers on that bright loveliness in the eternal cold." The Defense Department built a network of linked computers called Arpanet, the precursor of the Internet, which first demonstrated to the public in 1972 such uses as electronic mail. The U.S. government launched the first military satellite in 1957, and by the 1970s commercial satellites were dramatically accelerating the speed with which information and communication could circle the globe. Such satellites, for example, were essential for CNN, which banned the word "foreign" from its first broadcast in 1980 as it sought to become the dominant news network worldwide with continuous updates twenty-four hours a day.[28]

Service industries from banking to insurance benefited from the greater efficiencies of automation in this decade. Contemporary commercial life in the United States soon became difficult to imagine without bar codes, the tiny Universal Product Codes (UPCs) that scan at retail checkout counters everywhere. Before

1974, they did not exist. IBM installed the first scanner system that year at Marsh's supermarket in Troy, Ohio, where it started up on June 26 by scanning a ten-pack of Wrigley's Juicy Fruit gum. UPCs radically improved inventory control for businesses, reduced theft of goods in transit, and speeded up the checkout process. Similarly, the term "banker's hours" began to lose its comfortable, 9–3 meaning in 1973 with the installation of the first automatic teller machine (ATM) at the Rockville Center branch of New York's Chemical Bank. Within a few decades, ATMs could be found from Antarctica to northernmost Norway and would greatly facilitate international travel and tourism.[29]

No technological innovation of the 1970s was as important as the advent of the personal computer (PC), a huge step beyond the enormous mainframe computers that preceded them. Beginning in the early 1970s, integrated circuits on tiny silicon chips enabled the creation of microprocessors. In 1976, Steve Jobs and Steve Wozniak, high school friends and college dropouts, formed Apple Computer in Cupertino, California, and soon released their first product, the Apple 1 computer kit. A year earlier, Bill Gates had incorporated Microsoft to provide the programming software for the imminent computer revolution, beginning with an early Altair 8800 microcomputer. Microsoft's operating systems were soon powering the PCs coming off the assembly lines of IBM and rival companies. Wal-Mart installed its first computer network linking its proliferating stores to corporate headquarters in Bentonville, Arkansas, in 1977. In terms of increasing productivity and efficiency, it is difficult to imagine a more significant development than the widespread use of personal computers in homes and businesses. In combination with the developing Internet, PCs became the very symbols of global interconnection. In an era of economic crisis and growing support for deregulation, science in the 1970s declined as a national and public project, such as in the form of NASA's funding, but boomed as a private and individual project, such as in the computer industry.[30]

A revealing measure of fuller U.S. integration into the world economy in the 1970s was the threefold increase in the value of imported manufactured goods as a percentage of domestic manufactures, from 14 percent in 1970 to 40 percent in 1979. A product "made in China" a century and a half earlier had almost certainly been a rare luxury item like porcelain or silk, a stark contrast to the rising river of imported goods now flowing into the United States. And increasing international trade flowed in both directions. Just as imports' share of American car purchases rose from 8 percent to 22 percent and German automaker Volkswagen opened its first U.S. assembly line in Pennsylvania, by 1981, Ford was producing more cars abroad than it did at home. McDonald's, the largest maker of the most iconic American product, the hamburger, began a relentless march across the globe when it opened its first franchises outside North America in 1971. At the other end of the range of consumer goods, when elite California cabernet sauvignon and chardonnay, for the first time, bested France's finest wines in a 1976 blind tasting in France, the so-called Judgment of Paris, it opened another avenue for U.S. exports.[31]

Several aspects of American popular culture had long appealed to audiences around the world, particularly Hollywood films and jazz and rock 'n' roll music. In 1979, a new kind of American entertainment product began to seep into Asia. The National Basketball Association (NBA), perched on the edge of new popularity with the imminent arrival of charismatic stars Magic Johnson, Larry Bird, and Michael Jordan, sent the Washington Bullets to China to play the national Chinese team in an exhibition. Just six years after the last U.S. combat troops left Vietnam, and only three years after the death of Chinese Communist leader Mao Zedong, a new realm of international commerce beckoned American entrepreneurs, one that would lead within a generation to Yao Ming becoming the first Chinese star playing in the NBA, and China emerging as the NBA's largest overseas market. In that same year of 1979, U.S. trade across the Pacific to Asia for the first time exceeded that across the Atlantic to Europe, a gap that more than doubled during the following decade and a half.[32]

The intensified international trade of the 1970s depended upon swift and efficient transportation of goods across long distances. Air freight for high-value and perishable products was central. The booming international sushi industry, for example, evolved from the new Boeing 747, a wide-body jumbo jet designed to hold two shipping containers side-by-side in its hold; the first Japan Air Lines 747s in the early 1970s carried home north Atlantic salmon from eastern Canada and New England. On April 17, 1973, Federal Express, a brand new small company, delivered 186 packages to 25 U.S. cities, flying fourteen small planes out of Memphis International Airport, a hub chosen for its central location and record of almost never closing due to bad weather. FedEx expanded rapidly and internationally, followed by United Parcel Service and DHL; by 1988, FedEx was delivering one million packages a day all over the world. Because ships carried more than 90 percent of the world's international merchandise by volume, the development of standardized shipping containers marked perhaps the most important innovation. Rather than laborious and expensive unloading and reloading in ports, where goods moved from train or truck to boat and from boat to train or truck, the new container system allowed for a single packing and unpacking by shippers. Cranes then handled all intermediary steps in the global chain of transportation. Labor costs—and potential disruptions—plummeted. North Carolina trucking company owner Malcolm McLean pioneered the system in the mid-1950s by using old truck trailers, and international use of containers followed in 1966. But only in 1970 was a full set of international standards for containers adopted, similar to the standardization of railroad track widths in the late 1800s. Then the new system became truly global. Oakland built a huge container facility in its port in 1972, and Los Angeles and Long Beach became the nation's two busiest ports, another indicator of the scale of the Pacific trade.[33]

A key strand of the developing web of global economic integration in the 1970s was the ease of transporting people as well as goods. Two airplanes stood out as symbols. First, in March 1970, the Boeing 747 lifted off into duty as the first wide-bodied passenger plane, increasing the number of comfortable seats available to tourists and businesspeople, particularly for flights from New York to European capitals. Second, the supersonic Concorde began regular trans-Atlantic air service in 1976, flying from New York and Washington to London and Paris in half the time of regular jets. The Concorde epitomized the breaking down of international barriers of time and space, making it possible for a person to depart from the United States and arrive in Europe in a mere three hours. Like satellites, the new plane made the world seem smaller. Air travel overall increased impressively in this era. Passenger miles traveled on domestic U.S. flights jumped fivefold between 1960 and 1980. The five million Americans who traveled overseas in 1970 grew to eight million in 1980, while the two and a half million visitors to the United States at the start of the decade increased to eight million at its end.[34]

The increased interweaving of the U.S. economy with the world economy required a language in which to communicate. French had been the language of international diplomacy and business as late as the nineteenth century, when English began to overtake it as the British Empire expanded its power. This process continued in the twentieth century, the British accent changing to an American accent along the way. One final development was necessary for English to emerge as a truly global language after the 1960s: the electronic revolution that gave birth to computers and the Internet was based primarily in the United States, a key influence on the vocabulary and syntax of computer use and the World Wide Web. From the 1970s on, English surged forward with little competition as the preeminent language of diplomacy, commerce, media, popular culture, advertising, and international travel and safety. Ambitious people everywhere learned English.[35]

The process of globalization that advanced in the 1970s had limitations and problems. One was the insufficient diffusion of English. "Unclear English accents and terminology" among the pilots and the control tower contributed significantly to the worst accident ever in aviation history, a crash of two Boeing 747s on a runway in Spain's Canary Islands in 1977 that killed 583 people. Other problems resulted from the now more rapid spread of pathogens and fauna. Human Immunodeficiency Virus (HIV) apparently spread from a very isolated environment in central Africa to Haiti and eventually to the United States, where it began appearing in the form of Acquired Immunodeficiency Syndrome (AIDS) in the late 1970s, soon moving on to become a deadly worldwide scourge. The 1972 détente between the United States and the Soviet Union accidentally brought a species of comb jelly from eastern North American estuaries, where it was inconspicuous and inoffensive, in ballast water of ocean-going vessels shipping U.S. grain to the Soviet Union. Arriving for the first time in the Black Sea, it reproduced with gusto, consuming the foods there that had previously sustained a large anchovy population. Within a few years, the comb jelly constituted most of the biomass in the Black Sea, the anchovies were gone, the anchovy fishing industry had dried up, and another small blow had been struck against the weakening Soviet economy. An even more grim outcome arose from the problems of misuse of the newly international media, particularly television, by terrorists seeking publicity, most notably the Black September operatives who murdered Israeli athletes and coaches at the 1972 Munich Olympics and the slew of subsequent international hijackings. Globalization found particular opposition from those concerned with the environment and the rights of working people, as chapter 5 will explore. But overall, the intensified processes of global economic integration in the 1970s dovetailed with the concurrent rising enthusiasm for free markets, deregulation, and the retreat of national governments.[36]

From Citizenship to Deregulation

Faced with economic hardship, declining faith in government, and a movement to promote freer markets as the best path forward, many Americans turned increasingly in the 1970s toward the private sphere of consumerism. Advertising expenditures grew by 50 percent as an encouragement in a down economy to keep buying—tickets for the new blockbuster-style movies, for example. But how could they afford it? Edith Bunker, the seemingly clueless but often quite perceptive mother in the popular television show, *All in the Family*, explained it as well as anyone: "With credit, you buy everything you can't afford." The Master Charge credit card appeared in the late 1960s and took off in popularity during the 1970s, changing its name to MasterCard in 1979 and competing with the new Visa credit card created in 1975 out of the older and more limited BankAmericard system. The explosion in consumer debt that followed became a familiar tale to most American households. Grocery stores began staying open all night, partly out of recognition that shoppers would come at all hours, and partly because they already had people working in the stores doing nightly restocking anyway. Safeway, Kroger, and others contributed thereby to the trend of expanding commerce into more and more sectors of American life. President Jimmy Carter, concerned by the nation's historic shift since 1971 to importing more than it exported and worried about the moral implications of a culture focused on material gratification, called on his fellow citizens to restrain themselves. "Too many of us now worship self-indulgence and consumption," he warned the nation in his prominent "crisis of confidence" speech on July 15, 1979. But Americans largely rejected Carter's call for restraint, instead turning the next year to Ronald Reagan, with his exuberant optimism about the future of the American material good life. "Growth for the sake of growth is the ideology of the cancer cell," writer Edward Abbey argued in 1977, but fewer and fewer Americans by the late 1970s dissented from the desire for unrestrained economic growth and the logic of the free market.[37]

A recent body of social science research, primarily by political scientists, has demonstrated that the early 1970s marked the beginning of a long-term retreat by the federal government from the lives of its younger and less advantaged citizens and of a long-term decline in civic engagement by such citizens. Social Security and Medicare continued to hold older Americans in a close relationship with Washington, and affluent Americans, as always, continued to use the political process to protect their

interests. But other citizens experienced decreasing daily influence from their government. The federally mandated minimum
wage, for example, when adjusted for inflation, grew from 1938
to 1968 and then began a steady decline after 1970. Younger
and poorer Americans found that wages stagnated, employee
benefits dried up, unionization rates shrank, the differences in
wages between college graduates and high school graduates
spiked, and public aid to those in need tailed off. The broad
disillusionment with politics stemming from Watergate also
turned them to the private sphere. Women, for their part, moved
increasingly into the paid workforce, reducing the amount of
traditional volunteer work they had previously provided for the
society as a whole. As a result, younger and less affluent Americans participated less in the processes of political democracy,
from joining service organizations to doing volunteer work to
voting. The peak of civic engagement in public life in the United
States turned out to be the 1950s and 1960s—the era of PTAs,
Elks Clubs, and the Veterans of Foreign Wars—resulting from a
generation of Americans uniquely shaped by the New Deal and
World War II. By the early 1970s, the high tide of civic participation was beginning to recede.[38]

The situation in the United States was not unique, but it was
unusual. Political philosopher Francis Fukuyama has demonstrated that a pattern of disruption and readjustment in social
values unfolded across the industrialized world after the 1960s,
with families shrinking in size, the importance of kinship declining, and trust in institutions atrophying. Other major industrialized countries besides the United States encountered similar economic downturns in the 1970s that placed new stresses on the
relationship between governments and their citizens. The United
States since World War II, however, had been at one extreme
among industrialized nations in offering few of the universal
benefits and services to its citizens that were common elsewhere,
from health insurance to child care. The American welfare state
emphasized categorical benefits, such as provisions for workers
or for veterans, while Western European welfare states moved

instead toward shared benefits for all citizens. So even before the 1970s, social protection and welfare spending by the French and British governments, for example, as a percentage of gross national product was notably greater than that by the U.S. government. After 1975, that gap widened further, the American share leveling off at 15 percent and the British and French climbing up to 25 percent and 30 percent, respectively. The American experience of the 1970s, in other words, pushed the nation even further down its distinctive path of intense individualism, declining political participation, and suspicion of government.[39]

Americans not only lost faith in government but also began to socialize with and trust each other less. Political scientists have carefully measured this decline in "social capital." Beginning in the early 1970s, citizens, on average, initiated a steady decline in visiting each other in their homes, socializing with neighbors, and eating family dinners together. The use of unlisted phone numbers and call screening increased sharply. The amount of time spent alone in cars grew rapidly, particularly for purposes of commuting to and from work. The practice of hitchhiking, once a common custom, almost disappeared. Rather than attending public meetings or serving in local organizations, Americans began cocooning at home and watching more television, particularly alone. "The link between increased television watching and decreased civic engagement," political scientist Robert Putnam wrote, "is unusually clear." A culture with less parent time at home, greater suburban space between houses, and more electronic entertainment was a recipe for increased social isolation—a less positive way of viewing individualism.[40]

Social critics have long argued that capitalism as an economic system has an unintended result of tending to erode the interpersonal ties and social trust that are necessary conditions for its success. The results of a relentless individual pursuit of wealth and free choice include a decline in social capital and a diminishing of its virtues, such as honesty, reciprocity, and keeping commitments, as conservative critics like Francis Fukuyama have observed. Maximum personal freedom does not fit easily with community responsibility; they are inherently conflicting values. Technological innovations like those appearing in the 1970s provided classic examples of the "creative destruction" that economist Joseph Schumpeter noted was a central dynamic of the capitalist marketplace, so it is not surprising that disruptions in the economy would also affect the realm of social relationships, including what Fukuyama called the "extreme forms of individualism that appeared during the 1970s." The shift in emphasis from active citizenship to individual consumption, from the public sphere to the private sphere, marked a trade-off between the values of individualism and the values of community.[41]

This shift in values underpinned deregulation, the most important policy initiative of the second half of the decade. From 1975 to 1980, the federal government retreated from much of its prominent role in overseeing the transportation, communications, banking, and energy sectors of the American economy. The movement for deregulation reversed most of a century of efforts to use the U.S. government as a balancing force against too great corporate power, from the Progressive era in the early twentieth century, to the New Deal in the 1930s, to the Great Society of the 1960s. But deregulation was not a right-wing plot. It was a bipartisan initiative, begun during the Ford administration, embraced by Jimmy Carter, and expanded by Ronald Reagan. It drew strength from the persistent inflation pervading the economy, which made more competitive pricing very attractive. It had support not only in the White House but also in Congress and even in many of the federal regulatory agencies themselves. Alfred Kahn, appointed chair of the Civil Aeronautics Board (CAB) by Carter, argued for the superiority of open markets because "the optimum outcome" of competition in any industry "cannot be predicted." Deregulation appealed to both the Right and the Left: the Right saw the regulatory system in principle as inefficient and unnecessary, and the Left viewed the regulatory agencies as favoring the industries they oversaw rather than protecting the interests of average citizens as consumers. "We believe that we ought to get the Government's nose out of the private enterprise of this country," Carter told fellow Democrats in 1980. A Reagan adviser explained that "by making their own choices in the free marketplace," consumers themselves "become the regulators."[42]

While President Ford and Congress in 1975–76 began reducing the authority of the Interstate Commerce Commission over interstate trucking and railroads, from rates to routes, it was air travel that proved the most visible part of the transportation sector. Air travel might be thought of as the second phase of transportation in the long-term history of globalization: water travel had integrated the world economy from Columbus's day up to the 1930s and remained important thereafter, but air travel now surpassed it, and airline deregulation in the 1970s further accelerated this process. Senator Edward Kennedy (D-MA), a preeminent liberal, held a crucial set of hearings into the state of the airline industry in 1975. Kennedy generally supported a strong federal regulatory presence, but like other New Deal-style liberals he also believed in competition rather than monopolies as beneficial to consumers. Aided by legislative assistant Stephen Breyer, the future U.S. Supreme Court Justice, Kennedy's hearings revealed to the public the large inefficiencies and high fares in the industry that resulted directly from the Civil Aeronautics Board's efforts to protect existing airlines. From 1950 to 1974, the CAB had turned down all seventy-nine new carrier applications. The results included fares that were at least 40 percent higher than they would have been in a more competitive environment, plus planes being flown—inefficiently—with scores of empty seats, a phenomenon that would be hard to imagine later, after thirty years of deregulation. Airlines were eager for more flexibility in setting prices in order to sell more seats, particularly in a recession. Consumers wanted lower prices, particularly in a period of high inflation.[43]

Congress responded with the Airline Deregulation Act of 1978, phasing out the CAB and ushering in much less restricted competition. That summer, there were suddenly eighteen different fares on the New York-London route, a phenomenon famil-

FIGURE 3.1.
Airline deregulation in 1978 launched the modern era of price competition
and busy planes. Courtesy *Time*, August 14, 1978.

iar to a later generation but utterly novel at the time. The first discount airline, People's Express, began flying in 1981, precursor to Southwest, Jet Blue, and others to follow. The average price that a passenger paid per mile on domestic U.S. flights began a steady decline of 51 percent over the next three decades, when adjusted for inflation. Travelers, in sum, got what they most wanted: lower fares. Airlines did reasonably well, too. Even in a fiercely competitive environment, they filled more and more seats with paying passengers: 55 percent in 1975, 60 percent in 1980, 70 percent in 1995, and 77 percent in 2005. Deregulation ended the more elegant style of early air travel, a function of its expensive character. Flying became more widely accessible and more common, but also more crowded and less pleasant. Consumers were getting what they paid for.[44]

Deregulation rolled through other industries as well, including natural gas and electricity. The U.S. Postal Service lost its monopoly on delivering letters in 1979. Lifting restrictions on competition among telephone service providers resulted in an 85 percent decline in the average price of an international phone call from New York to London. A "Sagebrush Rebellion" of large ranchers in Nevada even convinced their state legislature to pass a law in 1979—never tested in court—claiming ownership of all the federal lands in Nevada managed by the Bureau of Land Management, an ultimately futile effort to then get the state to sell them off to private citizens. This was taking deregulation to the point of privatization. The financial industry moved in a similar direction. The 1975 Securities Acts Amendments deregulated the New York Stock Exchange, where 80 percent of the dollar value of stock trading occurred, by eliminating fixed brokerage rates and other anticompetitive practices. The resulting drop in rates and rise in trading volume, combined with novel computerized information technology, reflected a new era of more active citizen engagement in the financial markets. Relaxed banking regulations after 1977 allowed small-deposit savings account owners to begin investing in higher-profit enterprises such as Treasury bills and money-market mutual funds.

The landmark Supreme Court decision in *Marquette v. First of Omaha* (1978) essentially deregulated credit card interest rates by allowing companies to issue credit cards in states like South Dakota that had the fewest or no restrictions on interest rates, but to market the cards to consumers all over the country. It was the domestic equivalent of banks going offshore to avoid taxation. And it accelerated the metastasizing of credit cards and credit card debt that soon came to define much of the American economy.[45]

The new logic of deregulation also ended the international system of fixed exchange rates for national currencies. Ever since the Bretton Woods agreement of 1944, named for the New Hampshire mountain resort where it was hammered out, other currencies had been linked to the dollar at fixed rates while the dollar was set at $35 per ounce of gold. But much had changed in the intervening twenty-seven years, including resurgent Japanese and Western European economies and a weakening dollar, thanks to the Vietnam War and domestic spending. Perhaps the clearest indicator of ebbing American economic dominance came in 1971, when imports exceeded exports for the first time in the twentieth century, a historic shift. Faced with few options and a wave of investors seeking to turn in dollars for gold, President Nixon broke the Bretton Woods system by taking the United States off the gold standard, ending the promise of exchanging dollars for gold ("as good as gold"), and creating a new system of floating currency exchange rates. Internationally, money was now deregulated. International investors responded by driving down the value of the dollar. From $35 per ounce, gold soared to $800 per ounce in 1980, a decline in the value of the dollar to roughly one-twenty-fifth of its former value. International markets were now deciding the worth of the currency. Along with the oil shocks of the decade, this shift to the logic of the market introduced considerable instability and unpredictability into international trade and strongly stimulated the growth of the financial industry, as investors rapidly shifted large pools of money around the world in a continuous quest for maximum profits.[46]

MARKET SOLUTIONS FOR EVERY PROBLEM

Public policy turned to market-based approaches throughout American society during the 1970s, beginning with the fundamental issue of who would bear arms to defend the nation. For most of U.S. history, the military draft had been a wartime exception until the Cold War, when it became the norm even in peacetime. The U.S. escalation of the conflict in Vietnam after 1965 and declining popular support for the war effort at home and within the ranks after 1968 created enormous stress. Resistance to the draft soared. "A crisis in morale and discipline" plagued the army in Vietnam, a *New York Times* reporter wrote in 1971, as gradual withdrawals of American troops made clear that the United States was no longer trying to win the war. "The men themselves are fed up with the war and the draft, questioning orders, deserting, subverting, smoking marijuana, shooting heroin, stealing from their buddies, hurling racial epithets and rocks at their brothers." Fraggings—killings of one's own officers—jumped fourfold, to 425, from 1969 to 1971. Back home, opposition to the draft among the young spanned the political spectrum. The conservative Young Americans for Freedom called it "involuntary servitude," the liberal National Student Association declared that "conscription is immoral," and radical protesters organized public burnings of draft cards. The random nature of the lottery system and its various exceptions for such factors as education undercut the idea that sacrifice for the nation was being equally shared by young men from all backgrounds.[47]

At this lowest point of morale inside the military and of popular support from the outside, how was the nation to shore up its armed services? It turned to the free market. No longer would military service be considered a fundamental obligation of all male citizens. It would be provided by volunteers, by individuals choosing to enlist. The armed forces, President Nixon contended on the campaign trail, were "the only employers today who don't have to compete in the job market. . . . They have been able to ignore the laws of supply and demand." A new all-volunteer army would be "more competitive with the attractions of the civilian world," including higher pay and increased benefits. Nixon agreed with young Americans "who recognize the draft as an infringement on their liberty—which it is." Nixon and his economic advisers argued that the free market, in which individuals made their own choices based on their own best economic interests, would be fairer and more efficient than the Selective Service System's exemptions and draft. The new volunteer army replaced the draft in 1973. General Walter Kerwin assured Congress that the change "should enable us to turn the corner and bring this level of indiscipline down." The officers in charge of its implementation understood, however, that successful recruiting in competition with private employers would require more than just attractive wages and benefits. It needed advertising. The army would be a product and its future soldiers would be customers. "In relying on the tools and techniques of a consumer market to help fill its ranks," historian Beth Bailey concluded, the American military "replaced public portrayals of shared sacrifice and obligations with a language of consumer dreams and images of individual opportunity."[48]

The creation of the all-volunteer U.S. armed forces in 1973 solved the problem of resistance to the draft, but it also provided the most dramatic example of the shift from citizenship to consumerism, from the common good to individual choice. By ending the constant inflow of new draftees, the new military distanced itself further from the citizenry as a whole. It created the potential for the kind of "standing army" that the nation's founders had warned against two centuries earlier and even a mercenary army, as the Persian Gulf War of 1990–91 suggested, where other nations contributed money to help pay for the presence of U.S. troops. For most middle-class Americans, soldiers were admired from a distance and war became increasingly a form of entertainment, in movies and video games. The same was true for the most educated and wealthiest Americans. "Since Vietnam," historian Andrew Bacevich demonstrated, "the American elite has largely excused itself from military service," including both Democrats such as President Bill Clinton (an antiwar protester) and Republicans such as Vice President Dick Cheney (who had "other priorities"). During the Cold War, veterans made up 75 percent of a typical U.S. Senate and more than 50 percent of a typical U.S. House of Representatives; by 2001, those numbers dropped to 36 percent and 29 percent, respectively. The 1970s was the tipping point. The all-male class of 1956 at Princeton University had 450 of its 750 members serve in the military after graduation; in 2004, 8 of 1,000 graduates enlisted. The volunteer military of the 2000s would not look much like average America, where 46 percent of citizens have studied at the undergraduate level, but only 6.5 percent of eighteen- to twenty-four-year-olds are enlistees. Market logic brought mostly poorer Americans into the armed services. African Americans roughly doubled their portion of military personnel between 1970 and 1980, due both to limited employment options in recessionary times and to relatively equal treatment within the military, a leader among institutions in promoting people of color. Women's portion of military personnel jumped fivefold in the 1970s. By recruiting women as well as men, the armed services doubled the size of their pool and kept average qualifications and test scores much higher than they would have been otherwise.[49]

Market logic won out in how to provide the manpower for national security, and it also pushed forward in the central matter of how—and how much—to fund government. Lower taxes were the answer. Shrinking government budgets was the most direct way to reduce the reach of the regulatory agencies and relief programs of the liberal welfare state. Rather than all citizens paying collectively for services provided for everyone, the powerful anti-tax movement of the 1970s aimed to reduce such services and let individuals pay for what they themselves used. Individual choice would replace collective ideas about the common good. The explosive inflation of 1973 to 1977 boosted the popularity of reducing taxes, particularly among senior citizens on fixed incomes and middle-class folks who saw their economic security waning, and particularly in states like California and Massachusetts where property values and taxes had soared.

"No, thanks—I'm a libertarian."

FIGURE 3.2.
The increasing disparagement of government
in the 1970s raised questions about the appropriate boundaries between the public and
private realms of American life. Courtesy
David Sipress/*The New Yorker.*

Under growing economic pressure, these mostly white taxpayers saw themselves as being forced, through taxes, to pay for
medical and other services for other disproportionately black
and Latino people, which they could hardly still afford for
themselves. Americans actually paid the lowest per capita taxes
of citizens of any industrialized nation in the 1970s, except perhaps Japan, but they complained the most loudly about "high
taxes." Feeling squeezed and resentful, already skeptical about
their government, they moved decisively toward an even more
individualistic, anti-tax perspective.[50]

　　The tax revolt found its first real traction in California with
the momentous passage of Proposition 13 in 1978. Anti-tax cru-
saders Howard Jarvis and Paul Gann led a forceful campaign
that won popular approval by a 2–1 margin, cutting property
taxes by more than 50 percent and severely limiting future tax
increases. One Californian called it "the Watts riot of the white
middle-class," a powerful expression of rage parallel to that of
the impoverished black residents of south-central Los Angeles in

1965. Proposition 13 made no effort to replace lost revenues, forcing state and local governments to simply slash an array of services. The curtain came down on two decades of California's efforts to build a social democratic state in health care, public works, welfare provision, and the promotion of organized labor, and one of the leading state educational systems in the nation began a steady decline. While individual property taxes had indeed grown very rapidly in recent years, the share of state taxes paid by businesses declined precipitously from 46 percent in 1967 to 28 percent in 1979. But Proposition 13 turned taxpayers against the public sector, not against corporate interests.[51]

Proposition 13 served as merely the opening shot in a larger anti-tax war. Over the following four years, from 1978 to 1982, similar tax-cutting and tax-limitation referendums passed in eighteen other states as diverse as Utah, Maine, Washington, Missouri, Alaska, Massachusetts, and Montana. The campaign aimed not only at local property taxes and state income taxes, but also at federal levies. Strong bipartisan majorities in the U.S. Senate and the U.S. House of Representatives approved a cut in the top federal capital-gains tax rate from 49 percent to 28 percent, despite the opposition of the Carter administration, whose spokesman referred to it as "the Millionaire's Relief Act of 1978." And the stage was set for a newly elected President Reagan to push through Congress in 1981 a major reduction in the top federal income tax bracket from 70 percent to 50 percent. From a peak of 94 percent during World War II, that top federal income tax bracket continued to drop until it reached 35 percent in the early 2000s. Because top income and capital-gains brackets affect only the wealthiest Americans, these tax reforms disproportionately benefited those who were already the most affluent. Wealth began to shift up the economic ladder as government revenues fell.[52]

The logic of free markets also limited Congress's efforts to reform the financing of election campaigns. In 1974, Congress passed amendments to the Federal Election Campaign Act that established a system of public financing for presidential races and limits on contributions by individuals and political action committees, as well as limits on the amounts individuals could spend on their own campaigns. The new law required the public disclosure of campaign contributions and created the Federal Election Commission as an independent regulatory watchdog. The goal was a more transparent system, where the natural tendency of money to flow to those with political power would be checked by public knowledge and by specific dollar limits. In the critical test case of *Buckley v. Valeo* (1976), the U.S. Supreme Court upheld most of the new rules as constitutionally grounded in the state's interest in limiting corruption, but the Court overturned the limits on an individual's spending on his or her own campaign as an overriding matter of free expression guaranteed by the First Amendment. In essence, the Court decided there was a free market for public speech and any individual could buy as much of it as he or she wanted to. The one limitation would be if public financing were accepted. *Buckley v. Valeo* limited the impact of campaign finance reforms by giving wealthier people an incentive to run for office. It was no surprise that within a generation, most U.S. senators were millionaires and most successful U.S. House races would require raising almost a million dollars.[53]

The logic of the free market shaped public policy on the issue of abortion in similar fashion. Here the roles of Congress and the Supreme Court were reversed from the campaign finance issue, with the Court leading the way and Congress then intervening to create a new compromise. After the *Roe v. Wade* decision in 1973, abortion opponents organized to prevent federal funds from being used to pay for abortion procedures, either through the Medicaid system for indigent patients or through the system of military hospitals for the many young women now serving in the armed forces. Beginning in 1976, Congress each year attached the Hyde Amendment, named for lead sponsor Rep. Henry Hyde (R-IL), to the Medicaid appropriation bill, prohibiting with very few exceptions the use of federal dollars for abortion, a practice upheld by the Supreme Court in *Harris v. McRae* (1980). Hyde and his allies hoped ultimately to stop all abortions. The practical result, however, was a classic market solution: a pregnant woman might have an abortion, but only if she could pay for it. The right to have an abortion is thus really a privilege for those who can afford it, rather than an absolute right such as the right to vote or speak freely. A reporter at a press conference asked President Carter if this were really fair. "Well, as you know, there are many things in life that are not fair, that wealthy people can afford and poor people can't," Carter replied.[54]

Indeed, American women's lives in the 1970s might be seen more broadly as reflecting the prevailing turn toward the operation of the free market, greater individual choice, and a receding government. Women's continued entry into the workforce put them in larger numbers into the paid labor market, where their identity as individual workers contended with any previous identity within a family unit. Women's sexual lives were essentially deregulated, both through the ending of restrictions on access to birth control in the Supreme Court's decision in *Eisenstadt v. Baird* (1972) and the legalization of abortion one year later in *Roe v. Wade*. Women's marriage arrangements—men's, too, of course—were deregulated by the development of no-fault divorce laws across the country, beginning in California in 1970. Divorce became much more common because people chose increasingly to pursue individual happiness rather than to remain in unhappy marriages. The emphasis on personal liberation pervaded the decade, bringing the market mentality—of individual choice among a growing array of options—more fully into the most intimate of relationships.[55]

The mechanisms of the free market moved to the forefront of American sports, too. In 1970, when baseball still reigned as "America's national pastime" and the National Football League and the National Basketball Association had not yet matched its popularity, major league baseball enjoyed an exemption from U.S. antitrust laws. It was known as the "reserve clause," and it bound each player to one team. The team could play him or trade him to another team, but the player himself had no say in where he worked at any point in his baseball career. The system preserved stability on teams' rosters and probably bolstered fans' loyalties as a result, in contrast to a later era of "free agency" when players frequently changed teams. But the reserve clause certainly prevented players from operating as free individuals within a competitive labor market. Outfielder Curt Flood, traded to the Philadelphia Phillies in 1969 after twelve years as a star player for the St. Louis Cardinals, refused to move to Philadelphia. He retired instead. But he refused to go quietly. Flood sued baseball commissioner Bowie Kuhn for the right to be a free agent and negotiate his own contract. Flood, who was black, understood that as a well-remunerated and high-profile sports star, his was not a typical labor dispute, but he noted in a much-quoted interview with sportscaster Howard Cosell that "a well-paid slave is nonetheless a slave." The case of *Flood v. Kuhn* made its way to the U.S. Supreme Court, which upheld the reserve clause in 1972. But baseball's anti-competitive system was nonetheless on its last legs. Three years later, an arbitration panel ruled that pitchers Andy Messersmith and Dave McNally were free agents, opening the door to the powerful winds of the free market and competitive bidding.[56]

A similar story unfolded in the realm of retirement planning. How people could afford to live after they quit working had become an increasingly central policy issue in the United States, as the twentieth century progressed and citizens lived longer and longer, life expectancy growing from forty-seven to seventy-seven years. The Social Security system established in 1935 provided a very modest source of income, and most American workers after 1945 came to rely on company pension programs run by their employers. Pensions were also usually modest but guaranteed; they involved no risk for retirees and no need to manage investments. This began to change, not surprisingly, in the 1970s. As manufacturing jobs disappeared, the pension system began to wither. In 1978, Congress added section 401(k) to the Internal Revenue Code. This voluntary retirement fund option was at first intended to supplement existing pension plans and to allow executives to tuck extra compensation in tax-deferred accounts. But the law turned out to be the beginning of the end of the entire system of professionally managed pensions providing benefits to retirees. Employers realized how much cheaper 401(k)'s were for them than traditional pensions, since many workers did not participate in voluntary plans and employers thus did not have to make matching contributions. In the early 1980s, three of five workers had a traditional pension plan and one of five had a 401(k); by the early 2000s, these ratios had reversed. Political scientist Jacob Hacker identified this change as part of a "great risk shift" from the government and employers to individual workers. Individuals increasingly managed their own retirements, from contributions to investments, leaving them more in charge but less economically secure, as the calamitous drop in 401(k) values in 2008–2009 highlighted. They were in the market now.[57]

In the early 1970s, the logic of free markets also replaced government intervention in determining how racial desegregation in America's schools would or would not continue. The U.S. Supreme Court had declared segregated schools unconstitutional in 1954, but policies to actually implement that decision developed slowly, reaching their apex in two other decisions by the high court. In *Swann v. Charlotte-Mecklenburg Board of Education* (1971), the Court ruled that, if necessary, school districts should bus students across town in order to achieve "the greatest possible degree of actual desegregation," regardless of difficulty, since "all awkwardness and inconvenience cannot be avoided in the interim period when remedial adjustments are being made to eliminate the dual school systems." In *Keyes v. School District No. 1 of Denver* (1973), the Court extended the same logic to non-Southern districts without a history of separate school systems that had allowed de facto segregation within their boundaries. But after this the tide turned against the use of busing to integrate the nation's schools. Later that same year, in *San Antonio Independent School District v. Rodriquez* (1973), the Court found that while racial integration might be essential for equal educational opportunities, starkly unequal financial resources for schools were constitutionally acceptable—specifically, that Texas did not violate the equal protection clause of the Fourteenth Amendment by allowing large disparities in local school funds, and districts therefore did not need to share their resources more equally. A minimally decent education was all that the Constitution required for citizens, not actually equal educational opportunities.[58]

While the *San Antonio* decision eliminated any need to share wealth across school district lines, *Milliken v. Bradley* (1974) determined there was also no constitutionally sanctioned need to share students across district lines in the pursuit of educational desegregation. In a 5–4 decision, the Court overturned a Detroit area busing plan that would have combined the mostly black city school district with the districts of three mostly white surrounding counties. The Justices ruled that lower courts could not order busing across district lines unless all affected districts were guilty of segregation, which was very difficult to prove in a nearly all-white suburb. This decision was a turning point in the federal judiciary's view of racial issues, the Court as a whole no longer trying to remedy the origins of residential segregation and instead accepting the reality of racially separate suburbanization. *Milliken v. Bradley* allowed people to go to school in the districts where they could afford to buy or rent a dwelling. This was the logic of the market and consumer preference—in this case, the real estate market. In combination with the *San Antonio* decision, *Milliken* established that there was no constitutional right to an equal education for all citizens, just the possibility of moving to a wealthier school district if one could afford it.[59]

A Freer Market, A Coarser Culture

The ascendancy of the idea of unrestricted individual choice in the 1970s spelled trouble for traditional community restraints on potentially offensive words and actions. The range of personal bodily practices widened, as the long hair, unruly clothing, nudity, and more expressive language that appeared in the counterculture at the end of the 1960s spread further into the mainstream. Illegal drugs became commonplace in middle America, not just in certain neighborhoods of large cities. Vocabulary previously considered vulgar began seeping into public conversation, not yet "motherfucker" but "ass," "butt," "pissed off," "screw," and the beginnings of what novelist Tom Wolfe would later call "the fuck patois" in which that word is used interchangeably as noun, adjective, adverb, and exclamation, in addition to verb. Self-discipline was out; self-expression was in. Older Americans, in particular, worried that the decline in self-restraint of an increasingly individualistic culture made Americans less respectful of each other and of traditional authorities.[60]

The freer market in sexuality captured the most public attention. "It was during the 1970s, not the 1960s, that sex outside marriage became the norm," historians Beth Bailey and David Farber wrote. Rising rates of divorce and cohabitation combined with greater acceptance of sex as important for personal happiness to reduce marriage's status as the premier venue for sexual expression. It was obvious to children and adolescents that adults had sex outside of the context of marriage, and they followed suit. Sex seemed to be newly ubiquitous in the culture, or at least much less hidden than in the past. Whether denouncing or celebrating the new trend, Americans talked about it and, in a common phrase of the era, "did it." Books such as *The Joy of Sex* and *Everything You Always Wanted to Know about Sex* became runaway best sellers and were quite explicit; a decade earlier, they would have been considered pornographic. An increasingly public erotic culture flourished in districts like New York's Times Square. For Manhattan residents inclined in that direction, the decade marked what historian Peter Braunstein has called "an unprecedented mass experiment in hedonism." The Bicentennial year seemed to epitomize the era, from the best-selling and explicit *Hite Report* on female sexuality, to the sex scandal involving powerful U.S. Congressman Wayne Hays (D-OH) and his assistant Elizabeth Ray, to Jimmy Carter's campaign interview with *Playboy* magazine in which the born-again Christian admitted, "I've committed adultery in my heart many times." By the early 1980s, mainstream advice columnists Ann Landers and "Dear Abby" were writing frankly about sexual scenarios, and bumper stickers associating occupations with sexual performance became commonplace: "Firemen have long hoses," and "Teachers do it with class." The formerly shocking had become cute.[61]

In no realm was the coarsening—or liberating—quality of America's free-market culture more obvious than the metastasizing pornography industry, particularly films. Pornography involved the portrayal of explicit and graphic sexual behavior, particularly genitalia, separated from emotion and relationships. What was new in the 1970s was not pornographic materials themselves but rather their introduction into the mainstream of American culture. New graphic magazines like *Penthouse* and *Hustler* made the older *Playboy* seem more modest than risqué. Under pressure to grant directors more artistic freedom and to accommodate shifting cultural values, Hollywood adopted in 1968 a new motion picture rating system of "G," "PG," "R," and "X," placing sexually graphic movies on a continuum and ending the previous production code in which all films had been considered family-friendly and "adults-only" films had been seen as deviant and separate. Several films from Sweden and Denmark that arrived in the United States in 1969 and 1970 received "X" ratings for their "hard-core" portrayals of non-simulated sex on screen; these films purported to be documentaries on the recent legalization of pornography in Denmark.[62]

The mainstreaming of hard-core pornography reached a new high—or low—with the appearance of *Deep Throat* in 1972. This 62-minute film left nothing to the imagination with its continuous close-ups of the most intimate sexual organs and acts. It was the first hard-core film to reach millions of middle-class Americans, women as well as men, and to be reviewed in mainstream newspapers, including the *New York Times*, which labeled it "porno chic." Celebrities such as Johnny Carson and Jacqueline Onassis were seen slipping into Manhattan's New Mature World Theater to see it. It went on to play in mainstream movie houses and on college campuses across the country. *Deep Throat* became so widely familiar that reporters Bob

Woodward and Carl Bernstein used it as the nickname for their secret Watergate informer, knowing that any reader would understand the reference. The film cost just $24,000 to make and—ahem—grossed over $100 million, dramatically demonstrating how profitable a freer market in American popular culture could be.[63]

The brief period of "porno chic" in the early 1970s included similar films such as *Behind the Green Door* (1972) and *The Devil in Miss Jones* (1973), but it also overlapped with new standards for frank sexual depiction among regular Hollywood filmmakers. *Last Tango in Paris* opened in the United States in 1973, the first graphically erotic film with a major star, Marlon Brando, who one year earlier had won an Oscar as best actor for his role in *The Godfather*. With Brando crossing over in the critically acclaimed *Last Tango*, the distinction between adults-only X-rated films and regular films was much less clear than it had been. The U.S. Supreme Court's decision in *Miller v. California* (1973) decentralized the regulation of obscenity, leaving the difficult definition of obscenity—once famously framed by Justice Potter Stewart as "I know it when I see it"—to local community standards. What was obscene in one jurisdiction might be acceptable in another, such as rural Utah and New York City, while standards across the country were clearly evolving from just a few years earlier. "One startling aspect of porn," *Time* magazine observed, "is its new social acceptability." Nowhere was this clearer than in Manhattan, where the number of pornographic businesses rose from nine in 1965 to 245 in 1977.[64]

At this point, new technology intervened to boost the already robust growth of the sex film industry. In 1975, videocassette recorders came on the market with the Video Home System (VHS) format, followed the next year by the competing Betamax format. Both allowed viewers to watch whatever films they wanted in the privacy of their own households. Viewing pornography no longer required a trip out into public to a theater. Adult cinemas closed by the hundreds. Pornography came home instead. It was privatized. Between 1975 and 1982, por-

FIGURE 3.3.
The increasingly explicit sexual character of American popular culture reached new heights in the 1970s and included a now vast pornography industry. Courtesy *Time*, April 5, 1976.

nographic films were estimated to account for as much as 80 percent of videocassette sales. By the end of the 1970s, 40 percent of all VCR owners admitted to buying or renting an X-rated film, and more than 15 million hard-core videos were being rented each week, feeding a now enormous industry that was grossing $2 billion annually. The growth of cable television, particularly premium channels, and the development of the Internet soon created vast new profitable media for pornography, which came to occupy a large if not always acknowledged part of American popular culture.[65]

"America is deep into its Age of Porn," *Time* announced in an April 1976 cover story. "How will the current avalanche of porn change America? Many who oppose censorship now wonder if the mounting taste for porn is a symptom of decay, of corrosive boredom, of withdrawal from social concern for obsessive personal pleasures." Meeting consumers' tastes, however, was precisely what markets were supposed to do. There was a demand for sexually explicit materials, and a supply arose to meet it. Diminished oversight by the government allowed this exchange to function efficiently, with satisfaction for customers and profits for successful entrepreneurs. The market, in this case, was distributing goods in a way that undercut traditional conservatives' goal of preserving and improving the virtue of the nation's citizens. Edmund Burke's warning remained prescient, that "before we risk congratulations" for the liberty of individuals to do what they please, "we ought to see what it will please them to do."[66]

It pleased Americans as well to take up gambling in the 1970s. Like pornography, gambling had a long history of association with organized crime and just as long a history as an object of condemnation for its moral impact on people. While gambling had always had its proponents and participants, from friendly basement poker games to sleek international high rollers in Monaco casinos, mainstream American opinion before the 1970s tended to view it as an at least slightly illegitimate and usually illegal activity. The most notable exception was Nevada, which had legalized gambling in 1931 in response to the Depression and the need for state revenue. In the more permissive era now dawning four decades later, gambling began to spread. Modern lotteries appeared first in New Hampshire in 1964 and then took off with New York's legalization of off-track betting in 1970, followed by Massachusetts's scratch-off instant game in 1974 and New York's lottery in 1978. By the end of the decade, nearly the entire Northeast was open to lotteries, followed by the West and the more traditionally religious South and Midwest in the 1980s, where riverboat casinos spread south from Iowa and Illinois to states down the Missouri and Mississippi rivers. Native American tribes also tapped into this new source of revenue by opening up casinos and large bingo parlors in the 1980s and 1990s.[67]

The biggest step toward making gambling widely acceptable in American society came from New Jersey voters in a 1976 referendum allowing the establishment of casinos in Atlantic City. The goal was to revitalize a declining resort town, creating jobs and generating new revenue for the state through taxes on the new operations, in an era of high unemployment and rising voter resentment of property and income taxes. Most fundamentally, the large casinos that began to open in Atlantic City in May 1978—the first outside of Nevada—reflected shifting American attitudes about personal behavior, a growing inclination to let individuals do what they wanted to do and buy what they wanted to buy, as long as it did not obviously hurt other people. There was clearly a market for gambling, and New Jersey was much closer to the population centers of that market, particularly New York and Philadelphia, than were the Western deserts of Nevada. Within a few years, Atlantic City was welcoming twice as many visitors as Las Vegas and nearly as much casino revenue, counted in the billions rather than millions of dollars. Rather than Americans having to go to Las Vegas, Las Vegas seemed to be coming to them. The urban revitalization that promoters promised for the rest of decaying Atlantic City did not materialize, however, beyond the limited blocks of the casinos themselves. Visitors came just to gamble and then left.

Casino workers lived mostly in the suburbs and surrounding small towns. Gambling turned out to be a private activity, whatever its morality and impacts on the families of gamblers, one profitable for the industry but not effective for rebuilding a community. *Money* magazine in 1988 ranked Atlantic City dead last in its "best places to live" in the United States.[68]

The coarsening American popular culture visible in the rapid growth of the gambling and pornography industries also became apparent in rising crime rates and, beginning in the mid-1970s, a sharp increase in rates of incarceration. Both violent and nonviolent crime doubled in the 1960s and nearly doubled again in the 1970s. The trend was particularly evident in the impersonal setting of major cities, where the economic frustrations of the 1970s exacerbated existing problems of poverty. Several serial killers gained notoriety in mid-decade, including John Wayne Gacy, Ted Bundy, and David Berkowitz. Anxieties that American society might be coming apart at the seams reached an apex in 1977, when New York City's overnight blackout during a heat wave unleashed a terrifying flood of looting, including more than a thousand fires being set and $1 billion in damages. Despair about the condition of the nation's cities deepened. A new genre of guidebooks on the best small towns to move to began with David and Holly Franke's *Safe Places* (1971) and boomed with Rand McNally's first edition of *Places Rated Almanac: Your Guide to Finding the Best Places to Live in America* (1981).[69]

How Americans responded to the reality and perception of rising crime revealed the same individualist ethics that were spreading with the logic of the market into all arenas of social policy. Prisons entered a period of rapid growth in the mid-1970s. After fifty years of stable incarceration rates, and even a small decline from the 1960s to the early 1970s, the number of inmates in state and federal prisons nearly doubled from 300,000 in 1974 to 540,000 in 1980. The trend continued, putting 2.2 million people behind bars by 2007, a fivefold increase in the average incarceration rate of most of the twentieth century. Sociologist James Q. Wilson, an influential thinker in the "get tough on crime" trend of the 1970s, explained the new approach in 1975: "Wicked people exist. Nothing avails except to set them apart from innocent people." A new emphasis on punishment and retribution—on making individuals pay for their crimes—replaced the older, Great Society-era aim of rehabilitation, of helping prisoners turn their lives around in order to reintegrate readily into society after release, an approach that remained the norm in Europe. The "penitentiary," whose goal was to make prisoners penitent, might have been better renamed the "retributionary."[70]

The toughening stance against crime had bipartisan support. Republicans made better political use of citizens' concerns about law and order, but many Democrats moved in the same direction. Critics on both the Right and the Left, for example, helped erode the traditional practice of indeterminate criminal sentencing that had given judges and parole boards flexibility in determining specific sentences for individuals, allowing consideration of their cases' particular circumstances. The Right found that the system let too many criminals off lightly, while the Left believed that poor and black defendants received unfair prison terms. Seventeen states abolished or limited parole during the 1970s, followed by another sixteen by 2000. The most prominent example was the Rockefeller drug laws passed in New York in 1973, strongly promoted by generally moderate Republican governor Nelson Rockefeller, which provided mandatory sentences and even mandatory life sentences for selling drugs stronger than marijuana. Imprisonment for drug crimes soared from 11 percent of sentences in 1970 to 34 percent in 1996. Sentencing policies within the United States did not become monolithic. States like Maine and Minnesota more closely resembled Sweden in their incarceration rates, while Louisiana and Texas looked more like Russia, China, or Saudi Arabia. But by the end of the 1970s, the United States, on average, had moved sharply away from the norms of other industrialized Western nations in its use of prisons.[71]

The core market logic of individuals getting what they chose by their actions, without government softening the consequences, appeared most clearly in the 1970s shift back strongly in favor of capital punishment. From World War II up to the early 1970s, the United States followed the broader pattern of Western democracies that were moving away from the use of the death penalty, the ultimate denial of the possibility of rehabilitation. In Western Europe, individual nations outlawed capital punishment by 1981, with France using the guillotine for the last time in 1977, while executions tapered off in the United States until the federal courts declared a moratorium in 1967. In 1972, the U.S. Supreme Court in *Furman v. Georgia* found federal and state capital punishment laws permitting wide discretion in applying the death penalty to be "arbitrary and capricious" and therefore in violation of the Eighth Amendment's ban on cruel and unusual punishment. The *Furman* decision reflected a growing national consensus that the disproportionate execution of African Americans—54 percent of all criminals killed between 1930 and 1967, five times their proportion of the population—was clear evidence of the death penalty being used unfairly. Rather than a final turn away from capital punishment, like Western European nations, however, the *Furman* decision turned out instead to be a minor detour on the path to renewing executions. Several states rewrote their capital punishment laws to reduce the prospect of discrimination, and the Supreme Court in *Gregg v. Georgia* (1976) and a handful of similar cases the same year found them constitutional. In January 1977, the state of Utah ended the life of Gary Gilmore, the first U.S. execution in a decade and the start of a cascade of more than a thousand death penalties carried out over the next three decades.[72]

The controversial nature of the renewed death penalty in the United States—due to its racially discriminatory history, Europe's abolition of it, and its inherent finality—meant that for the Supreme Court, as legal historian Franklin Zimring noted, "the substantive law and procedure in state death cases became the most frequent business of that court in the two decades after

1976." The Justices were not pleased with this development and sought to loosen the ties between their jurisdiction and appeals of state death penalty cases. The result was a kind of deregulation of death: a disinclination to intervene in the decisions of state courts. This was one way to ease the tension between the declining hegemony of an activist federal government, a key theme of the decade, and the simple reality that the state's deliberate taking of a citizen's life represented the most visible form of governmental power. The other way to reduce this tension was the symbolic privatization of executions, wherein prosecutors and courts deemphasized the public demonstration of government power through punishment and retribution, instead favoring a new emphasis on serving the interests of those closely related to the victims of capital murders. The defense of capital punishment became less about preserving the safety of society and, for the first time in American history, more about helping the particular family and close friends left behind by the crime to find psychological "closure." Service to private, symbolic victims replaced service to society as a whole. Even in the most awesome use of state power over an individual, the taking of a life, the government role was downplayed and the private sphere emphasized.[73]

Individual choice and the values of the marketplace seized the rhetorical high ground in the 1970s, paving the way for the dissolution of much of the New Deal political order that had permeated American life for two generations. Sustained economic decline weakened the claim of government on citizens' loyalties. Instead, from filling the ranks of the nation's armed forces to managing school desegregation, from tax rates to baseball contracts, from free speech practices to abortion policies, from X-rated films to the gambling industry, Americans during this decade embraced anew the mechanisms of supply and demand and the priority of the private realm of individual choice over the public realm of shared community commitments. Inflation and unemployment undercut the idea of effective government management of the economy, like a persistent riptide reshaping the sand on a beach. A new consumerism began to develop, rooted in fierce price competition, expanding world trade, and shrinking labor unions, best embodied by a new company out of Bentonville, Arkansas. Founded a few years earlier and spreading rapidly by the late 1970s, Wal-Mart's hyper-efficient management gave its customers "always low" prices and the convenience of shopping for most household needs in a single store. It was the wave of the future and it was building fast.[74]

One ironic result of the successes of the liberal New Deal order in propelling so many Americans up into the middle class by the 1960s was that many of them came eventually to forget the role that government played in their ascent. Government employment, the protection of unions, veterans' benefits, and health care and pensions for retirees dropped off the radar as many citizens came to view themselves alone as the successful authors of their fortunate circumstances in what was so often called the richest nation in history. Steady economic growth in the 1950s and 1960s made redistributive policies such as welfare acceptable to a majority of voters, but the end of growth in the early 1970s placed Democratic Party liberalism and activist government on the defensive. Reviving the economy became the top priority, freer markets the favored means. Unrestrained individualism flavored American culture and institutions ever since. Taking a global view, Francis Fukuyama observed that "the tendency of contemporary liberal democracies to fall prey to excessive individualism is perhaps their greatest long-term vulnerability, and is particularly visible in the most individualistic of all democracies, the United States." Both the Left and the Right contributed to the effort to free the individual from restrictive rules, though they did so with different emphases: the Left wanted people to be free to choose their lifestyles, while the Right wanted people to be free to do what they wished with their money. The foundation for a neoliberal order was in place by the end of the 1970s. With communitarian critics on the Right regretting the onset of a coarser, more sexualized public culture and those on the Left disliking the diminishing concern for the poor, the new market values represented not a simple victory for either Right or Left, but a celebration of individual freedom over traditional community restraints. A similar process was under way on a global scale, as we shall now see.[75]

Chapter 4

THE RETREAT OF EMPIRES AND THE GLOBAL

ADVANCE OF THE MARKET

ACROSS THE POLITICAL SPECTRUM, Americans tend to think of their country and their history as exceptional. From the fortuitous geographical buffer of two vast oceans to a founding Constitution that emphasized liberty, from a robust base of natural resources to regular inflows of industrious immigrants, the United States has appeared to most of its citizens and to many foreign observers as a land uniquely blessed with wealth and freedom. But the American story is not separate from the larger narrative of world history. Historians of U.S. foreign relations have long made this point, and other historians of the United States have more recently begun to develop a similar perspective.

The United States in the 1970s did not stand apart from the rest of the world but fit into the broader tale of global history. Because of the diversity of the Earth's societies in political and social development, all nations and peoples in this era did not march in lockstep with each other; as the Cold War and other conflicts revealed, trends around the globe at the time seemed to be heading in very different directions. But in retrospect, it is now possible to see that the 1970s American story of moving simultaneously toward greater egalitarianism and toward greater faith in the free market fit with a similar pattern taking shape around the world, one emphasizing human rights and national self-determination, on the one hand, and the declining legitimacy of socialism and government management of economies, on the other.[1]

The Soviet Union was the biggest loser. Committed denier of

human rights to its own citizens, imperial opponent of self-determination throughout the eastern half of Europe, and center of command economies and socialist history across the twentieth century, the regime in Moscow in the 1970s seemed to reach the apex of its world influence and then begin a rapid descent toward oblivion. Marxism made new gains in revolutionary circumstances across the Southern Hemisphere. Communists seized control of Cambodia and all of Vietnam in 1975; Marxists won out in newly independent Angola and Mozambique in the same year and soon thereafter in Ethiopia; and the leftist Sandinista National Liberation Front overthrew the intensely pro-American dictatorship of Anastasio Somoza in Nicaragua in 1979, while leftist rebels threatened to seize control of the government in nearby El Salvador. From the Soviet KGB on the Left to American neoconservatives on the Right, many observers thought—briefly—that the Soviets were advancing, an idea punctuated by the Soviet invasion of Afghanistan in December 1979.

This apparent advance, however, turned into a retreat and then a rout. For anticommunists, it turned out to have been darkest just before dawn. Even before the Red Army bogged down in Afghanistan, economic decline was undercutting the legitimacy of Soviet rule at home, while the human rights conventions signed as part of the Helsinki Final Act in 1975 opened new space for political dissent in the USSR and in Communist-ruled Eastern Europe. Even the supposed advance of Soviet influence into the Third World was not so clear. Egypt, for example, sent home Soviet advisers in 1972 and instead developed a close relationship with the United States, which Cairo recognized as offering much greater leverage in their regional contest with Israel. For at least a generation, Americans had believed Communism to be a single unified threat to U.S. interests, a hostile conspiracy straddling Eurasia and headquartered in Moscow. But by 1969, Chinese and Soviet troops were instead skirmishing with each other along their common border. In 1972, President Nixon's visit to Beijing initiated a tacit U.S.-Chinese alliance against the USSR. And in 1979, Chinese and Communist Vietnamese troops clashed in a brief border war. As the 1970s revealed to Americans, Communists were not at all united, and they could even serve as unofficial allies of the United States. Indeed, Communists by 1979 were hardly even still Communists, in light of the pro-market reforms begun in China. The Soviet empire was in deep trouble, and market forces were infiltrating into what had recently been, under Mao Zedong, the most fiercely anti-capitalist nation on Earth. One can interpret these events as the tragic ebbing of communitarian and altruistic values, or as the wondrous retreat of savage totalitarianism, or as something in between these two, depending on one's political stance, but one can hardly deny the retreat of empire and the advance of the market in the 1970s.

In Western Europe, as historian James Sheehan has shown, citizens since World War II turned away from the use of violence as a legitimate political weapon. The mid-1970s saw a surprisingly peaceful and swift transition from right-wing authoritarian regimes to stable democracies in Greece, Portugal, and Spain. The disinclination of Communist authorities in Eastern Europe to use force against a new dissident movement reflected a recognition of this shift toward greater respect for citizens' individual dignity and human rights. "Eurocommunism" emerged in this decade as an ephemeral reformist theme among Italian and Spanish Communists seeking to identify their Marxist convictions with Western European democratic practices, a specific rejection of anti-democratic Soviet-style Communism.[2]

The 1970s brought a definitive end to the largest imperial project of world history, the modern overseas empires managed by Western Europeans. The British, French, Spanish, Portuguese, Danes, Dutch, and Belgians had followed in the footprints of earlier great empire-builders such as the Romans and the Persians, sharing by force with Asians, Africans, Latin Americans, and Middle Easterners what they viewed as their superior civilization. Americans and Japanese had joined the process late. It was an enormous and often brutal undertaking. "The conquest of the earth," novelist Joseph Conrad wrote at the start of the twentieth century and the height of European dominion, "which mostly means the taking it away from those who have a different complexion or slightly flatter noses than ourselves, is not a pretty thing when you look into it too much." World War I ended the landed eastern empires—the Russian, Ottoman, Austro-Hungarian, and German—and World War II fatally weakened the overseas western empires, particularly the British and French. The Asian colonies broke free in the late 1940s, followed by most of Africa by the mid-1960s. In the 1970s the final blow landed, liberating the colonies of southern Africa and undermining the internal colonialism of apartheid South Africa. The new governments of these postcolonial territories often leaned Left, at least at first, due to their unhappy experiences with capitalism in the form of colonialism. But they sought primarily to stay out of the Cold War and take advantage of it when possible, just as the American revolutionaries had done in 1776 in claiming their own independence during the global struggle between Britain and France. James Madison reminded his fellow delegates to the Constitutional Convention in Philadelphia that throughout history great powers tended to seek each other's destruction, often benefiting weaker nations: "To this principle we owe perhaps our liberty."[3]

National self-determination won out as the guiding principle of contemporary world governance. Traditional hierarchies of power and authority lost their legitimacy in the public sphere of the new age of egalitarianism. Injustices and abuses of power endured, of course, but from the 1970s onward, governments around the world were increasingly expected to defer at least publicly to international norms of dignified treatment of nations and individuals. Yet the nationalist perspectives of peoples all over the world in the 1970s, from capitalists in the West to socialists in the East and South to religious revolutionaries in Iran (as chapter 5 will show), blinded most observers to the largest picture of all: that not only would empires fall, but capitalism and its market values would eventually flow into every nook and cranny of an increasingly integrated international structure. The process of globalization that accelerated in the 1970s carried consumer goods and services around the world, spreading the powerful idea that markets alone were the best solver of problems.[4]

THE EMERGENCE OF HUMAN RIGHTS

Respect for nations and respect for individuals did not always mesh. National governments could gravely mistreat their own citizens. The egalitarianism that spread around the world in the 1970s thus had a tension built into it: all nations, including the newest and least powerful just emerging from colonial rule, deserved respect as self-governing entities, free from undue outside influence, yet all individuals also deserved respect for their physical and moral dignity, thereby necessarily limiting what an autonomous government could do to its own citizens. This tension was reflected in the founding charter of the United Nations, which declared in 1945 that it was based both "on the principle of the sovereign equality" of all member nations and "on the dignity and worth of the human person." During the 1970s, a growing international consensus about the importance of human rights sometimes cut against the grain of national sovereignty.[5]

The modern idea of people having individual rights that could not be overridden by the community or the state emerged in the revolutionary atmosphere of the late 1700s. Moral autonomy was the key: people who were seen as having the ability to reason and the independence to decide for themselves should be allowed to govern themselves. Initially, these criteria excluded those without property, women, children, the insane, and the enslaved, but over the next century and a half all mentally competent adults came to be seen as deserving inclusion. The American Declaration of Independence of 1776 and the French Declaration of the Rights of Men of 1789 publicly asserted a new kind of sovereignty, of Americans from the foreign rule of the British Crown and of the French people from the traditional French monarchy. By redefining sovereignty and where it came from, the American and French Revolutions established a radically new basis for government, one that guaranteed universal rights for citizens. Eliminating torture and including non-Catholics as citizens, the French Revolution even guaranteed citizenship status for executioners and actors, professions formerly excluded for killing for a living and for pretending to be someone else—a reform in the spirit of later American actor-politicians such as Ronald Reagan and Arnold Schwarzenegger.[6]

Some of the late-eighteenth-century revolutionaries worried about the potential implications of this new understanding of human rights. It seemed there might be no clear way to limit the logic of inclusion and equality. "Depend upon it, Sir," John Adams wrote to a friend in 1776, "it is dangerous to open so fruitfull a Source of Controversy and altercation, as would be opened by attempting to alter the Qualifications of Voting. There will be no End of it. New Claims will arise. Women will demand a Vote. Lads from 12 to 21 will think their Rights not enough attended to, and every Man, who has not a Farthing, will demand an equal Voice with any other in all Acts of State." Adams saw the future clearly. Next came the abolition of slavery in Latin America, the British Empire, and the United States, along with the ending of serfdom in Russia. Women won the right to vote across the West. The Nazi Holocaust in World War II led to the 1948 Universal Declaration on Human Rights of the United Nations. The decolonization of the Third World and the civil rights movement in the United States then put teeth in the UN's assertion that "all human beings are born free and equal in dignity and rights," and subsequent movements for the rights of women, homosexuals, and the disabled pressed the same logic further forward. The new emphasis on human rights that blossomed in the 1970s resulted from the confluence of these events: the background of the Holocaust, the end of formal racial inequality (that had dampened Western interest in talking about human rights), the Soviet denunciation of Stalin and the dissolution of the labor camps, and the onset of détente. In addition, the new satellites that became common by the late 1960s allowed nearly instant sharing of images around the world, increasing the flow of information that would be crucial for human rights consciousness and activism.[7]

The influential new human rights community that coalesced in the 1970s was global in its reach and its perspective. These activists worked primarily in non-governmental organizations (NGOs) rather than governments themselves, which tended to be jealous of their sovereignty and inclined to respect the sovereignty of other governments. Human rights activists directly challenged the legitimacy of national policies regarding labor, immigration, women, free speech, and torture. They rejected the Cold War distinction of repressive Communists and virtuous anticommunists (or the opposite view, within the Soviet bloc), focusing instead on concrete abuses by regimes of all ideologies. Key recruiting tools included the brutal 1973 coup in Chile, the publication in 1974 of Aleksandr Solzhenitsyn's *The Gulag Archipelago* about the Soviet labor camps, and the human rights guarantees embodied in the Helsinki Accords of 1975. For Americans, the withdrawal of U.S. combat troops from Vietnam by 1973 reduced the fever of domestic political conflict and opened new ideological space for a more comprehensive consideration of human rights problems. Activists rejected not just the Cold War but also the détente policies associated with Richard Nixon and Henry Kissinger from 1972 to 1976, which they saw as eliminating moral concerns from international politics. In a sense, human rights activists took the language of the Cold War utterly seriously—about the freedom and dignity of the individual—and applied it to all sides. They emphasized abuses by governments, but their emergence also responded to the sharp rise in international terrorism and its targeting of innocent civilians by nonstate actors in the 1970s, most notably against Israel and that nation's supporters.[8]

Amnesty International (AI) became the largest and best known of the more than fifty human rights organizations functioning by the end of the 1970s. AI first opened its doors in London in 1961 but almost closed them six years later because of funding problems. In the United States, AI then grew from

6,000 members in 1970 to 35,000 in 1976. Amnesty International used information to pressure governments to improve their treatment of dissidents. Between 1970 and 1977, when it was awarded the Nobel Peace Prize, AI adopted more than fifteen thousand political prisoners and helped half of them win release. Imprisoned in 1975 for union-organizing work in the Dominican Republic, Julio de Peña Valdez described his experience with the organization: "When the first two hundred letters came, the guards gave me back my clothes. Then the next two hundred letters came and the prison director came to see me. . . . The letters still kept arriving and the President called the prison and told them to let me go. After I was released, the President called me to his office. . . . He said, 'How is it that a trade union leader like you has so many friends all over the world?'" Human Rights Watch engaged in similar work, and *Human Rights Quarterly* began publication in 1979.[9]

These activists "devised ways to collect accurate accounts of some of the vilest behavior on earth that no one had bothered to document before," historian Kenneth Cmiel wrote. "They invented ways to move this information to wherever activists had some chance to shame and pressure the perpetrators. Theirs was a politics of the global flow of key bits of fact." In the more repressive environment of the Soviet bloc, courageous dissidents built similar organizations, including the Moscow Human Rights Committee launched in 1970 and, after the Helsinki Accords, Charter 77 in Prague to monitor the progress of human rights within Czechoslovakia. Soviet bloc activists found refuge in the Soviet government's desire to preserve détente and its trade and strategic benefits, and thus its disinclination to crack down as severely on dissent as it had in the past. Other activists looked beyond lobbying and publicity to take direct action in humanitarian crises around the globe, and to speak clearly in favor of human rights. Splitting off from the older International Committee of the Red Cross, Médecins Sans Frontières (Doctors Without Borders) began operations in 1971 to provide medical relief in disaster zones and "to bear witness publicly to the plight of the people it assists," rather than following the Red Cross's traditional path of avoiding criticism of the government policies that were often creating those disasters. One measure of the enduring impact of Médecins Sans Frontières was the elevation of Bernard Kouchner, the organization's founder, to become the Foreign Minister of France in 2007.[10]

The growing constituency for human rights found a crucial voice within the U.S. government in Rep. Donald Fraser of Minneapolis. The Minnesota Democrat chaired the first congressional hearings on the topic in 1973 and issued a major report the next year. "We are, indeed, facing a global human rights crisis," he announced, noting the combination of a lack of freedom under Communist regimes, "single-party dominance" in the newly independent nations of Africa, and increasing polarization in Latin America between Left and Right "with rightist governments sanctioning torture and killing," most notably in Chile and soon in Argentina. Congressional hearings on human rights abuses multiplied between 1974 and 1976, partly in response to information publicized by AI and other activists. In 1975, Congress for the first time linked U.S. foreign aid to human rights practices of recipient nations, leading within two years to reductions in assistance to eighteen countries. In 1978, Argentina lost all of its U.S. military assistance. Concern about human rights abuses crossed ideological lines, with members of Congress on both the Left and the Right working together to promote decent treatment of dissidents.[11]

The most prominent congressional effort to punish human rights abuses came in the 1974 Jackson-Vanik Amendment, named for Sen. Henry Jackson (D-WA) and Rep. Charles Vanik (D-OH), which made most-favored nation (MFN) trade status for the USSR dependent on Soviet liberalization of emigration restrictions on Jews. Efforts by Soviet Jews to leave for Israel increased sharply in the wake of Israel's victory in the 1967 Six-Day War, and the Soviets placed a "diploma tax" on them, purportedly to recoup some of Moscow's investment in these citizens' educations. Americans, both Jews and gentiles, were dismayed at this "Jews for cash" policy and demanded that the Soviets not be allowed to continue benefiting from the 1972 U.S.-Soviet détente

trade agreements. The Jackson-Vanik Amendment, passed unanimously in both houses of Congress and reluctantly signed by
President Ford, was their weapon. Secretary of State Kissinger
was not pleased: this was precisely the kind of moralistic med-
dling that he wanted to eliminate from U.S. Soviet relations, for
he feared it would undercut the mutual benefits of détente. But
Jackson-Vanik made clear that religious freedom and freedom of
immigration were central elements of human rights.[12]

The principle of human rights found its most powerful pro-
ponent in President Jimmy Carter. The born-again Christian and
civil rights supporter, later to be known for his extensive post-
presidential humanitarian work abroad, did not create the
human rights agenda of the U.S. government. NGOs and Congress had been the real initiators. But Carter did make the issue
central to the Executive branch's approach to foreign relations
for the first time. He campaigned in 1976, the same year Amnesty International opened its Washington lobbying office, as an
antidote to the corruption of Watergate and the amorality of
Nixon and Kissinger's foreign policy. While Nixon and Kissinger believed that only the external behavior of other governments mattered to the United States, Carter insisted that nations' internal behavior was also a concern for Americans and
the world as a whole. Where Nixon and Kissinger sought to
pursue U.S. interests by focusing solely on how governments
operated outside their borders, Carter believed that American
interests included the decent treatment of all peoples everywhere. In his first public address as president, Carter made clear
that he meant U.S. behavior as well: "We will not behave in
foreign places so as to violate our rules and standards here at
home." He created a new office of human rights within the State
Department.[13]

In practice, the Carter administration had great difficulty rec-
onciling these principles with the records of certain U.S. allies
abroad, such as Iran under the Shah, South Africa under apartheid, several Latin American nations under military dictator-
ships, and China as it evolved into a de facto American ally. The
president also wound up his term with a resurgent Cold War, a
Soviet occupation of Afghanistan, and a spike in U.S. military

spending. But along the way, particularly during his first two years in the Oval Office, Carter did earn high marks for reducing tensions in the Middle East through the Camp David accords, arranging the return of the Panama Canal to Panamanian sovereignty, and promoting a reduction in nuclear weaponry, all of which aimed at peacemaking and the promotion of human welfare.[14]

All of this human rights activism, along with the unfolding movements for women's and gay rights and the environment, suggests that the 1970s served as a robust period of egalitarian reform. In these years, Western Europeans came increasingly to view human rights as an essential component of being culturally "European," most notably by eliminating capital punishment from their penal codes. They completed the decriminalization of homosexual behavior, and the conservative Roman Catholic countries of Italy, Spain, and Portugal legalized divorce. Women's rights were central to a meaningful definition of human rights, evident in French and British legislation mandating equal treatment in employment. Restrictions on the availability of contraception and abortion began to disappear across Western Europe during this decade.[15]

Yet it was in the Soviet bloc that human rights activism in this decade had its greatest impact, revealing the moral hollowness at the core of the Communist project. The Soviet government helped bring this calamity down upon itself by initiating a pan-European set of negotiations over three years (1972–75), with a culminating treaty signed in Finland by the USSR, the United States, and thirty-five other nations, known as the Helsinki Final Act or simply the Helsinki accords. The Soviets won greater trade with Western Europe along with official Western recognition of the 1945 borders in Eastern Europe, thus providing international legitimacy for the continent's Communist governments, particularly East Germany. In exchange, the Soviets agreed to commit to "respect for human rights and fundamental freedoms, including the freedom of thought, conscience, religion, or belief" and "non-intervention in internal affairs" of other nations.[16]

It proved to be a fateful deal for the USSR. "In the long

run," historian Vladislav Zubok wrote, "the commitments to human rights embedded in the act proved to be a time bomb under the Soviet regime." As part of the agreement, the Soviet government published the entire text of the Helsinki Final Act in the official newspaper *Pravda*. Dissidents seized on the new guarantees to expand their criticisms of Communist rule. Next door in Eastern Europe, dissidents realized that the Soviets had essentially given up the Brezhnev Doctrine of intervening at will to protect other Communist governments, and they stepped up organizing. Helsinki watch groups sprouted across the Communist landscape, building alliances with their Western equivalents. Détente-era loosening of restrictions on travel and cultural exchanges continued. A young Communist Party official named Mikhail Gorbachev, for example, took his first trip outside the Soviet bloc in 1976, visiting France and later Italy and returning home deeply impressed by the cultures, freedom, and wealth that he experienced firsthand. Hawkish American observers, including the editorial pages of both the *New York Times* and the *Wall Street Journal*, opposed the Helsinki accords for granting recognition to oppressive regimes, not recognizing at the time—like the Soviet government—the power of the new human rights promises for opening up change from within Communist countries. They later changed their minds. Norman Podhoretz, editor of the neoconservative journal *Commentary* and a ferocious critic of the Helsinki process, admitted in 2005 that the accords "put a very powerful weapon in the hands of the dissidents" and "instead of ensuring the permanence of the Soviet empire, contributed to its eventual demise."[17]

European Empires and Southern Africa

The story of imperial retreat in the 1970s puts the relationship of Europeans with Africa at center stage. European contacts with Africa traced to the beginning of human history, when the first *homo sapiens* traveled out of eastern Africa and some of them populated the region north of the Mediterranean Sea. In the longest time frame, that is, Europeans *were* Africans, or at least were their descendants. They came back, however, as conquerors, both the ancient Greeks colonizing around the eastern Mediterranean and the Roman Empire encompassing the entire northern littoral of the African continent. After the Middle Ages, an era when Muslim empires centered east of the Mediterranean dominated much of Africa and parts of Europe, improvements in sailing technology allowed European adventurers of the 1400s to explore farther abroad than ever before. Portuguese sailors pushed southward down the west coast of Africa, crossing the equator to where the stars they sailed by were "upside down" in the Southern Hemisphere. In 1488, just four years before Christopher Columbus and his ships reached the Americas, Bartol-omeu Dias and his crew rounded the Cape of Good Hope and sailed into the Indian Ocean. They established the first European contacts with the southern tip of Africa, the fateful beginning of five hundred years of white dominion in the region.[18]

The next several centuries witnessed the explosive growth of the African slave trade across the Atlantic by European kidnapper-merchants. Until the middle of the nineteenth century, European settlements on the African continent remained few and primarily coastal. The interior was forbidding to non-indigenous folk, particularly the Sahara and Kalahari deserts in the north and south, and tropical diseases such as malaria in the center. But medical breakthroughs such as the discovery of quinine (a key ingredient in the tonic water that British imperialists added to their gin) to counteract malaria and the development of powerful new weapons such as Gatling guns, along with burgeoning intra-European imperial competition, led to intensive penetration of the continent by the northern invaders. At the Berlin Conference of 1884–85, the great powers drew a new map of Africa by dividing it into European colonies. White rule was at flood tide. Only Ethiopia held out, defeating an invading Italian army at the Battle of Adowa in 1896 and preserving the hope of African self-rule.[19]

Then the three-decade European "civil war" from World War I through World War II devastated the militaries and treasuries of the colonial powers, as well as their confidence in the idea of European cultural superiority. Between 1940 and 1980, more than eighty colonies around the world, most in Africa, gained their formal independence from European overlords, incorporating nearly 40 percent of the world's population (a figure that would be much higher if it included the unofficially colonized Chinese). Early Western domination of the UN General Assembly dissipated by the late 1960s. In the wake of the Holocaust and decades of nationalist organizing in the colonies, Europeans turned their energies away from colonial grandeur and dominion abroad and toward building social stability and material comfort at home. Western Europe's demographic shortfall from deaths and a lack of births during the two world wars led to a kind of reversal of the colonizing process, in which immigrants from beyond the continent were recruited as labor and contributed mightily to the economic miracle of a rebuilt Western Europe. The number of foreign workers reached a high point in 1973, "the best bargain Europe ever made," historian Tony Judt wrote, "and the final, enduring advantage of imperial conquest."[20]

The struggle against colonial rule that culminated in the 1970s had effects that reached beyond national liberation. In the sphere of literature and epistemology, a new scholarly approach known as postcolonialism sought to correct the ongoing biases that accompanied and justified European colonization of most of the Earth's surface over the previous five hundred years and that survived the formal demise of empires. Edward Said's *Orientalism* (1978) was the founding text, revealing how previous Western histories of the Middle East had served as an arm of the colonizing process, rendering non-Europeans in primitive terms in order to justify their conquest by the imperialists as a beneficial development. Related calls to "decolonize the mind" emphasized the enduring intellectual and psychological power of colonial forms of knowledge. Feminists' contemporaneous request for equality between the sexes while respecting their differences seemed to them analogous to anticolonialists calling for equality for all peoples and nations while respecting their differences. In the sphere of popular culture, Jamaica's reggae music leapt into world popularity in the 1970s, first Jimmy Cliff's soundtrack to the 1973 film *The Harder They Come* and then Bob Marley's 1976 top-ten album *Rastaman Vibration*, giving young Westerners a new and easy way to identify with people of color abroad. Marley brought recognition to the anti-colonial politics and magnetic music of the island's countercultural Rastafarians, who looked to independent black Ethiopia for inspiration.[21]

In the sphere of international politics, the departure of European rulers sometimes removed a common enemy from peoples who did not share a strong sense of national identity. East Pakistan, for example, won its own war of independence against West Pakistan in 1971, creating the new nation of Bangladesh. In seemingly stable Canada, Quebec separatism grew sharply during the decade. Several major Canadian corporations and thousands of English-speaking residents began leaving Montreal, a key step on the path to Toronto's eventual emergence instead as the nation's premier city. In 1977, Quebecois voters went beyond the national policy of bilingualism by making French their official language, and in a referendum two decades later came within a whisker of choosing to separate from the rest of the country. The logic of a narrower political identity flowed directly from the struggle for decolonization and national self-determination.[22]

In southern Africa, the last redoubt of white colonial rule, the great engine of European overseas empires ground to a halt in 1975. The Portuguese, the first to arrive in the region half a millennium earlier, were the last to go. Partly, Portugal held on longest because it remained neutral during the World War II and thus avoided the devastation that even the winners experienced. Partly, Portugal lasted longest because it made the most dramatic commitment to settling in Africa in the twentieth century of any European power. After centuries of paying little attention to its colonies, the Portuguese sent thousands of families to Angola and Mozambique and invested heavily in colonial infrastructure such as roads, ports, railways, and telecommunications in the decades after 1945, precisely when the other imperial powers were headed in the opposite direction: out of Africa. The dictatorial regime of Antonio Salazar announced in 1951 that the overseas territories were not colonies but actually integral parts of Portugal itself, similar to the way the French viewed Algeria. The Lisbon government called this imagined transcontinental character of an essential Portuguese nation "lusotropicalism," a supposedly uniquely non-racist and egalitarian quality of the Portuguese people, and a rhetorical device to try to fend off calls for decolonization.[23]

Angolans and Mozambicans were unconvinced of Portuguese virtue in this regard. Insurgent warfare against the colonial overlords began in 1961. Left-leaning Portuguese military officers, dismayed at the seemingly endless conflicts to the south, eventually overthrew the right-wing dictatorship in Lisbon in 1974 and quickly negotiated an end to the wars with the insurgents. Portugal withdrew its military forces and ended the last major colonial campaign abroad by a European army. In Maputo, a new leftist government took power in 1975, while in Luanda, the Ford administration through the CIA tried briefly to prevent the same development by supporting the most anti-Soviet groups within the anti-Portuguese coalition. Here the anticolonial, pro–human rights environment of American politics in the mid-1970s made a difference. The U.S. Congress, wary of another commitment like Vietnam, angry about Nixon and Kissinger's support for the brutal coup in Chile, and unhappy about the revelations of CIA and FBI abuses and the criminality of the Watergate scandal, put its foot down against CIA involvement in Angola. The Tunney and Clark Amendments cut off U.S. aid to Angola, at least until President Reagan managed to briefly renew some assistance to anticommunist forces a decade later. But the hand of Europe was gone, the world's oldest empires retired.[24]

The descendants of Europeans remained, however, particularly in two final white settler states: Rhodesia and South Africa.

In Rhodesia, whites made up just 5 percent of the population, and they could see the writing on the wall, as independence and black rule swept down the continent toward them in the early 1960s. In 1965, they took their stand. Determined to forestall any version of decolonization that included majority rule, Prime Minister Ian Smith announced a "Unilateral Declaration of Independence" from Britain. For the next fourteen years, Rhodesia's whites ruled the territory on their own, unrecognized by other governments. The British refused to intervene militarily to put down the coup as they had done to crush unrest in Kenya a decade earlier; too many British felt too close to too many British-descended Rhodesians to make such action politically viable in London. Instead, the British government enacted economic sanctions against Smith's new government.[25]

For their part, the black majority of Rhodesians supported insurgents who took up arms against the settler regime in 1966, creating internal pressure to match the external pressure of sanctions. Tens of thousands died in the fighting, mostly Africans. "I think I first realized something was wrong when our next-door neighbor, oom Piet Oberholzer, was murdered," began Peter Godwin's memoir of growing up white on a remote farm in the southeastern part of the country. He was six years old at the time, fascinated and horrified to see Oberholzer's body "lying on the tar road . . . with the bone handle of a hunting knife sticking out of his chest" and a message reading "Viva Chimurenga!" The white police were mystified by the term and turned to a black underling for explanation. "Well, sah, it is the word for the old Shona rebellion in 1896. But I think it can mean any rebellion. Maybe this is a new rebellion?" Indeed it was. Then the liberation of neighboring Mozambique in 1975 opened a new front for guerilla infiltration into the country, ratcheting up the pressure another notch. Negotiations in London in 1979 led, at last, to the end of white rule the following year and the change of name from Rhodesia to Zimbabwe. Two decades later, gross corruption and misrule eventually dragged the country down, but at the end of the 1970s, with Bob Marley appearing in concert to celebrate independence under majority rule, Zimbabwe stood as a symbol of freedom and hope to much of the world.[26]

South Africa was the toughest nut to crack. With a white population of close to 15 percent, a sophisticated military, the wealthiest and most industrialized economy on the continent, and a long history of independence (a result of rebelling against Europe earlier in the twentieth century, when white minority rule was still widely seen as normal and acceptable), South Africa stood as the final outpost of legalized white rule over people of color. The Portuguese left in 1975, the Rhodesians gave up in 1979, but the white South Africans endured. They kept control of their thinly populated colony next door, Southwest Africa (Namibia), too. The Pretoria government crushed all dissent and built the world's most rigid form of racial segregation and inequality, the system of apartheid. The regime drove the African National Congress, an organization founded on the principles of nonviolence and racial reconciliation, into exile and into insurgent warfare, locking up its leader, Nelson Mandela, in 1962 for a prison term that lasted more than twenty-seven years. South Africa developed a nuclear weapons capability in order, presumably, to defend its way of life even to the point of massive human destruction.[27]

In this decade of a rising egalitarian tide, however, not even apartheid's rulers proved immune. They held onto power a little longer, but by the end of the 1970s they could clearly see the twin threats that were bound to bring them down eventually. From the outside, criticism was building rapidly, followed a few years later by comprehensive economic sanctions. Soviet-bloc critics had long condemned South Africa's racial policies, an easy point-scoring rhetoric in light of apartheid's intertwining with anticommunism, and the United Nations regularly rebuked Pretoria for violations of its citizens' human rights. In the 1970s, many Western nations, led by Sweden, moved beyond words to provide actual assistance to liberation groups such as the African National Congress, thus balancing older Soviet military aid to insurgents. In the United States, the Congressional Black Caucus began in 1971 to give an organized voice within the government to black interests, including anti-apartheid lobbying, and widespread student protests convinced prominent American universities to divest their stock holdings in companies doing business with South Africa at the end of the decade.[28]

From inside South Africa, the other, larger threat to apartheid appeared on June 16, 1976, when thousands of young students marched in Soweto to protest authorities' efforts to require the use of the Afrikaans language in half of school classes. Violence ensued and the police cracked down ferociously, killing at least dozens and perhaps hundreds of black South Africans. But police brutality could not put the genie of dissent back in the bottle this time. The Soweto uprising was the first blow in what became a regular cycle of protests against apartheid from 1976 on, leading to global outrage at the police response, an official state of emergency a few years later, deepening economic and social disarray, withdrawal from Namibia, and, by 1990, an official renunciation of apartheid and the release of Mandela from prison. The final victory over formal white colonial rule in its last settler form grew directly from the courageous actions of township youths in the 1970s.[29]

THE SOVIET EMPIRE

For a brief period in the 1970s, the Soviet Union seemed to be expanding rather than shrinking its influence abroad. The USSR had pulled roughly even with the United States in the nuclear arms race. Hardliners on both sides of the Cold War took note of Marxist victories in Vietnam, Cambodia, Angola, Mozambique, Ethiopia, and Nicaragua, compared those to U.S. retrenchment, and predicted more heady days to come for Moscow. They were wrong. Historian Nancy Mitchell has observed the intriguing contrast "between the prevailing perception at the time—that the Soviet Union was repeatedly besting the United States—and reality: the Soviet Union lost ground in the late 1970s and was on the threshold of its last decade" of existence. Having cut ties with Israel in 1967 and having their advisers kicked out by Egypt in 1972, the Soviets found their influence in the Middle East limited to the most radical Arab governments at the very moment when those regimes had been crushed by the Israeli military. The Islamist revolution next door in Iran in 1979 provided cold comfort, as anti-Soviet as it was anti-American. Soviet influence in Asia was checked by an increasingly powerful and hostile China, vivid proof of international Communism's profound divisions. Moscow had been no help to Salvador Allende in Chile as South America moved to the right. Marxist advances in some parts of Africa were balanced by failures in other parts, and even the temporary successes were driven primarily by Cuban rather than Soviet determination. Eastern Europe, meanwhile, experienced economic decline and renewed anti-Soviet organizing. The Soviet Union had long had a double empire—the internal one of the non-Russian parts of the USSR and the external one of Eastern Europe—and both elements began to fray badly before the 1980s.[30]

The aging, sclerotic Soviet leadership tried to prop up the system from which it benefited. Moscow was now more than fifty years past the revolutionary hopes and fervor of 1917, and the distance showed. Communist Party head Leonid Brezhnev awarded himself more than one hundred medals for heroic patriotism, an apt symbol of the corruptions of power. With little experience in foreign policy before his promotion within the Politburo, Brezhnev sent Soviet tanks to crush the brief reformist socialist movement of the "Prague spring" in Czechoslovakia in 1968. Under the so-called Brezhnev Doctrine, the USSR would not allow Eastern European governments to leave the Communist fold or even to embrace serious reform. Brezhnev then felt secure enough to pursue détente with the United States in 1972, winning trade and technology benefits and slowing the growth of military spending.[31]

But Brezhnev was steering a slowly sinking ship. He declared capitalism "a society without a future," utterly failing to grasp that system's durability and adaptability. A few years later, historian Stephen Kotkin had the opportunity to help shepherd

Soviet dignitary Yegor Ligachev, then the second most powerful figure in the Politburo, around New York City on a visit. Kotkin recalled explaining to Ligachev "the vast universe of private small businesses and immigrant-run eateries for hours on end, only to have him ask over and over again who in the government was responsible for feeding the huge urban population." A lifetime in the Soviet Union had made it nearly impossible for Ligachev even to imagine the operation of a market system. Similarly, by the 1980s the Soviet newspaper *Pravda* declared that "rock and roll"—long a bête noire of capitalist degradation for the Soviet leadership—"has a right to exist but only if it is melodious, meaningful, and well-performed." This was more than a decade into the popularity of wildly indecorous bands from Kiss to the Sex Pistols. Soviet leaders seemed to have little idea of the deluge of uncontrolled market forces about to pour down on them.[32]

The fortunes of Soviet Communism depended on the fortunes of capitalism, which socialism was built to oppose and ultimately replace. The problem for the USSR, Kotkin wrote, was that "the differences between capitalism in the Great Depression and capitalism in the post-war world were nothing short of earth shattering." Rather than sliding from its traumatized situation in the 1930s into a final death spiral, as Joseph Stalin predicted, capitalism instead revived in the 1940s and roared to extraordinary success in the 1950s and 1960s, marked by welfare state security combined with affordable housing in comfortable suburbs, steadily rising standards of living, and increasingly inclusive democratic institutions and governance. Nikita Khrushchev, the head of state between Stalin and Brezhnev, promised in 1961 that "Communism will win" in the competition with capitalism for "a higher standard of living, greater assurance for the future, freer access to education and culture, [and] more perfect forms of democracy and personal freedom." He could not have been more wrong.[33]

Soviet central planning worked adequately for producing simple goods such as steel, but the highly centralized command economy prevented the innovations central to the Western shift to an economy driven by technological creativity and a decentralized service sector. The result was a yawning chasm of difference between East and West in consumer goods, personal freedom, and material quality of life, as the increased travel abroad allowed by détente revealed to a growing number of Soviet citizens. Shoddy goods and food shortages accompanied the slowing Soviet economy in the 1970s. The lack of incentives in the Communist bloc inspired the popular joke: "You pretend to work; we pretend to pay you." Much of the terror and repression of an earlier era drained away, replaced by the grayness and drabness of economic stagnation. People had fewer children. From the late 1960s to the early 1980s, Soviet per capita alcohol consumption quadrupled. Eastern Europeans, for their part, borrowed heavily from Western Europe in order to buy some of its consumer goods. Only a brief boost in oil production from new wells in western Siberia, at just the moment when world oil prices were soaring, kept the Soviet economy from declining more rapidly still.[34]

More important for weakening the Soviet empire in the 1970s—more than setbacks abroad, economic stagnation, and benighted leadership—was the full revelation to the world of the horrors of Soviet governance. The new international emphasis on human rights and the Helsinki process gave support and some protection to courageous dissidents such as physicist Yuri Orlov, physician Yelena Bonner, and her husband, nuclear physicist Andrei Sakharov, who won the Nobel Peace Prize in 1975. Novelist Aleksandr Solzhenitsyn provided perhaps the gravest blow to the moral legitimacy of Communist rule when he published *The Gulag Archipelago* in France on December 28, 1973, after smuggling the manuscript out of the USSR.[35]

Solzhenitsyn was a complicated figure. A dedicated Marxist as a young man, he had served with distinction in the Red Army as a commander of an artillery battery from 1942 to 1945. But in a letter to a friend he expressed unorthodox opinions, and the friend reported him to the authorities. Solzhenitsyn spent the next eight years in the vast internal Soviet prison system known as the Gulag that spread eastward across Siberia. While incarcerated, he became a Russian Orthodox Christian, exchanging Marx for Jesus. Later, he was able to publish a riveting account of the prison camps in fictionalized form as *One Day in the Life of Ivan Denisovich*, thanks to Khrushchev's need during the brief reformist period of the early 1960s for a book to indict Stalin's repressiveness. This extraordinary event in Soviet literary history won Solzhenitsyn the Nobel Prize for literature in 1970. But *The Gulag Archipelago* went much further, using his own experiences plus extensive research and interviews with hundreds of other former political prisoners to explain in comprehensive detail and scope the system's brutal mechanisms of interrogation, incarceration, forced labor, and execution. With authority and precision, Solzhenitsyn exposed what writer David Remnick called "the inherent illegitimacy of the regime and every Soviet leader including Lenin."[36]

The publication of *The Gulag Archipelago* was a turning point in twentieth-century history. The Soviet system of governance stood condemned before world opinion. The Politburo responded by exiling Solzhenitsyn on February 13, 1974, and stripping him of his citizenship, but it was far too late. Whatever elements of moral authority Moscow had once retained fell away. The democratic Left in the West, already shaken by the Soviet repression of the Czech uprising in 1968 and by reports of Communist brutalities in the Cultural Revolution unfolding in China, and about to learn of the genocidal savagery of the Cambodian Communists, the Khmer Rouge, shed its last illusions about Communism. State socialism was revealed as what historian Tony Judt, himself a man of the Left, called a barbaric fraud, built on slave labor and mass murder. The timing of the publication of *The Gulag Archipelago* helped assure that the anti-imperial reformist spirit of the early 1970s in the United States, visible in the investigations of the CIA and the new focus on human rights, did not take the form of any greater sympathy for the Soviet system. Instead, all empires—European, Soviet, American—stood exposed as illegitimate.[37]

Solzhenitsyn himself wound up living quietly for most of the next twenty years in the small town of Cavendish, Vermont. He remained a distinctive figure who identified in some ways with the Russian nationalism and even monarchism of the Czarist era before the Bolshevik Revolution, and who considered Americans insufficiently anticommunist. He disliked the materialism and "all-permissiveness" of the West. Indeed, he told graduates at Harvard University in 1978, the West now stood at "the abyss of human decadence" and "in its present state of spiritual exhaustion does not look attractive." Solzhenitsyn moved back to Russia in 1994 after the end of Communist rule.[38]

The Soviets crossed their own imperial Rubicon in central Asia in the last week of the decade. On December 25, 1979, the first airlifts of Red Army troops who would eventually number over 100,000 landed in Kabul. They were there to prop up a wavering Communist regime that had taken power in Afghanistan in a coup a year earlier, to the total surprise of Moscow, which first learned of the event from a Reuters news agency bulletin. Americans were incensed and fearful at this first Soviet military operation outside of the Warsaw Pact region since World War II. Surely this meant Communism was literally on the march, probably on the way to the oil wealth of the Persian Gulf? Neoconservatives raged at the Soviet aggression, some even discovering a new cause among Muslim Afghan insurgents calling themselves mujahideen. Fritz Ermath, a Soviet expert on the National Security Council, summed up Washington's concern: "The invasion sharply increases the prospect of eventual Soviet military domination of the greater Middle East and the US exclusion from the region." The Carter administration declared the defense of the Persian Gulf region from outside aggression to be a core U.S. interest, withdrew the SALT II treaty from Senate consideration, ratcheted up defense spending, and boycotted the 1980 Moscow Olympics. The president himself admitted that he had failed to understand fully the aggressive nature of the Soviet regime and called the invasion "the greatest threat to peace since the Second World War," an interpretation that omitted the wars in Korea and Vietnam. A renewed Cold War loomed.[39]

From Moscow, these same events looked very different. Defensive about human rights, aware of their declining economy, and concerned about Islamist organizing in their own central Asian republics, Soviet leaders watched with trepidation as Khomeini's revolution unfolded across the border in Iran. If Americans, halfway around the world, were anxious about events in Iran, the Soviets were much more so. They feared the spread of Islamist revolution into neighboring Afghanistan, where the mujahideen had been organizing for years, as the next step in a march of political Islam that could lead to the Soviet Union itself. They hoped to avoid being drawn into Afghanistan's internal struggles, but ultimately decided they could not afford to stay out. "Under no circumstances may we lose Afghanistan," Foreign Minister Andrei Gromyko told his colleagues in Moscow in 1979.[40]

The stakes were high but, like Americans going to war in Vietnam in 1965, the Soviets could imagine only victory over the technologically inferior forces of guerilla fighters in a much smaller country. Brezhnev anticipated just a brief incursion into Afghanistan. "It'll be over in three to four weeks," he told his ambassador to the United States, Anatoly Dobrynin. The Politburo failed utterly to understand the depth of Afghan nationalist and religious resistance to the Communist regime and its Soviet supporters, and the scale of assistance the mujahideen would receive from the United States and several wealthy Muslim nations. The Soviet invasion inflicted enormous damage on Afghan society but bogged down in what became a decade of stalemated counterinsurgent warfare against a hostile population. It was a recipe for disaster and became the Soviets' "Vietnam," gravely weakening support at home for the Soviet regime and leading directly to the disintegration of the Soviet empire in 1989 and the Soviet Union itself in 1991.[41]

The failure of the Red Army in Afghanistan meant that the Soviets would not use force again in Eastern Europe when the final struggle to throw off Communist rule began. "The quota of interventions abroad has been exhausted," KGB chief Yuri Andropov told an aide in 1980, as the momentous effort to roll back the Soviet empire took hold first in Poland. The enduring

Roman Catholicism of most of the Polish population provided a tangible alternative way of living and center of power, in the form of the Church. The significance of the spiritual grounding of Polish resistance became clear after Karol Wojtyla, the Cardinal of Cracow, was elected Pope as John Paul II on October 16, 1978. He returned triumphantly to Poland for the first time as Pope in June 1979, drawing enormous crowds and encouraging them to make no compromises with Marxism and Communist rule, to stand together in nonviolent resistance, and to grant no legitimacy to the official atheists of the Communist Party. Devout Polish Catholics had long seen themselves as the embattled eastern front of the true Church, "the Christ among nations." Now they had a renewed national destiny: to begin the peaceful rollback of the Soviet empire.[42]

The primary mechanism was labor organizing. Following in the footsteps of earlier worker unrest in 1970 and 1976, dissident laborers met at the front gate of the Lenin shipyards in Gdansk in December 1979 to express their unhappiness with food shortages and deteriorating working conditions. They formed Solidarity, the first labor union ever in a Communist state, and led a large strike at the Lenin shipyards in August 1980. The Polish government officially recognized Solidarity in September—an extraordinary, if implicit, admission of failure by a Communist regime whose entire avowed purpose was to defend the interests of workers. Ten million Poles quickly joined the new union. The Warsaw government eventually instituted martial law to restore control of the workplace, but the deed was done: Poles had stood up en masse to reveal their government as a sham, and the Soviets had done nothing to help the regime. "The Polish people," historian Matthew Ouimet wrote, "had forced the Soviet colossus into an imperial retreat from which it would never recover." Socialist internationalism was dead. The Brezhnev Doctrine was defunct. The Soviet Union was withdrawing from its empire. Within nine years, Communism would disappear from Poland and the rest of Eastern Europe, and two years later the internal empire of the USSR itself would collapse.[43]

The American Empire

One unanticipated result of the end of the Cold War was the ebbing of American defensiveness about being an imperial nation. From their origins in successful revolution against European colonial control in the 1770s, Americans tended to see themselves in political terms as the world's leading *anti-imperialists*. They had, after all, set the model for throwing off European rulers. There were debates: all other great nations at the time were imperialist, and there was considerable admiration for the British despite the wars of the Revolution and 1812. Thomas Jefferson spoke of building "an empire for liberty" by expanding westward across the continent, an oxymoron that obscured the reality of conquering new lands and new peoples. The slogan "Manifest Destiny" captured the widespread sense that the fate of America in the 1840s was to reach from the Atlantic to the Pacific. But few Americans were fully comfortable with the idea of empire.

The swift U.S. seizure of overseas colonies in 1898, particularly the Philippines and Puerto Rico, stimulated serious national debate about whether this action threatened or fulfilled the national sense of destiny. Theodore Roosevelt, for one, had few doubts about his nation's growth: "The simple truth is there is nothing even remotely resembling imperialism in the development of the policy of expansionism which has been part of the history of America since the day she became a nation." A generation later, prominent journalist Walter Lippmann shared Roosevelt's confidence but not his views. "The rest of the world will continue to think of [America] as an empire," he wrote. "Foreigners pay little attention to what we say. They observe what we do." British historian Niall Ferguson later called the United States an "empire in denial." During the Cold War decades after 1945, such language was associated with dissent on the Left and largely ignored by policymakers and the public. But the disappearance of the Soviet Union in 1991, along with the invasion of Iraq in 2003, paved the way for the production of an entire shelf of books with titles that included the words "America" and "empire" together, encompassing a wide range of views about the relative virtues of that combination. It may have been primarily an informal empire, one grounded less in direct governance of overseas territories and more in dominant military, economic, and cultural influence, but observers across the political spectrum were finally inclined to call it an empire.[44]

Just as it did for the European and Soviet empires, the decade of the 1970s proved to be a turning point for the American empire. The long advance of American influence abroad slowed and seemed, briefly, to stall. Relative economic decline explained part of this development. The U.S. trade balance turned negative in 1971 as Americans consumed more goods from abroad than they exported, a symbol of self-indulgence that belied an older emphasis on Yankee frugality and self-sufficiency stemming from the colonial era. That same year, the shrinking value of the dollar forced the Nixon administration to end the post–World War II Bretton Woods system of fixed exchange rates that had ensconced the dollar as the world's central currency. Political crises in the Middle East involving Israel and its neighbors in 1973 and Iran in 1979 revealed the sharply rising U.S. dependence on foreign oil for the sustenance of Americans' daily lives. A slowing economy at the start of the decade tipped into a deep recession in 1974 and unemployment rose steeply. A rising inflation rate then piled onto the existing problems to create stagflation, the grimly unprecedented combination of stagnation and inflation that shaped most Americans' memories of the 1970s thereafter. This darkening economic picture was particularly important for explaining the decline of the American empire because of that empire's mostly noncolonial nature and its grounding instead in free trade and the cultural influences carried on the backs of consumer goods shipped abroad.[45]

Defeat in Vietnam explained much of the rest of the stalling of American imperial advance in this era. The histories of the War of 1812 and the Korean War, both closer to draws than either victories or defeats, belied the common belief among Americans that their country won all its wars, but the failure to sustain a noncommunist South Vietnam certainly shocked a country accustomed to dominance in world affairs since World War II. Historian Richard Drinnon in 1980 called South Vietnam "our lost colony," the beginning of a rolling back of American expansion abroad. From 1973 to 1975, as the last U.S. combat troops came home and then the last American personnel were rescued by helicopter while Communist forces advanced on Saigon, Americans experienced a kind of national identity crisis. They learned that their nation was perhaps less history's special nation, a benevolent promoter of democracy everywhere, and perhaps more like other great powers, with many of the same strengths and problems. For some, the United States now looked like a defeated imperial power in economic decline and rife with political corruption all the way up to the White House. The 50,000 young Americans who had fled to Canada to avoid the draft, from this view, seemed more sensible than unpatriotic. For others, the Vietnam syndrome of public unwillingness to support the use of American military force abroad was a terrible outcome. "The United States cannot afford to be a second-rate power," Senator Jesse Helms of North Carolina declared in 1976, "but unfortunately, that seems to be what we are becoming." The failure to hold the line against Communist advance in Vietnam did not lead to Communist victories elsewhere across Asia beyond Indochina—the "falling dominoes" feared by many supporters of the war—but there was no question that U.S. influence overseas was, at least for now, on the wane.[46]

Revelations of anti-democratic behavior abroad by the U.S. government in pursuit of Cold War ends contributed to the decline in public support for U.S. actions overseas. American atrocities against Vietnamese villagers at My Lai, which came to light in November 1969, opened the floodgates to investigations of other government actions. The CIA's Phoenix program in South Vietnam turned out to be a tool of large-scale assassination of government opponents by the U.S. ally, the Saigon regime, whose undemocratic and deeply corrupt character came fully to light in the Academy Award–winning documentary film *Hearts and Minds* (1974). An entire series of covert operations by the CIA, including coups and assassination attempts, bubbled to the surface in 1974–75, rewriting the history of U.S. support for antidemocratic regimes throughout the Third World during the Cold War, from the Shah of Iran in 1953 to Augusto Pinochet in Chile in 1973. Such imperial behavior had the power to shock Americans still imbued with the Cold War idea of their nation as benevolent and generous, a bulwark of decency against Communist perfidy. Congress, the branch of government in closest contact with the public, reacted by trying to restrict what became widely known as "the imperial presidency," by outlawing U.S. aid to insurgents in Angola, and by tying foreign assistance to respect for human rights.[47]

The Nixon and Ford administrations' policies of détente with the Soviet Union (1972–75) and opening relations with China had mixed implications for imperial behavior. On one hand, lessening tensions with the other great powers meant backing away from direct imperial confrontations that could escalate to major wars. Military spending might also be reduced, enabling greater emphasis on domestic concerns. On the other hand, détente included recognizing the spheres of influence of the other powers and reducing criticism of their practices within those spheres. Détente, in this sense, was quite different from the moral universalism of an emphasis on human rights. Nixon and Kissinger could peacefully negotiate with their ideological opposites from Moscow and Beijing while simultaneously continuing the fighting in Vietnam, promoting the overthrow of the elected Chilean government of Salvador Allende, and supporting repressive regimes of the right from the Shah's Iran to apartheid South Africa. This tactical reality helps explain the lack of enthusiasm from more liberal Americans for defending détente when neoconservatives began attacking it vocally by 1974.

The traditional Right, for its part, feared Soviet nuclear might and distrusted any deals with Communists, while neoconservatives added a particular concern about the United States after Vietnam no longer defending its allies with sufficient vigor, particularly Israel. Both conservative groups thought the CIA was underestimating the size of the Soviet nuclear arsenal. Together, these political activists helped move the Republican Party away from détente by the electoral season of 1976, when Ronald Reagan in the Republican primaries attacked President Ford as supposedly weak on foreign policy and supposedly guilty of letting the United States slide into second place in military strength. Ford eked out a victory in the New Hampshire primary by one percentage point in late February, but a few weeks later, Reagan won the North Carolina primary, only the third time in U.S. history that a challenger had defeated an incumbent president in a primary. As the competitors headed next to Florida, Ford told an interviewer, "We are going to forget the word détente." Toughness and assertiveness were back as a theme, at least on the Republican side, a sign that the American imperial style might return someday, if Jimmy Carter's human rights emphases did not win an enduring popular majority.[48]

The United States suffered other losses of influence abroad in the later years of the 1970s, markers of the retreat of the American empire. They happened on Carter's watch, so he received much of the blame—or credit—but they mostly arose from longer-term developments rather than from specific actions or inactions of the U.S. president. Carter reminded Americans that "the United States cannot control events within other nations." One such event was the American agreement to turn over control of the Panama Canal eventually to Panama. The Carter administration completed negotiations that had been ongoing for twelve years, ever since an outbreak of anti-American demonstrations in Panama had revealed the depths of Panamanians' resentment of American control of a 10-mile-wide strip through the middle of their country—roughly akin to another nation operating the Mississippi River and a few miles of land on either side. Carter's chief negotiator on the Canal issue, Sol Linowitz, noted that its status "significantly affects the relationship between this country and the entire Third World" since those nations looked upon "our position on the Canal as the last vestige of a colonial past that evokes bitter memories and deep animosities." Life in the Panama Canal Zone had long been very comfortable for Americans but bitter for Panamanians, who felt like second-class citizens in their own country. And the narrow, sixty-three-year-old Canal's strategic significance was fading, as it could no longer accommodate the largest oil tankers. The Carter administration signed the Panama Canal Treaties in 1977 and barely managed to win their ratification by the Senate in 1978. Opposition was fierce, though not always well informed. A 1975 public opinion poll of Americans regarding who owned the Panama Canal revealed that 44 percent did not know and 22 percent were wrong, guessing everyone from Arab nations to Israel to Cuba. But a large majority opposed Panamanian control by 1978, after intense lobbying and publicity from opponents such as Reagan ("We built it. We paid for it. It's ours."). Reagan's aide David Keene explained later, "The Panama Canal issue had nothing to do with the canal. It said more about the American people's feelings about where the country was, and what it was powerless to do."[49]

A second loss of influence for the United States happened just north of the Canal a year later. The intensely pro-American Somoza family had ruled Nicaragua since the 1930s, when the U.S. Marines had installed it in power. By the 1970s, the dictatorship of Anastasio Somoza had produced great inequality and widespread opposition, which was kept in line with the brutal political police known as the National Guard. The inept government response to a major earthquake in 1972 that devastated much of the capital city of Managua, particularly the blatant theft of international relief funds by officials, stimulated new organizing against the government. Moderate opponents increasingly joined the left-wing Sandinista National Liberation Front in their armed struggle to overthrow Somoza. The Sandinistas were more diverse and complex than their later critics understood; they combined Marxism, Roman Catholicism (particularly the liberation theology prominent in Latin America since 1968), and nationalism (indicated by their name, a tribute to Augusto Sandino, a Nicaraguan general who had fought against the U.S. Marines occupying the country in the 1930s). But no one doubted that their victory, achieved with Somoza's flight into exile in Miami on July 17, 1979, represented the elimination of a longstanding regional outpost of U.S. influence. Even in what its citizens considered their own "backyard," the American empire was in retreat.[50]

An even more dramatic case of diminishing American influence unfolded in the same year halfway around the world in Iran. The strategic stakes were extremely high, due to Iran's vast oil reserves. The United States had defended the Shah, Reza Pahlavi, and Western access to Iranian oil back in 1953 when the CIA organized a coup against the popular nationalist prime minister, Mohammad Mussadiq, after he nationalized the nation's oil fields. It was a history to which few Americans paid any attention. Iranians, however, suffered mightily under the Shah's dictatorial rule, particularly at the hands of his personal political police, SAVAK, which detained—and, typically, tortured—some 50,000 political prisoners by the late 1970s. The Shah's wealth grew fantastically during the 1970s, thanks to the eightfold increase in the price of petroleum. He made efforts to modernize the Iranian economy but failed to benefit the deeply poor average citizens while creating a sycophantic luxury class whom journalist Ryszard Kapuscinski called the "petro-bourgeoisie." The Shah, Kapuscinski observed, "forgot that we are living in times when people demand rights, not grace"—that is, not just the supposed generosity of a wealthy benefactor. Opposition grew rapidly, coalescing behind the charismatic leadership of Ayatollah Ruhollah Khomeini, who returned from exile as soon as vast street protests and a wavering army drove the Shah into exile in January 1979. Under Khomeini, the broad revolutionary coalition quickly frayed and religious radicals won out, creating the Islamic Republic of Iran, the first modern theocratic state. U.S. intelligence officials utterly failed to anticipate this development. "We were just plain asleep," CIA chief Stansfield Turner admitted.[51]

In November 1979, after Carter allowed the ailing Shah to enter the United States for cancer treatment, Khomeini's followers responded by overrunning the U.S. embassy in Tehran, which they accurately viewed as a center of CIA activity, and seizing fifty-two American hostages, whom they paraded before the media's cameras and held for over a year. William Dougherty, a CIA case officer and one of the hostages, was new in Iran and did not speak Farsi, a situation that offended his captors, for whom it was "beyond insult for that officer not to speak the language or know the customs, culture, and history of their country." To them, it was the typically disdainful act of a distant imperial power. Now radical Iranians had struck back at "the Great Satan," Khomeini's term for the hated United States that had so long supported the Shah. Americans, in their turn, now became frustrated, enraged, and humiliated. ABC News introduced *Nightline*, a nightly news program that focused on the hostages, keeping public unhappiness with the situation at a steady boil. After Carter finally approved a military operation six months later to free the hostages, mechanical problems en route forced planners to abort the mission, and a helicopter-airplane collision in the desert south of Tehran killed eight U.S. soldiers. America's humiliation was complete. From all directions, it seemed, from Iran in the Middle East and Indochina in Asia, from Nicaragua in Central America and Angola in southern Africa, the United States was retreating from its global empire of influence.[52]

THE ISRAELI EXCEPTION

Israel was the exception that proved the rule about the decline of empires during the 1970s. While the Europeans, the Soviets, and the Americans withdrew from positions abroad or found their global reach undercut at home, the tiny Jewish state in the Middle East moved in the opposite direction. It consolidated its control of new territories won in battle in 1967 by sending Zionist settlers out to establish new colonies in the lands it had recently occupied. The Portuguese were leaving their colonies in Africa, the Soviets were watching the spread of opposition in the eastern European states they had occupied since 1945, and the Americans were retreating from newly hostile countries that had previously been U.S. allies, but the Israelis were directly bucking the international trend toward self-determination by openly expanding their own very small empire. Israel's recent history explained this distinctive behavior.

Zionism emerged at the end of the nineteenth century as a movement to establish a national homeland for the Jewish people, a safe haven from the persecutions they suffered under the rule of others, particularly in Eastern Europe and Russia. This was a movement for self-determination of a people who, though they had lived in diaspora around the world since their expulsion from the ancient land of Israel by the Roman Empire almost two thousand years earlier, preserved a common religion and language and other elements of a common culture. Zionism was a struggle for justice for an oppressed people who lived primarily under the rule of imperial European powers, and thus fit with other movements for national liberation in the same era, such as the founding of the National Association for the Advancement of Colored People (NAACP) in the United States in 1909 or the African National Congress in South Africa in 1912. What complicated the Zionist story was the absence of most Jews from the land known as Palestine for so many centuries, and the presence of the Arab people there known as the Palestinians. The process of building a Jewish homeland meant importing mostly European Jews into mostly Palestinian lands, a process that accelerated as World War II approached. This seemed, particularly to Arabs, a new case of European colonial settlement.

Then came the Holocaust. Nazi Germany's mass murder of most of Europe's Jews seemed, to Zionists and to many other observers, the most undeniable evidence imaginable of the legitimacy of an independent Jewish state, a place for surviving Jews finally to be safe. The Arab view that Palestinians should not pay the cost for European atrocities had little influence in the immediate aftermath of the war, as Britain withdrew from its imperial management of the territory and Zionists declared the establishment of the new state of Israel, recognized immediately by the United States and the Soviet Union. The war that ensued in 1948 between Arabs and Jews resulted in a victory for

Israel and the displacement of roughly a million Palestinian refugees. Occasional renewed skirmishing over the next two decades finally led to the momentous Six-Day War of 1967, a stunningly swift and complete Israeli victory over its Arab neighbors that brought new Palestinian lands (three times the size of Israel proper) under Israeli control: the West Bank, Gaza, the Golan Heights, East Jerusalem, and the Sinai peninsula. The Sinai was gradually returned to Egypt, but the other four became known as the Occupied Territories. It was Israeli policy toward these lands that set it at odds with the global trend away from empire in the 1970s.[53]

Rather than withdrawing from these territories, where almost all the inhabitants were Palestinian, in any sort of a peace-for-land negotiation, Israel dug in. The Labor Party government, which had dominated Israeli politics since 1948, swiftly annexed East Jerusalem, reunifying the city. Next, small settlements by mostly young, devout Orthodox Jews appeared in the Golan Heights, Gaza, and particularly the West Bank. Over time, these mushroomed into an empire of hundreds of suburban garrisons, bolstered by secular Israelis seeking cheaper housing, which eventually included more than 400,000 Israeli citizens. Such massive settlement created "facts on the ground" that would be difficult to undo, precisely the goal of supporters of what they called Greater Israel, the biblical Promised Land stretching from the Jordan River to the Mediterranean Sea. For Palestinians, other Arabs, and most of the United Nations, this represented another round of colonization of Palestinian lands, a second stage of imperial expansion adding to the "Nakba" (catastrophe) of 1948. International opinion regarding the region's conflicts had long favored Israel, seen as the home of history's most deserving victims, but after 1967 began to swing toward the Palestinians, with the exception of the United States.[54]

Public opinion in Israel, though not unanimous, generally supported the settlements, as did the Tel Aviv government through the provision of financial assistance and military security. Two factors in the 1970s intensified Israeli popular approval of the expansion. One was the rise of international terrorism. Some observers called the publicized slaughter of civilians for political ends "the poor man's atomic bomb." "Terrorism first became a global, not just a local, phenomenon in the 1970s," historian Akira Iriye noted, a means of using the newly international media to gain publicity for one's cause. Attacks occurred in several countries in Europe, in particular, but Israel proved to be the prime target, for the 1967 war and subsequent occupation of Palestinian territories drove some Palestinians to new levels of desperation. Hijacking airplanes emerged as a favored tactic, particularly flights by the Israeli national airline El Al (the screening of airline passengers began as a result). Israeli commandos dramatically liberated a Belgian Sabena plane full of passengers that had been commandeered to Tel Aviv's airport in May 1972 by the Palestinian nationalist group Black September.[55]

The murder of Israeli athletes and coaches a few months later at the Summer Olympics in Munich riveted Israelis and Jews everywhere. So did images of celebrations at the burial in Libya of five of the murderers, where German authorities sent their bodies at the Tripoli government's request after their deaths in a shootout with police. "We are all Black September," the crowd in Tripoli chanted. The same slogan echoed in rallies across the Arab world. Israelis and their government hardened their determination to protect their own citizens at all costs. In a private meeting with the families of Munich victims, Israeli Prime Minister Golda Meir promised, "I've decided to pursue each and every one" of the people involved in the planning and carrying out of the attack. "We will chase them to the last." Deterrence, not just revenge, was the goal. A clear message was to be sent about the personal consequences for perpetrators of future terrorist attacks.[56]

The other factor besides terrorism that consolidated public opinion in Israel in support of keeping the Occupied Territories was the Yom Kippur (October) War. The coordinated attack by the Egyptian and Syrian armies in October 1973 aimed to retake the lands lost six years earlier and to erase the humiliation that the Israeli Defense Forces had inflicted on the larger Arab armies. This was an Arab state action, paralleling the Palestinian non-state terrorist actions. The new assault almost overran Israel. Israelis, Jews, and other supporters briefly contemplated the very real prospect of the ending of the state of Israel. Though Israel rebounded to restore its antebellum position with the aid of U.S. equipment, the experience was a watershed moment in the creation of a firm and unwavering pan-Jewish sense of identity with Israel. Regardless of their degree of assimilation in other nations and regardless of other citizenships, most Jews around the globe identified anew with Jewish culture and history, with the experience of the Holocaust and survivorship, and with the state of Israel.[57]

The issue of the Occupied Territories came to be viewed primarily through the lens of how they might help in the preservation of Israel. Nowhere was this truer than the United States, home to roughly as many Jews as Israel itself. For American Jews, the Munich massacre and the October War solidified a connection with the modern state of Israel that had previously been more tenuous. In Israel, the turn to a fiercer, more defensive posture toward its neighbors helped lead to the first defeat of the Labor Party in 1977 and the election of the conservative religious coalition Likud and new Prime Minister Menachem Begin, a refugee from Poland whose family was slaughtered in the Holocaust. Likud's enthusiasm for Jewish settlements throughout what it saw as all the Land of Israel sealed the policy of expanding Israel's small empire. The Camp David accords of 1978 wound up focusing mostly on producing an Israeli-Egyptian peace through the return of the Sinai, with little real impact on the more populous Palestinian Occupied Territories.[58]

The exceptional character of Israel's expansion at a time of general imperial retraction produced a stinging backlash in 1975 when the UN General Assembly passed, by a 72–35 vote, a resolution condemning Zionism as "a form of racism and racial discrimination." The resolution called attention to Israel's military occupation of Palestinian lands and the second-class status of Arabs living inside Israel, which contrasted starkly with the nation's 1950 Law of Return that made Jewish immigrants from anywhere else in the world citizens upon arrival. In the twentieth century, Israel was the only case of colonial settlement accomplished by a diasporic community rather than by an empire's citizens occupying imperial lands, and the only successful case of nation-building by settlers. Zionism had used a colonial strategy to create a national home and was now continuing that strategy in a postcolonial world. For most Israelis, the UN resolution merely underlined how they could depend only on themselves for protection in a world plainly hostile to them. As if to emphasize this point, the hijacking of Air France Flight 139, originating in Tel Aviv, unfolded just a few months later, culminating in the dramatic rescue of Jewish captives by Israeli commandos at Entebbe in Uganda. The world might condemn Israel, but Israel would protect its own.[59]

Only the United States defended Israel almost unequivocally. The United States "does not acknowledge, it will not abide by, it will never acquiesce in this infamous act" of declaring Zionism to be racist, declared U.S. ambassador to the UN, Patrick Moynihan, a hard-nosed Irish American from New York's rough Hell's Kitchen neighborhood who had also been a Harvard professor. Moynihan considered the UN resolution tantamount to, in his wife Elizabeth's words, "the lunatics . . . taking over the asylum." Moynihan's response embodied a shift by the American public in the first decades after World War II from a broad anti-Semitism and tendency to see Jews as passive victims of the Nazis, to a new respect for Israel—and, by extension, for Jews as a whole—as a land of tough, successful pioneers rather like early American settlers, bringing European civilization to new lands where they confronted existing inhabitants.

In the United States, the newly inclusive rhetoric about "the Judeo-Christian tradition" that had first been heard in the 1940s was now mainstream. Open discrimination against Jews decreased rapidly, measurable from workplaces to social clubs to escalating rates of Jewish marriage to gentiles. The U.S. government developed increasing strategic ties with Israel, as the Jewish state emerged after 1967 as a regional superpower in the critical Middle East. The oil crisis of 1973–74 boosted anti-Arab sentiments among Americans, giving them a new appreciation for Israel's perspective, as did the Iranian seizure of American hostages in 1979 (most Americans being unaware of the distinction between Iranians and Arabs). Given their own frustrations with projecting military might abroad in this decade, from Vietnam to the hostage rescue effort in Iran, Americans tended to admire highly Israel's successes, particularly the stunning operation at Entebbe in 1976. In the popular film *Black Sunday* (1977), for example, a plot by Arab terrorists to attack the Super Bowl is only foiled at the last minute by Israeli intelligence agents who have replaced their ineffectual American counterparts. Support from the United States served to highlight the exceptional nature of Israel's situation in the world in the 1970s, a distinctive case of imperial expansion paradoxically grounded in a quest for national self-determination.[60]

THE RETREAT OF THE STATE

While one major trend of world history in the 1970s was the promotion of egalitarianism through the ending of empires and the growing concern for human rights, the other central theme of the decade on a global scale was the beginnings of the retreat of the state from the management of national economies and the provision of social welfare for its citizens. Like all global processes, the shift toward market economies and a more laissez-faire style of governance was partial rather than absolute. It developed further and faster in some areas than in others, and it may yet be reversed in the future. But a generation later, hindsight revealed clearly that the 1970s marked a turning point in attitudes toward government. After a century of governments, particularly in the industrialized nations, developing as a provider of social benefits and security, they began in this decade of recession and inflation to be seen increasingly as, in historian Tony Judt's words, "a source of economic inefficiency and social intrusion best excluded from citizens' affairs wherever possible." Gone were memories of the political and social traumas of mass insecurity that had defined such earlier eras as the 1890s and 1930s and that had given rise to systems of social security and subsequent prosperity. The welfare state's role of providing services from universal medical services to free education, from old-age pensions to subsidized public transportation, instead came under withering criticism. This discounting of the state from the 1970s onward, Judt noted, "has become the default condition of public discourse in much of the developed world."[61]

In place of the positive view of government social provision and economic management that had prevailed in both capitalist and socialist spheres for most of the twentieth century, a new emphasis emerged on policies of deregulation, privatization, reducing social spending, and cutting taxes. The public sphere shrank; the private sphere expanded. Reducing economic regulation by national governments contributed directly to the accelerating globalization of this era, particularly the rapid flow of investment capital across borders and corporations' increasing tendency to move operations to countries with lower labor costs. Pressure and publicity from international human rights organizations provided another new kind of restraint on the autonomy of national governments. The ebbing of national economic independence in a period of growing global economic integration limited the political options of individual states to address such problems as inequality within their borders. States were increasingly at the mercy of international money markets, whose influence corroded citizens' sense of having a distinctive destiny as a national community. While economic liberalization spread across the capitalist world, China led the socialist world toward its own rendezvous with the market. Beginning in the People's Republic in 1978 and proceeding into Eastern Europe in the next decade, state socialism was hollowed out and then rejected, bringing down the entire system of central bureaucratic planning and provisioning for all aspects of daily life. By the end of the 1970s, the shift away from state control of the economy on

both sides of the Cold War represented what Stanford University economist John McMillan called "history's biggest-ever experiment in economics."[62]

A critical disjuncture between expectations and reality helped
drive this change. In Western Europe, for example, the quarter-
century from 1948 to 1973 marked "a period of extraordinarily
rapid change and a veritable golden age of economic growth,"
in economist Barry Eichengreen's words. Sheltered partly by the
United States taking on the region's defense costs, Europeans
rebuilt from the devastation of World War II new societies of
mass consumption and material comfort. World energy consumption nearly doubled in these years, as the Soviets and even
nonaligned nations acknowledged the high U.S. standard of living and degree of consumer choice and sought to compete with
the Americans. Yet these elevated hopes and expectations of material well-being deteriorated rapidly in the 1970s, thrown back-
wards by the double blows of economic recession and price inflation. Inflation in Western Europe averaged 11 percent during
the decade, reaching 24 percent in Britain in 1975. Unemployment soared, increasing tenfold in France from the 1960s to the
early 1980s. By the late 1970s, a growing sense of crisis in the
welfare states undermined public confidence in the effectiveness
of government management of the economy and provision of
social services.[63]

The hardest blow of all came from skyrocketing oil prices.
All that energy consumption of the previous quarter-century
suddenly became terribly expensive. Oil prices soared tenfold,
from $3 per barrel in 1973 to $30 per barrel in 1980. Americans, who imported about a third of their oil, were hit hard, but
Europeans and Japanese, who imported nearly all of their oil at
the start of the decade, were hit harder. The oil crises of the
1970s reflected two major developments. One was the steady
decline of the U.S. share in world petroleum production from
more than 50 percent in 1950 to just 20 percent in 1972, along
with a similar decline in the U.S. share of proven oil reserves
from 46 percent on the eve of World War II to 6 percent in 1972.
Americans were consuming more and more and producing, pro-

portionally, less and less. The nations of the Middle East and North Africa replaced the United States, producing 41 percent of the world's oil in 1972 and sitting on top of almost two-thirds of proven global reserves.[64]

The second development that underlay the oil crises of the 1970s was the growing organization of the Arab nations, led by Libya's Muammar Gaddafi, and their swift nationalization of the holdings of the international oil companies in OPEC member nations. The equity participation of the international oil companies in those countries fell from 94 percent in 1970 to 12 percent in 1981. OPEC member states were retaking control of their own resources. This marked a partial countercurrent against the general shift toward markets and liberalizing international trade and investment in these years. The oil embargo of Israel's allies in 1973–74 by the Arab members of OPEC can be seen, in some regards, as one of the few major victories of a non-Western nation or nations over Western ones since the Japanese defeat of Russia at the Tsushima Straits in 1905. The embargo and the oil nationalizations represented a further step in the process of decolonization, a dramatic demonstration of national autonomy on the part of former imperial provinces. The second oil crisis of the decade stemmed from the Iranian revolution of 1978–79, which seemed to most Iranians a similar act of taking back their nation and its natural resources from a Shah they viewed as a tool of the West.[65]

Declining confidence in the welfare state reshaped Britain more than any other European state. Hand-in-hand with the United States, the British moved dramatically in the late 1970s to reduce the presence of government in daily life. Margaret Thatcher led the way. After serving in Parliament for sixteen years, the Oxford-educated shopkeeper's daughter became Education Minister and earned a reputation as a tough-minded administrator able to make large budget cuts by tough tactics such as ending free milk in school lunches, which won her the nickname "Maggie Thatcher Milk Snatcher" from critics. She won the leadership post in the Conservative Party in 1974 and went on to be elected in 1979 the first female prime minister in the long history of that nation. Thatcher proved a fierce critic of the welfare state, much influenced by free-market economists Friedrich von Hayek and Milton Friedman. She blamed Britain's profound economic stagnation and inflation squarely on what she considered too great taxation and too much state dominance of the private sector. While appealing to Victorian values and patriotism, she promoted individualism and entrepreneurship, forthrightly proclaiming the positive moral impact of capitalism as the only viable avenue to the production of wealth for the nation. Her government sold off the state ownership share in an array of industries: British Petroleum, British Aerospace, British Telecom, British Steel, British Gas, airports, and government housing. Many citizens admired her firm hand against the large public-sector employee strikes that roiled British society in the late 1970s. The most radical advocate of laissez-faire economics to take power in modern Europe, Thatcher won wide admiration for her ability to govern forcefully, including an upturn in the British economy after 1981. She promoted individualist ethics above all, while demoting the role of government and state-centered ideas of the common good. Britain's continuing status, despite imperial decline, as one of the world's small handful of most economically and militarily powerful nations rendered Thatcher's influence significant.[66]

Nowhere in the world in the 1970s was centralized state control of the economy rolled back as forcefully as in the Southern Cone of South America. The democratic election of socialist Salvador Allende as president of Chile in 1970 roused enormous opposition in Washington as well as in the Chilean military and among conservative and affluent sectors of Chilean society. President Nixon told aides, "No impression should be permitted in Latin America that they can get away with this, that it's safe to go this way." The Allende government nationalized several foreign-owned copper mining operations, including those of U.S.-based Kennecott and Anaconda corporations. The socialist regime cited foreign companies' long records of enormous profits extracted from Chilean soil, which it considered excessive.

One of Anaconda's lawyers seemed to agree, admitting privately: "We used to be the fucker. Now we're the fuckee."[67]

Then a U.S.-backed military coup in 1973 overthrew Allende and became synonymous with the abuse of human rights. The resulting dictatorship of General Augusto Pinochet gained infamy for its brutality toward political dissidents of any kind. In Chile, the free market did not fuse with greater individual freedoms. Pinochet brought into his government a group of Chilean free-market economists from Catholic University in Santiago, who had been trained in Milton Friedman's program at the University of Chicago. They helped privatize Chile's social security system; they reversed Allende's nationalizations and opened up new public resources in timber and fishing to private access; and they promoted foreign investment and freer trade, guaranteeing the right of foreign companies to take home profits from operations in Chile. Socialism south of Cuba disappeared.[68]

The ferocious anticommunism that seized power in Chile radiated outward across the continent in the 1970s. In late 1975, intelligence officers from most South American nations met in Santiago and launched Operation Condor, a region-wide alliance of governments working together to crush leftist resistance movements and even centrist rivals seeking to restore constitutional governments. Operation Condor had the domino effect in the region of promoting military coups. It reached as far as Washington, where Chilean agents murdered Allende's former foreign minister, Orlando Letelier, and his American aide in 1976, on affluent, embassy-filled Massachusetts Avenue. In the same year in Argentina, a military coup ushered in perhaps the most murderous regime in modern South American history, which "disappeared" tens of thousands of suspected leftists in the so-called dirty war that lasted until 1983. Nixon and Kissinger, in particular, supported the military rulers of Chile and Argentina as well as others in the region, and Central America (with the exception of Nicaragua) also saw U.S.-supported regimes fend off leftist opponents, most bloodily in Guatemala and El Salvador. In all of these cases, promoters of the free market won out, defeating defenders of centralized state economic management.[69]

CHINA AND THE HOLLOWING OUT OF SOCIALISM

Nothing confirmed the world turn toward markets by the late 1970s as dramatically as the path taken by the government of China. No country was larger, no regime more unremittingly hostile to capitalism. After consolidating its victory in the Chinese civil war in 1949, the Communist Party had moved with ideological clarity and revolutionary fervor to erase from Chinese society what it considered the corrupting influence of capitalism. Mao Zedong and his allies succeeded to a remarkable extent. They eradicated private property and collectivized agriculture and industry, even at the cost of millions of deaths by starvation during the Great Leap Forward era of the late 1950s. Aligned uneasily with fellow Communists in Moscow, Beijing fought the United States to a standstill in Korea earlier in the decade. Tensions with the Soviets grew more public after 1960, partly for reasons of competing national interests, but partly due to China's fierce commitment to socialism in the face of what it saw as a growing Soviet inclination to compromise with the hated capitalist bloc. No government on Earth was more opposed to free markets. In 1966, Mao—determined to keep China from sliding into Soviet-style "revisionism"—set off a decade of domestic turmoil by instigating the Cultural Revolution, a new wave of socialist enthusiasm among Chinese youth that targeted supposed dissenters. Facing economic stagnation at home and increasing conflict abroad with the Soviet Union, including military skirmishes on their common border in 1969, the Chinese government took two major steps in the 1970s to improve its deteriorating strategic situation.[70]

First, Mao decided to warm up relations with the United States. Concluding that the Soviets next door now constituted the greater danger of the two superpowers, the previously highly ideological Chinese government put theoretical principles aside and found common ground with the capitalist Americans. Mao feared a Soviet attack on China and wanted U.S. assistance should it come, a complete reversal of Chinese expectations for the superpowers. He would use the "faraway barbarians" to balance the "near barbarians." He hoped for technological assistance from the more sophisticated industrial nations as well as shared information from U.S. intelligence services. Mao found willing partners in Nixon and Kissinger. The fact of Chinese and Soviet soldiers shooting and killing each other convinced Nixon that the abstract notion of tensions between the two great Communist powers had become a hard reality and a major U.S. opportunity. Chinese-American negotiations began quietly in Warsaw in 1970, followed by Kissinger's secret visit to China the following year. Nixon's very public trip to Beijing in 1972, the first ever by a U.S. president, then opened a new era by ending twenty-three years of hostility between the two nations. As Kissinger wrote privately to the president about China and the United States a year later, "We have now become tacit allies." Under Mao's leadership, China took a major first step: it was still sticking with a command economy at home, but it was realigning itself internationally.[71]

The second step on China's path to reform came only after the deaths of Mao and his influential lieutenant, Zhou Enlai, in 1976. Chinese society was traumatized by ten years of upheaval during the Cultural Revolution. In the early 1970s, a series of coups and countercoups by political leaders around the ailing Mao created widespread doubts about the wisdom of the ruling Communist Party. Mao's heir-apparent, Lin Biao, lost out to rivals and died in a plane crash in 1971, confusing peasants who first heard him praised to the heavens and then, overnight, vilified. "I had felt faithful to Mao," one peasant recalled, "but that Lin Biao stuff affected my thinking." Another remembered that "the Lin Biao affair provided us with a major lesson. We came to see that leaders up there could say today that something is round; tomorrow, that it's flat. We lost faith in the system." If the nation's main enemy, the United States, was now a kind of ally and the nation's main ally, the Soviet Union, was now the pri-

*"I'm as aware of the evils of Communism as anyone,
but good God, when you think of eight hundred million
Chinese in terms of franchises . . ."*

FIGURE 4.1.
The sheer size of China's population had long
mesmerized foreign businesses. By the end of
the 1970s, market-oriented reforms began to
move the country toward making some of
those earlier fantasies into reality. Courtesy
Donald Reilly/*The New Yorker*.

mary enemy, what else might change? Within the Party leadership, a year of intense struggle for control followed Mao's death.
Deng Xiaoping finally won out and placed China officially on
the road to market reforms in late 1978.[72]

Foremost a nationalist, Deng declared that China "is fully
twenty years behind the developed countries in science, technology and education" and made clear that modernizing the Chinese economy was his highest priority. He was acutely aware
of the economic success of nearby Japan and the small "Asian
tigers" of South Korea, Taiwan, Hong Kong, and Singapore.
Modernization for China required access to industrial technol-

ogy through better relations with the United States, Japan, and Western Europe. Beijing bought its first jumbo jets from Boeing and arranged with Coca-Cola to open a bottling plant in Shanghai. "I'm as aware of the evils of Communism as anyone," one wealthy American said to another in a *New Yorker* cartoon of the era, "but good God, when you think of eight hundred million Chinese in terms of franchises. . . ." Deng also recognized that modernization required the use of at least some of the competitive incentives of capitalism: private property, entrepreneurial opportunities, and profit-making. In some regards, the Party leadership was merely running to keep up with changes on the ground among local Chinese farmers. In Anhui province in the south, for example, farmers had responded to drought and the threat of starvation early in 1978 by secretly experimenting with changing from collective farming to individual property rights. They had considerable success. "You can't be lazy when you work for your family and yourself," one of the farmers observed, embracing a market-oriented logic that was anathema to traditional Communist Party dogma. But the Party itself in 1979 admitted for the first time that Mao had made errors in the past, particularly the collectivization program of the Great Leap Forward. Between 1978 and 1984, in the most populous country in the world, one where 80 percent of the people worked on the land, real income in farm households rose 60 percent. The agricultural communes were dismantled. It was the start of what economist John McMillan has called "the biggest anti-poverty program the world has ever seen."[73]

The two-part Chinese reform that began in the 1970s, transitioning out of a state-run command economy and opening ties with the West, had global implications. The greatest enthusiast for the Soviet road to modernity was now moving away from state planning in its pursuit of economic growth. This provided a model to Communist regimes from Eastern Europe to Africa to end Soviet-style economic systems. Under Deng's leadership, China also reduced and ultimately stopped its aid to revolutionary regimes and movements abroad. Instead, the People's Republic began to build a web of human connections with the

United States that eventually became the most important bilateral trade relationship in the world. Nixon's trip to China was preceded by a brief visit of American table tennis players ("ping-pong diplomacy") and followed by other exchanges of professionals, students, and eventually tourists. With the formal exchange of ambassadors in 1979 came also tours of China by the Washington Bullets of the National Basketball Association and by the master violinist Isaac Stern, each symbolizing important parts of the Western culture that for the Chinese had been strictly forbidden for a generation. Professor Chen Lin began hosting China's first television program teaching English, a language that had placed many practitioners in China in serious peril a few years earlier during the Cultural Revolution. Deng Xiaoping himself spent a week touring the United States and charmed Americans, donning a ten-gallon hat and wielding a six-shooter at a Texas barbecue and dancing with Mickey Mouse at the Magic Kingdom in Orlando. The savvy Chinese leader was stunned by the technological sophistication and productivity of U.S. farms and factories, and returned home even more determined to modernize the Chinese economy rapidly using whatever capitalist incentives were required, even if doing so was masked rhetorically as "socialism with Chinese characteristics." A few years later, the common use of a new official slogan suggested the revolutionary (or counterrevolutionary) nature of China's changes: "To get rich is glorious."[74]

Deng's visit to the United States in early 1979 had an additional purpose of gaining tacit acceptance by the Carter administration of the imminent Chinese attack on its Communist neighbor, Vietnam. This brief invasion reflected growing tensions between the two countries over another Communist neighbor, Cambodia. China supported the Khmer Rouge government of Cambodia and resented Vietnam's brief recent occupation of part of Cambodia, which political scientist Benedict Anderson called "the first large-scale conventional war waged by one revolutionary Marxist regime against another." Nationalism, not Marxism, was the order of the day. So Americans, just six years out of their own war against Vietnam, now watched China—the nation President Johnson had claimed was the real threat Americans were meeting when they had gone to war in Vietnam—invade Vietnam. And China was sliding fast toward capitalism. The world had turned upside down.[75]

The present tends to look different in retrospect. From the perspective brought by the passage of time, historians can recognize patterns that were not visible at an earlier moment. So it was with the world in the 1970s. At the time, Americans and other observers could not easily step out of the Cold War framework that had shaped their understanding of the United States and so much of the world for the previous thirty years. They saw evidence of American decline and assumed it meant Soviet advance; they saw capitalism adrift and assumed it meant socialism was on the rise. The stories of Vietnam and Nicaragua in this decade turned out to be temporary, however, their significance more linked to the anti-imperialist struggles for national self-determination in Afghanistan and Poland than to any rising socialist tide. The tale of China proved to be a more accurate indicator of future world developments, not Mao's enthusiasm for socialist revolution but Deng's commitment to market incentives. Soviet hopes for an enlarging sphere of Communist influence turned out to be in vain, a reality that was being fleshed out well before the arrival of Ronald Reagan in Washington.

The world did not march in lockstep down the capitalist road to free markets. Revolutionary regimes in Luanda, Hanoi, Managua, and Phnom Penh were determined to build socialism in their own different ways. The Soviet Union's widely acknowledged parity in nuclear weapons with the United States by the early 1970s gave strategic weight to the Communist sphere, a point that the détente process underlined. In Western Europe, leftist terrorists created anxieties, and governments outside of Great Britain were slow to limit the robust welfare state systems they had built. In similar fashion, the widespread movement toward national self-determination and human rights had its limitations, ranging from repressive national governments to the problematic case of Israel's territorial expansion. The histories of nations are too often written as if all citizens move together in a unified way, with too-common generalizations about "the United States," "China," or "Chile," and the same can happen with histories of the globe. That is not the intention here. But the evidence does suggest a broad tale of transition in the 1970s as empires of all ideological stripes found themselves under renewed pressure and human rights gained new international prominence, and as market values replaced communitarian hopes across the world. The lure of capitalist economic growth and particularly of consumer culture, for which the United States remained the cutting edge, turned out to be growing, not shrinking.[76]

Chapter 5

RESISTANCE TO THE

NEW HYPER-INDIVIDUALISM

NOT EVERYONE found comfort in the increasingly though not fully entwined enthusiasms for greater human equality and the marketplace that took shape in the 1970s. An unfettered individualism, with all progressively more welcome to participate as autonomous buyers and sellers, was emerging as the central feature of contemporary American culture and gaining traction around the globe, but it deeply troubled certain observers. Some of the objections came from predictable if diverse corners. Socialist revolutionaries from Vietnam to Angola to Nicaragua, for example, saluted equality, at least in principle, but rejected the market and restricted private property. They fought for a collectivist future that they believed would offer greater justice and less exploitation, but it was a fight they clearly would be losing within a decade.

Labor union organizers in the United States, the traditional core of domestic collective action, struggled similarly in the 1970s to hold on to the benefits of collective bargaining. But they watched their memberships decline steadily, victims of the shift from manufacturing to service work and of the nimbleness of capital in an increasingly integrated global economy. Strikes and protests by public service employees in New York City and elsewhere during the economic trauma of 1974–75 alienated much of a shell-shocked public. The AFL-CIO and its supporters among more liberal Democrats in Congress understood that free markets were likely to benefit those with capital much more than those without it. But they were powerless to stop the hemorrhaging of union membership and influence. The very idea of a unified "working class" essentially disappeared in the 1970s.[1]

Meanwhile, as described in chapter 2, on the anti-egalitarian front, white racists, male chauvinists, and opponents of homosexuality endured, bolstering some of the ranks of the Republican Party. They steadily lost the cultural high ground and most legal decisions, however, and they began articulating their concerns in less openly racial and gendered language. By the end of the twentieth century, opposition to full human equality was losing its appeal, particularly among younger Americans, a sign of where the future was headed.

The two most significant and enduring forms of dissent against the new hyper-individualism came, in different ways, from environmentalists and religious fundamentalists. The powerful new wave of environmental activism that emerged in the late 1960s and early 1970s focused on the degradation of natural resources, both in the United States and around the world. From this green perspective, the unrestrained consumption encouraged by the free market was grossly irresponsible and unsustainable. What industrial society needed was to repair its ruinous relationship with the earth, air, and water, to replace exploitation with balance. From an ecological perspective, the Cold War competition of Soviets and Americans for greater economic output and ever-larger nuclear arsenals was a tragedy, one demonstrated in polluted waters from the Great Lakes to the Arctic Sea, in government mismanagement from Los Angeles smog and sprawl to the draining of the Aral Sea, in nuclear accidents from Three Mile Island to Chernobyl.

Under capitalism, it has been said, man exploits man, whereas under communism, it's the reverse. From the perspective of natural resource damage, something similar was true. There was little comfort in Karl Marx's writings or in Soviet leader Nikita Khrushchev at the United Nations promising to out-produce the West: "We will bury you!" In comparison to Communist revolutionaries, most environmentalists, particularly those associated with large mainstream organizations such as the Sierra Club and the National Wildlife Federation, seemed like unthreatening moderate reformers from middle-class and affluent backgrounds, while more radical direct-action groups such as Greenpeace and Earth First! had relatively few members. But at its heart, environmentalism represented a truly subversive critique of the enthusiasm for free markets. Greens focused on often-ignored "negative externalities": the considerable social and ecological costs of consumption not reflected in market prices, such as pollution and resource depletion. Collective responsibility needed to replace individual choice; careful environmental regulation had to restrain free enterprise. Communism largely disappeared by the 1990s, but environmentalism remained, in its different way, a potentially significant brake on the logic of markets.[2]

The second significant and sustained source of resistance to the newly inclusive individualism of the market was the resurgence of religious fundamentalism in the 1970s. Across the Christian, Jewish, and Muslim landscapes of the decade, militant forms of piety bloomed as embattled religious activists fought back against what they saw as advancing secular societies and institutions bent on destroying their essential spiritual identities. The religious revival took different forms and adopted different strategies in different countries, ranging from a politically influential new alliance of evangelical Protestants and conservative Roman Catholics in the United States, to an aggressive Israeli settler movement in the Palestinian Occupied Territories, to an Islamic revolutionary takeover of the government of Iran and insurgency in Afghanistan.

These movements varied in their estimations of the legitimacy of existing governments. But these activists shared a common yearning for a partially imagined earlier era of superior religious righteousness, one of greater deference to male elders and authorities and of less egalitarianism. They were determined to move out of their traditional sphere of countercultural separatism and into the public realm of political engagement, driven by what they saw as a crisis of dire secular threat that could no longer be avoided. And they specifically rejected the kind of unrestrained marketplace individualism of people choosing their own codes of moral behavior, even as they tended to accept marketplace individualism in the economic sphere. Godly moral behavior, they believed, had to be legislated and enforced. Religious fundamentalists reversed the very meaning of freedom from that of contemporary secular culture: being completely free meant actually being enslaved to one's hedonistic desires (ultra-Orthodox Jews referred to secular Jews as "free" because they had thrown off the yoke of Torah and mitzvoth, or religious commandments), while Christian fundamentalists spoke of being "yoked to God" and being "yoked together" in the work of the Lord. This militant piety emphasized the faith of individuals, but it placed them within the mutual obligations of a larger community of believers. The way of the Cross, like the way of jihad, had no obvious common ground with the way of the shopping mall, even if many religious activists, particularly in the United States, readily made peace with free-market capitalism and saw entrepreneurship as embodying biblical values.[3]

The international reemergence of religious fundamentalism in the 1970s surprised most observers. Their reaction recalled Thomas Jefferson's unfounded confidence that his own earlier era marked the decline of evangelical enthusiasm, when he wrote in 1822: "I trust that there is not a young man now living in the United States who will not die an Unitarian." The quarter-century from 1945 to 1970 enjoyed secular success and confidence around the globe, from great economic growth and national independence in Asia and Africa to men walking on the surface of the moon. Both sides in the Cold War emphasized rising standards of living and technological innovations in their competition to claim the mantle of European modernity after Europe's self-destruction in World War II. They focused on the here and now. The Soviets proclaimed religion a distraction, Marx's "opiate of the masses," while American leaders saluted the importance of religious faith but wrapped that value within a larger package of national virtues. The leaders of the newly independent nations of the Muslim crescent from Morocco to Indonesia were strongly secular in orientation; they aimed to build their own versions of the industrial North's success with science and nationalism. Then came the 1970s, bearing oil crises, inflation, economic stagnation, and growing evidence of the corruption and failure of secular leaders from Moscow to Washington to Tehran. Religious people across the Abrahamic faiths found their confidence in existing governments shaken and began to call for religious revitalization, a renewed spiritual identity that challenged national loyalties and offered a very different critique of capitalism from that of traditional socialism. In the United States, this shift brought to the White House the first evangelical Christian president of the modern era, Jimmy Carter, a man of environmental sympathies who embodied the strengths of religious people as well as the tensions between a spiritual orientation and the emerging new ethic of market-oriented individualism.[4]

THE ENVIRONMENTALIST CHALLENGE

The strength of environmentalist activism in the 1970s derived from the widespread visible evidence of deleterious human impact on the natural world. Things were changing and not in a happy way. A century of industrialization had remade American landscapes, waterways, and skies. Pollution seemed to be the price of economic growth. In 1969, a blowout from an offshore oil drilling operation soaked the picturesque beaches of Santa Barbara with 4.2 million gallons of crude oil. A few months later, the oil-slicked Cuyahoga River in Cleveland caught fire, prodding the Federal Water Pollution Control Administration to concede "the lower Cuyahoga has no visible signs of life." Behind the visible degradation of the natural world lay the core problem of population growth. An increasingly industrial, urban society of 76 million people in 1900 doubled in size by 1950 and expanded by another third by 1970. Then during the 1970s, the U.S. population grew another 11 percent, reaching 227 million at the end of the decade. With three times as many Americans as at the beginning of the twentieth century, the country's consumption of natural resources soared. Metropolitan areas stretched as suburbs sprawled; the burning of coal and oil rose steadily; forests retreated under siege as smog and water pollution spread. World population grew even faster, from 2.5 billion in 1950 to 4.0 billion in 1970. The so-called Green Revolution of higher crop yields through scientific management enabled this growth, although it required a vast increase in the use of chemical fertilizers and pesticides with consequent runoff pollution. In terms of food production, the Green Revolution was like adding an extra continent of North America's size and fertility to the Earth.[5]

Rapid population growth stimulated tremendous anxiety by the late 1960s, visible in the reception of Stanford University biologist Paul Ehrlich's best-selling book, *The Population Bomb*. Prominent conservative columnist George Will cited Thomas Jefferson's concern about the moral impact of urbanization on what he had seen as the unique virtue of the American people: "When they get piled upon one another in large cities, as in Europe, they will become corrupt as in Europe." Previous efforts to promote population control had often been racist, paternalistic, and even brutal, as historian Matthew Connelly showed in his important recent study, *Fatal Misconception*, and some of the direst predictions of imminent environmental destruction due to population growth did not pan out. But the central factor in the degradation of the natural environment by the 1970s was the unprecedented and still-growing number of human beings crowding the planet.[6]

The new wave of environmentalism arose in direct response to the extraordinary economic growth of the quarter-century after World War II. Global economic output nearly tripled, with pollution increasing in tandem. One measure of human impact in this era came from the two trans-Atlantic raft trips of Norwegian adventurer and scientist Thor Heyerdahl: while in 1950–51 he saw no sign of human pollution, on his second voyage, in 1969, he encountered oil slicks more than two-thirds of his days at sea as well as plastic debris bobbing on the waves. Another measure was world use of artificial fertilizer, which soared from 4 million tons in 1940 to 150 million tons in 1990, altering the chemical makeup of the Earth's soils ("chemotherapy of the land") and waters.[7]

The Cold War that shaped the politics of this era encouraged greater extraction of energy sources and other natural resources to feed the burgeoning aerospace, electronics, and petrochemical industries. The right-wing John Birch Society, figuring that all subversives were in league together, denounced the April 22, 1970, Earth Day as a thinly veiled attempt to honor Vladimir Lenin's birthday, but Communists matched capitalists step for step in the push to harness nature for human benefit—and built an even grimmer record of polluting land, water, and air. "Grow up to be good revolutionaries," Argentine leftist Che Guevara instructed his children. "Study hard to be able to dominate the techniques that permit the domination of nature." Soviet leader Nikita Khrushchev agreed: "Growth of industrial and agricultural production is the battering ram with which we shall smash the capitalist system." Environmentalists were distrusted in every Cold War camp as undercutting national strength, including Third World countries for which greater economic growth was a future aspiration rather than a current problem. Indian nationalist organizer Mohandas Gandhi, however, had warned back in 1928 of where modern economic growth might ultimately lead: "God forbid that India should ever take to industrialism . . . If an entire nation of 300 million took to similar economic exploitation, it would strip the world bare like locusts."[8]

Among the most significant environmental impacts of the postwar economic boom and the scientific research accompanying it in industrial countries was remarkable success in greatly reducing infectious disease. At the same time science offered up a new threat to public health in the form of nuclear weapons, it dramatically bolstered the personal health of individuals against virulent microbes. Antibiotics became common after 1943, followed in the next two decades by anti-viral vaccines against polio, measles, diphtheria, tetanus, and influenza. Smallpox, an epic killer for millennia, was driven to global extinction by 1980. Average life expectancy worldwide gained twenty years between

"I remember when there was no damn environment."

FIGURE 5.1.
Earlier failure to consider environmental damage while making public policy came to seem
obviously irresponsible to most Americans in
the 1970s. Courtesy David Sipress/*The New
Yorker.*

1920 and 1990. In the United States, as the population survived
much longer, non-communicable diseases such as heart disease
and cancer emerged as the most common causes of death. The
liberal and then extravagant use of antibiotics in this era, however, encouraged the development in the 1970s of the first
multiple-drug-resistant bacteria. Bacteria evolved extremely
rapidly, some of them mutating in ways that allowed them to
survive the antibiotic onslaught. Malaria cases spiked again in
the same decade as a result of mosquitoes developing resistance
to the pesticide DDT, and the first incurable strains of tuberculo-
sis appeared in South Africa in 1977. Resistant infections challenged scientists to what became an open-ended arms race with
evolving bacteria. The environmental impacts of human society
remained impossible to fully predict and elusive to control.[9]

The greatest human impact of all was global warming. In
1974, scientists first postulated not only that the atmospheric
ozone layer helping protect the Earth from ultraviolet rays was
thinning, but that chlorofluorocarbons (CFCs) such as Freon,

widely used in cooling systems and aerosol sprays since the 1930s, were a primary culprit. Releases of CFCs into the atmosphere had been fairly modest in 1950 at 20,000 tons; by 1970, the figure reached 750,000 tons per year. Sharply elevated rates of skin cancer in Southern Hemisphere countries like Australia helped confirm Freon's connection to ozone depletion, which led to a series of international bans on the production of CFCs. Also in the 1970s, James Hansen and other climate scientists first warned that the burning of fossil fuels was releasing carbon dioxide into the atmosphere that contributed to a growing "greenhouse effect." The Earth was getting warmer, on average, at a faster rate than natural cycles would have accounted for, and human activity—all those people burning all those fossil fuels—was the key variable. In 1979, the National Academy of Science first studied the issue of human-generated carbon dioxide in the atmosphere. It found "no reason to doubt that climate changes will result and no reason to believe that these changes will be negligible."[10]

Over the next generation, global warming emerged as the foremost environmental challenge for humankind. Economists and other observers joined environmentalists in characterizing global warming as a classic example of an "externality," an unintended side effect of a market transaction that affects others whom the decision-makers do not compensate. In other words, people pay a price for a good (here, an energy source) that does not fully reflect its true costs. "Our emissions affect the lives of others," former World Bank chief economist Sir Nicholas Stern later declared bluntly. "When people do not pay for the consequences of their actions, we have market failures. This is the largest market failure the world has seen." Free enterprise was not entirely free for the larger community, in this case for humankind as a whole, and environmentalists were among the first to recognize and publicize this reality.[11]

While old-fashioned coal remained a major energy source, oil emerged as the central fossil fuel of the twentieth century. From World War I forward, petroleum increasingly powered the world's modern transportation systems. Nowhere was this truer than in the United States, whose economy and culture came to hinge on the individual freedom of the automobile and the distribution of goods by truck. In the 1920s, best-selling author Bruce Barton called gasoline "the juice of the fountain of youth," the very symbol of American freedom, energy, and youthfulness. American oil fields, particularly in Texas and Oklahoma, produced more barrels than anywhere else on Earth throughout the first half of the century. From 1950 to 1973, the real cost of energy actually declined annually by 5 percent. Vast oil use was built into the U.S. economy. Four times as many cars and trucks cruised American roadways in 1973 as in 1945. From 1956 to 1970, the U.S. government invested $70 billion in highways versus just $1 billion in railways. Europeans after World War II, with their denser populations and smaller landscapes, took a more balanced approach by developing roadways and railways together, but they, too, developed a profound dependency on oil. Whereas in 1950, oil provided just 8.5 percent of Europe's energy needs, by 1970 it provided 60 percent. Inexpensive fuel underpinned the industrial world's great economic expansion of the quarter century after World War II.[12]

The era of cheap energy shuddered to a halt in October 1973 when the Arab OPEC nations began a five-month embargo of oil shipments to the United States and other Western nations that supported Israel in the brief Arab-Israeli war. World petroleum prices shot up 400 percent practically overnight. The Iranian revolution six years later again disrupted oil production and export from a major source, further jolting international markets. By 1980, the barrel of oil that had cost less than $3 in 1970 commanded $31.[13]

The two Middle Eastern oil crises of the 1970s caused particular disruption to the United States because they intersected with a historic turning point in the supply of oil for American consumers. U.S. domestic oil production peaked in 1970 and began to decline steadily thereafter. But demand for oil kept rising. On a bar graph, the two lines that had long run parallel now separated dramatically, one continuing upward and the other falling off. Here was the newfound U.S. vulnerability. If

Americans merely consumed roughly what they produced, they would have developed no large dependency on oil from outside sources. Before this decade, the United States was in fact already using more oil than it could drill at home; it imported 21.5 percent of its oil in 1970. But now declining domestic production drove that number skyward, reaching 47 percent in 1977. Outside of the United States, the story was similar. Surging energy prices stimulated inflation and hurt average people around the globe. Western Europeans were even more dependent on imported oil than was the United States, as the economic shocks rolling through their countries in the 1970s revealed.[14]

The crucial question for the United States was how it would respond to the challenge of uncertain energy supplies and higher prices. One option was to use less and find alternatives. Environmentalists made this argument with great enthusiasm, pointing out the benefits of energy conservation for foreign policy as well as for clean air and water ("a gallon saved is a gallon produced"). Physicist Amory Lovins of the Rocky Mountain Institute was the most important voice calling for a "soft energy path" of conservation and efficiency rather than the traditional "hard energy path" of reliance on fossil fuels. In a much-discussed article in the journal *Foreign Affairs* in 1976, Lovins explained in precise fashion how energy-saving measures could contribute directly to environmental preservation and national security. Many political leaders in both parties seemed to agree at least in part with this logic. Congress passed a national 55-mile-per-hour speed limit to conserve gasoline. In his first state of the union address in 1975, President Ford acknowledged that "in all honesty, we cannot put all of the blame on the oil-exporting nations. We, the United States, are not blameless. Our growing dependence upon foreign sources has been adding to our vulnerability for years and years, and we did nothing to prepare ourselves for such an event as the embargo of 1973." Conservation efforts initiated in the 1970s included more energy-efficient appliances, cars, homes, and manufacturing systems, which succeeded in reducing U.S. oil demand by one-sixth between 1977 and 1985. Renewable sources such as hydropower, solar panels, and wind farms experienced a brief boost with federal tax incentives. President Carter put solar panels on the White House in 1977, and implored his fellow citizens to conserve energy.[15]

The other option for how the United States and the rest of the world would respond to the new energy situation was not to use less but to produce more. One result of sharply rising petroleum prices was to provide an incentive for finding new oil fields. The massive stimulus to new drilling was most readily visible in such places as Alaska, Alberta, the Gulf of Mexico, the North Sea, Angola, and particularly western Siberia, where giant operations boosted the Soviet Union for a period to the status of the world's second largest producer. A campaign to derive petroleum from oil shale on the western slope of the Rocky Mountains helped create a brief boom in Colorado that brought dramatic growth to the formerly provincial town of Denver, which surpassed Kansas City in this decade as the largest city between Chicago and San Francisco.[16]

The preference for finding more energy rather than conserving known resources appealed to a powerful American tradition of growth and development, and it became increasingly associated by the end of the decade with the business-oriented Republican Party. The Reagan administration of the 1980s had little interest in energy efficiency or conservation. Indeed, Reagan even removed Carter's solar panels from the White House roof, and he kept taxes on gasoline at one-eighth the average amount of those in other industrialized nations. Two decades later, the Republican choice of two former oil business executives, George W. Bush and Richard Cheney, for president and vice president, illustrated the durability of this new partisan alignment, as did chants of "drill, baby, drill" at Republican rallies in the 2008 presidential campaign of John McCain and Sarah Palin.[17]

The most dramatic alternative source of fuel was nuclear energy, and the number of nuclear reactors in the United States grew from 55 in 1976 to 104 by the end of the century. France and Japan invested even more heavily in this new source. But the U.S. expansion was misleading, the result of earlier construction contracts being completed. In 1973, Arizona Public

Service ordered the last nuclear reactor that would be built for more than a generation. Attractive for not burning fossil fuels, nuclear power was burdened by enormous construction expense and the production of highly radioactive waste. Despite large federal subsidies for research and development, waste storage, and liability, nuclear energy remained prohibitively expensive. Environmentalists and other local activists organized a vigorous anti-nuclear power movement in the mid-1970s, particularly the Clamshell Alliance in New Hampshire and the Abalone Alliance in California. The accidents at Three Mile Island in 1979 and Chernobyl in 1986 undercut remaining popular support for expanding the industry further.[18]

The roots of environmentalism extended far back in American history to colonial and early national botanical observers such as William Bartram and John James Audubon and nineteenth-century transcendentalists such as Ralph Waldo Emerson and Henry David Thoreau. At the dawn of the twentieth century, Sierra Club founder John Muir worked to encourage important land conservation efforts by policymakers, including President Theodore Roosevelt and U.S. Forest Service chief Gifford Pinchot. For the much more widespread environmental movement that took shape in the late 1960s and particularly the 1970s, events since World War II were most influential. Living under the threat of nuclear annihilation made these activists acutely aware of the vulnerability of human habitation on the Earth. They shared a growing unhappiness at the desecration of nature by industrial society, articulated by economist John Kenneth Galbraith in his best-selling book *The Affluent Society*, with its description of cities "made hideous by litter, blighted buildings, billboards, and posts for wires that should long since have been put underground." *Apollo 8* astronauts brought home their "Earthrise" photograph in 1968. Humans had come an almost unbelievable distance from hunting and gathering days to be able to take such a photograph, yet the blue-green Earth hanging alone in the dark universe rendered the fragility of humankind's only home starkly clear as never before. The two U.S. *Viking* probes that landed on Mars in 1975 and the 1977 *Voy-*

ager spacecraft that closely photographed outer planets found
no signs of life elsewhere. Humans were on their own.[19]

Or were they? Central to much of modern environmentalism
was a quest for connection to larger spiritual truths and wisdom. Rather than seeing people as crude dominators and ex-
ploiters of the natural world, environmentalists sought to understand humanity in its larger context. Most immediately, this
meant thinking ecologically. During the 1970s, new terms like
"ecosystem" and "biosphere" became common. Recycling paper,
plastic, and metal waste began to be widely viewed as a virtuous
civic duty. New departments sprang up in universities such as
ecology and human biology, and environmental consciousness
began to reshape the contours of older academic disciplines
from architecture to engineering. Context mattered anew. Even
Republican President Richard Nixon called for a new, commu-
nally minded ethic of land management. "Traditionally, Americans have felt that what they do with their own land is their
own business," Nixon declared in 1970. "The time has come
when we must accept the idea that none of us has a right to
abuse the land, and that on the contrary society as a whole has
a legitimate interest in proper land use."[20]

For many Americans, the quest for environmental context
and understanding led beyond human community to a divine
connection and human responsibility for preserving God's creation rather than destroying it. Careful contemplation of the
natural world had long included concern for what Christians
and others called stewardship. One of the clearest manifesta-
tions of this element in modern environmentalism was the popularity of Annie Dillard's book, *Pilgrim at Tinker Creek*, the
1974 Pulitzer Prize winner for nonfiction, which lyrically linked
back-to-the-land consciousness with a contemplative focus on
divine creation.[21]

The 1970s in the United States generally marked a period of
movement toward deregulation and freeing up entrepreneurial
energies and capital from government management, a reversal
from the preceding decades of the New Deal to Great Society.
This process did not proceed in lockstep, however. In the first

years of the 1970s, a burst of legislative and administrative initiatives on environmental and health matters formed a last advance before the broader retreat, somewhat akin to the last shots of a fireworks display going up while the show as a whole is ending, or a few higher waves breaking up on the sand while the tide is actually beginning to go out.

The National Environmental Policy Act of 1970 (NEPA) required federal agencies to assess and report on the likely environmental impacts of their actions. NEPA also created the Council on Environmental Quality within the White House to advise the president on environmental initiatives. Later that year, the new Environmental Protection Agency (EPA) was established with strong bipartisan support. The EPA coordinated national environmental policy and enforced other laws and regulations soon established to protect clean air and water, preserve endangered species, limit the release of toxic chemicals, ban leaded gasoline, and increase fuel efficiency in the nation's automobile fleet. And Congress created the Occupational Safety and Health Administration to monitor and enforce rules protecting the health and safety of workers on the job.[22]

Such reforms marked an important environmental advance, though not an absolute victory. Critics noted, for example, that the considerable gains in efficiency in overall energy use that began to emerge in the late 1970s were more than offset by greater overall energy demand by the 1990s. The gains in efficiency in automobile engines were soon swallowed up by vehicles being made heavier and more powerful, and simply by more and more of them being manufactured, both in the United States and abroad.[23]

Environmentalists had sometimes been viewed as affluent liberals concerned about preserving far-off wilderness areas. But the immediate significance of environmental damage was brought home to Americans during the second half of the 1970s through great publicity about toxic chemical waste, particularly polychlorinated biphenyls (PCBs). First produced in 1929, this clear viscous liquid had been used for decades as an insulating material in electrical equipment and a stabilizer in lubricants, paints, pesticides, and food packaging. PCBs turned out to be carcinogenic, however, as researchers discovered by the early 1970s. They had spread around the globe, from the Arctic to Antarctica; they tended to move up the food chain, concentrating in humans; and they were present in mothers' breast milk, imperiling infants. Investigations in 1975 revealed that General Electric had, over decades, dumped more than a million pounds of PCBs into the Hudson River upstream from New York City, a casual by-product of its manufacturing plants in Fort Edwards and Hudson Falls. Congress responded by passing the Toxic Substance Control Act in 1976 to ban future production of the chemical. But PCBs were already widely spread and the challenges in containing their potential damage to people and wildlife remained monumental. Efforts by some companies to avoid the higher costs of the new regulations for safer disposal increased the challenge. The Ward Transformer Company of Raleigh, for example, paid a waste-hauler to spend two weeks in the summer of 1978 illegally dumping PCB-contaminated liquid waste along 240 miles of rural road shoulders in central North Carolina.[24]

The subject of toxic waste splashed on to the front pages of the nation's newspapers in 1978 with the story of Love Canal. Ironically, William Love had begun digging his canal in the town of Niagara Falls, New York, back in 1894 as part of a utopian industrial development that would rely on clean hydropower and create inexpensive housing for workers with abundant communal green space. He ran out of money. The Hooker Chemical Company eventually bought the unfinished, 16-acre canal and filled it with 43 million pounds of PCBs and other corrosive industrial wastes between 1942 and 1953, by-products of the industrial boom of World War II. Then the company sold the site to the Niagara Falls School Board for $1 and a release from liability. The town built an elementary school there and sold the surrounding area for housing development. By the early 1970s, as if in a horror movie, this pleasant middle-class neighborhood was under assault from the ground. Black sludge seeped into basements. Asphalt streets buckled, stank, and sometimes caught on fire. Children at the school suffered from unusually high rates of asthma and cancer. Mothers in the neighborhood miscarried and delivered babies with uncommon birth defects.[25]

Full-time homemaker Lois Gibbs and her family moved into a house in Love Canal in 1974. Her son Michael was then a healthy one-year-old. Over the next four years, Michael developed epilepsy, asthma, liver and urinary tract disorders, and skin diseases. A local newspaper article in 1978 about the toxic-waste dump and its potential health effects convinced her to do something. "I was incredibly shy. All I wanted to do was get Michael out of that kindergarten," she recalled. But the school board denied her petition to transfer her son from the school due to health problems because "if it was unsafe for my kid then it was unsafe for all four hundred-some children and they were not about to close the school because of one hysterical housewife." Gibbs and her neighbors began organizing a campaign to do just that and to force public authorities to clean up the toxic waste on top of which they lived. Three months later, the state of New York agreed to evacuate 240 families and compensate them for their property, and the story made headline news across the nation. EPA studies soon revealed chromosomal damage in local residents. In 1980, the Carter administration declared a state of emergency for the neighborhood and evacuated the remaining families.[26]

Love Canal became a synonym for the buried costs of industrial development and the failure of unregulated industry to preserve Americans' health and well-being. Toxic waste was another externality—another factor not readily calculated in a market transaction—that could gravely injure innocent bystanders. The worst consequences of industrial pollution had often been shielded from mainstream view by locating them in poor or obscure locations, but Love Canal was different: a middle-class white neighborhood with intact families living what seemed like prototypical American lives, only to be devastated by environmental damage. Environmental protection now seemed elemental and obvious as a national requirement. Lois Gibbs and her fellow organizers helped move environmental issues from a distant issue to an immediate concern, from a rich person's issue to an average American's concern. The EPA announced that the United States had between 32,000 and 50,000 major hazardous waste sites, and Congress created a so-called Superfund in 1980 to facilitate their cleanup. Residents of Love Canal had been hesitant initially to question authorities, living quietly with their growing anxieties for years, many of them, like Gibbs's husband and family, benefiting from good jobs in the chemical industry. But once organized and committed, the female-dominated activist leadership found their lives upended. Gibbs's own marriage became a casualty of her new political work, as she was no longer able or willing to be at home doing all the child care and providing timely dinners as she once had. Her husband found himself having to cook and do his own laundry, and, she recalled, "suddenly he was babysitting, because men don't take care of children, they baby-sit. Only women are parents." They each wound up happily remarried. Environmental activism converged at Love Canal with the rising egalitarianism of the decade.[27]

The Alaska oil pipeline provided one other prominent environmental battleground in the 1970s. At first, the new environmental impact statements required under NEPA seemed to imperil the massive project, but the oil crisis of 1973 eased federal approval of the pipeline. Construction began that winter amidst sharply rising unemployment, creating more than 20,000 jobs and luring waves of mostly young men from the lower 48, including a young George W. Bush on summer break from Harvard Business School. Oil began to flow to Valdez in 1977. With access to oil assured, the other half of the de facto compromise proceeded. Congress passed the Alaska National Interest Lands Conservation Act in 1980, tripling the amount of U.S. public land protected from development. This largest zoning act in history designated ten new national parks (including the largest, the Wrangell-St. Elias), monuments, and recreation areas, and set aside nearly a third of the state from development. Many Alaskans resented the restrictions at first, although many came to appreciate the bill in subsequent years. Congressman Morris Udall (D-AZ), a prime mover of the legislation, wryly recalled

FIGURE 5.2.
Alaska embodied the decade's tension between developing fossil-fuel energy reserves and protecting wildlife and wild lands. A young bull moose crosses under
the Trans-Alaska Pipeline in January 1977. Courtesy Alaska State Library,
Trans-Alaska Pipeline Construction Collection, 1976–1977, ASL-P2-6-57.

visiting the state in the mid-1980s and getting a warmer reception than earlier: "Just like in the 70s, everyone waves at me, but
this time all five fingers are extended."[28]

While Lois Gibbs and other activists helped ground environmentalism in the immediacy of local settings in the United States,
there was no issue more inherently transnational and international. Pollution and global warming had no respect for national
boundaries. Indeed, Communist Party leaders of the Soviet bloc
were even less accountable to their peoples and did little to shield
them from the toxic wastes of their industrialized command
economies. Centralized authorities in the Communist countries
casually poisoned whole forests, river systems, and shorelines. By
the late 1980s, economic historian Barry Eichengreen wrote,
"wide swaths of Eastern Europe and the Soviet Union had become toxic wastelands." Air pollution ate away at the marble

exterior of the magnificent Acropolis in Athens, and Michelangelo's famed statue of David was moved indoors in Florence.[29]

But people everywhere began to resist this degradation of their air, water, and land, and they began to do so with particular vigor in the 1970s. After Sweden in 1967 and the United States in 1970 created the first national environmental agencies, other countries followed suit. The UN's first Conference on the Human Environment met in Stockholm in 1972. International environmental accords followed, including agreements on dumping at sea, on Antarctica, and on the Baltic and Mediterranean Seas, the latter leading to new municipal sewage treatment plants from Marseilles to Alexandria. Rampant smog convinced Japan to pass tough new anti-pollution laws in 1970, and Tokyo responded to the 1973 oil crisis by committing swiftly to energy conservation and the construction of dozens of new nuclear power and hydropower plants. New international organizations promoted global consciousness of environmental damage, most notably Greenpeace, founded in British Columbia, Canada, in 1970. In 1972, the Club of Rome, a Europe-based global think tank, issued a widely publicized report, *The Limits to Growth*, on the impossibility of indefinite unlimited economic growth in a world of finite natural resources. This widespread shift in awareness of the need for environmental protection around the early 1970s embodied one of the most significant popular political mobilizations of the century, originating in the industrialized centers of pollution but appearing elsewhere, too.[30]

While environmentalism became a burgeoning force in American politics and culture in the 1970s, much of its drive was diverted into individual lifestyle choices. It offered a potentially deeply subversive critique of the ascending values of radical individualism, particularly the idea of unrestricted free markets. As one of the most prominent earlier American conservationists, Aldo Leopold, wrote, "all ethics rest upon a single premise: that the individual is a member of a community of interdependent parts." But in practical terms, beyond an important set of new governmental restraints on the most egregious forms of pollution, no significant Green Party emerged to seriously challenge the growing deregulation of American capitalism. More radical environmentalists such as deep ecologists or Earth First! organizers remained few. Increased fuel efficiency was soon drowned in rising energy demands and larger cars. The foundations of modern American life—an oil-based, automobile-centered, suburban, industrial culture—remained largely unchanged. Instead, the new environmental consciousness became manifest primarily in a series of what were really consumer choices for healthier personal lifestyles: jogging and running, a decline in smoking, self-propelled outdoor recreation like hiking and cycling, outdoor education like Outward Bound, organic produce and gardening, health-food stores and restaurants, and the back-to-the-land movement. Such changes made great differences in the quality of life for individuals, an achievement not to be downplayed, but this shift unfolded within the parameters of the marketplace, creating profitable new corporations from Nike to Whole Foods, rather than reconfiguring the fundamental structure of an economy grounded in market values.[31]

Religious Resurgence at Home

The other force besides environmentalism that offered a potentially serious challenge to the new orthodoxy of inclusive market-oriented individualism was religion. The 1970s witnessed an extraordinary and unpredicted spiritual resurgence across the great monotheistic faiths, Christianity, Judaism, and Islam. This wave primarily took the form of fundamentalism, a vigorous and combative assertion of religious truth against increasingly secular, scientific, and materialistic societies. In the United States, the New Christian Right insisted on bringing certain biblical principles to bear on a policymaking sphere they believed was dominated by "secular humanism." These primarily Southern and Midwestern activists focused on issues of personal morality, particularly sexual behavior and prayer in schools. If a key feminist slogan in this era was "the personal is political," for these Christian evangelicals the personal was spiritual. They also embodied a commitment to being straightforward and earnest. While not lacking in humor, they tended to be serious because they saw the stakes of daily life as ultimately high: eternal life versus eternal damnation. They rejected the ironic stance of so much of modern life in the United States: the wink-wink knowingness, the common sexual innuendos, the moral relativism, the jaded sense in the backwash of the Vietnam War and the Watergate scandal that corruption was everywhere. They stood out for the clarity of their beliefs in an era defined by uncertainty. Conservative and evangelical Christians in fact affirmed that people were inherently corrupt— that is, sinful, or separated from God by their self-centeredness— but believed that salvation from sinfulness was readily available through committing one's life to following Jesus. "Accepting Jesus as your Lord and Savior" was the central phrase of the born-again movement, a choice to be made by each individual.[32]

Religious revivalism was, of course, not a new phenomenon in the United States in the 1970s. Waves of religious enthusiasm had washed across American soil for centuries, from the Pilgrims landing on the chilly shores of Cape Cod in the 1620s to the Second Great Awakening of the early 1800s. The phrase "fundamentalism" stemmed from the publication between 1910 and 1915 of a series of pamphlets explaining what the Presbyterian authors at Princeton Theological Seminary called the "Fundamentals" of the Christian faith, such doctrines as the virgin birth of Christ and the inerrancy of scripture, a response to the rise of liberal theology and the Social Gospel movement. Much of the language of the Cold War after 1945 contrasted American godliness with Soviet atheism. The mid-1950s saw "In God We Trust" inscribed on U.S. currency and "one nation under God" added to the Pledge of Allegiance. Evangelist Billy Graham's crusades won great publicity after 1949.[33]

It is nonetheless true that from the 1920s through the 1960s, Protestant fundamentalists tended to remove themselves from mainstream American culture and American politics. They sought purity in a largely separate and spiritually oriented culture, protected from the corrupting influences of worldly life. And it was this trend that began to change in the 1960s and

particularly the 1970s in direct response to certain developments: Supreme Court decisions removing prayer from public
schools, the sexual revolution, feminism, the gay rights movement, the explosive growth of pornography, and the legalization
of abortion. Fundamentalists now found some of their core values directly challenged by what they viewed as an aggressive
secularism, and they had to respond. Leaders of the New Christian Right also shared the broader conservative anxiety about an
American retreat from world leadership, seeing the United States,
for all its problems, as a crucial Christian influence in a hostile
and Communist-influenced international system. Pat Robertson
argued that "the Iranian captivity symbolized a growing sense of
the nation's helplessness before her enemies," while Jerry Falwell
declared that the United States was now "at the threshold of
destruction or surrender."[34]

The top-down organization of the New Christian Right, with
Falwell, Robertson, and other prominent television ministers al-
lying with politicians like Senator Jesse Helms, sometimes obscured the wide scope of evangelical Christianity in the United
States by the late 1970s, as well as that movement's place within
a still-broader popular quest for spiritual regrounding. The fundamentalist resurgence fit in with the capacious spirit of searching for authenticity and truth that helped define so much of
youth culture in the 1960s and early 1970s. Some found meaning in politics, from the Students for a Democratic Society (SDS)
on the left to Young Americans for Freedom (YAF) on the right.
Some sought insight by using psychedelic drugs. Others aimed
for the realm of the spirit, visible in the wide interest in Zen Bud-
dhism, Native American religious traditions, and new syncretis-
tic cults such as Jim Jones's Peoples' Temple of San Francisco,
which moved to Guyana and disappeared in a horrific act of collective suicide in 1979 (from following orders to drink poisoned
Kool-Aid—thus the subsequent phrase "drinking the Kool-Aid"
for any form of blind following of destructive leadership).

This collective search for truth was not restricted to young
people, and its greatest result by far was the new wave of evangelical Christianity, most of it in the form of fundamentalism and

much of it funneled into support for conservative political positions. In the mid-1970s, pollster George Gallup, Jr., found that one-third of adult Americans—50 million—described themselves as "born again," defined as having experienced "a turning point in your life when you committed yourself to Jesus Christ." While intensely individual experiences, these conversions took place most commonly within the community setting of the rapidly expanding evangelical and fundamentalist churches, not the declining mainline churches. The sense of community provided by these churches tended to be far stronger than in the moderate-to-liberal mainline Protestant congregations. Indeed, political scientist Robert Putnam described these churches as some of the most cohesive non-ethnic communities in America.[35]

A crucial step in the mobilization of conservative Christians in the political sphere came with a 1978 IRS ruling regarding the tax status of private schools established at or near the time of public school desegregation. So-called white-flight academies proliferated across the South in the 1960s and 1970s as a tactic to avoid racial integration. The IRS, with the approval of the administration of rural Georgian President Jimmy Carter, published new, stricter guidelines for private schools to prove their non-discriminatory policies and thus preserve their tax-advantaged position. This seemed to make basic sense: with racial discrimination now illegal, tax law should not favor institutions that continued to practice racial discrimination. But many conservative Christians saw private, explicitly Christian schools as not fundamentally about racial separation, but about educating their children with openly religious values rather than with the secular values of the now prayer-free public schools.

The debate about race versus religion in private schools in the South was complicated and not easily resolved. Conservative white Christians clearly viewed private schools and home-schooling as ways to defend themselves and their families against, as historian Joseph Crespino put it, the "pervasive and indiscriminate egalitarianism in modern America." In other words, racial integration constituted at least part of what threatened defenders of Christian private schools. The IRS ruling angered these fundamentalists, shattering their assumption that they could isolate themselves within their own institutions and teach what they wished to their own children, at least with the benefit of tax-free status. Long distrustful of the federal government, fundamentalists now saw themselves under attack and responded fiercely to defend their core values and identity.[36]

Fundamentalists were hardly the first Americans to believe their faith demanded political engagement. From its beginning, the Puritan settlement of Massachusetts sought to create a polity in line with God's commandments. Much subsequent political activism by people of faith looked closer to liberalism than conservatism, from the struggle to end slavery to the Social Gospel movement of helping the poor at the turn of the twentieth century. Christian campaigns for social justice reached a peak with the civil rights movement of the 1950s and 1960s, an effort rooted in Southern African American churches and prominently featuring clergymen as leaders. It was precisely the victory of such campaigns, along with the dramatic cultural shifts regarding youth, sexuality, and women, that tipped the balance of Christian political activism from left to right by the 1970s. At the height of civil rights campaigning in 1965, Falwell was still a segregationist, preaching that "we need to get off the streets and back into the pulpits and into our prayer rooms." This changed during the next ten years. Falwell turned his back on segregation, baptizing the first black members at Thomas Road Baptist Church and preaching in 1976 that "this idea of 'religion and politics don't mix' was invented by the devil to keep Christians from running their own country." In fact, the politics and policies of a leader now mattered much more than his personal religious practices. Falwell and most other evangelicals rejected the devout, born-again, long-married Carter in favor of the non-church-attending divorcé Ronald Reagan in the 1980 election.[37]

The New Christian Right mobilized supporters with the clarity of its vision. Fundamentalist leaders did not hem and haw. They did not hedge. What was wrong with America, they said, was the absence of prayer from schools and the presence of perverse and immoral sexual behavior almost everywhere, from pornography and heterosexual intercourse outside marriage to homosexuality and abortion. God's laws had been shoved aside in modern life, they believed. Richard Nixon was famous in this era for understanding the power of resentment in politics, of knowing who hates whom. There was equal power in knowing who hates what. Baptist minister and Arkansas governor Mike Huckabee would later campaign for the presidency in 2008 by frequently asserting, "I'm a conservative, but I'm not mad at anybody," a tacit acknowledgment of the rage associated with contemporary conservatism. In the 1970s, this anger focused on the new, less restrained sexual culture grounded in relative rather than absolute ethics. Evangelical intellectual Francis Schaeffer, in his influential 1976 book *How Then Should We Live?*, quoted former U.S. Supreme Court chief justice Fred Vinson on how "nothing is more certain in modern society than the principle that there are no absolutes." Schaeffer rejected "this curious mark of our age: The only absolute allowed is the absolute insistence that there is no absolute."[38]

A much smaller Christian Left continued to focus on public-sphere issues of peace and social justice rather than private-sphere issues of personal behavior. These activists ranged from Quakers and some Roman Catholics, to mainline Protestant denominations such as the United Church of Christ and Episcopalians, to the intentional Christian community that moved from Chicago to Washington, DC, in 1975, known as Sojourners. The collective sins of racial inequality, poverty, and war troubled them most deeply of all. Organizers on the religious Left and Right used fundamentally different frames of reference for how to address the issue of godly living: the context of the broader society and its socioeconomic structures, versus the context of the individual. The New Christian Right was not unconcerned with poverty and the Christian Left did care about individual ethical behavior, of course. This was not a case of complete opposites, but of radically different emphases in how to apply the Christian gospel to the sphere of daily life. While Sojourners leader Jim Wallis railed against child poverty rates that were "appalling in the richest nation in world history," Pat Robertson denounced feminism and homosexuality as scourges of modern American life. The New Christian Right generally celebrated the accumulation of wealth and found its support in rural, small-town, and suburban places, while Sojourners "shared a commitment to live and work in a poor urban neighborhood."[39]

In the long sweep of American history, nothing was more remarkable about the New Christian Right than the alliance created between fundamentalist Protestants and conservative Catholics. Distrust of Catholics had long been near the core of Protestant American identity, and anti-Catholic sentiment had nearly helped defeat John Kennedy's presidential bid in 1960. Being Catholic in the United States in the 1950s meant an awareness of being part of a minority held apart from the mainstream by its beliefs, rituals, and food taboos. But Catholic distinctiveness diminished rapidly in the next two decades, swept away by a Cold War emphasis on a common "Judeo-Christian tradition" and Catholic anticommunism, and by the rising tide of egalitarian inclusiveness from the 1960s onward. The reforms of the Vatican II conferences reduced Catholic-Protestant differences by having priests face the congregation and speak in English rather than Latin. Attendance at confession declined, as did the avoidance of meat on Fridays. Catholics were encouraged to no longer hold themselves separate from the societies in which they lived. The Vatican downplayed some of the rigid hierarchy of Catholicism, emphasizing the Church as "the people of God" moving through history rather than an unchanging hierarchical pyramid with Rome at the apex. American lay Catholics' accelerating assimilation was also evident on issues of birth control, where they began to act as though the celibate Pope and clergy perhaps did not know much about sex. By the end of the 1970s, Catholics for the first time were using contraceptives as frequently as other Americans.[40]

Abortion provided the lynchpin for the new coalition of fundamentalists and conservative Catholics. The Catholic hierarchy opposed the *Roe v. Wade* decision of 1973 from the beginning, but conservative Protestants were slower on the uptake. In fact, the Southern Baptist Convention had passed a mildly pro-abortion rights resolution two years earlier and reaffirmed it in 1974. Evangelical theologian Harold O. J. Brown explained that "a lot of Protestants reacted almost automatically—'If the Catholics are for it, we should be against it.'" But the Southern Baptists and other Protestants were in the midst of a rapid sea change, as fundamentalist leaders began to see abortion as closely related to the other sexual and gender issues they saw corrupting the nation, particularly homosexuality and feminism. Theologian Francis Schaeffer provided crucial leadership in this transition to what he called "co-belligerency," or working closely with conservatives of whatever religious beliefs on common moral issues. "If I live in a suburb and suddenly the sewer system begins to back up into the water system and all my neighbors are atheists," Schaeffer wrote, using an apt pollution metaphor, "it does not mean we cannot sign a petition together or go to the city council or the mayor, to say we want our water system fixed. I do not have to wait for them to become Christians [or evangelicals] to do that. It is the same for the issues we are discussing. We should be glad for every co-belligerent who will stand beside us." With secular humanism as a common enemy, conservative Protestants and Catholics joined political forces and sometimes shared mutual admiration. Falwell, for example, spoke of his hopes for the college he had founded in Lynchburg: "Liberty Baptist College is becoming to fundamentalist young people what Notre Dame is to Catholics."[41]

The Roman Catholic Church both internationally and in the United States began to move to the right in the late 1970s. Traditional Catholics were unhappy about many of the Vatican II reforms, which seemed to them to go too far in accommodating the institution of the Church to the mores of current society. Traditionalists were even less pleased with the rise of liberation theology in Latin America by the late 1960s, with its core belief that the Church should take a "preferential option for the poor." Many priests in the region began condemning economic injustice and militarism, sometimes using the language of Marxist analysis. The liberation theology movement within the Church reached a high-water mark with the Sandinista victory in Nicaragua in 1979 and the wave of support that followed the murder of Archbishop Oscar Romero in El Salvador a year later. But the elevation of Archbishop Karol Wojtyla of Cracow, Poland, to the papacy as John Paul II in 1978 changed all that. The first non-Italian Pope in 455 years, John Paul II was a man of great charisma and in essence a Roman Catholic fundamentalist, a fierce defender of the traditional Church and a multilingual, evangelical promoter of Catholicism around the world. He rejected any changes to the all-male and celibate nature of the Catholic priesthood, and he spoke passionately against abortion. His Polish background shaped his unstinting anticommunism; he moved quickly to winnow out liberation theology supporters by appointing traditionalists to influential positions within the Church's hierarchy. John Paul II stood out for his straightforward defense of the Christian faith and his opposition to the avowed godlessness of Communist governments.[42]

How did the new religious resurgence in the United States mesh with the rising hyper-individualism of inclusive egalitarianism and market values? It was not immediately obvious that it should fit very well. Columnist James Kilpatrick wrote in 1978 that he and other social conservatives "believe that a civilized society demands orders and classes, that men are not inherently equal." Laissez-faire capitalism made sense to entrepreneurial conservatives, but religious conservatives seemed more concerned about improving and enforcing personal moral behavior—and enforcement typically required more government, not less. The business wing of the developing Republican coalition talked about the freedom of individuals from government restrictions and taxation, but conservative Catholics and Protestants spoke of the family, not free-floating individuals, as the central pillar of society, the crucial bulwark to defend. Evangelical Christians across the political spectrum shared Jim Wallis's concern that America "becomes less and less communal every day," a casualty of "a harsh and cruel individualism." Faith was, of course, a personal and individual matter, but serious followers of Jesus had to wrestle with his condemnations of luxury, exploitation, and wealth, and his commandments to care for the poor and focus on the well-being of others. The Pope regularly criticized what he saw as the injustices in capitalist societies like that of the United States. Francis Schaeffer warned against "a life made up of things, things, and more things—a success judged by an ever-higher level of material abundance."[43]

A quick survey of Christianity's traditional "seven deadly sins" suggests potential conflicts with the market's purpose of meeting appetites of all kinds. Lust? Pornography abounded. Gluttony? Fast food fed the obesity epidemic. Greed? Materialism was rampant. Pride? People deserved what they had—or did not have. Envy? Competition anchored the market. Sloth? Perhaps this was an exception, since the market values seemed generally to promote diligence and effort, but gambling, at least, along with the growth of the financial markets struck many observers as shifts away from traditional production of goods of value. Wrath? Violence filled American films and shaped the more liberal use of profanity in daily language.

In addition to the libertarian values of the market, the new formal equality in American life also made conservative Christians uneasy. They considered obedience—to God—central to the Christian life. They had long valued traditional social hierarchies and deference to authorities, including the deference of young to old, female to male, poor to rich, and—in many cases—nonwhite to white. In the mid-1970s, 98 percent of opponents of the Equal Rights Amendment, male and female, were church members. The Catholic priesthood remained exclusively male, and eleven o'clock on Sunday morning generally carried on, observers noted, as the most segregated hour in America.[44]

But most of the elements of the religious resurgence made their peace with the new individualism, more readily with its market values than with its egalitarianism. They accepted, at least in principle, the formal equality of all people, though they tended to oppose governmental efforts to redress historic patterns of discrimination, such as school busing. In 1978, the conservative Church of Jesus Christ of the Latter-Day Saints (Mormons) finally eliminated its prohibition on people of color in positions of leadership, in step with its expansion of membership outside the United States and particularly into Latin America and Africa. In order to support their families, fundamentalist Protestant and conservative Catholic women went to work outside the home in growing numbers, exposing themselves to less hierarchical and less deferential environments and practices. Abortion opponents framed their argument as a defense of the lives of individual unborn children, a human rights imperative. And for all their hierarchical social traditions, evangelicals and fundamentalists were radically egalitarian in one crucial sense: they believed that each individual had equal access to God, and each individual soul was equally valuable in God's eyes. "You may be rich or poor," Bob Dylan sang in "Gotta Serve Somebody," a 1979 hit song during his born-again period, "but you're gonna have to serve somebody. Well, it may be the devil or it may be the Lord, but you're gonna have to serve somebody."[45]

Conservative religious activists adapted themselves readily to the values of free enterprise. From their decades of separatist culture, fundamentalists distrusted government already, and further disliked liberal policies regarding racial and sexual equality that they associated with Washington. As black Americans were increasingly included in the public realm of government programs, traditionally segregationist whites, many of them fundamentalists, found the private sphere even more attractive. They also felt that a secular government should not replace the religious community in providing for the needy. "Welfarism has grown because Americans have forgotten to tithe and give offerings," Jerry Falwell declared. The New Christian Right tended to associate economic success with spiritual salvation, with God granting material blessings to God's disciplined followers. "The New Christian Right of the 1970s and 1980s," Bethany Moreton concluded in her recent history of the Wal-Mart Corporation and Christian free enterprise, "combined religious efforts to regulate sex with an equally religious celebration of material comforts, self-expression, technological innovation, and secular success." The new suburban mega-churches that sprouted in the 1970s also embodied the customer-friendly style of American businesses with their emphasis on ease of access and ancillary services beyond just worship. Southern California even had one purely drive-in church, where worshippers did not get out of their cars. The ichthys, or Christian fish symbol, became a popular bumper sticker in this era. For Christian conservatives as for most Americans, Moreton observed, the free-market vision beginning in the 1970s "acquired over thirty-five years the status of common sense—a fact of nature as self-evident as gravity and considerably more certain than evolution." The blessing a Wal-Mart cashier accidentally but revealingly offered over her family's breakfast one morning summed this up: "Dear Father, we thank you for shopping Wal-Mart."[46]

Religious Resurgence in Israel

The story of renewed religious identity and organization in the 1970s was not confined to the United States or to Protestants and Roman Catholics. This development took shape as well across the varied landscapes of monotheism, including the Jewish state of Israel and the Muslim lands stretching from Morocco to Indonesia. Both Islamists and the Israeli settler movement came to prominence a generation after Arab independence and Israeli independence, both evidence of growing unhappiness with the rule of post-independence elites.

In Israel, three wars created a series of fears and opportunities. The 1948 war of independence established the modern state of Israel within borders that were difficult to defend against surrounding enemies. The country's narrow waist of just a dozen miles was vulnerable to an attack that might cut the nation in two. The Six-Day War of 1967 left Israel in control of territory more than three times larger than Israel's initial size, including Palestinian lands of the West Bank, Gaza, the Golan Heights, and East Jerusalem. Some euphoric Israelis saw this stunning development as God's blessing for the creation of a Greater Israel, and they initiated settlements in these Occupied Territories, with the tacit support of the Israeli government. Then the October War of 1973 saw Israel almost overrun, the country's very existence threatened in a way that inevitably reminded its citizens of the Holocaust a generation earlier. The long-ruling Labor Party was thrown onto the defensive, paving the way for the conservative, religious Likud coalition to win national elections in 1977. For a new generation of young, devout Israelis, the close call of the 1973 war was a warning to conquer and annex what they called "The Whole Land of Israel," from the Jordan River to the Mediterranean Sea including all the Occupied Territories, in order to provide defense in depth against future invasions, and to replace secularism in Israel with an aggressive religious form of Zionism.[47]

Bearded, skullcapped young Israeli men carrying rifles and rabbinical texts began spending the night in the Occupied Territories in the first months after the conclusion of the 1973 war. They and their supporters called themselves Gush Emunim, or Bloc of the Faithful. They seized attention by outmaneuvering Israeli troops in the territories, and by marching through Arab towns with the Israeli flag, puncturing tires and breaking windows. Their settlements proliferated across Palestinian lands, surrounding and penetrating hostile Palestinian populations. Eager for confrontation, Gush Emunim quickly emerged as the central radical religious and political movement in Israel. Gush Emunim activists sought to replace the current predominantly secular version of Zionism with a renewed religious version. They believed the opportunity from the 1967 war had almost been lost in 1973, and Jews now had to move swiftly to assure the defense of a Greater Israel. In words that echoed Islamists' concern for the Koranic law of sharia, Gush Emunim declared its goal "to elevate the Torah to a level at which it will no longer be an article of religion, manifested solely through synagogue services and study, but rather function as a platform for actual praxis of farmers and soldiers."[48]

The efforts of Gush Emunim and other settlers to accustom Israelis to the idea of the territories as Jewish land received a major boost from the election of Menachem Begin and Likud in 1977. Begin supported annexation of the West Bank. The young radicals actually found their influence diminishing, however, once the new prime minister took office, as they found themselves differing with Likud on tactical issues regarding negotiations with the Arab states. But their activism had without doubt helped shift the entire tenor of Israeli politics regarding the Occupied Territories during the critical years of the mid-1970s. They had created new "facts on the ground," particularly in the West Bank, that made any future Israeli withdrawal vastly more complicated and unlikely. In addition, their conservative religious perspective made them openly critical of secular Western materialism and the pursuit of individual self-fulfillment. They called instead for a renewed obedience to God's commandments in a reinvigorated community of Jewish faithfulness.[49]

Not all devout Orthodox Jews agreed with the settlement projects for expanding the state of Israel. Some even opposed Zionism itself for creating a secular state that claimed the loyalty of Jews whom they believed should be loyal only to God. They preferred to wait for God alone to reestablish a righteous nation of Israel. The ultra-Orthodox, or haredim (from the Hebrew term for "tremble," as in "you who tremble at His word," from the book of Isaiah), distinguished themselves not only from gentiles but also from most Jews by their distinctive attire, pious attitudes, and dissenting worldview. They rejected the compromise of most contemporary Jews who accommodated themselves to modern life while preserving elements of a distinct Jewish culture. They tended instead to look back to pre-modern Eastern Europe, before the Enlightenment and the pogroms and the Holocaust, as the ideal Jewish society of authentic religious practice. The haredim were small in number: 30 percent of Orthodox Jews, who were themselves just 15 percent of the world's 12 million Jews, who were in turn only a small fraction of 1 percent of the world's population. But the haredim had disproportionate influence in Israel as a visible minority who reminded religious Jews of the dangers of too close identification and cooperation with the state of Israel. And they shared with other devout Jews a commitment to the values of the spirit, not of the marketplace, and to the practice of community and "a rejection of emphasis on the freedom of the individual," as historians Samuel Heilman and Menachem Friedman wrote.[50]

The religious resurgence in Israel in the 1970s received enthusiastic support from three important constituencies in the United States. First, the U.S. government shifted from what had been a sometimes prickly relationship in the past with Israel to a close strategic alliance in this decade. Israel's anticommunism and growing regional military might made it an attractive balance against Arab regimes with links to the Soviets, such as in Iraq and Syria. Second, fundamentalist Christians began overcoming their historic anti-Semitism, in an era of rapidly diminishing discrimination against Jewish Americans, to identify increasingly with Israel as a pro-American and anticommunist society. The New Christian Right believed that Israel had a role of ultimate eschatological significance to play: it would be the site of God's final battle and victory at Armageddon, the precursor to the Second Coming of Christ. Third, Jewish Americans in this decade significantly strengthened their identification with Israel and its fate. Neoconservatives, who were disproportionately Jewish (though most American Jews remained liberals), vigorously promoted the closer U.S.-Israeli strategic ties visible in the crucial American resupply of military equipment that helped Israel survive the 1973 war. Israel came to figure more prominently in the public discourse of the Jewish-American community, whose number of five million was roughly equivalent to the number of Jews in Israel. The overwhelming majority of the world's Jews lived in either Israel or the United States.[51]

Jewish-American support for Israel had, of course, been very important from that nation's establishment in 1948, but emotional ties to the Zionist project grew significantly more intense between the late 1960s and the late 1970s. First came the spectacular victory and expansion in the 1967 Six-Day War, stunning observers everywhere and evoking pride in Jews abroad. Then the near-destruction of Israel in the 1973 October War scared Jews in the United States, who had begun taking Israel's existence for granted, and rallied them to its defense.

Historian Peter Novick demonstrated the remarkable, and

somewhat delayed, attention to the Holocaust that emerged in American society in the 1970s, among both Jews and gentiles. For the first twenty years after 1945, Jewish Americans had tended to focus their energies on American society, working for and savoring rapid advances in assimilation and declines in discrimination. They were not victims of the Nazis, not primarily supporters of a distant Middle Eastern nation, not unwanted immigrants, but mainstream and remarkably successful American citizens. "No group in American society shared more wholeheartedly in this ebullient [postwar] mood than American Jews," Novick has written. The shift to greater memorializing of the Holocaust followed this era of strengthening Jewish stature in the United States and ultimately took the form of the United States Holocaust Memorial Museum in Washington, DC, chartered in 1980 by a unanimous act of Congress. Novick showed that the new attention to the Holocaust during the 1970s probably had little impact on actual U.S. government policy toward Israel, determined as it was primarily by strategic considerations, but the shift helped explain some of the powerful Jewish-American support for Israel in an era of expanding Israeli settlements and resurgent Jewish religious identity.[52]

The appearance of a revived Jewish fundamentalism during the 1970s remained, ultimately, a minor note in the lively symphony of Israeli society and in Jewish-American life. Haredim and the Orthodox activists of Gush Emunim—colonizers, as they were seen outside Israel—helped push Israeli politics to the right, and settlers in the Palestinian territories played an important role in hindering a peaceful solution to the core Israeli-Palestinian conflict over land and thereby contributed to the eventual growth of Muslim fundamentalism in Palestine in the form of Hamas. In addition, devout Jewish dissenters did not share the egalitarianism and market fundamentalism that was spreading in the United States and in much of the rest of the world in this era, and they yearned for greater community rather than unfettered individualism. But their activism did not undo the vitality of capitalism in Israel and its thriving market system, just as it did not alter the enthusiastically secular and individualistic character of so much of Israeli life. In similar fashion, the disproportionate success of Jewish Americans in the spheres of business and finance suggested thorough comfort with the growing market orientation of American life.

Religious Resurgence in the Muslim World

While religious fundamentalism helped reshape the contours of American and Israeli life in the 1970s, it became most powerfully associated with Muslim-majority countries in the arc of Islam from Morocco to Indonesia. Muslim fundamentalism arose from believers' acute awareness of the conflict between the true religion God had appointed and the actual historical development of the world God theoretically controlled. That actual world of modern nations was profoundly secular and dominated by non-Muslim nations—by unbelievers. Indeed, fundamentalists, though they yearned for an imagined pious past, represented a distinctly modern phenomenon themselves as a reaction against the crushing impact of the modernity project in colonized Muslim lands. European domination for more than a century had valued science, rationality, and technology, while marginalizing Islam and identifying it with backwardness, a far cry from Islamic culture's earlier status in the medieval era as home to the most sophisticated and advanced societies. Islam scholar Bruce Lawrence argued that fundamentalism in the Islamic lands "represents a delayed reaction to the psychological hegemony of European colonial rule" and could only appear in postcolonial, independent Muslim-majority nation-states. Islamic religious revival shared many features with other fundamentalisms, but it emerged in a different situation. Rather than trying to establish a niche in pluralist societies, it sought to rekindle entire societies' identity as Muslim, emphasizing their common heritage and sense of membership in a transnational umma, or community of the faithful.[53]

Hasan al-Banna was the founding father of Islamic fundamentalism. This young Egyptian trained as a teacher in Cairo and took his first job in the town of Ismailia in the Suez Canal Zone in the 1920s. A devout Sufi Muslim, al-Banna was dismayed by the degradation of the Muslims there, who were mired in poverty while the British and other Western expatriate residents lived in luxury and paid little attention to the local workers. Al-Banna admired Western science and technology but loathed the secular thrust of Western cultural dominance in Egypt, particularly its emphasis on alcohol and sexuality. "Just after the First World War and during my stay in Cairo," he wrote, "the wave of atheism and lewdness engulfed Egypt. It started the devastation of religion and morality on the pretext of individual and intellectual freedom. Nothing could stop this storm." These were moral concerns that Protestant fundamentalists in the United States in the same era shared. The West seemed to al-Banna to be on a new crusade to destroy Islam through corruption and unbelief. Europeans and Americans had "imported their half-naked women into these regions, together with their liquors, their theaters, their dance halls, their amusements, their stories, their newspapers, their novels, their whims, their silly games, and their vices." Worse than previous military campaigns, al-Banna concluded, was the European establishment of schools and cultural institutes "in the very heart of the Islamic domain, which cast doubt and heresy into the souls of its sons and taught them how to demean themselves, disparage their religion and their fatherland, divest themselves of their traditions and beliefs, and to regard as sacred anything Western."[54]

Al-Banna met this challenge in 1928 by gathering like-minded Egyptians into a new organization called the Society of Muslim Brothers, or Muslim Brotherhood. Their project was not one of political violence nor military revolution, but education. They sought to teach the nation anew the ways of Islam and thus produce a gradual reformation, a return of Egypt and all other Muslim-majority lands to their own religious and cultural traditions. The Muslim Brothers aimed to free Islamic nations from Western control by first bringing about a revolution in people's hearts and minds. They shared with their secular nationalist countrymen a rejection of European dominance, and secular nationalist leaders in Egypt and elsewhere at times tried to accommodate the Muslim Brotherhood and its spread to other Arab countries in the region. But al-Banna and his comrades had a very different goal in mind from that of secular politicians like Gamal Abdul Nasser, the Arab nationalist ruler of Egypt from 1954 to 1970. Nasser sought to modernize Egypt with hydroelectric power, literacy and film programs, nationalized industries, and a ban on the hijab and other traditional Islamic attire. He emphasized Arab socialism, a vision of strong modern states allied together under the umbrella of a secular Arab identity. The Muslim Brothers, by contrast, promoted a devout Islamic identity, and they came to embody the foremost opposition to the government in Egypt and neighboring lands. They built a thriving counterculture based on religious education and social welfare provision that helped undercut some of the legitimacy of the Egyptian state.[55]

Facing repression from the state, some Muslim Brothers took up arms and shifted from reform to revolution in 1948. In response, assassins gunned down Hasan al-Banna in 1949. In his place, intellectual and spiritual leadership shifted to Sayyid Qutb, who had just returned that year to Egypt from a two-year sojourn in the United States to study educational administration. The courtly, sensitive writer and teacher was dismayed by what he found there: a culture obsessed with material gratification and sensuality. Even in the church-filled and alcohol-free small town of Greeley, Colorado, where he was enrolled in the graduate program of the Colorado State College of Education (now the University of Northern Colorado), Qutb was appalled by what he viewed as Americans' vulgarity and the promiscuity evident even in church dances. He acknowledged that "the New World . . . is spellbinding" in its sheer vitality and wealth, but this was precisely what made it so dangerous in its potential allure to innocent Muslims. The very modernism of the United States offended Qutb, its secular materialism, individualism, and mixing of the sexes polluting the true religious faith he sought. "Humanity makes the gravest of errors and risks losing account of its morals," Qutb concluded, "if it makes America its model."[56]

Back home in Egypt, Qutb railed against Nasser's new secular regime and became a frequent sojourner in Nasser's grim prisons, where he was eventually executed for treason in 1966. Along the way, Qutb refined his analysis of the problem facing true Muslims. There was a broad, historic corruption afoot. Westerners had infused the region with their foreign cultures; the Ottoman Empire had vanished, abolishing in 1924 the Islamic caliphate and the Muslim unity it embodied; and the Soviet Union had imposed atheistic Communist rule on the Muslims across Central Asia. Now that Nasser ruled in Cairo, foreign domination itself was no longer the foremost danger. The central problem was that Islam, under secular nationalist rulers, had now fallen back into a state of "jahiliyya," the term for pre-Islamic pagan Arabia. The Indian Muslim revivalist Maulana Maududi had used the same term in the 1930s, and Qutb now made it central to Islamic fundamentalist analysis. True Muslims in the late twentieth century constituted a small minority in a secular world surrounded by only nominal and hypocritical "believers." The situation demanded a total revival of true Islam.[57]

Qutb's execution made him a martyr to many, and his influence only grew stronger in the difficult years that followed his death. His brother and fellow teacher, Muhammad, left Egypt for the safety of Saudi Arabia, where the students he affected most greatly at King Abdul Aziz University in Jedda included the young Osama bin Laden, already under the influence of the Muslim Brotherhood there. Ayman al-Zawahiri, the founder of Egyptian Islamic Jihad and later bin Laden's closest colleague in al-Qaeda, was determined to put Qutb's vision into action. A year after Qutb's death, the swift and utter victory of the Israeli military over the combined forces of Egypt, Syria, and Jordan in the 1967 Six-Day War cast a pall over these and other primarily Muslim nations. The expansion of Israeli rule into more Arab lands underlined the weakness of Arab nationalist governments from Cairo to Damascus. The limited employment opportunities for educated young people in these nations highlighted the lack of economic growth under secular Arab regimes. A generation after independence from colonialism, most Middle Eastern

governments seemed to offer their people only stagnant economies, bloated bureaucracies, authoritarian rule, and political repression. The oil crises of the 1970s exacerbated these problems
for nations such as Egypt that lacked major oil resources. Religious critics of the secular regimes grew more numerous and
prominent, from South Asia, where Pakistan's government adopted much of the fundamentalist vision, to North Africa, where
Egyptian jihadists in the military assassinated Nasser's successor, Anwar Sadat, in 1981. The explosion of Saudi Arabian oil
wealth after 1973 enabled Riyadh to fund strict Wahhabi Muslim schools abroad and promote Islamization across the region,
as the Al Saud family sought to preserve its own rule by buying
off potential religious dissenters at home. Secular authoritarianism was ebbing. Islamist revivalism flowed in to take its place.[58]

Islamism, the modern project to create radical Islamic governments, found its first and most significant success in Iran.
Enduring historical and theological differences divided the minority of Shi'a Muslims, centered in Iran, from the large majority of Sunni Muslims, particularly for religious fundamentalists
who considered such matters crucial to their identity. But the
goals of Sunni and Shi'ite revivalists were quite similar and part
of the same wave of rejection of secular Middle Eastern governments and Western influence. Shah Reza Pahlavi of Iran embodied such regimes. While claiming to be a devout Muslim, the
Shah owed his rule to the Americans who had returned him to
power in a 1953 coup. He remained very close to the United
States thereafter. The CIA maintained a huge presence in Tehran
and helped train SAVAK, the Shah's political police that was
infamous for its repression and torture of political dissidents,
including Islamists. In what he called the "White Revolution,"
the Shah sought for years to modernize Iran by buying elements
of an industrial economy from Western contractors and by eliminating vestiges of traditional, rural Iranian culture, such as the
veiling of women. Skyrocketing oil revenues in the 1970s made
the Shah unimaginably wealthy, but while he pampered his elite
supporters, called the "petro-bourgeoisie" by some critics, the
vast majority of Iranians remained poor and increasingly un-

happy with their circumstances in a nation that was piling up new wealth.[59]

The imminent victory of a diverse coalition of revolutionaries convinced the Shah in January 1979 to flee to Egypt, where he was welcomed by Anwar Sadat, another sign to Islamists of Sadat's secular character. Ayatollah Ruhollah Khomeini returned from exile abroad to lead the new government in Tehran. The ascetic Shi'ite cleric squeezed out leftist and centrist secular elements of the revolution, as he created the first theocratic state in the modern world. Khomeini was a charismatic and revered figure in Iran, "the most handsome old man I had ever met in my life," recalled Italian journalist Oriana Fallaci. "He resembled the 'Moses' sculpted by Michelangelo." Indeed, "people loved him too much. They saw in him another Prophet." The deep resentment Khomeini and his followers felt for the U.S. support of the Shah boiled over in the fall of 1979, when President Carter allowed the exiled ruler into New York for cancer treatment. Iranians wanted him returned home to stand trial. Radical student supporters of Khomeini then overran the U.S. embassy in Tehran and seized dozens of hostages, whom they held for over a year. Americans were enraged and humiliated. But most Iranians, who had long suffered under the Shah, had little sympathy. "We didn't expect Carter to defend the shah, for he is a religious man who raised the slogan of defending human rights," Ayatollah Husain Montazeri told an interviewer. "How can Carter, the devout Christian, defend the shah?" To the new government in Iran, everything American seemed corrupt, from its political leaders to its secular and hedonistic popular culture. And Khomeini's vision did not stop at Iran's borders. He sought to spread Islamist revolution throughout the region. Not since the Bolshevik Revolution of 1917 in Russia had the West been so ideologically challenged.[60]

In the same year that Shi'ite revolutionaries seized control of Iran, one of the two largest oil-producing nations in the world, Sunni Islamists almost did the same in Saudi Arabia, the other largest producer, just across the Persian Gulf. A small army of fervent Muslim rebels infiltrated and occupied the Grand

Mosque in Mecca and held it for two weeks, before the Saudi military was finally able to retake the vast complex with the covert assistance of French security advisers. The rebels viewed the ruling al-Saud family much as Egyptian jihadists saw Sadat's government: nominally Muslim, but ultimately secular and corrupted by deals with Israel and the West. This was what Sayyid Qutb had called jahiliyya, the corruption of Islam by Muslims themselves. And the Saudi case was even more portentous, for Saudi Arabia was not only the holder of the largest oil reserves in the world, but also the keeper of the two holiest places in Islam, Mecca and Medina. The rebels' sustained military campaign revealed the fragility of the Saudi government and the potential for further Islamist revolutions across the region. In Pakistan, a mob attacked and burned the U.S. embassy compound, murdering one American and nearly killing over one hundred more. In Saudi Arabia, the official religious authorities made a de facto pact with the country's rulers to support them in retaking the Grand Mosque, in exchange for the al-Saud family ending any further liberalization of Saudi society and using oil revenues to help spread Wahhabi Islam abroad.[61]

The Saudi Arabian and Pakistani governments were the largest outside supporters of the Afghan mujahidin, the Islamist rebels who had been fighting the Communist regime in Kabul since late 1978. The United States had also begun secretly aiding the mujahidin in July 1979. The Soviets were, in turn, determined to preserve Communist rule in Afghanistan, certain that they could not afford any further spread of Islamist revolution toward their own Muslim-majority Central Asian republics. The Soviet invasion in December 1979 set Afghanistan on the path to a generation of warfare and the eventual creation in 1996 of a particularly severe Islamist regime, the Taliban, whose Department of the Promotion of Virtue and the Prevention of Vice suggested— by its very name—their utter rejection of the secular individualism of Western capitalist society. Women, in particular, suffered grievously under the Taliban's rule. Carter's fiercely anti-Soviet national security adviser Zbigniew Brzezinski rejected the suggestion of an interviewer in 1998 that U.S. assistance to Islamists had turned out to be a poor choice. "What is more important to the history of the world? The Taliban or the collapse of the Soviet empire? Some stirred-up Muslims or the liberation of Central Europe and the end of the cold war?" While the demise of the USSR and the eclipse of the Cold War certainly marked an extraordinary moment in world history, the answer to Brzezinski's rhetorical question may or may not prove, in the long run, to be as obvious as he supposed. "Stirred-up Muslims" continued to provide the most powerful, committed, and widespread resistance to the egalitarian and market-driven individualism of the United States.[62]

JIMMY CARTER AS A MAN OF HIS TIMES

To Americans who lived through the 1970s, Jimmy Carter is a familiar if complicated figure. He served as president from 1977 to 1981, the first native of the Deep South to do so since Woodrow Wilson. He gained a reputation as, variously, an idealist, an industrious micro-manager, a global peacemaker, a weak leader, a victim of difficult circumstances, a conservative, a liberal, and the most internationally respected former U.S. president. About one aspect of Carter there was little doubt. "I have been accused of being an outsider and I plead guilty," he declared in a campaign advertisement in 1976. After a string of presidents who came to the job with experience in the federal government that stretched back more than sixty years, Carter became the first of a new breed from outside the Capitol Beltway, most of them, like Carter, former state governors. "Is he a true populist from something called the New South or yet another creature of the Eastern Establishment?" journalist Robert Scheer asked.[63]

Culturally, at least, Carter seemed to embody much of the non-judgmental diversity of the 1970s. He was very Southern and a serious evangelical Christian, yet, as his close political aide Hamilton Jordan noted, he did not seem self-righteous to those who knew him well. Rather, they considered him open-minded and generally tolerant of the different attitudes and behaviors of some of his young staff regarding matters such as sex and alcohol. In fact, Carter can be understood as an emblematic figure of the decade's major intellectual and cultural developments. The former peanut farmer and businessman believed in racial and gender equality and in human rights, while he also helped move the country onto a path of pro-entrepreneurial deregulation. At the same time, he shared many of the critiques of the new hyper-individualism with other environmentalists and religious enthusiasts. In a manner reminiscent of the title character of the popular film *Forrest Gump* (1994), who managed to pop up at major points throughout recent U.S. history, Carter carried within him the perspectives and sympathies of the ascending values in American public life, along with the hesitancies and dissents of the most thoughtful critics. It was no surprise that some observers found him sometimes vacillating or uncertain.[64]

The new formal equality in American life fit Jimmy Carter like a glove. The president with the diminutive first name who walked rather than rode in his inaugural parade, who preferred to carry his own bag, who disliked the honorific tune "Hail to the Chief," had strong egalitarian tendencies. He had grown up in segregated southwestern Georgia, the son of a successful farmer and businessman. His early racial moderation did not match the radicalism of the integrated Christian farming community of Koinonia seven miles away (led by Hamilton Jordan's uncle, Clarence Jordan), but the civil rights movement in his home state in the 1950s and 1960s helped free him up. As governor, he made the symbolic gesture of installing a portrait of Martin Luther King, Jr., in the rotunda of the state capitol in Atlanta, and opened state government to many more black employees. Carter developed close ties with Andrew Young, King's former assistant and a U.S. Congressman from Georgia, and other black leaders in Atlanta, and he won the 1976 Democratic primaries and the general election with strong majorities of African American voters.[65]

Carter's egalitarianism extended to changing gender roles, particularly for a white Southern male of his generation. He and his wife Rosalynn were genuine partners, and she became an unusually influential informal presidential adviser in the White House. Carter appointed an unprecedented number of women to his administration and the federal judiciary, including some outspoken feminists. And he made human rights a rhetorical centerpiece of his administration's foreign policy, evidenced in the new human rights office in the State Department and Andrew Young's appointment as ambassador to the United Nations. That he chose to deemphasize human rights with certain friendly governments—Iran under the Shah and China, among others—in order to preserve important security relationships limits but does not erase the importance of his promotion of human rights. At heart, Carter had profound internationalist sympathies, as the decades of peace and development work of his post-presidential career further revealed. In his Christian internationalist fashion, he believed that other peoples were inherently neither better nor worse than the American people, a fairly radical opinion for a U.S. president in the Cold War. Americans, he contended, had "no special claim to be God's chosen people."[66]

Just as Carter approved of the new egalitarian inclusiveness in American life, so, too, did he promote the turn to market values. Before entering politics, he had managed the family business of producing and marketing the essential ingredient in the all-American peanut butter sandwich. This was a president who understood intimately the details of profit margins, amortization, business taxes, and government inspections. Carter brought to the White House a depth of entrepreneurial experience and knowledge not seen there since Herbert Hoover fifty years earlier. He also entered the presidency in an era of stagflation and soaring energy costs, with a palpable national sense that the country could not afford to just continue along as before. He was the first Democratic chief executive since 1932 to lack a strong commitment to such New Deal norms as Keynesian economics and labor union support. Even more, he did not share the New Deal order's enthusiasm for the positive possibilities of government.

Carter emphasized the limits of federal resources. In sharp contrast to the last Democratic president, Lyndon Johnson, Carter declared in his first state of the union address: "Government cannot eliminate poverty or provide a bountiful economy or reduce inflation or save our cities or cure illiteracy or provide energy. And government cannot mandate goodness." Such pragmatic and moral initiatives had to come from the private sector instead, unleashed through market incentives. "I was eager," he recalled in his memoirs, to "deregulate banks, airlines, trucking, communications, and railways."[67]

Carter embodied the egalitarian, market-oriented individualism that was gaining ascendance in the United States at the time, but he also shared many of the values of its environmentalist and religious critics. His love of the natural world was grounded in a childhood life on a farm and in the woods of southwestern Georgia where he hunted and fished. He came to national politics with one of the strongest gubernatorial records on protecting natural resources. The green color of his 1976 campaign buttons foreshadowed early emphases of his presidential administration: the appointment of environmentalists to prominent positions, the creation of a new Department of Energy, attention to world population problems, and opposition to further construction by the Army Corps of Engineers of expensive, environmentally damaging dams in western states. Even amid the enormous challenges of high inflation and the Iran hostage crisis that would do so much to prevent his reelection in 1980, Carter managed two great environmental achievements during his last year in office. One was the creation of the Superfund to pay for the restoration of major hazardous waste sites. The other was the Alaska Lands Act, tripling the size of the national park system and preserving much of the spectacular beauty and wildlife of the nation's largest state.[68]

More than any other president before or since, Carter tried to focus Americans' attention on the issue of energy. "One of our most urgent projects is to develop a national energy policy," he told the nation two weeks after taking office. "We must face the fact that the energy shortage is permanent" and "all of us must learn to waste less energy." Conservation was crucial, from lowered thermostats to lowered speed limits. His administration created incentives for the development of solar and other alternative sources of energy. Oil reserves were finite, he told the nation two months later: "We are running out of petroleum." It was not a message either the American public or Congress was eager to hear, even though the president framed it as the "moral equivalent of war." Carter later confided to his diary: "It was like pulling teeth to convince the people of America that we had a serious problem." High prices proved to be the most effective incentive for consumers, helping U.S. oil use drop during the Carter years, only to edge steadily back up once prices came down in the 1980s. Carter's enthusiasm for other forms of fossil fuels such as coal and the development of shale oil placed him in partial conflict with environmentalists' agenda, but overall he ranked with Theodore Roosevelt as the greenest of American presidents.[69]

Finally, Jimmy Carter symbolized the resurgence of evangelical Christianity in the United States in the 1970s, though he did so in a manner that ultimately set him at odds with the emerging New Christian Right. He was the first president to refer to himself as a "born-again Christian" and to teach Sunday school while in office, to the sometime consternation and amusement of jaded Washington insiders. He was not a saint; he could seem imperious and self-righteous, and he did not suffer fools gladly. But his faith clearly informed his work. Jesus had said in the Sermon on the Mount, "Blessed are the peacemakers," and Carter pursued peacemaking, notably in the new accords with Panama about the Canal, in nuclear arms reduction talks with the USSR that ultimately foundered, and most prominently in the Camp David accords that created a peace treaty for the first time ever between Israel and an Arab nation, Egypt. No friend of socialism, the president still preferred reaching out to potential enemies such as the leftist governments of Angola, Vietnam, and Cuba: "Should we write them off permanently as enemies and force them to be completely under the control and influence of Communist powers, or should we start the process of giving them an option to be both our friends and the friends of others, hoping that they will come to a more democratic free society and join with us in making a better world?" Carter's long post-presidential career focused on diplomacy, peacemaking, and economic development in the world's poorest areas and eventually won him the Nobel Peace Prize in 2002. The way of Jesus, he believed, was the pursuit of peace and care for the poor.[70]

Carter's support from evangelical and fundamentalist Christians in 1976 fell away by 1980. They may have admired his personal piety and devoted family life, but members of the New Christian Right increasingly wanted national military strength and anticommunism rather than peacemaking, and—like many other Americans of the era—reassurance rather than challenge. They found this easier path in Ronald Reagan, who announced his candidacy for the White House in 1979 by rebuking those who told "our children not to dream as we once dreamed" and complimenting his fellow citizens: "I find no national malaise. I find nothing wrong with the American people." Carter was too serious a student of the Bible and too aware of contemporary problems for such facile comforts. While leaders of the New Christian Right such as Falwell and Helms used Christianity to justify the pursuit of economic self-interest and the promotion of free markets, Carter called Americans to common sacrifice in the face of serious challenges and limitations at home and abroad. In contrast to Reagan's assuaging Americans with promises of unlimited consumption, Carter asked for self-restraint and moderation. He was, in the most literal sense, more conservative than Reagan. He warned against the growing trend of self-indulgence and materialistic consumerism. Carter reiterated instead the central importance instead of conservation, of *not* consuming, "the most painless and immediate way of rebuilding our Nation's strength."[71]

It is no surprise that the doubts and uncertainties characterizing so much of American and international life during the 1970s included doubts and uncertainties about the emerging individualistic synthesis of formal equality and market values. This was even visible in the White House itself, where a Christian with an environmentalist bent struggled to reconcile his partial dissent from the new era he, as a human rights advocate and business-man, symbolized. The issues raised by environmentalists did not disappear with the end of the decade and the election of a new president, Ronald Reagan, who was openly hostile to the green movement.

One of the largest oil spills in history, the 1979 blowout of the Ixtoc I drilling rig off the coast of Tabasco in the Gulf of Mexico that created an oil slick the size of Connecticut, proved to be just one more incident in a long history of large-scale man-made pollution that has not ended. Some successful efforts at pollution mitigation recalled the *New York Times* headline re-garding Chicago's earlier water cleanup—"Water in Chicago River Now Resembles Liquid"—but these were relatively minor remediations on the margins of a global tapestry of increasing ecological damage. U.S. and world population numbers contin-ued to climb, as did the impacts of industrialization in China and elsewhere. Fossil-fuel burning continued to grow, eventu-ally rendering the evidence of global warming impossible for responsible political leaders to ignore, as the human experiment with the Earth proceeded on its nature-changing course.[72]

The religious fundamentalism that flowered in the late 1970s in the United States and abroad did not go away either. Ameri-cans remained by far the most religious people of any industrial-ized nation, more similar in this regard to Muslims in the Mid-dle East and Asia than to generally secular Europeans. During the Carter years, American policymakers tended to view Islamic fundamentalism as an inchoate and primarily anti-Soviet force, an ally in the Cold War. Even years later, Carter's national secu-rity adviser, Zbigniew Brzezinski, argued that the idea that Mus-lim fundamentalism might pose a threat to the world "is stupid. There isn't a global Islam." This may prove to be true in the long run, for local, national, and sectarian differences obstruct a uni-fied Islam, but there was little question after the first decade of the twenty-first century of Muslim fundamentalism's global impact.[73]

The broader religious resurgence of the era may also be seen as helping place the Soviet Union under ideological pressure by 1979, with a revived Roman Catholicism on its western front and a surging radical Islam on its southern front, both contributing mightily to the demise of the Soviet empire. The spiritual critique of market-based individualism extended also to Communist materialism. In its first public manifesto in 1985, the Islamic guerilla organization in Lebanon, Hezbollah, declared itself hostile to "both the USSR and the U.S., both capitalism and communism, for both are incapable of laying the foundations for a just society." Two decades later, in very similar fashion, Pope Benedict XVI condemned both capitalism and Marxism as "systems that marginalize God."[74]

For the most part, however, dissenters from the emerging ethic of inclusive hyper-individualism could not hold back the high tide of egalitarianism and capitalism that was rolling up the beach by the end of the 1970s. For all their various concerns about the neglect of community values, spiritual priorities, and environmental realities, these activists were fighting an uphill battle. In the United States, the New Christian Right wound up as the foot soldiers of a Republican Party that governed primarily in the interests of free markets and private enterprise, paying mostly lip service to the cultural concerns of conservative religious folk. Similarly in Israel, Orthodox activists did not approach undoing the individualistic culture of a vibrantly capitalist society. Only in the Muslim-majority nations did religious fundamentalists either gain state power, as in Iran and briefly Afghanistan, or threaten to do so, as in Pakistan and Saudi Arabia. How far this development might go remained to be seen.[75]

Chapter 6

MORE AND LESS EQUAL SINCE THE 1970S

"You can call me anything you want, but do not call me a racist." President George W. Bush was responding to accusations that the failure of the federal government to respond swiftly to the devastation of Hurricane Katrina in 2005 was partially due to the hardest-hit New Orleans residents being primarily poor and working-class African Americans—and likely Democratic voters, to boot. Bush's reply captured a fundamental truth about American public life in the new millennium. No label was more damaging to a public figure than being identified as racist. Even this conservative Texas Republican, whose party since 1964 had been associated with those white voters least sympathetic to black people, wanted nothing to do with it. He meant it. Bush's closest foreign policy adviser—and an intimate family friend—was Condolezza Rice, a black woman. His first secretary of state was Colin Powell, an African American. His sister-in-law, Columba Bush, was from Mexico. No simple good ol' boy from the patriarchal South, Bush was also comfortable with powerful women, including Rice and his influential domestic adviser, Karen Hughes.[1]

In 2008, American voters elected Barack Obama by a solid majority, putting the first African American in the White House. It did not mean that racial discrimination and prejudice had disappeared. It certainly did not mean that black economic disadvantage had ended. But the election did mark a level of white acceptance of blacks in positions of authority that would have seemed nearly unimaginable a generation earlier. Voters were also demonstrating a cultural inclusiveness, choosing this son of a Kenyan father and white American mother, a man who had grown up in Hawaii and Indonesia and who carried an Islamic middle name—Hussein—that was the very name of the tyrant in Iraq—Saddam Hussein—against whom the United States had just been at war. After the election, Americans of differing political stripes took comfort in the outcome. Obama's supporters were obviously pleased, as was most of the rest of the world. But even conservatives who voted against Obama pointed to the result as evidence of a striking degree of equality in American public life and opportunities. Observers in other countries rued the unlikelihood of electing a member of an ethno-racial minority to the top political office in their nations. Comedy writers for late-night television shows were perhaps less happy, at least professionally, finding little suitable target for satire in the new president. "Anything that has even a whiff of being racist, no one is going to laugh," explained Rob Burnett, an executive producer for the David Letterman show. "The audience is not going to allow anyone to do that."[2]

While American public life grew generally more inclusive and egalitarian after the 1970s, attitudes toward government regulation and taxation continued to slide further into negative territory. "You had an intellectual conviction that you did not need much regulation—that the market could take care of itself," recalled Paul Volcker, the chairman of the Federal Reserve from 1979 to 1987, as he later came to regret his own partial acceptance of that view after the economic crisis of 2008. Reagan's two terms in office and his dominance of the American political landscape in the 1980s elevated market values, while discrediting the role of the federal government as it had developed since the New Deal fifty years earlier. "Government's view of the economy could be summed up in a few short phrases," he explained in 1986. "If it moves, tax it. If it keeps moving, regulate it. And if it stops moving, subsidize it." Reagan's contrarian view of government epitomized mainstream American politics after 1980. This vision helped Republicans under the small-government leadership of Rep. Newt Gingrich of Georgia seize control of the U.S. House of Representatives in 1994 for the first time in four decades. The only non-Republican president elected between 1980 and 2008 was the self-proclaimed "New Demo-

crat" Bill Clinton, "new" for distancing himself from the New
Deal tradition, who still wound up spending most of his eight
years in the White House (1993–2001) in a defensive posture
toward a Republican-dominated Congress. Steep tax cuts in
2001 and 2003 were emblems of the George W. Bush administration's pro-market, anti-regulatory stance. Partisan gridlock in
Congress—from the 1995 shutdown of government services to
the 1998 impeachment of Clinton, to the nearly lockstep threat
of filibuster against Obama's initiatives by the opposition
party—contributed to a broadening public perception that government simply does not work well.[3]

"Politics moved right just as the culture moved left." This
evaluation of the 1980s by historian Robert Collins holds true
for the sweep of American life since the 1970s. Greater inclusiveness and formal equality were accompanied by growing distrust of government and the rise of market values. Over more
than three decades, the result was a more diverse public culture
in the realm of employment, entertainment, and politics, on the
one hand, and a more economically differentiated society, on
the other. Class differences widened, as measured by the distribution of income and wealth. But Americans had long been
loath to talk about class divisions, something associated for the
past century with Marxist analysis. Historian William Appleman
Williams referred to this resistance to discussing class as "the
Great Evasion" in American life. Rather than addressing growing economic inequality, Americans tended instead to celebrate
racial and ethnic diversity. Writer Walter Benn Michaels noted
how cultural liberalism and economic conservatism formed a de
facto alliance. It had become the contemporary American condition, the ground on which the vaunted American middle class
continued to shrink.[4]

EVIDENCE TO THE CONTRARY

It took little effort to find evidence of enduring inequality in the
United States, based on group identities such as race, ethnicity,

sex, disability, religion, and sexual orientation. For all the formal inclusiveness of public life, the actual private lives of Americans—like peoples anywhere—negotiated daily a wide array of prejudices and discriminatory practices. One saw this in household chores and caring for children: despite significant increases in men's contributions in these areas, women continued to shoulder the vast majority of domestic duties, even as they worked outside the home as much as men and were paid less for it, on average. Single-adult households with children, rising sharply in number, were usually headed by women. One saw this enduring prejudice in the lives of gays and lesbians: despite vast changes in their legal and moral status in American society, they still faced a threat of violence and condemnation unknown to most heterosexuals. One saw this among American Muslims and the hatred they encountered after the September 11, 2001, terrorist attacks by al-Qaeda on U.S. targets. And one saw this in the resentment and disrespect that Latinos often encountered from those who associated a Spanish surname or a Latino accent with undocumented immigration.[5]

African Americans remained the citizens most likely to experience direct discrimination on the basis of group identity. This was not surprising. Centuries of race slavery, segregation, and discrimination developed a robust foundation for anti-black prejudice, a reality weakened since the 1960s but not yet eliminated. The cornerstone was stolen labor. While white families built up inheritable wealth over generations, black families were largely prevented by bondage, law, and policy from doing so. In 2003, the median net worth of black households was 10 percent of that of white households. From the initial wellspring of this crucial disadvantage flowed a river of inequality: in health, education, social connections, self-esteem, employment, and opportunity. Prisons became more familiar to young black men, on average, than colleges. Black unemployment rates ran significantly higher than white unemployment rates. The growth of a robust black middle class in the past two generations was real and critically important, but it sometimes masked the enduring reality of poverty and discrimination. African American scholar

Stephen Carter explained that "America has two black communities, really, and one of them is falling further and further behind." Residential segregation by race changed only marginally in the past three decades. It remained profoundly easier to be white—and male—in the United States. Comedian Chris Rock made this point concisely with mainly white audiences: "None of you would trade places with me, and I'm rich!"[6]

Racial dislike and even hatred lingered since the 1970s like a persistent mist shrouding uncertain ground. At times the mist hardened into solid, brutal form, such as the vicious beating by police of unarmed motorist Rodney King in Los Angeles in 1991. After a bystander captured the traumatic scene on videotape, television viewers across the country and the world saw briefly the tense reality of black men's common experience with real or threatened physical force by the authorities. A year later, a jury with no black members acquitted the four officers on the videotape. African American rage at injustice exploded into a ferocious race riot in south-central Los Angeles, where racially targeted murder and mayhem flowed between blacks, whites, Asians, and Latinos. After 1992, racial violence was confined to smaller-scale incidents. In 1998, for example, three white men near Jasper, Texas, dragged an African American acquaintance to death behind a speeding pick-up truck, and in 2006, racial fights in a Louisiana high school divided the small community of Jena. White supremacist organizations continued to persist in places like northern Idaho, reminding African Americans and other Americans of color that some of their fellow citizens wished them only ill. Racial sentiment provided one ingredient in many citizens' opposition to Barack Obama, a fact expressed openly by some. A spike in racially explicit threats of violence against the president followed his election.[7]

Prejudice and discrimination against people of color could be found across the political spectrum, but one of the two major American political parties positioned itself as the voice of those white Americans least sympathetic to the concerns of African Americans. This is not to say that all Republicans were racist—hardly. But it does suggest why George W. Bush was defensive about accusations of racial neglect in the aftermath of Hurricane Katrina. The party of Abraham Lincoln had chosen since the early 1960s to position itself, above all, as the party of the white South and the white suburbs. Its leaders were often not shy about this strategy. In 1964, Barry Goldwater ran for president on a platform opposing the Civil Rights Act. In 1968, Richard Nixon endorsed a "Southern strategy" of pursuing segregationist voters. In 1980, Ronald Reagan opened his presidential campaign in Philadelphia, Mississippi, declaring his support for "states' rights" in a county known for the infamous murder of three civil rights workers only sixteen years earlier. In 1988, George H. W. Bush won the presidency after using a controversial advertisement linking his opponent to the release from jail of a convicted black murderer who then raped a white woman. In 1990, Jesse Helms won reelection to the Senate from North Carolina with an advertisement appealing explicitly to white resentment of affirmative action policies. In 2002, Senate majority leader Trent Lott of Mississippi publicly praised the 1948 white supremacist presidential candidacy of Strom Thurmond: "When Strom Thurmond ran for president, we [Mississippians] voted for him. We're proud of it. And if the rest of the country had followed our lead, we wouldn't have had all these problems over all these years." Other Republican leaders quickly distanced themselves from Lott's remarks, and he resigned from his leadership role. "But an important reason why both the White House and conservative pundits were so eager to condemn Trent Lott was not because Lott had long been out of touch with the party's values," historian Joseph Crespino wrote, "but because his remark crystallized so succinctly the reactionary populist resentment of the modern civil rights struggle and the important role that that antipathy has played in fueling modern conservative politics."[8]

Crespino and other careful observers noted the direct connection between white racial backlash since the 1960s and the declining status of government and the public sector. Put bluntly, as African Americans and other people of color were increasingly included in a formally egalitarian society, some of their white countrymen reacted by withdrawing their sympathies and votes from social welfare programs and from governmental operations in general. Historian Kevin Kruse identified this phenomenon in the case of Atlanta since the beginnings of desegregation in the 1950s. Longtime California newspaperman Peter Schrag described this development in the Golden State in the 1970s, where older white voters backed the tax revolt as they disengaged from key publicly funded mandates like the public schools and universities that had growing numbers of nonwhite students. By the early 2000s, various social science studies indicated that up to half of Americans' greater antipathy toward government spending on social services resulted from the nation's racial and ethnic diversity. This diversity undermined white support for collective funding of public goods of all kinds, from parks to food stamps to elementary schools. By contrast, European voters tended to see recipients of such goods as similar to themselves and thus more readily supported such spending. Meanwhile, white citizens in the United States responded to greater diversity in their society by withdrawing a portion of their support for the public sphere.[9]

Just as greater formal equality and inclusiveness in American society since the 1970s did not eliminate racial prejudice or racial gaps in wealth and education, the rise of free-market values did not eradicate Americans' dependence on and even affection for their government and its programs. In fact, as the U.S. population grew 36 percent from 1980 to 2010, the sheer size of federal, state, and local governments expanded as well. Like all bureaucracies, governments aimed above all to perpetuate themselves. It was the nature of large organizations. But governments also provided services, and citizens came to depend on those services much more than they sometimes liked to admit, and sometimes more than they realized. Foremost among the expenses of the U.S. government, besides payment on existing debt, was the vast military force that had bases in every state and on every continent abroad. No other nation since the demise of the Soviet Union approached the level of U.S. spending on military purposes. Indeed, the United States invested more in "defense" than the next ten largest national militaries *combined*. Yet there was little organized domestic opposition to the scale of this military spending, even after the end of the Cold War. Americans, by and large, seemed to have accepted, and to continue to support, an extraordinary global role for their military forces—that is, for the armed element of their government. Disproportionate military strength seemed to be part of the American identity. It also served as a kind of covert welfare system. Vast government spending on the military provided literally millions of jobs, in military service directly as well as in ancillary services around military bases, in military contracting, and in medical care for veterans. It was not the free market, and it was popular.[10]

The other largest federal outlays paid for domestic services directly affecting the lives of even more Americans. The Social Security system established in 1935 came to define, for most citizens, what their government owed them in retirement. After they retired and their paychecks disappeared, they counted on this federal program to provide for their most basic sustenance. Between 1980 and 2010, pensions disappeared for most American workers, leaving them dependent in retirement on their own savings—including 401(k) plans—and, above all, their Social Security check. The same was true for health-care insurance in retirement. Americans aged sixty-five and over, who typically required more medical care than younger citizens, came to depend on the Medicare system established in 1965. Indeed, their fierce and specific loyalty to Medicare sometimes conflicted head-on with their broad but vaguer support for "less government," lower taxes, and more leeway for the free market. One speaker at a 2009 town-hall meeting in Simpsonville, South Carolina, on health-care reform declared: "Keep your government hands off my Medicare!" Such confusion made sense for a citizenry committed to the benefits of specific government programs while supposedly disenchanted with the public sphere in general.[11]

Three decades of anti-regulatory rhetoric did not eliminate Americans' unthinking assumption that their government should protect them from harm on a daily basis. They bought meat and medicines in confidence that inspectors from the Food and Drug Administration were assuring their safety. They drove on highways and over bridges without wondering if they would hold up. They drank water from their kitchen taps without thinking if local officials were assuring its potability. They worked in factories in confidence that the Occupational Safety and Health Administration monitored dangerous machinery and materials. They boarded airplanes with the knowledge that pilots passed rigorous training tests and airplane equipment was regularly inspected by the Federal Aviation Administration. They lined up for seasonal flu shots when the Centers for Disease Control and Prevention recommended them. They dialed "911" when they were in trouble and simply assumed police, fire, and emergency personnel would respond immediately. In these and a myriad of other aspects of their daily lives, citizens did not rely—and would never have dreamed of relying—on a truly free market. They expected and demanded government protection. This is what taxes paid for. Taxes were the price of civilization.[12]

The rhetorical dominance of free-market values in American politics since the 1970s, then, masked some older, New Deal-style loyalties. The severe economic recession that began in December 2007 further tested Americans' commitment to a less regulated economy. The steep decline in real estate values, the rise in unemployment above 10 percent, and particularly the collapse and near-collapse of major investment banks shook people's faith in unregulated markets. Even the most ardent defenders of entrepreneurship were shocked. "A system Americans have trusted—the market—has failed in important ways," observed conservative columnist David Brooks. Former Federal Reserve chairman Alan Greenspan, a once revered figure, came under withering criticism, and conceded that "I have found a flaw" in the pro-market ideology that led him to make "a mistake" in trusting banks to protect the interests of their shareholders. "We are learning from [these events] that we need a more active and intelligent government to keep our mode of a capitalist economy from running off the rails," wrote federal

appeals court judge Richard Posner, a leading figure in the conservative Chicago school of economics. "The movement to deregulate the financial industry went too far by exaggerating the
resilience—the self-healing powers—of laissez-faire capitalism."
Only massive U.S. government intervention, begun by the Republican administration of George W. Bush and continued by
the Democratic administration of Barack Obama, kept the damage from growing much worse. The reputation of economist
John Maynard Keynes rose sharply in response.[13]

Some observers suggested that the recession that began in
late 2007 might mark the end of the deregulatory period since
the 1970s. Public opinion and political support may swing back
toward a more positive view of government management of the
economy, as indicated by Obama's election.[14] Only time will tell.
Regardless of whether this proves true, the era from 1980 to
2008 witnessed a full generation of dominant free-market values that reshaped the American political landscape, carrying
forward the anti-regulatory logic that seized the high ground in
the 1970s. Likewise, the reality of enduring challenges to egalitarianism since 1980 did not derail the dramatic progress of
growing inclusiveness in American society. The individualistic
emphasis of these twin values of the 1970s defined much of the
last thirty years of U.S. history.[15]

INCLUSIVENESS ASCENDING

American culture was significantly more liberal and open in
2010 than it had been in 1980. This was visible from matters
of music, movies, performance arts, and freedom of expression
to issues of gender, race, and sexuality. Women's breakthroughs
in the 1970s continued to reshape American life most dramatically of all. From a small minority of the paid workforce, women
came to hold half the nation's jobs. Women's average paychecks
lagged behind men's, but they were catching up. In 1970, 4 percent of husbands had wives who made more money than they
did; in 2007, 22 percent did. Women moved up into positions

of authority in the workplace in these years, from schools and hospitals to businesses and governments. They held 51 percent of professional and managerial positions in the U.S. economy in 2010. Ursula Burns became the first black woman to head a top 100 company when she took over as CEO of Xerox Corporation in 2009, succeeding another woman in the position, Anne Mulcahy. Americans in these years became accustomed for the first time to female authority over both women and men as a normal public phenomenon, a transition of vast historical significance.[16]

At the top echelons of political power, women became increasingly visible. Hillary Clinton narrowly missed the Democratic presidential nomination in 2008, while Sarah Palin won the Republican vice presidential nomination. Women as governors became standard fare, including the 1986 gubernatorial race in Nebraska that featured female candidates from both major parties. The number of women in the 535-member U.S. Congress rose from eleven to seventeen during the 1970s, and then leapt to ninety-one in 2009—still less than 20 percent, but increasing steadily. In 2007, Nancy Pelosi (D-CA) became the first female Speaker of the U.S. House of Representatives. The number of women elected to statewide executive offices went from 7 percent to 11 percent during the 1970s, and then zoomed to 25 percent by 2004. Sandra Day O'Connor's elevation to the U.S. Supreme Court in 1981 was followed by Ruth Bader Ginsburg in 1993, Sonia Sotomayor in 2009, and Elena Kagan in 2010. In the deeply symbolic U.S. military, the number of women rose steadily since the 1970s, including in the officer corps. The Persian Gulf War of 1991 marked a turning point, with women becoming more visibly identified as warriors by the public and popular culture. Despite an official ban on women serving in combat positions, they informally began doing precisely that in the unpredictable combat landscapes of Iraq and Afghanistan in the 2000s. They were "attached" rather than "assigned" to combat units, and they piloted aircraft into combat zones. Some also died there.[17]

Sex desegregation and the empowerment of women's public

lives began in schools. In 1970, women earned 43 percent of bachelor's degrees awarded; in 2001, they earned 57 percent. In 1970, women received 6 percent of professional degrees; in 2004, they received almost half. In 2002, Yale Law School enrolled its first class with a majority of women. The following year, Harvard Medical School did the same. Indeed, the success of female applicants to undergraduate institutions began to give them a slight competitive disadvantage, as male applicants benefited from colleges' efforts to preserve a roughly gender-balanced student body. Women's sweeping success in education penetrated the most elite circles. By 2007, half of the eight Ivy League universities had female presidents.[18]

In their personal lives, the struggle for women's equality pressed forward after the 1970s. Female athleticism boomed. During the 1971–72 school year, girls comprised just 7 percent of all participants in high school sports; in 2006–2007, they totaled 41 percent. Women's running took off. From 1971, when three women completed the second New York City Marathon, the number of female finishers soared to 11,715 in 2003. Roughly a third of the racers in New York for the annual event were now women. Pat Summitt built an extraordinarily successful women's basketball program at the University of Tennessee from scratch, bringing in an average of 14,000 fans for each home game in 2008–2009. The U.S. women's national soccer team won the Women's World Cup in 1999, attracting unprecedented public attention to the sport. Downhill skier Lyndsey Vonn's three consecutive World Cup overall titles in 2008–2010 and gold medal at the 2010 Vancouver Winter Olympics embodied the respect, media attention, and money that women athletes earned. One seventy-five-year-old fan of the 2008 national champion University of Nebraska women's volleyball team tried to explain to a reporter the power of a favorite photograph of her team celebrating together. "Every time I look or talk about that photo, I just weep. We were denied so much for so long." As a high school basketball player herself six decades earlier, Lynn Darling and her own teammates had different rules in gym class and were not allowed to run in basketball. "They wanted us to protect the uterus." Darling wiped her eyes. "It's true. Procreating. That was our purpose." Such a perspective seemed difficult to imagine for contemporary American women. Being female in the United States now meant a different relationship with one's body and different expectations.[19]

Providing equal protection to women also involved, in some cases, recognition of their distinctiveness from men. Most notable was their common status as primary targets of unwanted sexual advances and sexual assault. In 1986, for the first time, the U.S. Supreme Court established a workplace right to be free from "sexual harassment," a new term in American law. In *Meritor Savings Bank v. Vinson*, the Court ruled that unwanted sexual advances in the workplace constituted a form of sex discrimination against women and were thus illegal. Women had the right to be free of a hostile employment environment. This watershed decision eliminated the legal basis for the age-old attitude of "boys will be boys" and the double standard it allowed for appropriate behavior of men toward women, at least in the workplace. The new standard of freedom from sexual harassment—and the struggles that accompanied it—followed women into new employment situations, including the military services.[20]

Even those opposed to parts of the empowerment of women since the 1970s tended to frame their arguments in terms of individual rights. Anti-abortion activists, male and female, focused less on the obligations of motherhood and sexual responsibility, and more on the rights of the fetus as an "unborn child." The campaign to restrict access to abortion services centered on defending the fetus as an elemental matter of protecting human rights. This campaign did not (at least yet) succeed in overturning *Roe v. Wade*'s legalization of abortion, but it did manage to win new restrictions on the practice by individual states, most notably in the Supreme Court's decision in *Planned Parenthood of Southeastern Pennsylvania v. Casey* (1992). These activists called themselves "pro-life," to the dismay of observers who noted their strong tendencies to support capital punishment and to oppose government-provided child social services. "Pro-life" organizers seemed to some to care more about people before they were born than after they were born. But anti-abortion activists were resolute in their commitment to stopping what they saw as the taking of helpless individual human lives, and they succeeded in reducing the availability of abortion services.[21]

At the broadest level, women's position in all aspects of society—economic, political, social, cultural—across the industrialized world became much more equal to men's after the 1960s. Feminism helped shape the two predominant developments that drove this change. One was the rising tide of women entering the paid workforce as economies shifted from industry to information and services. With higher incomes, women were more independent; marriage declined in importance and divorce became more common. The second development was the ready availability of effective contraception, particularly the birth control pill. Women in industrialized countries now controlled their own reproduction and thus their lives to a greater extent than ever before in history. These factors liberated women as individuals, but altered traditional family structures and corroded traditional forms of authority that had held together families, neighborhoods, and even nations. By 2007, for the first time, the majority of adult American women lived without a spouse, either unmarried, separated, divorced, or widowed.[22]

A similar story of increasing public prominence unfolded for African Americans, male and female, after the 1970s. Nonblack Americans grew thoroughly accustomed to black successes in politics, business, education, the arts, sports, and entertainment. After the initial breakthroughs of the 1960s, African Americans became commonplace in positions of executive authority, particularly as mayors of large cities. In 2009, even the mostly white town of Philadelphia, Mississippi, renowned for its brutal hostility toward the civil rights movement in the 1960s, elected its first black mayor, James A. Young. At the state level, in 1989 Virginia's large white-majority citizenry made Douglas Wilder the first elected black governor in the nation. He was followed by Deval Patrick in Massachusetts and David Paterson in New York. Black officials rapidly lost their novelty at all levels of government. Their very normality helped set the stage for Obama's election to the presidency in 2008.

So did African American prominence in the cultural spheres of music, sports, literature, dance, and film. Nonblack Americans grew very much accustomed to listening to black musicians; they cheered for black athletes, including those in traditionally white leadership positions such as quarterback in football, and black coaches; they listened to television personalities like Oprah Winfrey; and they flocked to theaters to watch movie stars such as James Earl Jones and Denzel Washington. In a culture deeply influenced by Hollywood's images, Americans found nothing odd about Morgan Freeman playing the U.S. president in *Deep Impact* (1998). The mainstreaming of blacks in American public life changed advertising, which began to target black audiences and to use African American images. In the 2000s, the iconic figure of Betty Crocker on mashed-potato box covers was regenerated by computer to be darker and more ethnic-looking than the white, blue-eyed original of 1936. By the 2000s, mainstream television ads even casually included images of black men in the company of white women, a scene scarcely imaginable a few decades earlier. Marriage between members of different races, perhaps the most sensitive indicator of changing racial practices, increased fivefold between 1960 and 2000 and accounted for 8 percent of all marriages in the United States in 2010.[23]

Rising non-European immigration changed the public face of the United States as much as any other factor after the 1970s. Latinos—mostly but not exclusively from Mexico—became the largest racial or ethnic minority in the early 2000s. While anti-immigrant sentiment remained a serious force in American politics, Latinos' prominence as voters gained them newfound respect. Sonia Sotomayor was the first Latina or Latino elevated to the Supreme Court, and even those Republicans opposing her nomination in 2009 trod very carefully to avoid appearing in any way anti-Latino. Thirty Latinos served in Congress in 2010. In the high-tech world of Silicon Valley south of San Francisco, half the engineers by 2009 had been born overseas, particularly in China, India, and Russia. At the University of California at Berkeley, the nation's most prestigious public university, 46 percent of freshmen in 2006 were Asian American. The 2008 election brought two new ethnic breakthroughs in the U.S. House of Representatives: Steve Austria (R-OH), the first Filipino American, and Anh (Joseph) Cao (R-LA), the first Vietnamese American. Demographers estimated that 2010 was the first year in which the number of babies born to minorities outnumbered that of babies born to whites. In sheer numbers, the nation's future was destined for greater diversity.[24]

One of the most revealing statistics of the success of a minority group in American public life involved religion and the Supreme Court. In 2010, the retirement of John Paul Stevens left the Court without a single Justice who was a Protestant. The Founding Fathers would have been dumbfounded. Three Justices were Jewish: Ruth Bader Ginsburg, Stephen Breyer, and Elena Kagan. The remaining six were Roman Catholic, all appointed after 1985. In a nation with a long history of anti-Jewish and anti-Catholic discrimination, a land where Protestants still remained the large majority, this was a striking development. After the September 11 attacks of 2001, Muslims faced ongoing prejudicial treatment, as did non-European immigrants, but the entirely non-Protestant makeup of the nation's highest court suggested a much more inclusive view of minorities in American life than ever before.[25]

Gays and lesbians made the longest strides the fastest. In the early 1980s, they were still the most marginalized group in the United States, their legitimacy undercut by their absence from most anti-discrimination statutes and the disdain and violence they often encountered. Most homosexuals remained "in the closet," calculating accurately if sadly that keeping their sexual orientation private was safer for their economic, social, and physical well-being. The Supreme Court as late as 1986, in the case of *Bowers v. Hardwick*, declared that states could continue to outlaw private consensual sex between homosexual adults. Indeed, the swing vote in that decision, Justice Lewis Powell, told one of his clerks that he had never met a gay person. It turned out that the clerk was gay.[26]

The Court was slow to recognize rapid change coming on this issue. Through the 1990s, Americans learned that millions of their family members and friends were gay and mostly just got used to it. *Fortune* magazine in 1991 declared that "homosexuality, once a career-destroying secret, is coming out of the closet in corporate America." In 2000, Vermont passed the first state civil-union law to grant legal recognition to homosexual couples. The Supreme Court reversed itself in 2003 in *Lawrence v. Texas*, finding a right to privacy for consenting adult homosexuals. In 2009, Houston became the first of the nation's largest cities—in conservative Texas, to boot—to elect a gay mayor, Annise Parker. By 2010, five states and Washington, DC, had legalized same-sex marriage, as had ten other nations, including such traditionally Roman Catholic countries as Spain, Portugal, and Argentina. For the first time in its polling, Gallup found that a majority of Americans no longer considered gay and lesbian relationships to be immoral.[27]

The trajectory of public opinion about homosexuality was changing. By the early 2000s, younger Americans considered it much less of an issue than did their elders, and they supported the right to same-sex marriage by a large margin. This pointed to a future in which gays and lesbians were likely to become increasingly accepted as normal Americans. Even prominent conservatives and leaders of traditional institutions found their views on private adult sexual behavior changing. Republican Vice President Richard Cheney had an openly lesbian daughter. Right-wing organizer Phyllis Schlafly had a gay son. Republican senator and 2008 presidential nominee John McCain opposed having openly gay people serve in the U.S. military, but his wife and daughter became public proponents of the right to same-sex marriage. Chairman of the Joint Chiefs of Staff Admiral Mike Mullen, the nation's top uniformed officer, explained to Congress in 2010 the growing support in the Pentagon for eliminating the "Don't ask, don't tell" policy, which allowed homosexuals to serve in the military only so long as they kept their sexual orientation private. "It is my personal and professional belief that allowing homosexuals to serve openly would be the right thing to do. No matter how I look at the issue, I cannot escape being troubled by the fact that we have in place a policy which forces young men and women to lie about who they are in order to defend their fellow citizens." Mullen noted that he had "served with homosexuals since 1968" and that his views had evolved "cumulatively" and "personally" ever since. This was the case with most Americans.[28]

The story of greater formal equality and inclusiveness in public life was not unique to the United States in the decades after the 1970s. It was a global tale. It was also not simple and straightforward in its progression; the world was far too large and diverse for all societies to move in unison with each other. There were, for example, plenty of cases of ethnic hatred and violence, such as—just in the 1990s—the unraveling of the former nation of Yugoslavia, Hindu-Muslim riots in India, and the Hutu genocide of Tutsis in Rwanda. Nonetheless, while racism and xenophobia still stalked the contemporary world, it was true that their expression continued to lose acceptability. Australia renounced its informal "White Australia" policy and began to make a place for itself in Asian affairs and to accept Asian immigrants. White settler states New Zealand, Canada, Australia, and the United States all developed more respectful relationships with their indigenous populations of Maori, First Peoples, Aborigines, and Native Americans, respectively. Namibia threw off its colonial overlord, apartheid-era South Africa. And South Africa itself gave up apartheid in 1990, elected Nelson Mandela president in 1994, and became a model to the world—not a perfect model, but a model— of a relatively peaceful transition from racial authoritarianism to inclusive democracy.

Markets Persisting

The new multiculturalism visible from the 1970s on was closely connected to globalization. Information and people moved more often and more rapidly, linking cultures and nations more closely together than ever before. Immigration to the United

States rose sharply in the 1980s, 1990s, and 2000s. Computers, satellites, cell phones, cable television, and the Internet accelerated the pace and intensity of connection. The average real cost of air travel plummeted 60 percent between 1969 and 2009. English became the de facto second language almost everywhere. International telephone traffic tripled in volume during the 1990s, and then nearly doubled again by 2002. World trade as a percentage of world economic output tripled between 1945 and 1998. From 10 percent of the U.S. economy in 1979, imports grew to 17 percent in 2007. Across the globe, markets won out. Socialism retreated from Russia, Eastern Europe, China, and Vietnam, holding on only in the poorest backwaters of North Korea and Cuba. The growth of international trade and globalization surprised even the savviest of observers. Henry Kissinger had told the Chinese in 1972, when first negotiating the new Sino-American relationship: "The maximum amount of bilateral trade possible between us, even if we make great efforts, is infinitesimal in terms of our total economy." By 2009, it soared to $409 billion, and China was the second largest trading partner of the United States.[29]

The expansion of information-driven international markets brought rapid, even disorienting change to the economic landscape. The largest American corporations had long been a stable group, the top one hundred taking an average of thirty years to replace half their members during the period from 1917 to 1976, but from 1977 to 1998, it now took just twelve years. In 2007, for the first time ever, the iconic U.S. automobile companies that had so long dominated U.S. and world markets—General Motors, Ford, and Chrysler—sold fewer than half the vehicles bought by American consumers. Geographical distances no longer made the same sense. Telephone numbers halfway across the globe in the U.S.-occupied Green Zone of Baghdad received local American area codes, 703 (metropolitan Washington, including the Pentagon) and 914 (Westchester County, New York). Meanwhile, the labels of intensely familiar products like Coca-Cola shed any indication of an actual place (such as Atlanta, its historic headquarters), carrying instead just the virtual location of an 800 telephone number or a website. Union membership plunged from 29 percent of the U.S. workforce in 1973 to 12 percent in 2009, taking down health insurance and pension benefits for American workers and returning labor relations demographics to the pre–New Deal era.[30]

Disadvantages for workers were balanced, in the eyes of consumer-oriented Americans, by the benefits of the globalized marketplace and an increasingly deregulated economy. The continued spread of gambling epitomized the post-1970s emphasis on freedom for consumers. While at the end of the 1970s gamblers still had to travel to Nevada or Atlantic City to bet legally at a casino, by 2009 they could gamble in some form in forty-two states and in often-elegant Indian casinos in twenty-nine states. Government-owned slot machines tempted young soldiers on U.S. military bases around the globe.[31]

Restrictions on alcohol sales had been similarly loosened. Other than the creation of a national standard minimum age of twenty-one, buying liquor was much easier than it used to be. State lawmakers, in pursuit of new tax revenues and eager to please citizen-consumers, pared back traditional "blue laws" restricting alcohol sales. Bible-belt states like North Carolina gave up "brown-bagging" in restaurants for the profits of selling "liquor by the drink." In 2009, Mormon-dominated Utah eliminated its byzantine system of requiring bars to be member-only clubs, and Colorado joined the now large majority of states with open liquor stores on Sundays. Governments continued their retreat from many salients of their former role as moral policeman.[32]

The Republican Party became the most powerful promoter of freeing up consumers and markets. From 1980 to 2008, the GOP dominated national politics and helped force the Democratic Party also to the right. On no issue was this clearer than lowering taxes. With considerable Democratic support, Republicans led the campaign that successfully cut the top federal income tax rate in half, from 70 percent in 1980 to 35 percent in 2003. The maximum rate for federal capital gains taxes fell even more steeply, from 40 percent in 1978 to 16 percent in 2003.

The key reductions came under Republican president Ronald Reagan in 1981 and 1986 and Republican president George W. Bush in 2001 and 2003. More money stayed in citizens' pockets, particularly in those of the wealthiest Americans. Citizens affected by the top federal income tax bracket were a thin slice of the American population, the same elite who reaped the benefit of lower taxes on capital gains. It was a great era in which to be wealthy.[33]

Both parties joined in weakening government regulation of financial institutions. The Garn-St. Germain Depository Institutions Act of 1982 removed constraints on one formerly staid sector of the banking world, helping usher in the newly risky lending practices of savings-and-loans in the late 1980s, whose defaults wound up costing taxpayers $130 billion. Americans' debt levels climbed and their savings sagged. The 1999 repeal of parts of the Glass-Steagall Act allowed bank holding companies to own other financial companies, removing the wall between old-fashioned, conservative deposit banking and much higher-risk investment banking, and helping lead to the economic meltdown of 2008. President Bush tried but failed to push this logic even further by privatizing the Social Security system in the early 2000s.[34]

The Supreme Court came to share this more skeptical view of government regulation of corporate behavior. In *Citizens United v. Federal Election Commission* (2010), the Court ruled unconstitutional any restrictions on corporate spending in political campaigns, reversing decades of precedents. The largest companies now had to be treated just the same as individual citizens in the realm of political speech. "While American democracy is imperfect," Justice Stevens wrote in dissent, "few outside the majority of this court would have thought its flaws included a dearth of corporate money in politics." But the Court reflected its times. "With their pro-business jurisprudence, the justices may be capturing an emerging spirit of agreement among liberal and conservative elites about the value of free markets," wrote careful observer Jeffrey Rosen in the *New York Times*. "Many Democrats and Republicans, whatever their other disagreements, have come to share a relatively laissez-faire, technocratic vision of the economy and are suspicious of excessive regulations and reflexive efforts to vilify big business."[35]

The bandwagon of disdaining government and promoting privatization of the public sphere reached even to that most central purpose of the state: self-defense. The famous remark of the entrepreneurial character Milo Minderbinder in the satirical hit book and film *Catch-22* (1970) was intended to be absurd: "Frankly, I'd like to see the government get out of the business of war altogether and leave the whole field to private industry." But this increasingly described what actually happened in the U.S. military system by the time of the invasion of Iraq in 2003. Blackwater and other private security firms reaped enormous contracts for providing services that the U.S. military had formerly taken care of on its own. The privatization movement also swept into prison management as private companies began contracting with local governments to operate jails. And the same logic began winning out in transportation systems as well. By the early 2000s, intense freeway traffic congestion convinced half of the states to allow local transportation authorities to operate special, pay-as-you-go lanes or to let the private sector build and run separate roads.[36]

UNRESTRAINED CONSUMPTION

The twin beliefs that commerce was the most natural relationship between people, and that consumption was the most natural activity of individuals, came to dominate American life after the 1970s. Advertising linked commerce and consumption, and advertising spread pervasively in these decades. Yankelovich, a market research firm, estimated that a person living in a city in 2007 saw five thousand advertising messages a day, up from two thousand thirty years earlier. Advertisements showed up in places previously free from them—on the windows of public buses, before movies in theaters—and came on the television at louder volume than regular programming. Sports venues like college football bowl games, once revered for simple names linked to their geography (Cotton Bowl, Orange Bowl, Sugar Bowl), became advertisements: the Chik-Fil-A Bowl in Atlanta, the Tostitos Fiesta Bowl in Phoenix, and the Outback Steakhouse Gator Bowl in Jacksonville. And sports, from college basketball's "March Madness" to the National Football League, became bigger and bigger business. In the case of the Super Bowl, the advertisements sometimes became more the entertainment than the game itself.[37]

Higher education of the nation's youth reflected the now more visibly dominant ethic of consumerism. In 2010, 22 percent of college undergraduates were majoring in business, by far the most popular major on campus. The numbers majoring in the liberal arts and humanities, meanwhile, declined steadily. English majors dropped by half from 1971 to 2001. The number of MBA degrees increased more than fivefold in the same period. Some of this educational shift toward business reflected economic uncertainties and the need to pay off rising student debt. In 1979, the total yearly costs at a four-year public college or university averaged less than $3,000, of which the maximum federal Pell grant covered three-quarters; thirty years later, the average was $14,000, with a full Pell grant covering just one-third of it. But the shift to business reached beyond just economic need. There was a broader change in the values that college students expressed. UCLA students, for example, went from considering "becoming an educated person" or "developing a philosophy of life" to be their primary reason for attending college in the early 1970s to instead "making a lot of money" by the 1990s. Statistics from the U.S. Census Bureau tracked the same story nationally among college freshmen. In 1970, 79 percent said their major goal was to develop a meaningful philosophy of life; in 2005, 75 percent said it was to be financially very well off.[38]

The idea of unrestrained individual consumption seeped into the fabric of American society, most immediately in citizens' diets. From the late 1970s to the early 2000s, the percentage of Americans who were obese more than doubled. In 2010, fully two-thirds of Americans were either overweight or obese, half in each category. The average American male was seventeen pounds heavier in 2009 than in the late 1970s, and the average female, nineteen pounds heavier. This public health epidemic had many causes. New technologies involving corn syrup and palm oil made soft drinks and high-fat snacks cheaper, more accessible, and higher in calories. Soda swept past milk in popularity. Pizza's soaring sales tripled cheese consumption. Two-job families ate out more frequently, doubling the average fraction of calories from restaurant food, with its higher calories and fat and salt content. Americans ate take-out meals on average 125 times a year in 2008, up from 72 a generation earlier. And Americans smoked cigarettes less, a serious public health advance, but also one that removed a traditional substitute for eating. They also consumed larger portions. The standard-size bottle of Coke grew from 8 to 20 ounces; bagels and muffins bulked up; and fast-food burgers more than doubled in size. In 2004, one critic's response to the introduction by Hardee's of the 1,418-calorie Monster Thickburger, with 107 grams of fat, was: "Would you like a defibrillator with that?" The bottom line was that citizens, including children, ate more and exercised less, as an explosion of new entertainment options kept them indoors and seated in front of computer and television screens. Even their pets grew overweight, a result of more food and less exercise.[39]

Americans had grown more overweight than peoples of other industrialized nations, a change encouraged by American culture. Indeed, immigrants who came to the United States from elsewhere were rarely obese, but time on American shores tended to change that. After a decade in the United States, the foreign-born lost any earlier advantage. "Trends in obesity among immigrants may reflect acculturation and adoption of the U.S. lifestyle, such as increased sedentary behavior and poor dietary patterns," one prominent group of public health researchers observed. American culture also spread its influence abroad, and other nations were not immune to the same confluence of abundant fast food and proliferating indoor technological diversions. From France to China, from Sweden to Mauritania, from Egypt to Brazil, from Germany to Japan, average weights crept upward, a worrisome indicator of an increasingly global culture of personal consumption.[40]

The pursuit of self-satisfaction with food extended as well to sexuality. In traditional Catholic language, these were the temptations of gluttony and lust. In the contemporary United States, they became just part of the normal landscape of daily life. The loosening private sexual mores of the 1960s and 1970s pervaded public life as well. In the 1980s, Calvin Klein billboards marketed sex with models wearing only jeans. The line of acceptable public nudity and sexual behavior moved dramatically, making "PG" films look like "R" movies of a generation earlier. Openly sexual behavior became commonplace on television, including a vast new empire of on-demand and pay-per-view video, a third of which was sexually explicit programming. In 2007, sex entertainment industry producers began planning for on-demand live sex programming for hotel televisions. Erotic imagery pervaded mainstream American life.[41]

While the growth of pornography represented one end of a wide spectrum of changing sexual mores, at the center was a transformation of marriage and the family. After the 1970s the relationship between sex, marriage, and children was no longer straightforward. Dependable birth control meant that children were no longer an inevitable factor in marriage. The percentage of American babies born to single mothers doubled from 16 percent in 1978 to 32 percent in 1995. Divorce was now commonplace. The public increasingly accepted homosexuality as an option. The average age of Americans getting married increased by several years, as young women and men waited—but they did not necessarily wait to have sexual relationships. The net effect of such changes was that sex outside marriage became not just common, but widely accepted as normal rather than immoral.[42]

Many citizens were troubled by this development but unsure what, if anything, could be done about it. They elected supposedly conservative Republican leaders, several of whom, particularly in the early 2000s, became involved in public sex scandals of their own—among them Senator Larry Craig (ID), Senator David Vitter (LA), Representative Mark Foley (FL), Governor Mark Sanford (SC), and others. They were pleased by the nomination of the stridently conservative Clarence Thomas to the Supreme Court in 1991, only to learn of his habit of watching pornographic films and to be troubled by serious questions about his treatment of at least one female subordinate. They lobbied against sex education in schools, but some activists wound up introducing into public discourse precisely the kind of explicit, sexually charged language they deplored. The most notable example was the publication of extremely detailed and graphic impeachment charges against President Clinton for an affair with a White House intern. Even when trying to downplay sexuality, Americans seemed to wallow in it.[43]

The new indulgence of the market ethos included not only the realms of gluttony and lust, but also what the traditional Church called wrath. Violence—anger translated into physical action—became a mainstay of entertainment. Tens of millions of Americans played luridly violent video games such as "Grand Theft Auto" and "Call of Duty." The United States had significantly higher homicide rates than other industrialized nations. The United States also had the loosest gun laws and highest levels of gun ownership in the industrialized world, an orientation that grew stronger in the 2000s as activists pressed state legislatures to ease restrictions on openly carrying weapons. The gun-slinging world of Western movies drew closer to current reality. Hollywood films continued to set the national standard for entertainment, one increasingly soaked in blood. Watching films made before the late 1960s seemed like looking into an alternative universe of modesty and restraint. From mainstream movies to horror films, the silver screen poured forth the infliction of pain and destruction. "Bloodletting, sadism and slaughter are now taken for granted," wrote David Thomson, one of the most astute critics of modern film. "In term of the cruelties we no longer notice, we are another species."[44]

Hollywood set standards of entertainment for the world as well as the country, as it had since the 1920s. American films remained one of the nation's most lucrative and influential exports. Hollywood stars were global celebrities. The explicit violence and sexuality of blockbusters, from *Terminator* and *Lethal Weapon* in the 1980s to *Lord of the Rings* and *Avatar* in the 2000s, splashed on to movie screens on every continent. Even one of the last socialist holdouts caved in. Within a decade after Americans departed from Vietnam in defeat, some Vietnamese were complaining that their revolutionary leaders had instead brought in Soviets who were merely "Americans without dollars." Vietnam's citizens turned out to prefer foreigners with more to offer. The United States and Vietnam reopened diplomatic relations in 1995, and the United States quickly emerged as Vietnam's largest trading partner. By 2007, residents of Ho Chi Minh City flocked to plush new cinemas to see films like *Pirates of the Caribbean* with high-tech soundtracks and all the popcorn and super-size soft drinks they wished to buy.[45]

An enjoyment of violence did not extend to sympathy for those breaking laws. The renewed American individualism rejected liberal criminology and its emphasis on social environments. Individuals were to be held strictly responsible for their actions, through tough drug-sentencing guidelines and stiff mandatory sentences from "three-strikes" laws. The U.S. prison population began to grow sharply in the mid-1970s. Up until then, American incarceration rates had remained stable throughout the twentieth century, and had been in line with the rates in other industrialized nations. Indeed, in the nineteenth century, Europeans had come to the United States to study its penal system. "In no country is criminal justice administered with more mildness," Alexis de Tocqueville wrote after touring American penitentiaries in 1831. After the 1970s, however, Americans lost interest in penitence in those penitentiaries and grew disillusioned with rehabilitation. They wanted punishment for individuals who chose to break the law.[46]

While Europeans continued their more moderate treatment of prisoners, including putting an end to capital punishment, which they tended to view as a medieval atrocity, Americans turned in the opposite direction. The United States put more of its citizens to death than any countries other than China and Iran. In 2009, it was the only nation in the Western Hemisphere to execute its own citizens, almost half of them in Texas. From 380,000 inmates in 1975, the overall U.S. prison population soared to 2.3 million in 2008, a quarter of them for nonviolent drug offenses. This was the highest total number and the highest incarceration rate of any nation. "We have 5 percent of the world's population and 25 percent of the people in prison," U.S. Senator Jim Webb (D-VA) observed. "Either we're the most evil people on earth, or we're doing something wrong."[47]

Whether or not there was something wrong, the harsh new American prison regime that developed after the mid-1970s was distinctive among industrialized nations. It targeted juveniles as well. The United States was one of a small handful of countries that gave life-without-parole sentences to some people who committed crimes before the age of eighteen. In 2005, the other such countries combined for a total of twelve such sentences. The United States had 2,200, including more than 350 for people whose crimes had been committed when they were fifteen or younger. Prison sentences in general in the United States were significantly longer on average than elsewhere. And lengthy sentences and mass incarceration added to class and racial inequalities, due to the 30–40 percent average reduction in a person's annual earnings that a prison record caused. These policies also indirectly helped increase inequality through the disenfranchisement of felons and ex-felons (disproportionately black and likely Democratic voters), a tipping factor of a few percentage points in the close elections of recent history. A study in 2007 demonstrated three specific impacts of these disenfranchisements of voters: George W. Bush would not have been awarded Florida's crucial electoral votes in the protracted 2000 presidential contest, sending Al Gore to the White House instead; seven modern Republican senators would not have won their initial elections; and the tax cuts of 2001 and 2003 that shifted wealth upward would have been much more difficult to enact. American prison policies across three decades revealed a culture comfortable with incarceration and its costs, emphatic about people being free to do what they chose and to pay for the consequences when they chose wrong.[48]

INEQUALITY RISING

The single most significant result of the victory of market values in U.S. public policy since the 1970s was a steady rise in economic inequality. The gap between rich and poor grew wider, startlingly so at times, and the bulk of the vaunted American middle class saw its economic security begin to slip away. This process was not always obvious, masked by several concurrent developments. First, globalized manufacturing and trade patterns kept downward pressure on prices of consumer goods, from milk to toys to airline tickets to computers. A larger market meant more competition in many sectors of the economy. Imports from low-wage countries like China and Mexico stayed relatively inexpensive. Second, the credit industry expanded its reach dramatically. Americans built up impressive debt loads on credit cards, supplementing their home mortgages and car loans. They bought what they could not formerly afford and preserved an outward appearance of economic good health. Average household debt grew by 80 percent between 1990 and 2005. Third, a traditional cultural style of social egalitarianism restrained some demonstrations of material excess by wealthy citizens. Just as working-class kids dressed in middle-class styles, so did many elite kids. Fitting in remained a goal in a society where most people claimed to be "middle class." Flaunting of wealth was common enough, from mansions and yachts to jewelry and cars, but social pressure to conform provided a measure of balance to the public behavior of at least some elites.[49]

Regardless of such constraints, however, the distance between the richest and poorest Americans, measured in simple dollars and cents, grew vast from the 1970s on. The widely shared income gains of the decades from 1946 to 1976 disappeared, replaced by dramatic increases for those citizens at the top. Between 1979 and 2007, the share of national income going to the richest 1 percent of families grew from 9 percent to 24 percent (an increase of 150 percent in one generation), the largest share for them since 1928. In the same years, the share of national income accruing to the poorest 90 percent of families dropped from 66 percent to 50 percent. According to the U.S. Census Bureau, in 2009 the gap between the richest and poorest Americans reached its widest amount on record. The shift during the later years and further up the chain was even more dramatic. Between 1992 and 2007, the bottom 90 percent of Americans watched their real incomes rise by 13 percent, compared with an increase of 399 percent for the top four hundred individuals. Between 2002 and 2007, the top 1 percent of households doubled their share of the total national income. By 2010, the top 0.1 percent of Americans—fewer than a third of a million people—were earning as much as the bottom 120 million of their fellow citizens. "At the same time that the rich have been pulling away from the middle class," observed financial columnist James Surowiecki, "the very rich have been pulling away from the pretty rich, and the very, very rich have been pulling away from the very rich."[50]

The increasingly information-driven U.S. economy placed a premium on education. While college graduates and those with advanced degrees saw their real income increase by a quarter in these decades, workers with high school diplomas felt a drop of 2 percent, and high school dropouts experienced a remarkable 18 percent decrease. Political leaders, particularly Republicans, took no action to mitigate this trend toward inequality. Instead, they cut federal taxes in 2001 and 2003 in a manner that gave 62 percent of the benefits to the wealthiest 20 percent of Americans by 2010, and they allowed the federal minimum wage in 2006 to reach its lowest inflation-adjusted value since the 1940s.[51]

Many factors contributed to this widening gap. Lower numbers of unionized workers, high divorce rates, and elevated incarceration rates all depressed family incomes. Quick to shift production sites in a more globalized economy, corporations were able to keep wages lower even when worker productivity picked back up after its 1973–79 lull, thus boosting company

"There, there it is again—the invisible hand of the marketplace giving us the finger."

FIGURE 6.1.
American workers were not sure that the pro-market reforms of the 1970s would benefit them. Indeed, the
next three decades saw a dramatic shift of shares of national income and wealth moving up the socioeconomic
scale to more affluent Americans. Courtesy Charles Bar-
sotti/*The New Yorker.*

profits. Employee benefits like retirement plans and health insurance coverage also shrank dramatically as a result of corporate cost-cutting, reducing security even for workers still on the
job. Not surprisingly, poverty rates in the United States, which
had dropped by half between 1959 and 1973, began rising
again, reaching 15 percent in 1994 and remaining at 13 percent
in 2008 (or higher, using unofficial rates). The rate was 18 percent for minors; nearly one in five American children were growing up in poverty in the new millennium. Most other industrialized nations experienced similar trends after the 1970s, but only
the United Kingdom came close to matching the sharp increase
in economic inequality in the United States. The United States
had the most uneven distribution of wealth of any industrialized
nation.[52]

"What I want to see above all," President Reagan declared in
a speech in 1983, "is that this remains a country where someone

can always get rich." Income statistics made it clear that Reagan's wish remained fulfilled a generation later. Indeed, wealth, a person's accumulated and inherited assets, provided a clearer indicator of one's real economic condition than income, a person's intake of money in a given year. Wealth was more unequally distributed than income. In 2007, the top 1 percent of American households owned 34.5 percent of the nation's wealth. The next 19 percent of households owned 50.5 percent of the wealth. So the bottom 80 percent—four out of five citizens—shared just 15 percent of the nation's private assets. This kind of skewing of the distribution of wealth was similar to the distribution in the poorest nations, though of course those countries had less total wealth to skew. The maldistribution of wealth shaped American society in a myriad of ways, from the wildly unequal endowments of the top two dozen universities compared to those of the next several hundred, to the opening of still more exclusive downhill ski resorts such as Beaver Creek, Colorado, and Deer Valley, Utah, to the multimillion-dollar cost of winning election to the U.S. Senate, to the proliferation of gated residential communities and luxury yachts. Even the *Wall Street Journal*, the nation's leading mouthpiece for the virtues of entrepreneurial capitalism, acknowledged in 2005 "a widening rich-poor gap" and admitted that "the level of [socioeconomic] mobility in the U.S. has been stuck over the past three decades, and some studies suggest mobility in continental Europe is higher." The future of the land of opportunity was unclear.[53]

In 1896, Merrill Gates, a distinguished educator and president of Amherst College, addressed the question of how to assimilate Native Americans more fully into mainstream American society. Capitalist values were crucial. "To bring him out of savagery into citizenship we must make the Indian more intelligently selfish," Gates wrote. "We need to *awaken in him wants*" that would create "an Indian wearing trousers with a pocket in them, and with a *pocket that aches to be filled with dollars*." Such awakened wants and aching pockets were in plentiful supply in the later era after the 1970s. Young and old Americans alike, according to surveys, placed a premium value on "being very well off financially." The "small is beautiful" movement of the late 1960s and early 1970s ultimately succumbed, among the vast majority of citizens, to the "bigger is better" movement of sport utility vehicles, larger houses, super-sized restaurant portions, and broader waistlines—a truly expanding America. To compete for student applicants, universities by the new millennium began to build luxurious facilities, from cosmopolitan dining services to spa-style recreation emporiums. The average American increased the amount of garbage thrown out each day by more than 50 percent between 1975 and 2005. More than three-quarters of respondents told pollsters in 2005 that "Americans overconsume," but when asked the follow-up question, "Do you think we should change that?" the majority agreed, "No, it's one of the great things about being American." In the late 1970s, President Carter called for common sacrifice to meet a national crisis of energy; after the terrorist attacks of September 11, 2001, President Bush asked for no sacrifice at all by average voters. "Get down to Disney World in Florida," he told citizens, urging them to restore confidence in air travel and the U.S. economy by flying and shopping. "Take your families and enjoy life the way we want it to be enjoyed." The words "common" and "sacrifice" rarely appeared together any longer in the national lexicon.[54]

Instead, Americans by the early 2000s spoke a more distilled version of their traditional language of individualism. They lived in bigger houses, on average, with smaller families, farther out in expanding suburbs. More than most peoples, Americans moved to new places for jobs and often lived far from extended family. Their nuclear families unraveled frequently, nearly half of marriages ending in divorce. Individuals in a culture that celebrated individual fulfillment, they found the inevitable sacrifices of married life difficult to reconcile with their own happiness. They had fewer children, and many more of those grew up with only one parent. Forty percent of all births were to unmarried women, a figure more than twice as large as in 1980. Americans valued privacy, or at least personal space. Ninety percent drove to work, the vast majority of them alone. Fewer than 5 percent used public transportation to get to their jobs. They seemed to appreciate the autonomy of their cars and being free of other people in close proximity. The same was true with Americans' primary forms of entertainment, televisions and computers, used mostly in isolation. "Technology has privatized our leisure time," Harvard political scientist Robert Putnam observed. "The distinctive effect of technology has been to enable us to get entertainment and information while remaining entirely alone." Americans remained famously friendly, according to foreign visitors, but the institutions and habits of contemporary American society pulled them increasingly apart from each other.[55]

OUT OF THE 1970s emerged the dominant contemporary American values of formal equality and free-market economics. Few would disagree that the United States became a more inclusive society while also one more deeply skeptical about the benefits of activist government, just as none would deny the reality, on the world stage, of the crumbling of colonialism and the retreat and near-collapse of socialism. But what was the precise relationship between these two developments? How were the simultaneous flowerings of egalitarianism and free-market values related to each other?

Both commitments had deep roots in the American past and had long helped shape the nation's politics and culture. The shedding of formal systems of social hierarchy was a continuing process, one that did not begin in the 1970s but did accelerate dramatically during that decade. The rejection of collective enterprise reflected an enduring belief in limited government and entrepreneurial virtue, a view that soared in popularity and political traction during these years. Some of the overlap of these two commitments was coincidental, the result of historical circumstances in different spheres that happened to unfold in the same era. The struggle for social equality and inclusion did not arise directly from changes in attitudes about the public and private spheres. And the push for economic deregulation and privatization was not simply a reaction to increasing egalitarianism.

But the two developments were related. Each principle tended to support the other, particularly in a culture as traditionally individualistic as that of the United States. A political economy rooted in free markets provided benefits for buyers and sellers alike, and the larger the market, the better. It made no economic sense to exclude potential customers or workers on the basis of a group identity such as race or sex. The dramatic evidence of globalization from the 1970s onward underlined this essential logic of contemporary capitalism: profitability meant expanding markets, selling goods and services to everyone everywhere. The creative destruction that accompanied capitalism pulled down old barriers between peoples, whether national, racial, or any other kind. The green of currency was the only color that mattered.

Formal equality had less direct correlation to market values. The Soviet Union, after all, outlawed racial discrimination decades earlier than the United States, and American Communists were among the most vociferous early twentieth-century opponents of discrimination. Indeed, much of the rhetoric of the Cold War focused on the question of which side more truly believed in, and lived out, a commitment to treating all people equally. So egalitarianism could point in either direction regarding command versus market economies. In the case of the United States, the enduring values of protecting private property and pursuing socioeconomic mobility meshed relatively easily with the elimination of legal discrimination, resulting in a purified inclusive version of individualism.

Ultimately, equality and markets were linked by a growing conviction among Americans and others that the end of legal discrimination assured that most remaining inequalities were natural and reasonable, the result of differences in ability and ambition. "A society free not only of racism but of sexism and of heterosexism is a neoliberal utopia," writer Walter Benn Michaels observed, "where all the irrelevant grounds of inequality (your identity) have been eliminated and whatever inequalities are left are therefore legitimized." The United States across the last several decades may have become "a much more unequal country" in economic terms, as prominent conservative columnist David Brooks noted, but it was an inequality that forty years of changing public values had helped to make acceptable in a culture that lays great claim to equal opportunity for its citizens. A considerable gap remained between the formal equality of citizens and the actual inequalities of opportunity visible in the lives of rich and poor children. Americans were indeed more equal, and less equal, than they used to be.[1]

Affirmative action provided one arena for a potentially direct conflict between the values of non-discrimination and free-market competition. In the 1970s, Allan Bakke, a white former engineer, applied for admission to the University of California–Davis medical school and was twice rejected, despite having test scores significantly higher than those of several minority applicants who were admitted. Bakke appealed the decision all the way to the U.S. Supreme Court, whose split decision in 1978 articulated the precise dilemma of the two principles involved. The Court threw out the medical school's specific quota of sixteen places (out of one hundred) for nonwhite candidates as itself a form of illegal discrimination, and ordered that Bakke be admitted to the program. But the Court also articulated a new purpose and legal justification for the preferential programs known collectively as affirmative action. Race-conscious criteria could not be used to compensate for racial injustice in the past. Instead, race could be one of many factors—along with geography, interests, income, and the like—used to foster a diverse student body that enhanced the education of all current students. Diversity to benefit all replaced compensation for a few.[2]

The Court's 5–4 majority in the *Bakke* case demonstrated acute sensitivity to the idea of using contemporary, benevolent race consciousness to overcome the effects of earlier, malevolent race consciousness. But they saw no other way. Dozens of generations of stolen labor in slavery and impoverishment through Jim Crow underlined the truth of President Johnson's 1965 speech: "You do not wipe away the scars of centuries by saying: Now you are free to go where you want, and do as you desire, and choose the leaders you please. You do not take a person who, for years, has been hobbled by chains, liberate him, bring him up to the starting line of a race, and then say, 'you are free to compete with all the others,' and still justly believe that you have been completely fair." In the Bakke decision, Justice Harry Blackmun agreed: "In order to get beyond racism, we must first take account of race. There is no other way. And in order to treat some persons equally, we must treat them differently." Blackmun concluded: "We cannot—we dare not—let the Equal Protection Clause perpetuate racial supremacy."[3]

The Supreme Court, along with outside sympathizers, assumed that affirmative action would not be needed for longer than a generation, certainly not permanently. White Americans remained skeptical of a policy that seemed to many of them a kind of reverse discrimination. Most did not believe they should be held responsible for the collective sins of their parents and ancestors. Some black Americans, such as Supreme Court Justice Clarence Thomas, agreed. They disliked the idea of a vague racial favoritism that cast doubt on their individual achievements. In the meantime, the racial categories used for affirmative action had the unintended consequence of also making some 80 percent of the 35 million immigrants arriving in the United States between 1970 and 2000 eligible for some preferential treatment that had been designed originally for native-born African Americans. The results included both a much more diverse society and growing public opposition to affirmative action policies, evident in the elimination of race as a factor in public university admissions by legal statute in the two most populous states, California and Texas. However, Michigan and other states preserved affirmative action, supported by affidavits from the U.S. military and major U.S. corporations and narrowly upheld in a 5–4 Supreme Court decision in *Grutter v. Bollinger* (2003). The tentative status of affirmative action early in the new millennium reflected both Americans' belief in formal equality and their belief in the market mechanism of straightforward competition.[4]

In the legislative and political sphere, each of the two dominant themes of post-1970s America had a political party as its spokesperson. While Democrats and Republicans shared more common ground on these issues than they like to admit, particularly around election time, each party evolved to focus on one above all. Democrats became the party of equality. They sometimes talked tough on crime and national security and they even balanced the national budget for a few years in the late 1990s, but their core common ground emerged more and more clearly as a broad inclusiveness. Democrats were liberals, or at least liberals were Democrats. Gay rights, women's equality, civil rights, and environmentalism became their touchstones. Cultural concerns replaced the older, labor union-oriented economic concerns of the New Deal coalition. Markets were good; so was free trade. And Presidents Clinton and Obama strongly promoted international trade. But equality ruled the roost in the Democratic caucus.

Republicans, for their part, carried the real torch for free markets. They were "conservative," at least in the oxymoronic sense that promoting capitalism somehow conserved anything. They aimed for a government whose primary purpose was to serve the interests of business, which they believed to be the interests of all Americans. Building wealth and supporting investment created jobs; the private sector always acted more rationally and efficiently than government; wealth and a high material standard of living merited praise and admiration, and were available to all who worked hard enough—these assumptions were at the core of the contemporary GOP. Republicans officially praised equality and many of them believed in it sincerely, as it fit with the libertarian leaning that shaped much of the party's policies. But free markets ruled in the Republican caucus.[5]

The two major political parties, then, each reflected a central political belief of the American electorate in the new millennium. This helps explain some of the closeness of so many elections and the inability of either party to dominate completely the American political landscape. Americans believed in equality and they believed in free markets, and they were not fully comfortable choosing one over the other.

In the cultural realm, the forty years after 1970 brought a remarkable reversal of how the public and private spheres of American life were understood. Things were turned inside out. What had once been considered fundamental matters of public policy at the broadest national level—military service, welfare provision, taxation—were increasingly privatized or shrunken.

Conversely, what had once been viewed as matters of essential privacy—sexual behavior, vulgar language, family relationships, and religion—became normal parts of public conversation, mainstream entertainment, and politics. The values of what sociologists sometimes called "expressive individualism" reoriented American life toward the realm of the personal, the immodest, the self-celebrating, and the gratification-seeking, and away from the realm of concern for others, with its older values of community, self-sacrifice, and self-restraint. This was not a complete switch, a substitution of one for the other. But it was a historical process, a marked shift that reshaped, for better or worse, the nation's culture and politics.[6]

Out of the 1970s came a fundamental change in what Americans considered natural or commonsensical. The more communal values of the mid-twentieth century ebbed, particularly the idea that citizens should act collectively, through the mechanisms of government action and taxpayer funding, to reduce the most egregious forms of poverty and extreme economic inequality. This older perspective understood that deep inequality corresponds to serious social problems that diminish the quality of life across society. Such collective enterprise and purpose by the new millennium, however, were no longer seen by most voters as natural and right, but rather as an artificial intrusion into the more efficient realm of private enterprise. Into the place of ebbing communitarian values flowed instead a new assertion of the naturalness of markets, corporations, and the pursuit of self-interest. Americans across the political spectrum resented taxes and mistrusted the public sphere. They lived in a society where government's primary purpose was to facilitate citizens' individual pursuit of their own material aggrandizement, and most of them found it difficult to imagine a higher purpose for democratic governance. More inclusive and respectful in some regards, American life had grown harsher and cruder in others.[7]

NOTES

PREFACE

1. Bruce Cockburn, "Northern Lights," *Dancing in the Dragon's Jaws* (Columbia Records, 1979).

INTRODUCTION

1. Michiko Kakutani, "Two Perceptions of the Mellow Decade as Anything But," *New York Times*, March 21, 2006 (Doonesbury); Christopher Cappozzola, "'It Makes You Want to Believe in the Country': Celebrating the Bicentennial in an Age of Limits," in Beth L. Bailey and David Farber, eds., *America in the Seventies* (Lawrence: University Press of Kansas, 2004), 29–30 (Ford). On New York City, see Ken Auletta, *The Streets Were Paved with Gold: The Decline of New York, An American Tragedy* (New York: Random House, 1979).

2. "Honor, Then and Now," *Stanford Magazine*, September/October 2003, p. 72 (students); Joe Queenan, "The Decade That Won't Die," *New York Times Book Review*, December 2, 2007, 50–51. On divorce and families, see Natasha Zaretsky, *No Direction Home: The American Family and the Fear of Decline, 1968–1980* (Chapel Hill: University of North Carolina Press, 2007). On films, see Peter Lev, *American Films of the 70s: Conflicting Visions* (Austin: University of Texas Press, 2000); and David A. Cook, *Lost Illusions: American Cinema in the Shadow of Watergate and Vietnam, 1970–1979* (New York: Scribner, 2000). Illegal drug use continued to grow throughout the decade, peaking in 1979. Marie Gottschalk, *The Prison and the Gallows: The Politics of Mass Incarceration in America* (New York: Cambridge University Press, 2006), 33.

3. Andreas Killen, *1973 Nervous Breakdown: Watergate, Warhol, and the Birth of Post-Sixties America* (New York: Bloomsbury, 2006), 2; David Kennedy, "Editor's Introduction," to James T. Patterson, *Restless Giant: The United States from Watergate to Bush V. Gore* (New York: Oxford University Press, 2005), xii; Bailey and Farber, "Introduction," in *America in the Seventies*, ed. Bailey and Farber, 1; Philip Jenkins, *Decade of Nightmares: The End of the Sixties and the Making of Eighties America* (New York: Oxford University Press, 2006); David Frum, *How We Got Here: The 70's: The Decade That Brought You Modern Life (For Better or Worse)* (New York: Basic Books, 2000); Thomas Hine, *The Great Funk: Falling Apart and Coming Together (on a Shag Rug) in the Seventies* (New York: Sarah Crichton Books, 2007); Andrew J. Edelstein and Kevin McDonough, *The Seventies: From Hot Pants to Hot Tubs* (New York: Dutton, 1990).

The best overviews of the decade are Bruce J. Schulman, *The Seventies: The Great Shift in American Culture, Society, and Politics* (New York: Free Press, 2001); Edward D. Berkowitz, *Something Happened: A Political and Cultural Overview of the Seventies* (New York: Columbia University Press, 2006); Peter N. Carroll, *It Seemed Like Nothing Happened: America in the 1970s* (1982; reprinted with new preface, New Brunswick, NJ: Rutgers University Press, 1990); Bailey and Farber, eds., *America in the Seventies*.

For an introduction to the now blossoming literature on the rise of conservatism, particularly in the 1970s, see Laura Kalman, *Right Star Rising: A New Politics, 1974–1980* (New York, Norton, 2010); Bruce J. Schulman and Julian E. Zelizer, eds., *Rightward Bound: Making America Conservative in the 1970s* (Cambridge, MA: Harvard University Press, 2007); Donald T. Critchlow, *The Conservative Ascendancy: How the GOP Right Made Political History* (Cambridge, MA: Harvard University Press, 2007); Thomas Byrne Edsall and Mary D. Edsall, *Chain Reaction: The Impact of Race, Rights, and Taxes on American Politics* (New York: Norton, 1991); E. J. Dionne, Jr., *Why Americans Hate Politics* (New York: Simon & Schuster, 1991).

4. Two solid recent overviews are Maurice Isserman and Michael Kazin, *America Divided: The Civil War of the 1960s*, 3rd ed. (New York: Oxford University Press, 2007); Robert M. Collins, *Transforming America: Politics and Culture in the Reagan Years* (New York: Columbia University Press, 2007).

5. An intriguing new study of the U.S. place in global history is Daniel Sargent, "From Internationalism to Globalism: The United States and the Transformation of International Politics in the 1970s" (Ph.D. dissertation, Harvard University, 2008). On American exceptionalism, see Thomas Bender, *A Nation Among Nations: America's Place in World History* (New York: Hill and Wang, 2006); Daniel T. Rodgers, "Exceptionalism," in Anthony Mohlo and Gordon S. Wood, eds., *Imagined Histories: American Historians Interpret the Past* (Princeton, NJ: Princeton University Press, 1998); Seymour Martin Lipset, *American Exceptionalism: A Double-Edged Sword* (New York: Norton, 1996). Michael Kammen has noted how the crises of the early 1970s stimulated the rise of a sustained intellectual dissent against the very idea of American exceptionalism by 1975. Kammen, "The Problem of American Exceptionalism: A Reconsideration," *American Quarterly* 45, 1 (March 1993): 11–16.

6. Ryan Sager, *The Elephant in the Room: Evangelicals, Libertarians, and the Battle to Control the Republican Party* (Hoboken, NJ: Wiley, 2006).

7. Louis Menand, "The Seventies Show," *New Yorker*, May 28, 2001, pp. 130–31.

8. Killen, *1973 Nervous Breakdown*, 1; Bailey and Farber, "Introduction," in *America in the Seventies*, ed. Bailey and Farber, 2.

9. Robert J. Samuelson, *The Good Life and Its Discontents: The American Dream in the Age of Entitlement, 1945–1995* (New York: Times Books, 1995), 51; James Reston, "War Leaves Deep Mark on U.S.," *New York Times*, January 24, 1973, p. 1; Elizabeth Drew, *American Journal: The Events of 1976* (New York: Random House, 1977), 3; Christopher Cappozzola, "'It Makes You Want to Believe in the Country': Celebrating the Bicentennial in an Age of

Limits," in *America in the Seventies*, ed. Bailey and Farber, 38–39. One emblematic example of the turn to social history was Lawrence Goodwyn's *Democratic Promise: The Populist Moment in America* (New York: Oxford University Press, 1976), nicely representative of its time: rethinking older assumptions, granting respect and dignity to those formerly dismissed or despised (agrarian radicals in the South and the Midwest in the late 1800s), skeptical of traditional elites and social hierarchies, and enthusiastic about reform from below, about democracy as something common people create together rather than something others give to them.

10. William Graebner, "America's Poseidon Adventure: A Nation in Existential Despair," in *America in the Seventies*, ed. Bailey and Farber, 158; Peter Novick, *The Holocaust in American Life* (Boston: Houghton Mifflin, 1999); Piers Paul Read, *Alive: The Story of the Andes Survivors* (Philadelphia: Lippincott, 1974); Nando Parrado, *Miracle in the Andes: 72 Days on the Mountain and My Long Trek Home* (New York: Crown, 2006); Sue Halperin, "Virtual Iraq," *New Yorker*, May 19, 2008, p. 32.

11. Graebner, "America's Poseidon Adventure," 183. Of course, many antibusing activists, such as Louise Day Hicks in Boston, were female. See Ronald P. Formisano, *Boston Against Busing: Race, Class, and Ethnicity in the 1960s and 1970s* (Chapel Hill: University of North Carolina Press, 1991).

12. Doug Rossinow, *The Politics of Authenticity: Liberalism, Christianity, and the New Left in America* (New York: Columbia University Press, 1998).

13. *Blazing Saddles* went on to become the most financially successful Western film ever, due to DVD rental profits that reached $48 million. David A. Cook, *Lost Illusions: American Cinema in the Shadow of Watergate and Vietnam, 1970–1979* (New York: Scribner, 2000), 182.

14. David J. Hoeveler, *The Postmodernist Turn: American Thought and Culture in the 1970s* (Boston: Twayne, 1996); Collins, *Transforming America*, 148–49; Tony Judt, "Edward Said: The Rootless Cosmopolitan," in *Reappraisals: Reflections on The Forgotten Twentieth Century* (New York: Penguin, 2008), 164.

15. Tom Wolfe, "The 'Me' Decade and the Third Great Awakening," *New York*, August 23, 1976, pp. 26–40; Dana Spiotta, *Eat The Document* (New York: Scribner, 2006), 200; David Herzberg, "'The Pill You Love Can Turn On You': Feminism, Tranquilizers, and the Valium Panic of the 1970s," *American Quarterly* 58, 1 (2006): 79–103; Jeremy Black, *Altered States: America since the Sixties* (London: Reaktion, 2006), 65; Andrew J. Cherlin, *The Marriage-Go-Round: The State of Marriage and the Family in America Today* (New York: Knopf, 2009).

16. Suzanne Mettler, *Soldiers to Citizens: The G.I. Bill and the Making of the Greatest Generation* (New York: Oxford University Press, 2005), 4; Robert D. Putnam, *Bowling Alone: The Collapse and Revival of American Community* (New York: Simon & Schuster, 2000); Jimmy Carter, "Address to the Nation on Energy and National Goals," July 15, 1979, *Public Papers of the Presidents*, accessed at http://www.presidency.ucsb.edu/ws/index.php?pid =32596&st=&st1; Christopher Lasch, *The Culture of Narcissism: American Life in an Age of Diminishing Expectations* (New York: Norton, 1978), 4–5.

Valium turned out to be addictive, and the FDA in 1980 began requiring that it and other anxiety medications come with a warning that "anxiety or tension associated with the stress of everyday life usually does not require treatment with an anxiolytic." Louis Menand, "Head Case," *New Yorker*, March 1, 2010, p. 73.

17. Donald T. Critchlow, *The Conservative Ascendancy: How The GOP Right Made Political History* (Cambridge, MA: Harvard University Press, 2007); Godfrey Hodgson, *The World Turned Right Side Up: A History of the Conservative Ascendancy in America* (Boston: Houghton Mifflin, 1996); Sean Wilentz, *The Age of Reagan: A History, 1974–2008* (New York: Harper, 2008); Sam Tanenhaus, *The Death of Conservatism* (New York: Random House, 2009); Schulman and Zelizer, eds., *Rightward Bound*; Edsall and Edsall, *Chain Reaction*. A fascinating interpretation of the role of Wal-Mart in smoothing the confluence of the conservative Christian and free-market wings of the Republican Party is Bethany Moreton, *To Serve God and Wal-Mart: The Making of Christian Free Enterprise* (Cambridge, MA: Harvard University Press, 2009). On enduring internal tensions within the Republican Party, see Sager, *The Elephant in the Room*.

18. Sara Evans, *Tidal Wave: How Women Changed America at Century's End* (New York: Free Press, 2003); Ruth Rosen, *The World Split Open: How the Modern Women's Movement Changed America* (New York: Viking, 2000); Winifred D. Wandersee, *On The Move: American Women in the 1970s* (Boston: Twayne, 1988).

19. Akira Iriye, *Global Community: The Role of International Organizations in the Making of the Contemporary World* (Berkeley: University of California Press, 2002); Samuel Moyn, *The Last Utopia: Human Rights in History* (Cambridge, MA: Harvard University Press, 2010).

20. Steve Friess, "Las Vegas Adapts to Reap Chinese New Year Bounty, *New York Times*, February 21, 2007 (Weidner); George M. Fredrickson, *Racism: A Short History* (Princeton, NJ: Princeton University Press, 2002), 143; Walter Benn Michaels, *The Trouble With Diversity: How We Learned to Love Identity and Ignore Inequality* (New York: Metropolitan Books, 2006), 75; David Harvey, *A Brief History of Neoliberalism* (New York: Oxford University Press, 2005).

21. "New Network Will Showcase Greed, Lust, Sex," *Wall Street Journal*, February 23, 2006, p. B1.

CHAPTER 1. CROSSCURRENTS OF CRISIS IN 1970S AMERICA

1. I am indebted to Professor Peter Wood of Duke University for conversations about this film.

2. Jefferson Cowie, "'Vigorously Left, Right, and Center': The Crosscurrents of Working-Class America in the 1970s," in *America in the Seventies*, ed. Bailey and Farber, 76; Graebner, "America's Poseidon Adventure," 163.

3. Louis P. Masur, *Runaway Dream: Born To Run and Bruce Springsteen's American Vision* (New York: Bloomsbury, 2009).

4. Among the best overviews of what Vietnamese called "the American War" are George Herring, *America's Longest War: The United States and Vietnam, 1950–1975*, 4th ed. (New York: McGraw-Hill, 2001); Marilyn B. Young, *The Vietnam Wars, 1945–1990* (New York: Basic Books, 1991); Robert D. Schulzinger, *A Time For War: The United States and Vietnam, 1946–1975* (New York: Oxford University Press, 1997); and Mark A. Lawrence, *The Vietnam War: A Concise International History* (New York: Oxford University Press, 2008).

5. Thomas Alan Schwartz, "'Henry, . . . Winning an Election Is Terribly Important': Partisan Politics in the History of U.S. Foreign Relations," *Diplomatic History* 33, 2 (April 2009): 174 (Kissinger and Nixon); Jeffrey P. Kimball, *Nixon's Vietnam War* (Lawrence: University Press of Kansas, 1998); Frank Snepp, *Decent Interval: An Insider's Account of Saigon's Indecent End Told by the CIA's Chief Strategy Analyst in Vietnam* (New York: Random House, 1977).

6. U.S. National Archives, "Statistical Information About Casualties of the Vietnam War," http://www.archives.gov/research/vietnam-war/casualty-statistics.html (accessed July 7, 2010); David M. Halbfinger, "Kerry's Antiwar Past Is a Delicate Issue in His Campaign," *New York Times*, April 24, 2004; Young, *The Vietnam Wars*, 255–57, 280; Michael Bilton and Kevin Sim, *Four Hours in My Lai* (New York: Viking, 1992); Kyle Longley, *Grunts: The American Combat Soldier in Vietnam* (Armonk, NY: M.E. Sharpe, 2008), 115–57. For an interpretation with a different emphasis, see Jeremy Kuzmarov, *The Myth of the Addicted Army: Vietnam and the Modern War on Drugs* (Amherst: University of Massachusetts Press, 2009).

7. Tobias Wolff, *In Pharoah's Army: Memories of the Lost War* (New York: Knopf, 1994), 23; Dwight Garner, "America Abroad," *New York Times*, July 9, 2008 (Melville); Albert J. Beveridge, "The March of the Flag," speech, September 16, 1898, http://www.historytools.org/sources/beveridge.html; *United States-Vietnam Relations, 1945–1967: Study Prepared by the Department of Defense* (Washington, DC: U.S. Government Printing Office, 1971); David Halberstam, *The Best and the Brightest* (New York: Random House, 1972); Yanek Mieczkowski, *Gerald Ford and the Challenges of the 1970s* (Lexington: University Press of Kentucky, 2005), 293–94.

8. Patterson, *Restless Giant*, 102.

9. Christopher M. Andrew, *The World Was Going Our Way: The KGB and the Battle for the Third World* (New York: Basic Books, 2005); Odd Arne Westad, *The Global Cold War: Third World Interventions and the Making of Our Times* (New York: Cambridge University Press, 2005); Piero Gleijeses, "Moscow's Proxy? Cuba and Africa, 1975–1988," *Journal of Cold War Studies* 8, 4 (Fall 2006): 98–146.

10. Robert David Johnson, "The Unintended Consequences of Reform: The Clark and Tunney Amendments and U.S. Policy toward Angola," *Diplomatic History* 27, 2 (April 2003): 224–26; Piero Gleijeses, *Conflicting Missions: Havana, Washington, and Africa, 1959–1976* (Chapel Hill: University of North Carolina Press, 2001), chapters 11–16.

11. H. W. Brands, *The Devil We Knew: Americans and the Cold War* (New

York: Oxford University Press, 1993), 137; Johnson, "Unintended Consequences of Reform," 234–38.

12. Margaret MacMillan, *Nixon and Mao: The Week That Changed the World* (New York: Random House, 2007); Michael Schaller, *The United States and China into the Twenty-First Century*, 3rd ed. (New York: Oxford University Press, 2002), 113 (Wherry); "Editorial Opinions in U.S. on Nixon Trip," *New York Times*, February 25, 1972.

13. Lorenz M. Lüthi, *The Sino-Soviet Split: Cold War in the Communist World* (Princeton, NJ: Princeton University Press, 2008); David A. Mayers, *Cracking the Monolith: U.S. Policy against the Sino-Soviet Alliance, 1949–1955* (Baton Rouge: Louisiana State University Press, 1986); Raymond L. Garthoff, *Détente and Confrontation: American-Soviet Relations from Nixon to Reagan*, rev. ed. (Washington, DC: Brookings Institution, 1994). Yugoslavia, where Communist partisans under Josep Tito seized power late in World War II without Red Army assistance, had long gone its own way, diverging from Soviet leader Joseph Stalin's policies enough to be ejected from the Comintern in 1948. But few Americans paid much attention to the Yugoslav exception of nationalist Communism independent from Moscow. See Lorraine M. Lees, *Keeping Tito Afloat: The United States, Yugoslavia, and the Cold War* (University Park: Pennsylvania State University Press, 1997).

14. Lyndon B. Johnson, "Peace Without Conquest," address at Johns Hopkins University, April 7, 1965, *Public Papers of the Presidents, 1965, Book I*, available at "The American Presidency Project," http://www.presidency.ucsb.edu/ws/index.php?pid=26877&st=&st1=.

15. Carroll, *It Seemed Like Nothing Happened*, 75 (Nixon); "In The World: A Time of Difficult Choices," *U.S. News and World Report*, July 5, 1976, p. 50.

16. Alastair Reid, "1973," in *Weathering: Poems and Translations* (New York: E. P. Dutton, 1978), 72–73; John Dinges, *The Condor Years: How Pinochet and His Allies Brought Terrorism to Three Continents* (New York: New Press, 2004); Hobsbawm, *The Age of Extremes*, 446.

17. *The Oxford History of the British Empire*, vol. 4, *The Twentieth Century*, ed. Judith M. Brown and Wm. Roger Louis (New York: Oxford University Press, 1998); Nikki R. Keddie, *Modern Iran: Roots and Results of Revolution* (New Haven, CT: Yale University Press, 2006); David Farber, *Taken Hostage: The Iran Hostage Crisis and America's First Encounter with Radical Islam* (Princeton, NJ: Princeton University Press, 2005); Yaroslav Trofimov, *The Siege of Mecca: The Forgotten Uprising in Islam's Holiest Shrine and the Birth of Al Qaeda* (New York: Doubleday, 2007).

18. Avi Shlaim, *The Iron Wall: Israel and the Arab World* (New York: Norton, 2000); Benny Morris, *Righteous Victims: A History of the Zionist-Arab Conflict, 1881–1998* (New York: Knopf, 1999); Gershom Gorenberg, *The Accidental Empire: Israel and the Birth of the Settlements, 1967–1977* (New York: Times Books, 2006); Michelle Mart, *Eye on Israel: How the United States Came to View the Jewish State as an Ally* (Albany: State University of New York Press, 2006); Melani McAlister, *Epic Encounters: Culture, Media, and U.S. Interests in the Middle East since 1945*, rev. ed. (Berkeley: University

of California Press, 2005), especially 155–97; David Schoenbaum, *The United States and the State of Israel* (New York: Oxford University Press, 1993); "Jewish Virtual Library," http://www.jewishvirtuallibrary.org/jsource/History/worldpop.html and http://www.jewishvirtuallibrary.org/jsource/Judaism/jewpop.html.

19. "4 Jets Hijacked; One, a 747, Is Blown Up," *New York Times*, September 7, 1970, p. 1.

20. Bernard Gwertzman, "Ford Congratulates Israel on the Raid," *New York Times*, July 5, 1976, p. 2; Aaron J. Klein, *Striking Back: The 1972 Olympics Massacre and Israel's Deadly Response* (New York: Random House, 2005); Max Hastings, *Yoni, Hero of Entebbe* (New York: Dial, 1979).

21. Bernard Bailyn, *The Ideological Origins of the American Revolution* (Cambridge, MA: Harvard University Press, 1967), 34–36, 55–59 (Bailyn), 93 (Eliot).

22. Dan T. Carter, *From George Wallace to Newt Gingrich: Race in the Conservative Counterrevolution, 1963–1994* (Baton Rouge: Louisiana State University Press, 1996), 54 (Buchanan); Stanley I. Kutler, *Watergate and the Fall of Richard Nixon* (St. James, NY: Brandywine, 1996), 21 (Dean and Nixon); Rick Perlstein, *Nixonland: The Rise of a President and the Fracturing of America* (New York: Scribner, 2008).

23. Lois G. Gordon and Alan Gordon, *American Chronicle: Six Decades in American Life, 1920–1980* (New York: Atheneum, 1987), 495.

24. Gordon and Gordon, *American Chronicle*, 513 (Goldwater); Mieczkowski, *Gerald Ford and the Challenges of the 1970s*, 21–22 (Cronkite and Ray); "Take My Vice President, Please!" *New York Times*, November 9, 1997, Sec. 4, p. 7 (Nixon).

25. Fraser and Gerstle, eds., *Rise and Fall of the New Deal Order*.

26. Merle Miller, *Plain Speaking: An Oral Biography of Harry S. Truman* (New York: Berkley, 1974). Bob Woodward's book, *The Brethren: Inside the Supreme Court* (New York: Simon & Schuster, 1979), similarly revealed less admirable details of how the nation's highest Justices sometimes operated.

27. Mieczkowski, *Gerald Ford and the Challenges of the 1970s*, 1, 28–31, 334; "Transcript of Foreign Affairs Debate Between Ford and Carter," *New York Times*, October 7, 1976, p. 36.

28. Jimmy Carter, "Address to the Nation on Energy and National Goals," July 15, 1979, *Public Papers of the Presidents, 1979, Book 2*, available at "The American Presidency Project," http://www.presidency.ucsb.edu/ws/index.php?pid=32596&st=&st1=; Burton I. Kaufman, *The Presidency of James Earl Carter, Jr.* (Lawrence: University Press of Kansas, 1993); Gary M. Fink and Hugh Davis Graham, eds., *The Carter Presidency: Policy Choices in the Post-New Deal Era* (Lawrence: University Press of Kansas, 1998).

29. Loch K. Johnson, *A Season of Inquiry: The Senate Intelligence Investigation* (Lexington: University Press of Kentucky, 1985), 9, 48–53; Kathryn S. Olmsted, *Challenging the Secret Government: The Post-Watergate Investigations of the CIA and FBI* (Chapel Hill: University of North Carolina Press, 1996), 140–43; U.S. Senate Select Committee to Study Governmental Operations with Respect to Intelligence Activities, *Alleged Assassination Plots In-*

volving Foreign Leaders, 94th Cong., 1st sess., November 20, 1975 (Washington, DC: U.S. Government Printing Office, 1975); U.S. House Select Committee on Intelligence, *CIA: The Pike Report* (Nottingham, UK: Spokesman Books, 1977); Philip Agee, *Inside The Company: CIA Diary* (New York: Stonehill, 1975); John Stockwell, *In Search of Enemies: A CIA Story* (New York: Norton, 1978). On film, see Cook, *Lost Illusions*, 200–202.

30. Johnson, *A Season of Inquiry*, 6 (quotation), 48–53.

31. U.S. Department of State, Foreign Relations of the United States, 1969–1976, vol. 17: *China, 1969–1972* (Washington, DC: U.S. Government Printing Office, 2006), 55; Peter Irons, *War Powers: How the Imperial Presidency Hijacked the Constitution* (New York: Metropolitan, 2005), 198–99; Meredith Fuchs, "The White House: Off Limits to Historians?" *Passport: Newsletter of the Society for Historians of American Foreign Relations* 39 (April 2008): 7; Julian E. Zelizer, *On Capitol Hill: The Struggle to Reform Congress and Its Consequences, 1948–2000* (New York: Cambridge University Press, 2004); National Security Archive, "The CIA's Family Jewels," http://www.gwu.edu/~nsarchiv/NSAEBB/NSAEBB222/index.htm.

32. Bruce Miroff, *The Liberals' Moment: The McGovern Insurgency and the Identity Crisis of the Democratic Party* (Lawrence: University Press of Kansas, 2007); Jefferson Cowie, "Nixon's Class Struggle: Romancing the New Right Worker, 1969–1973," *Labor History* 43, 3 (2002): 281.

33. Patterson, *Restless Giant*, 89; Hitchcock, *Struggle for Europe*, 5–6; Francis Fukuyama, *The Great Disruption: Human Nature and the Reconstitution of Social Order* (New York: Free Press, 1999), 50; Mieczkowski, *Gerald Ford and the Challenges of the 1970s*, 21; Putnam, *Bowling Alone*; Public Broadcasting System, "Politics and Government," http://www.pbs.org/now/politics/vote_pop/vote3.html; William A. Link, *Righteous Warrior: Jesse Helms and the Rise of Modern Conservatism* (New York: St. Martin's, 2008), 105 (Helms). For a useful summary of recent American conservatism, see Julian E. Zelizer, "Rethinking the History of American Conservatism," *Reviews in American History* 38, 2 (June 2010): 367–92.

34. Donald T. Critchlow, *Phyllis Schlafly and Grassroots Conservatism: A Woman's Crusade* (Princeton, NJ: Princeton University Press, 2005), 2 (Jepsen); Robert Entman and Bonnie Koenig, "The 'Conservative' Myth," *The Nation*, July 17, 1976, pp. 39–42 (Harris); Allan J. Lichtman, *White Protestant Nation: The Rise of the American Conservative Movement* (New York: Atlantic Monthly Press, 2008).

35. Rebecca Klatch, *Women of the New Right* (Philadelphia: Temple University Press, 1987), 4–5. On Reagan, see Lou Cannon, *Reagan* (New York: Putnam, 1982); Edmund Morris, *Dutch: A Memoir of Ronald Reagan* (New York: Random House, 1998); Kiron K. Skinner, Annelise Anderson, and Martin Anderson, eds., *Reagan, In His Own Hand: The Writings of Ronald Reagan That Reveal His Revolutionary Vision for America* (New York: Free Press, 2001). On the Republican Party's divisions, see Sager, *The Elephant in the Room*.

36. Kevin M. Kruse, *White Flight: Atlanta and the Making of Modern Conservatism* (Princeton, NJ: Princeton University Press, 2005), 9–11, 106–7,

132–33, 247; James N. Gregory, *The Southern Diaspora: How the Great Migrations of Black and White Southerners Transformed America* (Chapel Hill: University of North Carolina Press, 2005), 302; Thomas J. Sugrue, *Origins of the Urban Crisis: Race and Inequality in Postwar Detroit* (Princeton, NJ: Princeton University Press, 1996); J. Anthony Lukas, *Common Ground: A Turbulent Decade in the Lives of Three American Families* (New York: Knopf, 1985); John Egerton, *The Americanization of Dixie: The Southernization of America* (New York: Harper's Magazine Press, 1974); Peter Applebome, *Dixie Rising: How the South Is Shaping American Values, Politics and Culture* (New York: Times Books, 1996); Joseph E. Lowndes, *From the New Deal to the New Right: Race and the Southern Origins of Modern Conservatism* (New Haven, CT: Yale University Press, 2009).

37. Link, *Righteous Warrior*, 129, 170–73, 198–200.

38. Ibid., 131–65, 171, 178–80 (quotations at 171 and 180); Joseph Crespino, *In Search of Another Country: Mississippi and the Conservative Counterrevolution* (Princeton, NJ: Princeton University Press, 2007); Adam Clymer, *Drawing the Line at the Big Ditch: The Panama Canal Treaties and the Rise of the Right* (Lawrence: University Press of Kansas, 2008); John D'Emilio and Estelle B. Freedman, *Intimate Matters: A History of Sexuality in America* (New York: Harper & Row, 1988), 351–53.

39. Richard W. Stevenson and Adam Liptak, "Cheney Defends Expansion of Presidential Powers," *New York Times*, December 20, 2005; Link, *Righteous Warrior*, 189 (Helms); Anne Cahn, *Killing Détente: The Right Attacks the CIA* (University Park: Pennsylvania State University Press, 1998), 20, 36, 47, 49, 64–67; Justin Vaïsse, *Neoconservatism: The Biography of a Movement*, trans. Arthur Goldhammer (Cambridge, MA: Harvard University Press, 2010), 110–79; Jerry W. Sanders, *Peddlers of Crisis: The Committee on the Present Danger and the Politics of Containment* (Boston: South End Press, 1983).

40. Richard A. Easterlin, *Growth Triumphant: The Twenty-First Century in Historical Perspective* (Ann Arbor: University of Michigan Press, 1996), 1; McNeill, *Something New Under the Sun*, 15, 305; Jurgen Osterhammel and Niels P. Petersson, *Globalization: A Short History* (Princeton, NJ: Princeton University Press, 2005), 121; Barry J. Eichengreen, *The European Economy since 1945: Coordinated Capitalism and Beyond* (Princeton, NJ: Princeton University Press, 2006), 2; Kenneth T. Jackson, *Crabgrass Frontier: The Suburbanization of the United States*, (New York: Oxford University Press, 1985), 297–98; Dana Frank, *Buy American: The Untold Story of Economic Nationalism* (Boston: Beacon, 1999), chapter 5; Hobsbawm, *The Age of Extremes*, 261. The expansion of the American middle class in these years can be traced in William H. Chafe, *The Unfinished Journey: America since World War II*, 7th ed. (New York: Oxford University Press, 2010); and James T. Patterson, *Grand Expectations: The United States, 1945–1974* (New York: Oxford University Press, 1996).

41. U.S. Department of Labor, Bureau of Labor Statistics, www.bls.gov; Dean Baker, *The United States since 1980* (New York: Cambridge University Press, 2007), 45; Barry Bluestone, "Foreword," in Jefferson R. Cowie and Joseph Heathcott, *Beyond the Ruins: The Meanings of Deindustrialization*

(Ithaca, NY: ILR Press, 2003), viii; Laurence Veysey, "The Autonomy of American History Reconsidered," *American Quarterly* 31, 4 (1979): 456.

42. Edsall and Edsall, *Chain Reaction*, 105; Hodgson, *More Equal Than Others*, 16; Eichengreen, *The European Economy since 1945*, 7–8; Tony Judt, *A Grand Illusion? An Essay on Europe* (New York: Hill and Wang, 1996), 94; Mark Mazower, *Dark Continent: Europe's Twentieth Century* (New York: Knopf, 1998), 327–31; Bruce J. Schulman, "Slouching Toward the Supply Side: Jimmy Carter and the New American Political Economy," in *The Carter Presidency: Policy Choices in the Post-New Deal Era*, ed. Gary M. Fink and Hugh Davis Graham (Lawrence: University Press of Kansas, 1998), 63.

43. Larry M. Bartels, *Unequal Democracy: The Political Economy of the New Gilded Age* (Princeton, NJ: Princeton University Press, 2008), 45; Kevin P. Phillips, *American Theocracy: The Peril and Politics of Radical Religion, Oil, and Borrowed Money in the 21st Century* (New York: Viking, 2006), 40–41; William I. Hitchcock, *The Struggle for Europe: The Turbulent History of a Divided Continent, 1945–2002* (New York: Doubleday, 2003), 243–44; Judt, *A Grand Illusion* 94; Frederick Cooper, *Africa Since 1940: The Past of the Present* (New York: Cambridge University Press, 2002), 86–87, 93, 100; Stephen Kotkin, *Armageddon Averted: The Soviet Collapse, 1970–2000* (New York: Oxford University Press, 2001), 11–12.

44. David S. Painter, "International Oil and National Security," *Daedalus* 120, 4 (1991), 196–97; U.S. Department of Energy, Energy Information Administration, www.eai.doe.

45. Patterson, *Restless Giant*, 65; Mieczkowski, *Gerald Ford and the Challenges of the 1970s*, 198, 212–13 (first Ford); History News Network, February 27, 2006, http://hnn.us/articles/22084.html (second Ford); Phillips, *American Theocracy*, 31 (Barton); Hodgson, *More Equal than Others*, 13 (Gulf Oil executive). For a provocative comparison of the United States and Rome, see Cullen Murphy, *Are We Rome? The Fall of an Empire and the Fate of America* (Boston: Houghton Mifflin, 2007).

46. Philip Shabecoff, *A Fierce Green Fire: The American Environmental Movement*, rev. ed. (Washington: Island Press, 2003), 113; Mieczkowski, *Gerald Ford and the Challenges of the 1970s*, 246.

47. Elizabeth Kolbert, "The Road Not Taken," *New Yorker*, 27 March 2000, pp. 33–34 (Carter); *New York Times*, July 6, 2008, p. BU6; Phillips, *American Theocracy*, 55; Andrew Gordon, *A Modern History of Japan: From Tokugawa Times to the Present* (New York: Oxford University Press, 2003), 287–88; Matthew L. Wald, "Automakers Use New Technology to Beef Up Muscle, Not Mileage," *New York Times*, March 30, 2006 (EPA expert).

48. U.S. Department of Energy, Energy Information Administration, table 8.1, "Nuclear Energy Overview," http://www.eia.doe.gov/emeu/mer/pdf/pages/sec8_3.pdf; U.S. Nuclear Regulatory Commission, "Backgrounder on Radioactive Waste," http://www.nrc.gov/reading-rm/doc-collections/fact-sheets/rad waste.html.

49. J. Samuel Walker, *Three Mile Island: A Nuclear Crisis in Historical Perspective* (Berkeley: University of California Press, 2004); U.S. Nuclear Regulatory Commission, "Backgrounder on Chernobyl Nuclear Power Plant Ac-

cident," http://www.nrc.gov/reading-rm/doc-collections/fact-sheets/chernobyl-bg.html.

50. D. W. Meinig, *The Shaping of America: A Geographical Perspective on 500 Years of History*, vol. 4: *Global America: 1915–2000* (New Haven, CT: Yale University Press, 2004), 265–66; McNeill, *Something New Under the Sun*, 301; Painter, "International Oil and National Security," 197–99; Donald Worster, *Under Western Skies: Nature and History in the American West* (New York: Oxford University Press, 1992), 188–214.

51. Paul Volcker, interview with PBS, http://www.pbs.org/fmc/interviews/volcker.htm; Robert M. Collins, *Transforming America: Politics and Culture in the Reagan Years* (New York: Columbia University Press, 2007), 72; Economic History Services, "Measuringworth," http://www.measuringworth.com/inflation/; Baker, *The United States since 1980*, 46–47; Carroll, *It Seemed Like Nothing Happened*, 134 (Burns); Hitchcock, *The Struggle for Europe*, 314; Eichengreen, *The European Economy since 1945*, 30; Gordon and Gordon, *American Chronicle*, 513.

52. Paul Krugman, "The Big Disconnnect," *New York Times*, September 1, 2006; Eduardo Porter, "After Years of Growth, What About Workers' Share?" *New York Times*, October 15, 2006, Sec. 3, p. 3; Urie Bronfenbrenner, *The State of Americans: This Generation and the Next* (New York: Free Press, 1996), 54–55; Tom Kemp, *The Climax of Capitalism: The U.S. Economy in the Twentieth Century* (New York: Longman, 1990), 155; Bailey and Farber, "Introduction," in *America in the Seventies*, ed. Bailey and Farber, 1; Richard M. Abrams, *America Transformed: Sixty Years of Revolutionary Change, 1941–2001* (New York: Cambridge University Press, 2006), 215–16; Jacob S. Hacker, Suzanne Mettler, and Joe Soss, "The New Politics of Inequality: A Policy-Centered Perspective," in *Remaking America: Democracy and Public Policy in an Age of Inequality* (New York: Russell Sage Foundation, 2007), 7.

53. Peter Gottschalk, "Inequality, Income Growth, and Mobility: The Basic Facts," *Journal of Economic Perspectives*, 11, 2 (1997): 21; Amy Glasmeier, *An Atlas of Poverty in America: One Nation, Pulling Apart, 1960–2003* (New York: Routledge, 2005), xix, 39, 83–85; James T. Patterson, "Jimmy Carter and Welfare Reform," in *The Carter Presidency*, ed. Fink and Graham, 191.

54. Patterson, *Restless Giant*, 63 (Susan Ford); Kim Phillips-Fein, "Follow the Money," *Reviews in American History* 33, 3 (2005): 469; Barry Bluestone, "Foreword," in *Beyond the Ruins*, ed. Cowie and Heathcott, viii; Abrams, *America Transformed*, 117; Theodore Caplow, Louis Hicks, and Ben J. Wattenberg, *The First Measured Century: An Illustrated Guide to Trends in America, 1900–2000* (Washington, DC: AEI Press, 2001), 49; Patterson, *Restless Giant*, 62; Jefferson Cowie, "'Vigorously Left, Right, and Center': The Crosscurrents of Working-Class America in the 1970s," in *America in the Seventies*, ed. Bailey and Farber, 101.

55. Murphy, *Are We Rome?* 15 (MacMullen); Hacker et al., "New Politics of Inequality," 7; Margaret Weir, "The American Middle Class and the Politics of Education," in *Social Contracts under Stress: The Middle Classes of America, Europe, and Japan at the Turn of the Century*, ed. Olivier Zunz, Leonard J. Schoppa, and Nobuhiro Hiwatari (New York: Russell Sage Foundation,

2002), 191–92; Louis Hyman, "Debtor Nation: Personal Debt Practices and the Making of Postwar America" (PhD dissertation, Harvard University, 2009); Bartels, *Unequal Democracy*, 130; Paul Krugman, "Whining Over Discontent," *New York Times*, September 8, 2006; Tony Judt, "The Wrecking Ball of Innovation," *New York Review of Books*, December 6, 2007, p. 22.

56. Thomas A. Harris, *I'm OK, You're OK* (New York: Avon, 1969); Alex Comfort, ed., *The Joy of Sex: A Gourmet Guide to Lovemaking* (New York: Simon & Schuster, 1972); James L. Collier, *The Rise of Selfishness in America* (New York: Oxford University Press, 1991), 232; Eva S. Moskowitz, *In Therapy We Trust: America's Obsession with Self-Fulfillment* (Baltimore: Johns Hopkins University Press, 2001), chapter 7; Abrams, *America Transformed*, 8–9; Fukuyama, *The Great Disruption*, 36; Robert J. Ringer, *Looking Out for #1* (New York: Fawcett, 1977). For background on these issues, see Rochelle Gurstein, *The Repeal of Reticence: America's Cultural and Legal Struggles over Free Speech, Obscenity, Sexual Liberation, and Modern Art* (New York: Hill and Wang, 1996).

57. Center for Disease Control, "Advance Data from Vital and Health Statistics," October 27, 2004, www.cdc.gov/nchs/data; *Wall Street Journal*, December 12, 2006, p. D1; Melinda Beck, "A Salty Tale: Why We Need A Diet Less Rich in Sodium," *Wall Street Journal*, April 21, 2009, p. 1; Jane Brody, "You Are Also What You Drink," *New York Times*, March 28, 2007; Bill Marsh, "The Overflowing American Dinner Plate," *New York Times*, August 3, 2008; Michael Pollan, "Unhappy Meals," *New York Times Magazine*, January 28, 2007, p. 41.

58. Burkhard Bilger, "The Search for Sweet," *New Yorker*, May 22, 2006, p. 40; "Here's to Father of Light Beer," *Omaha World-Herald*, December 25, 2005, p. 11A.

59. Moosewood Restaurant, www.moosewoodrestaurant.com; Steven Shapin, "Paradise Sold," *New Yorker*, May 15, 2006, p. 84; Thomas McNamee, *Alice Waters & Chez Panisse: The Romantic, Impractical, Often Eccentric, Ultimately Brilliant Making of a Food Revolution* (New York: Penguin, 2007), 111; Harvey Levenstein, *We'll Always Have Paris: American Tourists in France since 1930* (Chicago: University of Chicago Press, 2004), 253–54.

60. Howard Schultz and Dori Jones Yang, *Pour Your Heart into It: How Starbucks Built a Company One Cup at a Time* (New York: Hyperion, 1997); Starbucks Company, www.starbucks.com; Bryant Simon, *Everything but the Coffee: Learning about America from Starbucks* (Berkeley: University of California Press, 2009). Three years earlier, in 1973, corrupt but clever Bordeaux wine merchants had been arrested for defrauding foreigners; the evidence included one vat of wine considered vastly inferior that was labeled "Salable as Beaujolais to Americans." Leonard Mlodinow, "A Hint of Hype, A Taste of Illusion," *Wall Street Journal*, November 14–15, 2009, p. W1.

61. Allan M. Brandt, *The Cigarette Century: The Rise, Fall and Deadly Persistence of the Product That Defined America* (New York: Basic Books, 2006), 237, 288–92 (Roper at 290), 303 (critic), 309, 436 (Super Bowl ad), 449–50; Caplow et al., *The First Measured Century*, 145.

62. James F. Fixx, *The Complete Book of Running* (New York: Random

House, 1977); Richard B. Stolley and Tony Chiu, *LIFE: Our Century in Pictures* (New York: Bulfinch, 1999), 345; James Surowiecki, "Turf War," *New Yorker*, June 10, 2002, p. 33; Jimmy Carter, *Christmas in Plains: Memories* (New York: Simon & Schuster, 2001), 115–16.

63. Annie Gilbert Coleman, *Ski Style: Sport and Culture in the Rockies* (Lawrence: University Press of Kansas, 2004), 198; Joshua L. Miner and Joseph R. Boldt, *Outward Bound USA: Crew Not Passengers*, 2nd ed. (Seattle: Mountaineers Books, 2002), 252–53; Yvon Chouinard, *Let My People Go Surfing: The Education of a Reluctant Businessman* (New York: Penguin, 2005), 31–54; *New York Times*, March 15, 2008, p. A15.

64. From the 1970s onward, critic Louis Menand observed, "a giant continent of mainstream entertainment has emerged of which parody is the foundation." "Parodies Lost," *New Yorker*, September 20, 2010, p. 110.

CHAPTER 2. THE RISING TIDE OF EQUALITY AND DEMOCRATIC REFORM

1. Murphy, *Are We Rome?* 193 (Pliny the Younger); Beth Bailey, "She 'Can Bring Home the Bacon': Negotiating Gender in Seventies America," in *America in the Seventies*, ed. Bailey and Farber, 107–8; Abrams, *America Transformed*, 215–16.

2. Andrew Delbanco, "The Universities in Trouble," *New York Review of Books*, May 14, 2009, p. 39.

3. "Senator Clinton Enters Hall of Fame," *Omaha World-Herald*, October 9, 2005, p. 9A; Sara Evans, *Personal Politics: The Roots of Women's Liberation in the Civil Rights Movement and the New Left* (New York: Knopf, 1979); Alice Echols, "'Nothing Distant about It': Women's Liberation and Sixties Radicalism," in *The Sixties: From Memory to History*, ed. David Farber (Chapel Hill: University of North Carolina Press, 1994), 149–74.

4. Laurel Ulrich, *Well-Behaved Women Seldom Make History* (New York: Knopf, 2007), 196.

5. Amy Erdman Farrell, *Yours in Sisterhood:* Ms. *Magazine and the Promise of Popular Feminism* (Chapel Hill: University of North Carolina Press, 1998).

6. Bailey, "She 'Can Bring Home the Bacon'," 123; Evans, *Tidal Wave*, 91–92; Lindsey, *The Age of Abundance*, 194.

7. For an intriguing recent example of brain research suggesting male-female differences in empathy, see Elisabeth Rosenthal, "When Bad People Are Punished, Men Smile (But Women Don't)," *New York Times*, January 19, 2006.

8. Critchlow, *Phyllis Schlafly*, 12 (Friedan); Bailey, "She 'Can Bring Home the Bacon'," 120–21. On the limits of women's identity politics, see Jocelyn Olcott, "Globalizing Sisterhood: International Women's Year and the Politics of Representation," in *The Shock of the Global*, ed. Niall Ferguson, Charles Maier, Erez Manela, and Daniel Sargent (Cambridge, MA: Harvard University Press, 2010), 281–93.

9. Elizabeth Kolbert, "Firebrand," *New Yorker*, November 7, 2005, p. 137;

Critchlow, *Phyllis Schlafly*, 229–44; Scott Kaufman, *Rosalynn Carter: Equal Partner in the White House* (Lawrence: University Press of Kansas, 2007); Donald G. Mathews and Jane Sherron De Hart, *Sex, Gender, and the Politics of ERA: A State and the Nation* (New York: Oxford University Press, 1990).

10. Cohen, *Consumers' Republic*, 369–70; Linda Kerber, "The Meanings of Citizenship," *Journal of American History* 84, 3 (December 1997): 841; Jefferson Cowie, "'Vigorously Left, Right, and Center': The Crosscurrents of Working-Class America in the 1970s," in *America in the Seventies*, ed. Bailey and Farber, 83 (National Airlines, flight attendant); Zelizer, *On Capitol Hill*, 185–86.

11. Bailey, "She 'Can Bring Home the Bacon'," 108–9; Patterson, *Restless Giant*, 54–55; Fukuyama, *The Great Disruption*, 106–29; Elizabeth L. Hillman, "The Female Shape of the All-Volunteer Force," in *Iraq and the Lessons of Vietnam*, ed. Lloyd C. Gardner and Marilyn B. Young (New York: New Press, 2007), 151; CRS Report for Congress, "Life Expectancy in the United States," August 16, 2006, http://aging.senate.gov/crs/aging1.pdf (accessed May 15, 2009). On the longer-term trend in twentieth-century women's paid employment in the United States, see William H. Chafe, *The Paradox of Change: American Women in the Twentieth Century* (New York: Oxford University Press, 1991).

12. D'Emilio and Freedman, *Intimate Matters*, 332 (quotation); Putnam, *Bowling Alone*, 197–98; Bailey, "She 'Can Bring Home the Bacon'," 114–15; Patterson, *Restless Giant*, 57. See also Hochschild, *Second Shift*, and Juliet B. Schor, *The Overworked American: The Unexpected Decline of Leisure* (New York: Basic Books, 1991).

13. Center for American Women and Politics, Rutgers University, www.cawp.rutgers.edu (accessed February 13, 2006); Caplow et al., *The First Measured Century*, 45; Lindsey, *The Age of Abundance*, 192.

14. Mark Chaves, *Ordaining Women: Culture and Conflict in Religious Organizations* (Cambridge, MA: Harvard University Press, 1997); Joshua L. Miner and Joseph R. Boldt, *Outward Bound USA: Crew Not Passengers*, 2nd ed. (Seattle: Mountaineers Books, 2002); Gordon and Gordon, *American Chronicle*, 547; Susan M. Hartmann, "Feminism, Public Policy, and the Carter Administration," in *The Carter Presidency*, ed. Fink and Graham, 230; "Women in the Courts," *New York Times*, July 5, 2005, p. A15.

15. Suzanne Mettler, *Soldiers to Citizens: The G.I. Bill and the Making of the Greatest Generation* (New York: Oxford University Press, 2005), 11; Caplow et al., *First Measured Century*, 55; Jenkins, *Decade of Nightmares*, 28; W. Michael Cox and Richard Alm, "Scientists Are Made, Not Born," *New York Times*, February 28, 2005, p. A25; *New York Times*, January 7, 2007; H. Michael Gelfand, *Sea Change at Annapolis: The United States Naval Academy, 1949–2000* (Chapel Hill: University of North Carolina Press, 2006), 131 (female graduate).

16. Evans, *Tidal Wave*, 94–96; Ulrich, *Well-Behaved Women*, 211 (Lerner, Bridenthal); Robert B. Townshend, "What's in a Label?" *Perspectives*, January 2007, p. 7.

17. Welch Suggs, *A Place on the Team: The Triumph and Tragedy of Title IX* (Princeton, NJ: Princeton University Press, 2005); Bailey, "She 'Can Bring Home the Bacon'," 108–9; Carl Bialik, "Narrowing the Gender Gap," *Wall Street Journal*, March 15, 2004, p. R9.

18. Arlene Blum, *Annapurna: A Woman's Place*, 20th anniv. ed. (San Francisco: Sierra Club Books, 1998), xvii (guide), 203; Arlene Blum, *Breaking Trail: A Climbing Life* (New York: Scribner, 2005); Monica Potts, "Dr. Vera Komarkova, 62, Botanist and Mountaineer," *New York Times*, June 26, 2005; Gail Collins, *When Everything Changed: The Amazing Journey of American Women from 1960 to the Present* (New York: Little, Brown, 2009), 245–46.

19. Caplow et al., *First Measured Century*, 69; Stephanie Coontz, *Marriage, A History: From Obedience to Intimacy, or How Love Conquered Marriage* (New York: Viking, 2005); Kaufman, *Rosalynn Carter*, esp. 32–33; Carter, *Christmas in Plains*, 104–5 (quotations).

20. Fukuyama, *Great Disruption*, 103; Caplow et al., *First Measured Century*, 79; Patterson, *Restless Giant*, 50–51.

21. Teresa A. Sullivan, Elizabeth Warren, and Jay Lawrence Westbrook, *The Fragile Middle Class: Americans in Debt* (New Haven, CT: Yale University Press, 2000), 174–75; D'Emilio and Freedman, *Intimate Matters*, 331; Lindsey, *The Age of Abundance*, 206.

22. Bailey, "She 'Can Bring Home the Bacon'," 115–16.

23. Alfred C. Kinsey, Wardell B. Pomeroy, and Clyde E. Martin, *Sexual Behavior in the Human Male* (Philadelphia: W. B. Saunders, 1948); Alfred C. Kinsey et al., *Sexual Behavior in the Human Female* (Philadelphia: W. B. Saunders, 1953); William H. Masters and Virginia E. Johnson, *Human Sexual Response* (New York: Bantam, 1966); Beth Bailey, *Sex in the Heartland* (Cambridge, MA: Harvard University Press, 1999); Patterson, *Restless Giant*, 46–48; Elana Levine, *Wallowing in Sex: The New Sexual Culture of 1970s American Television* (Durham, NC: Duke University Press, 2007); Caplow et al., *The First Measured Century*, 71.

24. Shere Hite, *The Hite Report: A Nationwide Study on Female Sexuality* (New York: Macmillan, 1976); Anne Koedt, "The Myth of the Vaginal Orgasm" (1970), available at Chicago Women's Liberation Union, "herstory project," http://www.cwluherstory.org/myth-of-the-vaginal-orgasm-2.html.

25. Boston Women's Health Book Collective, *Our Bodies, Ourselves* (New York: Simon & Schuster, 1973); Kathy Davis, *The Making of Our Bodies, Ourselves: How Feminism Travels across Borders* (Durham, NC: Duke University Press, 2007), 2; Lou Cannon, "Mrs. Ford to Undergo Breast Surgery Today," *Washington Post*, September 28, 1974, p. 1; Sandra Morgen, *Into Our Own Hands: The Women's Health Movement in the United States, 1969–1990* (New Brunswick, NJ: Rutgers University Press, 2002). *Our Bodies, Ourselves* was first published in 1970 by a small, countercultural publisher, the New England Free Press.

26. Lawrence Lader, *Abortion* (Indianapolis: Bobbs-Merrill, 1966); Douglas Martin, "Lawrence Lader, Champion of Abortion Rights, Is Dead at 86," *New York Times*, May 10, 2006; Linda Greenhouse, *Becoming Justice Black-*

mun: Harry Blackmun's Supreme Court Journey (New York: Henry Holt, 2005), 72–74, 98–99; U.S. Supreme Court, *Roe v. Wade*, 410 U.S. 113 (1973) (quotations).

27. Linda Greenhouse, "The Evolution of a Justice," *New York Times Magazine*, April 10, 2005, pp. 28–32; Greenhouse, *Becoming Justice Blackmun*, 72–75, 91, 137–38; Mary Ann Glendon, *Rights Talk: The Impoverishment of Political Discourse* (New York: Free Press, 1991), 56–57; Andrea Tone, *Devices and Desires: A History of Contraception in America* (New York: Hill and Wang, 2001), 238–39; Eyal Press, "My Father's Abortion War," *New York Times Magazine*, January 22, 2006, pp. 57–61.

28. Evans, *Tidal Wave*, 49; Susan Brownmiller, *Against Our Will: Men, Women, and Rape* (New York: Simon & Schuster, 1975); James Reston, Jr., *The Innocence of Joan Little: A Southern Mystery* (New York: Times Books, 1977); Fred Harwell, *A True Deliverance: The Joan Little Case* (New York: Knopf, 1979).

29. Linda Kerber, "The Meanings of Citizenship," 838; David Finkelhor and Kersti Yllo, *License to Rape: Sexual Abuse of Wives*, reprint ed. (1985; New York: Simon & Schuster, 1987), 170–72; New York Court of Appeals, *New York v. Liberta*, December 20, 1984, No. 597; Georgia Supreme Court, *Warren v. Georgia*, November 6, 1985, 336 S.E. 2nd 221; Diana E. H. Russell, *Rape in Marriage*, exp. and rev. ed. (Bloomington: Indiana University Press, 1990).

30. Carl Guarneri, *America in the World: United States History in Global Context* (Boston: McGraw-Hill, 2007), 272; Tony Judt, *Postwar: A History of Europe since 1945* (New York: Penguin, 2005), 488–90; Hitchcock, *The Struggle for Europe*, 263; Blum, *Breaking Trail*, 136; Blum, *Annapurna*, 23.

31. On women in Iran, see, for example, Azar Nafisi, *Reading Lolita in Tehran: A Memoir in Books* (New York: Random House, 2003).

32. Hodgson, *More Equal than Others*, 183; Newell G. Bringhurst and Darron T. Smith, eds., *Black and Mormon* (Urbana: University of Illinois Press, 2004); Andy Newman, "For Mormons in Harlem, A Bigger Space Beckons," *New York Times*, October 2, 2005; William L. Van Deburg, *New Day in Babylon: The Black Power Movement and American Culture, 1965–1975* (Chicago: University of Chicago Press, 1992); J. Anthony Lukas, *Common Ground: A Turbulent Decade in the Lives of Three American Families* (New York: Knopf, 1985).

33. W. Fitzhugh Brundage, *The Southern Past: A Clash of Race and Memory* (Cambridge, MA: Harvard University Press, 2005), 295–96; Robert J. Norrell, *The House I Live In: Race in the American Century* (New York: Oxford University Press, 2005), 277; Cowie, "'Vigorously Left, Right, and Center'," 91.

34. Daniel M. Cobb, *Native Activism in Cold War America: The Struggle for Sovereignty* (Lawrence: University Press of Kansas, 2008); "Alcatraz Is Not an Island," http://www.pbs.org/itvs/alcatrazisnotanisland/activism.html (accessed May 22, 2009); Dee Brown, *Bury My Heart at Wounded Knee: An Indian History of the American West* (New York: Holt, Rinehart, & Winston, 1970); Francis Jennings, *The Invasion of America: Indians, Colonialism, and*

the Cant of Conquest (Chapel Hill: University of North Carolina Press, 1975); Richard Drinnon, *Facing West: The Metaphysics of Indian-Hating and Empire Building* (Minneapolis: University of Minnesota Press, 1980).

35. Joe Starita, *The Dull Knives of Pine Ridge: A Lakota Odyssey* (New York: G. P. Putnam's Sons, 1995), 308. See also Tom Holm, *Strong Hearts, Wounded Souls: The Native American Veterans of the Vietnam War* (Austin: University of Texas Press, 1996).

36. Donald Worster, *Under Western Skies: Nature and History in the American West* (New York: Oxford University Press, 1992), 187; George Pierre Castile, *Taking Charge: Native American Self-Determination and Federal Indian Policy, 1975–1993* (Tucson: University of Arizona Press, 2006), 12–48; Timothy Egan, *The Good Rain: Across Time and Terrain in the Pacific Northwest* (New York: Knopf, 1990), 192; Paul Rosier, *Serving Their Country: American Indian Politics and Patriotism in the Twentieth Century* (Cambridge, MA: Harvard University Press, 2009), 270–77; U.S. Supreme Court, *United States v. Wheeler*, 435 U.S. 313 (1978).

37. Jeremi Suri, *Henry Kissinger and the American Century* (Cambridge, MA: Harvard University Press, 2007), 61–62. The history of such discrimination is mostly an ugly matter, but it could sometimes have its lighter moments. Future Arizona senator Barry Goldwater, son of a Jewish father and Episcopalian mother, reportedly responded to being told he couldn't play on a particular golf course by asking if, since he was half-Jewish, he couldn't play nine holes. Sager, *The Elephant in the Room*, 2.

38. Peter Novick, *The Holocaust in American Life* (Boston: Houghton Mifflin, 1999); Matthew Frye Jacobson, *Roots Too: White Ethnic Revival in Post-Civil Rights America* (Cambridge, MA: Harvard University Press, 2006); Alexander DeConde, *Ethnicity, Race, and American Foreign Policy: A History* (Boston: Northeastern University Press, 1992).

39. U.S. Supreme Court, *Carey v. Population Services International*, 431 U.S. 678 (1977); Richard K. Scotch, "American Disability Policy in the Twentieth Century," in *The New Disability History: American Perspectives*, ed. Paul Longmore and Lauri Umansky (New York: New York University Press, 2001), 375–92; Joseph P. Shapiro, *No Pity: People with Disabilities Forging a New Civil Rights Movement* (New York: Crown, 1993); *Wall Street Journal*, June 25, 2007, p. A12.

40. U.S. Census Bureau, www.census.gov/population/documentation/ www/twps0056/tab01.xls; Caplow et al., *The First Measured Century*, 17, 19; Patterson, *Restless Giant*, 25–26; EH.Net Encyclopedia, http://www.eh.net/ encyclopedia/article/cohn.immigration.us (accessed January 25, 2006); Mieczkowski, *Gerald Ford and the Challenges of the 1970s*, 293–94; Paul Spickard, *Almost All Aliens: Immigration, Race, and Colonialism in American History and Identity* (New York: Routledge, 2007), chapters 8–9. See also Carl J. Bon Tempo, *Americans at the Gate: The United States and Refugees during the Cold War* (Princeton, NJ: Princeton University Press, 2009).

41. Meinig, *The Shaping of America*, 237; Lizette Alvarez, "A Growing Stream of Illegal Immigrants Choose to Remain Despite the Risks," *New York Times*, December 20, 2006, p. A20; Guarneri, *America in the World*, 274;

Bertram M. Gordon, "The Decline of a Cultural Icon: France in American Perspective," *French Historical Studies* 22, 4 (Fall 1999): 625–26; Harvey A. Levenstein, *We'll Always Have Paris: American Tourists in France since 1930* (Chicago: University of Chicago Press, 2004), 234, 262. *Gourmet* magazine also dropped its monthly reviews of restaurants in France in the mid-1970s, replacing them with reviews of Californian restaurants—and with articles on other national cuisines, such as Chinese and Mexican. Levenstein, *We'll Always Have Paris*, 253–54.

42. Kristin Luker, *When Sex Goes to School: Warring Views on Sex—and Sex Education—since the Sixties* (New York: Norton, 2006); Herbie Hancock, "Hang Up Your Hang Ups," *Man-Child* (Columbia Records, 1975). Controversy over the choice-versus-genes question lingered for years, with science mostly undercutting this original conservative position—and helping change, by the 2000s, many conservatives' views. See chapter 6 and Vernon A. Rosario, *Homosexuality and Science: A Guide to the Debates* (Santa Barbara: ABC-CLIO, 2002).

43. Killen, *1973 Nervous Breakdown*, 47–48; Richards, *The Case for Gay Rights*, 74; Christopher Dickey, *Summer of Deliverance: A Memoir of Father and Son* (New York: Simon & Schuster, 1998); D'Emilio and Freedman, *Intimate Matters*, 324; "Gays on the March," *Time*, September 8, 1975; Jenkins, *Decade of Nightmares*, 28; Lindsey, *Age of Abundance*, 197; Collins, *Transforming America*, 134; David Eisenbach, *Gay Power: An American Revolution* (New York: Carroll & Graf, 2006), 221–90. On the centrality of sexual orientation in the shaping of the U.S. government in the twentieth century, see Margot Canaday, *The Straight State: Sexuality and Citizenship in Twentieth-Century America* (Princeton, NJ: Princeton University Press, 2009).

44. Peter Singer, *Animal Liberation: A New Ethics for Our Treatment of Animals* (New York: Random House, 1975).

45. Zelizer, *On Capitol Hill*, 1 (quotation), 2, 9, 177, 181–83; Cohen, *A Consumer's Republic*, 370; Public Citizen, http://www.citizen.org/about/ (accessed May 27, 2009).

46. Zelizer, *On Capitol Hill*, 108; Kalman, *Right Star Rising*, 143–46; Patterson, *Restless Giant*, 83; Mieczkowski, *Gerald Ford and the Challenges of the 1970s*, 67.

47. Zelizer, *On Capitol Hill*, 158 (Harris), 167–68, 170; Mieczkowski, *Gerald Ford and the Challenges of the 1970s*, 69 (O'Neill and Carter); Scott Shane, "For Some, Bypassing Controversy Recalls a Past Drama," February 6, 2006, *New York Times*, p. A18; Robert David Johnson, *Congress and the Cold War* (New York: Cambridge University Press, 2006), 242.

48. James Carroll, *House of War: The Pentagon and the Disastrous Rise of American Power* (Boston: Houghton Mifflin, 2006), 366 (first Carter); Mieczkowski, *Gerald Ford and the Challenges of the 1970s* (second Carter); Robert Scheer, "Jimmy, We Hardly Know Y'All," *Playboy*, November 1976, reprinted in *Thinking Tuna Fish, Talking Death: Essays on the Pornography of Power* (New York: Hill and Wang, 1988), 224–26 (quotations), 228–37; Elizabeth Drew, *American Journal: The Events of 1976* (New York: Random House, 1977), 68–69 (journalist).

49. Jimmy Carter, commencement address at Notre Dame University, May 22, 1977, available at The American Presidency Project, http://www.presi dency.ucsb.edu/ws/?pid=7552 (accessed May 28, 2009); H. W. Brands, *The Devil We Knew: Americans and the Cold War* (New York: Oxford University Press, 1993), 142–44; David Skidmore, *Reversing Course: Carter's Foreign Policy, Domestic Politics, and the Failure of Reform* (Nashville: Vanderbilt University Press, 1996), 41 (Vance); David F. Schmitz and Vanessa Walker, "Jimmy Carter and the Foreign Policy of Human Rights: The Development of a Post-Cold War Foreign Policy," *Diplomatic History* 28, 1 (January 2004): 113–43.

50. Skidmore, *Reversing Course*, 65, 70, 88, 97. See also Kathryn Sikkink, *Mixed Signals: U.S. Human Rights Policy and Latin America* (Ithaca, NY: Cornell University Press, 2004), and Smith, *Morality, Reason, and Power.*

51. Samuel Walker, *The Rights Revolution: Rights and Community in Modern America* (New York: Oxford University Press, 1998), 35; Collins, *Transforming America*, 183; Bailey and Farber, "Introduction," in *America in the Seventies*, ed. Bailey and Farber, 4–6. Political scientists have demonstrated that the class politics of the backlash were complicated, particularly over time, as income levels of white citizens remained strong predictors of their voting preferences—more affluent leaning Republican, less affluent leaning Demo-cratic. See Larry M. Bartels, *Unequal Democracy: The Political Economy of the New Gilded Age* (Princeton, NJ: Princeton University Press, 2008), chapter 3; Nolan McCarty, Keith T. Poole, and Howard Rosenthal, *Polarized America: The Dance of Ideology and Unequal Riches* (Cambridge, MA: MIT Press, 2006); Jeffrey M. Stonecash, *Class and Party in American Politics* (Boulder, CO: Westview, 2000).

52. Cowie, "'Vigorously Left, Right, and Center'," 83; Patrick Allitt, *I'm The Teacher, You're The Student: A Semester in the University Classroom* (Philadelphia: University of Pennsylvania Press, 2005), 128 (Nebraska legisla-tor); Patterson, *Restless Giant*, 22–23; Eric Porter, "Affirming and Disaffirm-ing Actions: Remaking Race in the 1970s," in *America in the Seventies*, ed. Bailey and Farber, 66–67; Link, *Righteous Warrior*, 195 (Helms). On the ori-gins of the backlash, see Sugrue, *The Urban Crisis*; Kruse, *White Flight*; Mi-chael W. Flamm, *Law and Order: Street Crime, Civil Unrest, and the Crisis of Liberalism in the 1960s* (New York: Columbia University Press, 2005).

53. Fred Fejes, *Gay Rights and Moral Panic: The Origins of America's De-bate on Homosexuality* (New York: Palgrave Macmillan, 2008), 134 (Fal-well), 137, passim; D'Emilio and Freedman, *Intimate Matters*, 346–47 (Bryant and Will); Link, *Righteous Warrior*, 178–79.

54. Phyllis Schlafly, "What's Wrong with 'Equal Rights for Women'?" Feb-ruary 1972, reprinted in *Debating the American Conservative Movement: 1945 to the Present*, ed. Donald T. Critchlow and Nancy MacLean (Lanham, MD: Rowman & Littlefield, 2009), 197–200 (first Schlafly); Critchlow, *Phyllis Schlafly and Grassroots Conservatism*, 216–17 (second Schlafly); Klatch, *Women of the New Right*, 129 (Marshner), 136; Mathews and De Hart, *Sex, Gender, and the Politics of ERA*, 158, 164–65.

55. Jacquelyn Dowd Hall, "The Long Civil Rights Movement and the Po-

litical Uses of the Past," *Journal of American History* 91, 4 (March 2005): 1260; Mathews and De Hart, *Sex, Gender, and the ERA*, 171.

56. D'Emilio and Freedman, *Intimate Matters*, 351–53.

57. Evans, *Tidal Wave*, 131–32 (*Daughters of Sarah*); Susan Moller Okin et al., *Is Multiculturalism Bad for Women?* (Princeton, NJ: Princeton University Press, 1999), 46 (al-Hibri).

58. Blum, *Annapurna*, xvii; "American Women," *Time*, January 5, 1976.

Chapter 3. The Spread of Market Values

1. William E. Leuchtenburg, "Jimmy Carter and the Post-New Deal Presidency," in *The Carter Presidency*, ed. Fink and Graham, 20 (Harrington); Osterhammel and Petersson, *Globalization*, 121; Easterlin, *Growth Triumphant*, 1; Gordon and Gordon, *American Chronicle*, 513 (Pan Am ad).

2. Fraser and Gerstle, eds., *The Rise and Fall of the New Deal Order*; Edsall and Edsall, *Chain Reaction*.

3. Hodgson, *More Equal Than Others*, 21–22; William H. Sewell, Jr., "AHR Forum: Crooked Lines," *American Historical Review* 113, 2 (April 2008): 399; David Reynolds, *One World Divisible: A Global History since 1945* (New York: Norton, 2000), 522–23.

4. Jackson, *Crabgrass Frontier*, 278; Christopher Rasmussen, "Lonely Sounds: Popular Recorded Music and American Society, 1949–1979" (PhD dissertation, Department of History, University of Nebraska–Lincoln, 2008); Collins, *Transforming America*, 152–55; Patterson, *Restless Giant*, 6.

5. George Will, "Land of Plenty," *New York Times*, June 9, 2007. On Las Vegas, see Hal Rothman, *Neon Metropolis: How Las Vegas Started the Twenty-First Century* (New York: Routledge, 2002), and Hal K. Rothman and Mike Davis, eds., *The Grit Beneath the Glitter: Tales from the Real Las Vegas* (Berkeley: University of California Press, 2002).

6. Harvey, *Neoliberalism*, 5; William J. Bernstein, *A Splendid Exchange: How Trade Shaped the World* (New York: Atlantic Monthly Press, 2008), 8 (Adam Smith).

7. Robert Kuttner, *Everything For Sale: The Virtues and Limits of Markets* (Chicago: University of Chicago Press), 34–35; Melvyn Leffler, "The Cold War: What 'Do We Now Know'?" American Historical Review 104, 2 (April 1999): 519 (Acheson); E. J. Hobsbawm, *The Age of Empire, 1875–1914* (New York: Vintage, 1989), 334; Daniel Yergin and Joseph Stanislaw, *The Commanding Heights: The Battle between Government and the Marketplace that Is Remaking the Modern World* (New York: Simon & Schuster, 1998), 66.

8. For more on the comparison of the eras after the 1970s and before the 1930s, see Bender, *A Nation Among Nations*, chapter 5. For a recent examination of pre-1970s free-market organizing, see Elizabeth Tandy Shermer, "Origins of the Conservative Ascendancy: Barry Goldwater's Early Senate Career and the De-legitimization of Organized Labor," *Journal of American History* 95, 3 (December 2008): 678–709. One exception to the general pattern of

challenging and diminishing the welfare state was the establishment of cost-of-living adjustments to Social Security, beginning in 1975.

9. Juliet Williams, "The Road Less Traveled: Reconsidering the Political Writings of Friedrich von Hayek," in *American Capitalism: Social Thought and Political Economy in the Twentieth Century*, ed. Nelson Lichtenstein (Philadelphia: University of Pennsylvania Press, 2006), 213–27; Alan Brinkley, *The End of Reform: New Deal Liberalism in Recession and War* (New York: Random House, 1995), 157–60; Yergin and Stanislaw, *The Commanding Heights*, 141–45; E. J. Hobsbawm, *The Age of Extremes: A History of the World, 1914–1991* (New York: Vintage, 1996), 409; Jennifer Burns, "Godless Capitalism: Ayn Rand and the Conservative Movement," in *American Capitalism*, ed. Lichtenstein, 271–90; Anne C. Heller, *Ayn Rand and the World She Made* (New York: Nan A. Talese/Doubleday, 2009); Jennifer C. Burns, *Goddess of the Market: Ayn Rand and the American Right* (New York: Oxford University Press, 2009).

10. Milton Friedman, *Capitalism and Freedom* (Chicago: University of Chicago Press, 1962); Yergin and Stanislaw, *The Commanding Heights*, 145–49; Michael Thompson, *The Politics of Inequality: A Political History of the Idea of Economic Inequality in America* (New York: Columbia University Press, 2007), 159; Doherty, *Radicals for Capitalism*, 454.

11. Milton Friedman and Rose Friedman, *Free To Choose: A Personal Statement* (New York: Harcourt Brace Jovanovich, 1980); Holcomb B. Noble, "Milton Friedman, Free Markets Theorist, Dies at 94," *New York Times*, November 16, 2006.

12. Alice O'Connor, "The Politics of Rich and Rich: Postwar Investigations of Foundations and the Rise of the Philanthropic Right," in *American Capitalism*, ed. Lichtenstein, 246–47; Alice O'Connor, "Financing the Counterrevolution," in *Rightward Bound*, ed. Schulman and Zelizer, 152–53; Sean Wilentz, *The Age of Reagan: A History, 1974–2008* (New York: Harper, 2008), 90; Phillips-Fein, *Invisible Hands*, 469–70. See also David M. Ricci, *The Transformation of American Politics: The New Washington and the Rise of Think Tanks* (New Haven, CT: Yale University Press, 2009).

13. Harvey, *A Brief History of Neoliberalism*, 43 (Powell), 49; Jeffrey Rosen, "Supreme Court Inc.," *New York Times Magazine*, March 16, 2008, 40; Nils Gilman, "The Prophet of Post-Fordism: Peter Drucker and the Legitimation of the Corporation," in *American Capitalism*, ed. Lichtenstein, 110; Bethany E. Moreton, "Make Payroll, Not War: Business Culture as Youth Culture," in *Rightward Bound*, ed. Schulman and Zelizer, 62; Moreton, *To Serve God and Wal-Mart*, 145–92.

14. Yergin and Stanislaw, *The Commanding Heights*, 60–64 (Nixon); Robert D. Lifset, "In Search of Republican Environmentalists," *Reviews in American History* 36, 1 (March 2008): 124.

15. Sager, *The Elephant in the Room*, 2 (Goldwater), 15–16 (first Reagan); Thomas Frank, *The Wrecking Crew: How Conservatives Rule* (New York: Metropolitan, 2008), 125 (second Reagan); Paul Krugman, "Seeking Willie Horton," *New York Times*, August 27, 2004 (Norquist).

16. Leuchtenberg, "Jimmy Carter and the Post-New Deal Presidency," 14–15 (Gillon and Schlesinger); Jimmy Carter, state of the union address, January 19, 1978, *Public Papers of the Presidency, 1978: Book 1*, available at The American Presidency Project, http://www.presidency.ucsb.edu/ws/index.php ?pid=30856&st=&st1= (accessed June 11, 2009). For a view emphasizing the durability of pro-New Deal, liberal values, see Timothy Stanley, *Kennedy vs. Carter: The 1980 Battle for the Democratic Party's Soul* (Lawrence: University Press of Kansas, 2010).

17. Barry Bluestone, "Foreword," in Cowie and Heathcott, *Beyond the Ruins*, ix; Lichtenstein, *State of the Union*, 215; Patterson, *Restless Giant*, 62; Paul Krugman, "The Big Disconnect," *New York Times*, September 1, 2006; Peter Gottschalk, "Inequality, Income Growth, and Mobility: The Basic Facts," *Journal of Economic Perspectives* 11, 2 (1997), 21; Zunz et al., *Social Contracts under Stress*, statistical appendix, 408. See also Judith Stein, *Pivotal Decade: How the United States Traded Factories for Finance in the Seventies* (New Haven, CT: Yale University Press, 2010).

18. Cowie, "'Vigorously Left, Right, and Center'," 96–97, 101 (quotation); Caplow et al., *The First Measured Century*, 49; Dana Frank, *Buy American: The Untold Story of Economic Nationalism* (Boston: Beacon, 1999), 132.

19. Suleiman Osman, "The Decade of the Neighborhood," in *Rightward Bound*, ed. Schulman and Zelizer, 109; Joseph A. McCartin, "'A Wagner Act for Public Employees': Labor's Deferred Dream and the Rise of Conservatism, 1970–1976," *Journal of American History* 95, 1 (June 2008): 123–48; Thomas J. Sugrue, "Carter's Urban Policy Crisis," in *The Carter Presidency*, ed. Fink and Graham, 137 ("terminal"); Charles R. Morris, *The Cost of Good Intentions: New York City and the Liberal Experiment, 1960–1975* (New York: Norton, 1980).

20. James N. Gregory, *The Southern Diaspora: How the Great Migrations of Black and White Southerners Transformed America* (Chapel Hill: University of North Carolina Press, 2005), 13, 38–39 (quotation), 322–23; D. W. Meinig, *The Shaping of America: A Geographical Perspective on 500 Years of History*, vol. 4, *Global America, 1915–2000* (New Haven, CT: Yale University Press, 2004), 260.

21. Raymond Arsenault, "The End of the Long Hot Summer: The Air Conditioner and Southern Culture," *Journal of Southern History* 50, 4 (1984): 597–628 (quotation at 598); John Egerton, *The Americanization of Dixie: The Southernization of America* (New York: Harper's, 1974).

22. Arsenault, "The End of the Long Hot Summer," 618.

23. Stephen Ohlemacher, "South, West Gain Population, Political Clout," *Lincoln Journal Star*, December 22, 2005, p. 4A; Phillips-Fein, *Invisible Hands*, 469.

24. William Brittain-Catlin, *Offshore: The Dark Side of the Global Economy* (New York: Farrar, Straus, and Giroux, 2005), 22–23 (Dow and Bank of America); Alison Frank, "The Petroleum War of 1910: Standard Oil, Austria, and the Limits of the Multinational Corporation," *American Historical Review* 114, 1 (February 2009): 16 (Smith); Sargent, "From Internationalism to Globalism," especially chapter 3 and conclusion.

25. *Wall Street Journal,* July 10, 2007, p. D5.

26. David Northrup, "Globalization and the Great Convergence: Rethinking World History in the Long Term," *Journal of World History* 16, 3 (2005): 249–67; Howard Brick, "The Postcapitalist Vision in Twentieth-Century American Social Thought," in *American Capitalism,* ed. Lichtenstein, 43.

27. Peter Novick, *That Noble Dream: The "Objectivity Question" and the American Historical Profession* (New York: Cambridge University Press, 1988), 300 (Schlesinger); Osterhammel and Petersson, *Globalization,* 20; Immanuel Wallerstein, *The Modern World-System* (New York: Academic Press, 1974). Some American conservatives continued to worry about negative associations with the word "capitalism," including the majority of the Texas Board of Education who in 2010 changed the state social studies standards to substitute the term "free-enterprise system" for all references to "capitalism." James C. McKinley, Jr., "Texas Approves Curriculum Revised by Conservatives," *New York Times,* March 12, 2010.

28. Sargent, "From Internationalism to Globalism," 1 (MacLeish); Internet Society, "A Brief History of the Internet," http://www.isoc.org/internet/history/brief.shtml (accessed June 15, 2009); Bruce Mazlish and Akira Iriye, eds., *The Global History Reader* (New York: Routledge, 2004), 4; Robert B. Reich, *Supercapitalism: The Transformation of Business, Democracy, and Everyday Life* (New York: Vintage, 2007), 56–60.

29. William Marling, *How "American" Is Globalization?* (Baltimore: Johns Hopkins University Press, 2006), 145, 182–83.

30. Meinig, *The Shaping of America,* 102; Pierre Lèvy, "Cyberculture," in *The Global History Reader,* ed. Mazlish and Iriye, 52; Moreton, *To Serve God and Wal-Mart,* 131–32.

31. Meg Jacobs, *Pocketbook Politics: Economic Citizenship in Twentieth-Century America* (Princeton, NJ: Princeton University Press, 2005), 264; Osterhammel and Petersson, *Globalization,* 25; Gordon and Gordon, *American Chronicle,* 556; Richard M. Abrams, *America Transformed: Sixty Years of Revolutionary Change, 1941–2001* (New York: Cambridge University Press, 2006), 117; James L. Watson, ed., *Golden Arches East: McDonald's in East Asia* (Stanford: Stanford University Press, 1997), 15; *Wall Street Journal,* May 2, 2006, p. 1.

32. Keith Bradsher, "NBA Makes a Big Move in China," *New York Times,* September 19, 2007.

33. Sasha Issenberg, *The Sushi Economy: Globalization and the Making of a Modern Delicacy* (New York: Gotham, 2007); Marling, *How "American" Is Globalization?* 16–174; Marc Levinson, *The Box: How the Shipping Container Made the World Smaller and the World Economy Bigger* (Princeton, NJ: Princeton University Press, 2006); Witold Rybczynski, "Shipping News," *New York Review of Books,* August 10, 2006, pp. 22–25; Bruce Stanley, "Ships Draw Fire for Rising Role in Air Pollution," *Wall Street Journal,* November 27, 2007, p. 1.

34. Levenstein, *We'll Always Have Paris,* 239; Caplow et al., *The First Measured Century,* 131, 231.

35. David Crystal, *English as a Global Language,* 2nd ed. (New York:

Cambridge University Press, 2003), 111–12, 121; Robert McCrum, *Globish: How the English Language Became the World's Language* (New York: Norton, 2010).

36. Crystal, *English as a Global Language*, 110; J. R. McNeill, "The Environment, Environmentalism, and International Society in the Long 1970s," in *The Shock of the Global*, ed. Ferguson et al., 263–78; Sargent, "From Internationalism to Globalism," epilogue.

37. Caplow et al., *The First Measured Century*, 260, 271; Jimmy Carter, "Address to the Nation on Energy and National Goals," July 15, 1979, *Public Papers of the Presidents, 1979: Book 2*, available at The American Presidency Project, http://www.presidency.ucsb.edu/ws/index.php?pid=32596&st=&st1= (accessed June 17, 2009); Andrew Bacevich, *The Limits of Power: The End of American Exceptionalism* (New York: Metropolitan, 2008); Edward Abbey, *The Journey Home: Some Words in Defense of the American West* (New York: Dutton, 1977), 183. Rising health-care costs and mortgages in an era of stagnating wages also contributed to growing consumer debt. See Teresa A. Sullivan, Elizabeth Warren, and Jay Lawrence Westbrook, *The Fragile Middle Class: Americans in Debt* (New Haven, CT: Yale University Press, 2000), chapter 1.

38. Mettler, *Soldiers to Citizens*, 4, 164–68; Theda Skocpol, *Diminished Democracy: From Membership to Management in American Civic Life* (Norman: University of Oklahoma Press, 2003); Putnam, *Bowling Alone*; *Lincoln Journal Star*, July 23, 2006, p. 11A.

39. Fukuyama, *The Great Disruption*, 4–5; Robert C. Lieberman, *Shaping Race Policy: The United States in Comparative Perspective* (Princeton, NJ: Princeton University Press, 2005), 78–80; Seymour Martin Lipset, *American Exceptionalism: A Double-Edged Sword* (New York: Norton, 1996), 26.

40. Mettler, *Soldiers to Citizens*, 4; Putnam, *Bowling Alone*, 44–45, 99, 142–43, 212–13, 238–240 (quotation), 255, 264.

41. Putnam, *Bowling Alone*, 282; Fukuyama, *The Great Disruption*, 6 (quotation), 15.

42. Phillip J. Cooper, *The War against Regulation: From Jimmy Carter to George W. Bush* (Lawrence: University Press of Kansas, 2009), passim; Cohen, *A Consumers' Republic*, 391–92 (Carter and Reagan adviser); Kuttner, *Everything for Sale*, 36–37; Martha Derthick and Paul J. Quirk, *The Politics of Deregulation* (Washington, DC: Brookings Institution, 1985), 124 (Kahn), 242; Alfred Kahn interview, "The First Measured Century," http://www.pbs.org/fmc/interviews/kahn.htm (accessed June 29, 2007); Shane Hamilton, *Trucking Country: The Road to America's Wal-Mart Economy* (Princeton, NJ: Princeton University Press, 2008), 224–31; Eduardo Canedo, "The Rise of the Deregulation Movement in America, 1957–1980" (PhD dissertation, Department of History, Columbia University, 2008). Even the 1978 Humphrey-Hawkins Full Employment Act, which seemed at first to promote government management of the economy at least regarding job growth, called for the federal government to rely primarily on the private sector to achieve its aim of job creation. The AFL-CIO admitted the final bill was "more symbol than substance." Cowie, "'Vigorously Left, Right, and Center,'" 98.

43. Kuttner, *Everything for Sale*, 256; Derthick and Quick, *The Politics of Deregulation*, passim, esp. 45–47, 75; Killen, *1973 Nervous Breakdown*, 17.

44. Gordon and Gordon, *American Chronicle*, 556; Alfred Kahn interview; Derthick and Quick, *The Politics of Deregulation*, 155; *Wall Street Journal*, July 21–22, 2007, p. A5; *New York Times*, May 21, 2006, p. 22.

45. Paul Krugman, "Who Was Milton Friedman?" *New York Review of Books*, February 15, 2007, pp. 29–30; Kuttner, *Everything for Sale*, 204; Meinig, *The Shaping of America*, 94; James Morton Turner, "'The Specter of Environmentalism': Wilderness, Environmental Politics, and the Evolution of the New Right," *Journal of American History* 96, 1 (June 2009): 130–37; Mark Dowie, *Losing Ground: American Environmentalism at the Close of the Twentieth Century* (Cambridge, MA: MIT Press, 1995), 90–91; Gregg A. Jarrell, "Change at the Exchange: The Causes and Effects of Deregulation," *Journal of Law and Economics* 27 (1984): 273–74; Jackson, *Crabgrass Frontier*, 299–300; Kevin P. Phillips, *American Theocracy: The Peril and Politics of Radical Religion, Oil, and Borrowed Money in the 21st Century* (New York: Viking, 2006), 290; U.S. Supreme Court, *Marquette v. First of Omaha*, 439 U.S. 299 (1978).

46. William Glenn Gray, "Floating the System: Germany, the United States, and the Breakdown of Bretton Woods, 1969–1973," *Diplomatic History* 31, 2 (April 2007): 295–323; Iriye, *Global Community*, 127; Collins, *Transforming America*, 101; Morris Berman, *Dark Ages America: The Final Phase of Empire* (New York: Norton, 2006), 56–57.

47. B. Drummond Ayres, "Army Is Shaken by Crisis in Morale and Discipline," *New York Times*, September 5, 1971; Beth Bailey, "The Army in the Marketplace: Recruiting an All-Volunteer Force," *Journal of American History* 94, 1 (June 2007): 48–49, 53 (Young Americans for Freedom and National Student Association); George Q. Flynn, *The Draft, 1940–1973* (Lawrence: University Press of Kansas, 1993).

48. Bailey, "The Army in the Marketplace," 48–51 (Nixon at 51); Matt Schudel, "Walter Kerwin," obituary, *Washington Post*, July 20, 2008. See also Beth Bailey, *America's Army: Making the All-Volunteer Force* (Cambridge, MA: Harvard University Press, 2009).

49. Bacevich, *The New American Militarism*, 26 (quotation), 27 (Cheney), 28; Murphy, *Are We Rome?*, 81–82; Caplow et al., *The First Measured Century*, 203–5; Elizabeth L. Hillman, "The Female Shape of the All-Volunteer Force," in *Iraq and the Lessons of Vietnam, or, How Not to Learn from the Past*, ed. Lloyd C. Gardner and Marilyn B. Young (New York: New Press, 2007), 151.

50. Abrams, *America Transformed*, 59; Cohen, *A Consumers' Republic*, 390–91; Eduardo Porter, "The Divisions That Tighten the Purse Strings," *New York Times*, April 29, 2007, Sec. 3, p. 4; Edsall and Edsall, *Chain Reaction*, passim.

51. "The Watts Riot of the White Middle-Class," *Sojourners*, July 1978, p. 5; Robert O. Self, "Prelude to the Tax Revolt: The Politics of the 'Tax Revolt' in Postwar California," in *The New Suburban History*, ed. Kevin M. Kruse and Thomas J. Sugrue (Princeton, NJ: Princeton University Press, 2006), 145,

158–59; Hodgson, *More Equal Than Others*, 43; Robert O. Self, *American Babylon: Race and the Struggle for Postwar Oakland* (Princeton, NJ: Princeton University Press, 2003), 319–25; Peter Schrag, *Paradise Lost: California's Experience, America's Future* (New York: New Press, 1998).

52. Edsall and Edsall, *Chain Reaction*, 131; Collins, *Transforming America*, 61.

53. U.S. Supreme Court, *Buckley v. Valeo*, 424 U.S. 1 (1978); Patterson, *Restless Giant*, 83; Hodgson, *More Equal than Others*, 31; Jeff Zeleny, "The Faint Hoof Beats? That's the Dark Horse," *New York Times*, February 3, 2007.

54. Linda K. Kerber, "Gender," in *Imagined Histories: American Historians Interpret the Past*, ed. Anthony Molho and Gordon S. Wood (Princeton, NJ: Princeton University Press, 1998), 49; U.S. Supreme Court, *Harris v. McRae*, 448 U.S. 297 (1980); Greenhouse, *Becoming Justice Blackmun*, 138–39; Connelly, *Fatal Misconception*, 334 (Carter).

55. Mary Ann Glendon, *Abortion and Divorce in Western Law* (Cambridge, MA: Harvard University Press, 1987).

56. Robert M. Goldman, *One Man Out: Curt Flood versus Baseball* (Lawrence: University Press of Kansas, 2008); U.S. Supreme Court, *Flood v. Kuhn*, 407 U.S. 258 (1972).

57. Center for Disease Control, "United States Life Tables, 2004," National Vital Statistics Reports, Vol. 56, No. 9, December 28, 2007, p. 34, table 12, available at http://www.cdc.gov/nchs/data/nvsr/nvsr56/nvsr56_09.pdf (accessed June 23, 2009); Jacob S. Hacker, *The Great Risk Shift: The New Economic Insecurity and the Decline of the American Dream* (New York: Oxford University Press, 2006); Jeff Madrick, "The Specter Haunting Old Age," *New York Review of Books*, March 20, 2008, p. 43; Eleanor Laise, "Big Slide in 401(k)s Spurs Call for Change," *Wall Street Journal*, January 8, 2009, p. A12.

58. U.S. Supreme Court, *Swann v. Charlotte-Mecklenburg Board of Education*, 402 U.S. 1 (1971); Jennifer L. Hochschild, *The New American Dilemma: Liberal Democracy and School Desegregation* (New Haven, CT: Yale University Press, 1984), 28 (quotation), 130; U.S. Supreme Court, *Keyes v. School District No. 1 of Denver*, 413 U.S. 189 (1973); U.S. Supreme Court, *San Antonio Independent School District v. Rodriguez*, 411 U.S. 1 (1973); Adam R. Nelson, *The Elusive Ideal: Equal Educational Opportunity and the Federal Role in Boston's Public Schools, 1950–1985* (Chicago: University of Chicago Press, 2005), 139–40, 162–64; Paul A. Scacie, San Antonio v. Rodriguez *and the Pursuit of Equal Education: The Debate over Discrimination and School Funding* (Lawrence: University Press of Kansas, 2006).

59. U.S. Supreme Court, *Milliken v. Bradley*, 418 U.S. 717 (1974); Matthew D. Lassiter, "'Socioeconomic Integration' in the Suburbs: From Reactionary Populism to Class Fairness in Metropolitan Charlotte," in *The New Suburban History*, ed. Kruse and Sugrue, 141; Kruse, *White Flight*, 257; Norrell, *The House I Live In*, 290–91; Hodgson, *More Equal than Others*, 181; Hochschild, *The American Dilemma*, 29–31.

60. Kenneth Cmiel, "The Politics of Civility," in *The Sixties: From Memory to History*, ed. David Farber (Chapel Hill: University of North Carolina Press,

1994), 263–90; David Farber, "The Silent Majority and Talk about Revolution," in ibid., 291–316; Tom Wolfe, *I Am Charlotte Simmons* (New York: Farrar, Straus and Giroux, 2004). This shift toward a coarser public culture does not imply an earlier tradition of absolute civility, as the examples of slavery and lynching demonstrate.

61. Bailey and Farber, "Introduction," in *America in the Seventies*, 6; D'Emilio and Freedman, *Intimate Matters*, 328–53; Alex Comfort, *The Joy of Sex: A Gourmet Guide to Lovemaking* (New York: Crown, 1972); David Reuben, *Everything You Always Wanted to Know about Sex: But Were Afraid to Ask* (New York: Bantam, 1971) (published originally in 1969 by a small publisher, but a much larger seller as a Bantam paperback); Peter Braunstein, "'Adults Only': The Construction of an Erotic City in New York during the 1970s," in *America in the Seventies*, ed. Bailey and Farber, 152; Shere Hite, *The Hite Report: A Nationwide Study on Female Sexuality* (New York: Macmillan, 1976); Robert Scheer, "The Playboy Interview: Jimmy Carter," *Playboy*, November 1976, pp. 63–86.

62. Cook, *Lost Illusions*, 70–71, 273; Braunstein, "'Adults Only'," 132.

63. Ralph Blumenthal, "Pornochic; 'Hard-core' Grows Fashionable—and Very Profitable," *New York Times Magazine*, January 21, 1973; Cook, *Lost Illusions*, 275; Lindsey, *The Age of Abundance*, 195; Killen, *1973 Nervous Breakdown*, 198.

64. "The Porno Plague," *Time*, April 5, 1976; *New York Times Magazine*, April 24, 2005, p. 12; U.S. Supreme Court, *Miller v. California*, 413 U.S. 15 (1973); Cook, *Lost Illusions*, 277–83; Killen, *1973 Nervous Breakdown*, 47.

65. Cook, *Lost Illusions*, 282–83; Braunstein, "'Adults Only'," 151; Joan Acocella, "The Girls Next Door," *New Yorker*, March 20, 2006, p. 148.

66. "The Porno Plague," *Time*, April 5, 1976; Abrams, *America Transformed*, 171–72.

67. David G. Schwartz, *Roll the Bones: The History of Gambling* (New York: Gotham, 2006), xviii, 433–36.

68. Bryant Simon, "Segregated Fantasies: Race, Public Space, and the Life and Death of the Movie Business in Atlantic City, New Jersey, 1945–2000," in *Beyond the Ruins*, ed. Cowie and Heathcott, 82–85; Schwartz, *Roll the Bones*, 425.

69. Edsall and Edsall, *Chain Reaction*, 112; Meinig, *The Shaping of America*, 265–66; James E. Goodman, *Blackout* (New York: North Point Press, 2003).

70. Marie Gottschalk, *The Prison and the Gallows: The Politics of Mass Incarceration in America* (New York: Cambridge University Press, 2006), 2–4, 22; Adam Liptak, "Inmate Count in U.S. Dwarfs Other Nations," *New York Times*, April 23, 2008; Jason DeParle, "The American Prison Nightmare," *New York Review of Books*, April 12, 2007, p. 33; Jenkins, *Decade of Nightmares*, 134 (Wilson); Joshua Guetzkow and Bruce Western, "The Political Consequences of Mass Imprisonment," in *Remaking America*, ed. Soss et al., 228–29.

71. Guetzkow and Western, "The Political Consequences of Mass Imprisonment," 228–33; Gottschalk, *The Prison and the Gallows*, passim; Killen,

1973 Nervous Breakdown, 209; Caplow et al., *The First Measured Century*, 225; Liptak, "Inmate Count in U.S. Dwarfs Other Nations."

72. U.S. Supreme Court, *Furman v. Georgia*, 408 U.S. 238 (1972); David M. Oshinsky, *Capital Punishment on Trial: Furman v. Georgia and the Death Penalty in Modern America* (Lawrence: University Press of Kansas, 2010); U.S. Supreme Court, *Gregg v. Georgia*, 428 U.S. 153 (1976); Gottschalk, *The Prison and the Gallows*, 228.

73. Franklin E. Zimring, *The Contradictions of American Capital Punishment* (New York: Oxford University Press, 2003), 1–64 (quotation at 9); David Garland, *Peculiar Institution: America's Death Penalty in an Age of Abolition* (Cambridge, MA: Harvard University Press, 2010).

74. See Bethany Moreton, *To Serve God and Wal-Mart: The Making of Christian Free Enterprise* (Cambridge, MA: Harvard University Press, 2009), and Hamilton, *Trucking Country*.

75. Suzanne Mettler, "When Government Withers," *Christian Science Monitor*, December 20, 2005; Edsall and Edsall, *Chain Reaction*, 105; Fukuyama, *The Great Disruption*, 10. On environmental impacts of the turn to unrestrained markets, see chapter 5.

Chapter 4. The Retreat of Empires and the Global Advance of the Market

1. Godfrey Hodgson, *The Myth of American Exceptionalism* (New Haven, CT: Yale University Press, 2009); Lipset, *American Exceptionalism*. On the recent turn to putting U.S. history in a global context, see Thomas Bender, *A Nation Among Nations: America's Place in World History* (New York: Hill and Wang, 2006), and Thomas Bender, ed., *Rethinking American History in a Global Age* (Berkeley: University of California Press, 2002). For the distinction between national self-determination and individual human rights, see Moyn, *The Last Utopia*.

2. James J. Sheehan, *Where Have All the Soldiers Gone? The Transformation of Modern Europe* (Boston: Houghton Mifflin, 2008), 185–87.

3. Joseph Conrad, *Heart of Darkness* (1902; New York: Modern Library, 1999), 7–8; Bender, *A Nation Among Nations*, 62 (Madison).

4. One measure of the increasing awareness of international norms of governmental behavior came from the new global surveys of public opinion begun by George Gallup in 1974. See Andrew Kohut and Bruce Stokes, *America Against the World: How We Are Different and Why We Are Disliked* (New York: Times Books, 2006), 7.

5. Charter of the United Nations, http://www.un.org/en/documents/charter/ (accessed April 14, 2010); Moyn, *The Last Utopia*; Kenneth Cmiel, "The Emergence of Human Rights Politics in the United States," *Journal of American History* 86, 3 (December 1999): 1231–50; Kenneth Cmiel, "The Recent History of Human Rights," *American Historical Review* 109, 1 (February 2004): 117–35; Bon Tempo, *Americans at the Gate*, chapter 6.

6. Lynn A. Hunt, *Inventing Human Rights: A History* (New York: Norton, 2007), 28–31, 147.

7. Hunt, *Inventing Human Rights*, 20, 147–48 (Adams); Samuel Walker, *The Rights Revolution: Rights and Community in Modern America* (New York: Oxford University Press, 1998), 48; Michael Cotey Morgan, "The Seventies and the Rebirth of Human Rights," in *The Shock of the Global*, ed. Ferguson et al., 237–50.

8. Cmiel, "The Emergence of Human Rights Politics in the United States," 1231–34.

9. Ian Parker, "Victims and Volunteers," *New Yorker*, January 26, 2004, p. 51 (Valdez); Stephen Hopgood, *Keepers of the Flame: Understanding Amnesty International* (Ithaca, NY: Cornell University Press, 2006), 140.

10. Cmiel, "The Emergence of Human Rights Politics in the United States," 1232 (quotation), 1234–36; Iriye, *Global Community*, 138; Morgan, "The Seventies and the Rebirth of Human Rights"; Doctors Without Borders, www.doctorswithoutborders.org (accessed April 14, 2010); James Traub, "Statesman Without Borders," *New York Times Magazine*, February 3, 2008, p. 48.

11. Donald M. Fraser, "Freedom and Foreign Policy," *Foreign Policy* 26 (1977): 140; Jack Donnelly, "Human Rights as an Issue in World Politics," in *The Global History Reader*, ed. Bruce Mazlish and Akira Iriye (New York: Routledge, 2004), 162; Van Gosse, "Unpacking The Vietnam Syndrome: The Coup in Chile and the Rise of Popular Anti-Interventionism," in *The World The Sixties Made: Politics and Culture in Recent America*, ed. Van Gosse and Richard R. Moser (Philadelphia: Temple University Press, 2003), 101–2; Cmiel, "The Emergence of Human Rights Politics in the United States," 1235–42.

12. Zubok, *A Failed Empire*, 231–34.

13. Jimmy Carter, inaugural address, January 20, 1977, available at the American Presidency Project, http://www.presidency.ucsb.edu/ws/index.php?pid=6575&st=&st1= (accessed April 14, 2010). For Carter's clearest public statement on human rights and foreign relations, see his commencement address at Notre Dame University on May 22, 1977, available at the American Presidency Project, http://www.presidency.ucsb.edu/ws/index.php?pid=7552&st=notre+dame&st1= (accessed August 5, 2009).

14. For an interpretation emphasizing the limits of Carter's success regarding human rights, see Kenton Clymer, "Jimmy Carter, Human Rights, and Cambodia," *Diplomatic History* 27, 2 (April 2003): 245–78. For a more positive evaluation, see David F. Schmitz and Vanessa Walker, "Jimmy Carter and the Foreign Policy of Human Rights: The Development of a Post-Cold War Foreign Policy," *Diplomatic History* 28, 1 (January 2004): 113–43.

15. David A. J. Richards, *The Case for Gay Rights: From Bowers to Lawrence and Beyond* (Lawrence: University Press of Kansas, 2005), 74; Fukuyama, *The Great Disruption*, 36; Judt, *Postwar*, 488–90; Hitchcock, *The Struggle for Europe*, 263; Carl Guarneri, *America in the World: United States History in Global Context* (Boston: McGraw-Hill, 2007), 272; Glendon, *Abortion and Divorce in Western Law*, passim.

16. Daniel C. Thomas, *The Helsinki Effect: International Norms, Human Rights, and the Demise of Communism* (Princeton, NJ: Princeton University Press, 2001), 3–4 (quotation), 34–36; Osterhammel and Petersson, *Globalization*, 142; Hitchcock, *The Struggle for Europe*, 301.

17. Zubok, *A Failed Empire*, 237–38; Morgan, "The Seventies and the Rebirth of Human Rights"; Yale Richmond, *Cultural Exchange and the Cold War: Raising the Iron Curtain* (University Park: Pennsylvania State University Press, 2003), 186–93; Wilentz, *The Age of Reagan*, 59 (Podhoretz); Thomas, *The Helsinki Effect*, 4, 91–92, 160–66, 204–5, 284; Douglas E. Selvage, "Transforming the Soviet Sphere of Influence? U.S.-Soviet Détente and Eastern Europe, 1969–1976," *Diplomatic History* 33, 4 (September 2009): 686.

18. On the broad sweep of human history and the rise of European power, see Jared Diamond, *Guns, Germs, and Steel: The Fates of Human Societies* (New York: Norton, 1997), and Alfred W. Crosby, *Ecological Imperialism: The Biological Expansion of Europe, 900–1900*, 2nd ed. (New York: Cambridge University Press, 2004). On the largest time frame for human history, see David Christian, *Maps of Time: An Introduction to Big History* (Berkeley: University of California Press, 2004).

19. David B. Abernethy, *The Dynamics of Global Dominance: European Overseas Empires, 1415–1980* (New Haven, CT: Yale University Press, 2000), 135–36.

20. Roland Burke, "From Individual Rights to National Development: The First UN International Conference on Human Rights, Tehran, 1968," *Journal of World History* 19, 3 (September 2008): 277–96; Sheehan, *Where Have All the Soldiers Gone?*, 169–71; Judt, *A Grand Illusion*, 102–3.

21. Edward W. Said, *Orientalism* (New York: Pantheon, 1978); Steven Davis, *Reggae Bloodlines: In Search of the Music and Culture of Jamaica* (Garden City, NY: Anchor, 1977).

22. *Wall Street Journal*, April 27, 2006, p. B4; Meinig, *The Shaping of America*, 380.

23. Jeanne Marie Penvenne, "Settling against the Tide: The Layered Contradictions of Twentieth-Century Portuguese Settlement in Mozambique," in *Settler Colonialism in the Twentieth Century: Projects, Practices, Legacies*, ed. Caroline Elkins and Susan Pedersen (New York: Routledge, 2005), 79, 84; Stephen C. Lubkemann, "Unsettling the Metropole: Race and Settler Reincorporation in Postcolonial Portugal," in ibid., 259; Abernethy, *The Dynamics of Global Dominance*, 148.

24. Marvine Howe, "Angola Pullout Marks End of a Vast African Empire," *New York Times*, November 11, 1975, p. 3; John A. Marcum, *The Angolan Revolution*, 2 vols. (Cambridge, MA: MIT Press, 1969–1978); William Minter, *King Solomon's Mines Revisited: Western Interests and the Burdened History of Southern Africa* (New York: Basic Books, 1986); Robert David Johnson, "The Unintended Consequences of Reform: The Clark and Tunney Amendments and U.S. Policy toward Angola," *Diplomatic History* 27, 2 (April 2003): 215–43.

25. Robert C. Good, *U.D.I.: The International Politics of the Rhodesian Rebellion* (Princeton, NJ: Princeton University Press, 1973). See also Prosser

Gifford and Wm. Roger Louis, eds., *Decolonization and African Independence: The Transfers of Power, 1960–1980* (New Haven, CT: Yale University Press, 1988).

26. Peter Godwin, *Mukiwa: A White Boy in Africa* (New York: Atlantic Monthly Press, 1996), 3, 11–12; Abernethy, *The Dynamics of Global Dominance*, 148; Minter, *King Solomon's Mines Revisited*.

27. Javan Frazier, "Atomic Apartheid: U.S.-South African Nuclear Relations from Truman to Reagan, 1945–1989" (PhD dissertation, Auburn University, 2006).

28. Piero Gleijeses, "Scandinavia and the Liberation of Southern Africa," *International History Review* 27, 2 (2005): 324–31; William Minter, Gail Hovey, and Charles Cobb, Jr., *No Easy Victories: African Liberation and American Activists over a Half Century, 1950–2000* (Trenton: Africa World Press, 2008); Thomas Borstelmann, *The Cold War and the Color Line: American Race Relations in the Global Arena* (Cambridge, MA: Harvard University Press, 2001).

29. Leonard Thompson, *A History of South Africa* (New Haven, CT: Yale University Press, 1990); Tom Lodge, *Black Politics in South Africa since 1945* (London: Longman, 1983).

30. Nancy Mitchell, review of Scott Kaufman, *Plans Unraveled: The Foreign Policy of the Carter Administration*, *International History Review* 31, 2 (June 2009): 464; Piero Gleijeses, *Conflicting Missions: Havana, Washington, and Africa, 1959–1976* (Chapel Hill: University of North Carolina Press, 2002); Zubok, *A Failed Empire*, 200, 247–54; Piero Gleijeses, "Moscow's Proxy? Cuba and Africa, 1975–1988," *Journal of Cold War Studies* 8, 4 (Fall 2006): 98–146; Andrew, *The World Was Going Our Way*.

31. Wilentz, *The Age of Reagan*, 105; Zubok, *A Failed Empire*, 201–3, 207–9.

32. Melvyn P. Leffler, *For the Soul of Mankind: The United States, the Soviet Union, and the Cold War* (New York: Hill and Wang, 2007), 255 (Brezhnev); Kotkin, *Armageddon Averted*, xi; Judt, *Postwar*, 602 (Pravda).

33. Kotkin, *Armageddon Averted*, 11–12, 20 (quotation), 23, 28, 31 (Khrushchev).

34. Barry J. Eichengreen, *The European Economy since 1945: Coordinated Capitalism and Beyond* (Princeton, NJ: Princeton University Press, 2006), 294–95; Robert W. Strayer, *The Communist Experiment: Revolution, Socialism and Global Conflict in the Twentieth Century* (Boston: McGraw-Hill, 2007), 156; Daniel Yergin and Joseph Stanislaw, *The Commanding Heights: The Battle between Government and the Marketplace That Is Remaking the Modern World* (New York: Simon & Schuster, 1998), 273; Judt, *Postwar*, 579 (joke).

35. On the dissident movement, see Joshua Rubenstein, *Soviet Dissidents: Their Struggle for Human Rights*, 2nd ed. (Boston: Beacon, 1985).

36. Yevgeny Yevtushenko, "Introduction," to Alexander Solzhenitsyn, *One Day in the Life of Ivan Denisovich* (1963; New York: Signet, 1998), xi–xvii; Richmond, *Cultural Exchange and the Cold War*, 189; David Remnick, *Lenin's Tomb: The Last Days of the Soviet Empire* (New York: Random House, 1993), 39.

37. Judt, *Postwar*, 559–63; Richard H. Pells, *Not Like Us: How Europeans Have Loved, Hated, and Transformed American Culture since World War II* (New York: Basic Books, 1997), 317.

38. Edward E. Ericson, Jr., "Introduction to the Perennial Classics Edition," in Aleksandr Solzhenitsyn, *The Gulag Archipelago, 1918–1956: An Experiment in Literary Investigation* (1973; New York: Perennial, 2002), xvi; "Solzhenitsyn Chronicled Soviet Cruelty," *Omaha World-Herald*, August 4, 2008, p. 2A (Solzhenitsyn); Kathleen Parthé, "The Politics of Détente-Era Cultural Texts: 1969–1976," *Diplomatic History* 33, 4 (September 2009): 723–33.

39. Matthew J. Ouimet, *The Rise and Fall of the Brezhnev Doctrine in Soviet Foreign Policy* (Chapel Hill: University of North Carolina Press, 2003), 89; Leffler, *For the Soul of Mankind*, 335–36 (quotations).

40. Ouimet, *The Rise and Fall of the Brezhnev Doctrine*, 92–97; Zubok, *A Failed Empire*, 225; Leffler, *For the Soul of Mankind*, 307 (Gromyko).

41. James Mann, *About Face: A History of America's Curious Relationship with China from Nixon to Clinton* (New York: Knopf, 1999), 110 (quotation); David N. Gibbs, "Reassessing Soviet Motives for Invading Afghanistan: A Declassified History," *Critical Asian Studies* 38, 2 (2006): 239–63.

42. Zubok, *A Failed Empire*, 265–67 (Andropov); Aleksander Smolar, "Towards 'Self-Limiting Revolution': Poland, 1970–1989," in *Civil Resistance and Power Politics: The Experience of Non-violent Action from Gandhi to the Present*, ed. Adam Roberts and Timothy Garton Ash (New York: Oxford University Press, 2009), 128 ("the Christ").

43. Ouimet, *The Rise and Fall of the Brezhnev Doctrine*, 113–16, 234, 243 (quotation); Timothy Garton Ash, *The Polish Revolution: Solidarity*, 3rd ed. (New Haven, CT: Yale University Press, 2002); Yergin and Stanislaw, *The Commanding Heights*, 263–65; Judt, *Postwar*, 585.

44. Dwight Garner, "America Abroad," *New York Times*, July 9, 2008; Paul Rosier, *Serving Their Country*, 2–3 (Lippmann), 14 (Roosevelt); Niall Ferguson, *Colossus*, cited in *New York Review of Books*, July 13, 2006, p. 54. For a sampling of the range of recent books on the American empire, see Maier, *Among Empires*; Murphy, *Are We Rome?*; Chalmers Johnson, *The Sorrows of Empire: Militarism, Secrecy, and the End of the Republic* (New York: Metropolitan, 2004); Niall Ferguson, *Colossus: The Price of America's Empire* (New York: Penguin, 2004); Rashid Khalidi, *Resurrecting Empire: Western Footprints and America's Perilous Path in the Middle East* (Boston: Beacon, 2004); Victoria de Grazia, *Irresistible Empire: America's Advance through Twentieth-Century Europe* (Cambridge, MA: Harvard University Press, 2005); Greg Grandin, *Empire's Workshop: Latin America, the United States, and the Rise of the New Imperialism* (New York: Metropolitan, 2006); Bernard Porter, *Empire and Superempire: Britain, America and the World* (New Haven, CT: Yale University Press, 2006).

45. Sargent, "From Internationalism to Globalism," chapter 3 provides a particularly insightful discussion of these events.

46. Richard Drinnon, *Facing West: The Metaphysics of Indian-Hating and Empire Building* (Minneapolis: University of Minnesota Press, 1980); John Hagan, *Northern Passage: American Vietnam War Resisters in Canada* (Cam-

bridge, MA: Harvard University Press, 2001), 3; Link, *Righteous Warrior*, 189 (Helms); Jeffrey A. Engel, ed., *The China Diary of George H. W. Bush: The Making of a Global President* (Princeton, NJ: Princeton University Press, 2008), 456.

47. Olmsted, *Challenging the Secret Government*; Arthur M. Schlesinger, Jr., *The Imperial Presidency* (Boston: Houghton Mifflin, 1973).

48. Cahn, *Killing Détente*, 20, 36, 47 (Ford), 64–65; John Ehrman, *The Rise of Neoconservatism: Intellectuals and Foreign Affairs, 1945–1994* (New Haven, CT: Yale University Press, 1995).

49. Skidmore, *Reversing Course*, 41 (Carter), 112 (Linowitz); Jason Colby, "Jim Crow Empire: Race and Nation Building in U.S.-Central American Relations, 1870–1940" (PhD dissertation, Cornell University, 2005); Walter LaFeber, *The Panama Canal: The Crisis in Historical Perspective*, updated ed. (New York: Oxford University Press, 1989), 158–64; Johnson, *Congress and the Cold War*, 235–39; Mieczkowski, *Gerald Ford and the Challenges of the 1970s*, 316 (Keene); Adam Clymer, *Drawing the Line at the Big Ditch: The Panama Canal Treaties and the Rise of the Right* (Lawrence: University Press of Kansas, 2008), 23 (Reagan). Clymer emphasizes the significance of the fight over the treaties for mobilizing the modern conservative movement, which can be understood, at least in part, as defending the American empire.

50. María Cristina García, *Seeking Refuge: Central American Migration to Mexico, the United States, and Canada* (Berkeley: University of California Press, 2006), 14–21; Walter LaFeber, *Inevitable Revolutions: The United States in Central America*, 2nd ed. (New York: Norton, 1993); William M. LeoGrande, *Our Own Backyard: The United States in Central America, 1977–1992* (Chapel Hill: University of North Carolina Press, 1998); John H. Coatsworth, *Central America and the United States: The Clients and the Colossus* (New York: Twayne, 1994). For a useful comparison of the operations of the Soviet and American empires in their closest respective regions of influence, see Jan F. Triska, ed., *Dominant Powers and Subordinate States: The United States in Latin America and the Soviet Union in Eastern Europe* (Durham, NC: Duke University Press, 1986).

51. Ryszard Kapuscinski, *Shah of Shahs* (New York: Vintage, 1985), 118; Nikki R. Keddie, *Modern Iran: Roots and Results of Revolution* (New Haven, CT: Yale University Press, 2006); Evan Thomas, "Counter Intelligence," *New York Review of Books*, July 22, 2007, p. 11 (Turner).

52. James A. Bill, *The Eagle and the Lion: The Tragedy of American-Iranian Relations* (New Haven, CT: Yale University Press, 1988); David Farber, *Taken Hostage: The Iran Hostage Crisis and America's First Encounter with Radical Islam* (Princeton, NJ: Princeton University Press, 2005); Thomas, "Counter Intelligence," 11 (Dougherty).

53. Benny Morris, *Righteous Victims: A History of the Zionist-Arab Conflict, 1881–1998* (New York: Knopf, 1999); Benny Morris, *1948: A History of the First Arab-Israeli War* (New Haven, CT: Yale University Press, 2008); Avi Shlaim, *The Iron Wall: Israel and the Arab World* (New York: Norton, 2000); Michael B. Oren, *Six Days of War: June 1967 and the Making of the Modern Middle East* (New York: Oxford University Press, 2002).

54. Frederic Hunter, "Israeli Ties with Black Africa Fray," *Christian Science Monitor*, January 3, 1973; Gershom Gorenberg, *The Accidental Empire: Israel and the Birth of Settlements, 1967–1977* (New York: Times Books, 2006); Joel Beinin, "When Doves Cry," *Nation*, April 17, 2006; Amos Elon, "What Does Olmert Want?" *New York Review of Books*, June 22, 2006, p. 53; Tony Judt, "Dark Victory: Israel's Six-Day War," in *Reappraisals: Reflections on the Forgotten Twentieth Century* (New York: Penguin, 2008), 279–81; Gilles Kepel, *The Revenge of God: The Resurgence of Islam, Christianity, and Judaism in the Modern World* (University Park: Pennsylvania State University Press, 1994), 154–60.

55. Akira Iriye, "Globalization as Americanization?" in *The Paradox of Global USA*, ed. Bruce Mazlish, Nayan Chanda, and Kenneth Weisbrode (Stanford: Stanford University Press, 2007), 42.

56. Aaron J. Klein, *Striking Back: The 1972 Munich Olympics Massacre and Israel's Deadly Response* (New York: Random House, 2005), 14–17, 24–26, 92, 97–98, 100 (Meir), 106–9, 206.

57. Robert Dallek, *Nixon and Kissinger: Partners in Power* (New York: HarperCollins, 2007), 522–23; Kepel, *The Revenge of God*, 140–42.

58. Peter Novick, *The Holocaust in American Life* (Boston: Houghton Mifflin, 1999); Avi Shlaim, *War and Peace in the Middle East: A Concise History*, rev. ed. (New York: Penguin, 1995), 50–52.

59. Paul Hofmann, "U.N. Votes, 72–35, to Term Zionism Form of Racism," *New York Times*, November 11, 1975, p. 1; Elkins and Pedersen, *Settler Colonialism*, 3; Gershon Shafir, "Settler Citizenship in the Jewish Colonization of Palestine," in ibid., 53–54; Jeffrey Goldberg, "Israel's Fears, Amalek's Arsenal," *New York Times*, May 17, 2009. Admiration at the tactical brilliance of the Israeli Defense Force was equally widespread and enduring. Thirty-two years later and halfway around the world, for example, when Colombian counterinsurgent forces freed political figure Ingrid Betancourt after six years of captivity at the hands of anti-government guerillas, she explained her response to a reporter: "This is a miracle, a miracle. . . . I think only the Israelis can possibly pull off something like this." David Luhnow and José de Cordoba, "Colombia Raid Frees U.S. Hostages," *Wall Street Journal*, July 3, 2008, p. A12.

60. Paul Hofmann, "UN Votes, 72–35, To Term Zionism Form of Racism," *New York Times*, November 11, 1975, p. 1; Tom Buckley, "Brawler at the U.N.," *New York Times*, December 7, 1975 (Moynihan); Michelle Mart, *Eye on Israel: How America Came to View the Jewish State as an Ally* (Albany: State University of New York Press, 2006); Jeremi Suri, *Henry Kissinger and the American Century* (Cambridge, MA: Harvard University Press, 2007), 61–62; McAlister, *Epic Encounters*, 125–97.

61. Judt, *Reappraisals*, 8–10.

62. McMillan, *Reinventing the Bazaar*, 196; Sargent, "From Internationalism to Globalism," conclusion; Osterhammel and Petersson, *Globalization*, 142–43.

63. Eichengreen, *The European Economy since 1945*, 2 (quotation), 8–11, 30; de Grazia, *Irresistible Empire*, 4–5, 11; Painter, "International Oil and

National Security," 195; Osterhammel and Petersson, *Globalization*, 134; Judt, *Postwar*, 453–64; Colin Jones, *The Cambridge Illustrated History of France* (New York: Cambridge University Press, 1994), 303; Bruce J. Schulman, "Slouching toward the Supply Side: Jimmy Carter and the New American Political Economy," in *The Carter Presidency*, ed. Fink and Graham, 63.

64. Hitchcock, *The Struggle for Europe*, 243–44; Painter, "International Oil and National Security," 195–97.

65. Yergin and Stanislaw, *The Commanding Heights*, 90.

66. Eichengreen, *The European Economy since 1945*, 280–81; Yergin and Stanislaw, *The Commanding Heights*, chapter 4; Judt, *Postwar*, 535–47; Janet Fink, "Welfare, Poverty and Social Inequalities," in *A Companion to Contemporary Britain, 1939–2000*, ed. Paul Addison and Harriet Jones (Malden, MA: Blackwell, 2005), 274–77.

67. Stephen Kinzer, *Overthrow: America's Century of Regime Change from Hawaii to Iraq* (New York: Times Books, 2006), 185–86.

68. Juan Gabriel Valdés, *Pinochet's Economists: The Chicago School of Economics in Chile* (New York: Cambridge University Press, 1995); Jeremy Adelman, "International Finance and Political Legitimacy: A Latin American View of the Global Shock," in *The Shock of the Global*, ed. Ferguson et al., 113–27.

69. John Dinges, *The Condor Years: How Pinochet and His Allies Brought Terrorism to Three Continents* (New York: New Press, 2004), 3–5, 10–11; Larry Rohter, "On Coup's Anniversary, Argentines Vow 'Never Again',," *New York Times*, March 25, 2006, p. A3; Melvin Small, "Spider-Man, Too," *Diplomatic History* 30, 3 (June 2006): 560–61; Greg Grandin, *The Last Colonial Massacre: Latin America in the Cold War* (Chicago: University of Chicago Press, 2006), 74.

70. Chen, *Mao's China and the Cold War*, 278; Jonathan D. Spence, *The Search for Modern China* (New York: Norton, 1990), 588–89; Roderick MacFarquhar, "The Succession to Mao and the End of Maoism, 1969–82," in *The Politics of China: The Eras of Mao and Deng*, 2nd ed. (New York: Cambridge University Press, 1997), 248–339; Roderick MacFarquhar, "Mission to Mao," *New York Review of Books*, June 28, 2007, pp. 69–70.

71. Patrick Tyler, *A Great Wall: Six Presidents and China* (New York: Public Affairs, 1999), 42, 50; Schaller, *The United States and China*, 166 ("barbarians"); Spence, *The Search for Modern China*, 629; Zubok, *A Failed Empire*, 210–11; MacFarquhar, "Mission to Mao," 70; James Mann, *About Face*, 8, 61 (Kissinger).

72. Spence, *The Search for Modern China*, 617.

73. Richard Baum, *Burying Mao: Chinese Politics in the Age of Deng Xiaoping* (Princeton, NJ: Princeton University Press, 1994), chapter 3; Hobsbawm, *The Age of Extremes*, 461 (Deng); Reynolds, *One World Divisible*, 403; Spence, *The Search for Modern China*, 657–58; *New Yorker*, August 5, 1972; Yergin and Stanislaw, *The Commanding Heights*, 197; McMillan, *Reinventing the Bazaar*, 94–95; Enrico Fardella, "The Sino-American Normalization: A Reassessment," *Diplomatic History* 33, 4 (September 2009): 555.

74. Odd Arne Westad, "The Great Transformation: China in the Long 1970s," in *The Shock of the Global*, ed. Ferguson et al., 65–79; Chen, *Mao's China in the Cold War*, 278; Mann, *About Face*, 8; David Barboza, "Isaac Stern's Great Leap Forward Reverberates," *New York Times*, July 5, 2009; Mei Fong, "Tired of Laughter, Beijing Gets Rid of Bad Translations," *Wall Street Journal*, February 5, 2007, p. A13; MacMillan, *Nixon and Mao*, 334 (slogan).

75. Benedict R. O'G. Anderson, *Imagined Communities: Reflections on the Origin and Spread of Nationalism*, rev. ed. (London: Verso, 1991), 1; Mann, *About Face*, 97; Schaller, *The United States and China*, 192. The new Communist government of Vietnam, facing considerable obstacles to postwar rebuilding, also began experimenting with economic reform and market incentives in 1979. See Bill Hayton, *Vietnam: Rising Dragon* (New Haven, CT: Yale University Press, 2010).

76. On the background of American consumer culture's influence abroad, see de Grazia, *Irresistible Empire*; Emily S. Rosenberg, *Spreading the American Dream: American Economic and Cultural Expansion, 1890–1945* (New York: Hill and Wang, 1982); Reinhold Wagnleitner, *Coca-Colonization and the Cold War: The Cultural Mission of the United States in Austria after the Second World War* (Chapel Hill: University of North Carolina Press, 1994).

Chapter 5. Resistance to the New Hyper-Individualism

1. An excellent brief summary of labor's decline in the 1970s can be found in Jefferson Cowie, "'Vigorously Left, Right, and Center': The Crosscurrents of Working-Class America in the 1970s," in *America in the Seventies*, ed. Bailey and Farber, 75–106. For greater elaboration, see Cowie, *Stayin' Alive: The 1970s and the Last Days of the Working Class* (New York: New Press, 2010). See also Joseph A. McCartin, "Turnabout Years: Public Sector Unionism and the Fiscal Crisis," in *Rightward Bound: Making America Conservative in the 1970s*, ed. Bruce J. Schulman and Julian E. Zelizer (Cambridge, MA: Harvard University Press, 2008), 210–26; and McCartin, "'A Wagner Act for Public Employees': Labor's Deferred Dream and the Rise of Conservatism, 1970–1976," *Journal of American History* 95, 1 (June 2008): 123–48.

2. McNeill, *Something New Under the Sun*.

3. Gabriel A. Almond, R. Scott Appleby, and Emmanuel Sivan, eds., *Strong Religion: The Rise of Fundamentalisms around the World* (Chicago: University of Chicago Press, 2003), 2, 37–41; Martin E. Marty and R. Scott Appleby, *Fundamentalisms Observed, The Fundamentalism Project*, vol. 1 (Chicago: University of Chicago Press, 1991), vii–viii; Bruce B. Lawrence, *Defenders of God: The Fundamentalist Revolt against the Modern Age* (Columbia: University of South Carolina Press, 1995), 100; Karen Armstrong, *The Battle for God: A History of Fundamentalism* (New York: Ballantine, 2000), vii–viii. Although there are problems with using the term "fundamentalist" for non-Protestants, historians Martin Marty and Scott Appleby observe, "[I]f the term were to be rejected, the public would have to find some other word if it is to

make sense of a set of global phenomena which urgently bid to be understood." They offer "revolutionary, neotraditionalist, religious radicalism" as an option, though the accuracy of the phrase is undercut by its literary infelicity, as they note. Marty and Appleby, *Fundamentalisms Observed*, viii.

4. Kepel, *The Revenge of God*, 2, 9; Westad, *The Global Cold War*, 94; Heather Sunderland, "The Problematic Authority of (World) History," *Journal of World History* 18, 4 (December 2007): 491–522; Lindsey, *The Age of Abundance*, 39 (Jefferson).

5. U.S. Census Bureau, *Statistical Abstract of the United States, 2003*, www.census.gov/statab/hist/HS-01.pdf (accessed January 24, 2006); Ohio History Central, "Cuyahoga River Fire," http://www.ohiohistorycentral.org/entry.php ?rec=1642 (accessed January 6, 2010) (Cuyahoga); J. R. McNeill, "The Environment, Environmentalism, and International Society in the Long 1970s," in *The Shock of the Global*, ed. Ferguson et al., 268; Nick Cullather, *The Hungry World: America's Cold War Battle against Poverty in Asia* (Cambridge, MA: Harvard University Press, 2010).

6. Paul R. Ehrlich, *The Population Bomb* (New York: Ballantine, 1968); George F. Will, "This, Too, Shall Pass Away," *Newsweek*, June 28, 1976; Connelly, *Fatal Misconception*.

7. McNeill, *Something New Under the Sun*, 25, 146.

8. Ibid., 332 (Guevara); Robert M. Collins, "Growth Liberalism in the Sixties: Great Societies at Home and Grand Designs Abroad," in *The Sixties: From Memory to History*, ed. David Farber (Chapel Hill: University of North Carolina Press, 1994), 15 (Khrushchev); Gottlieb, *Forcing the Spring*, 308; Shabecoff, *A Fierce Green Fire*, 107; Christian, *Maps of Time*, 475 (Gandhi); McNeill, "The Environment, Environmentalism, and International Society in the Long 1970s"; J. R. McNeill and Corinna R. Unger, eds., *Environmental Histories of the Cold War* (New York: Cambridge University Press, 2010).

9. Laurie Garrett, *The Coming Plague: Newly Emerging Diseases in a World Out of Balance* (New York: Farrar, Straus and Giroux, 1994); Richard Preston, *The Hot Zone* (New York: Random House, 1994); McNeill, *Something New Under the Sun*, 199–204.

10. McNeill, Something New Under the Sun, 113–14; Elizabeth Kolbert, "The Climate of Man—I," *New Yorker*, April 25, 2005, p. 58 (quotation).

11. John McMillan, *Reinventing the Bazaar: A Natural History of Markets* (New York: Norton, 2002), 119; John Cassidy, "High Costs," *New Yorker*, November 13, 2006, p. 35 (quotation). On global warming, see Bill McKibben, *The End of Nature* (New York: Random House, 1989); Elizabeth Kolbert, *Field Notes from a Catastrophe: Man, Nature, and Climate Change* (New York: Bloomsbury USA, 2006); David W. Orr, *Down to the Wire: Confronting Climate Collapse* (New York: Oxford University Press, 2009); James Hansen, *Storms of My Grandchildren: The Truth about the Coming Climate Catastrophe and Our Last Chance to Save Humanity* (New York: Bloomsbury USA, 2009).

12. Kevin P. Phillips, *American Theocracy: The Peril and Politics of Radical Religion, Oil, and Borrowed Money in the 21st Century* (New York: Viking, 2006), 31 (Barton); Jackson, *Crabgrass Frontier*, 297–98; David S. Painter,

"International Oil and National Security," *Daedalus* 120, 4 (1991): 196; Judt, *Grand Illusion*, 94. On the trucking industry, see Hamilton, *Trucking Country*. On oil in the twentieth century, see Daniel Yergin, *The Prize: The Epic Quest for Oil, Money, and Power* (New York: Simon & Schuster, 1991).

13. Kotkin, *Armageddon Averted*, 11–12; Phillips, *American Theocracy*, 40–41.

14. U.S. Department of Energy, Energy Information Administration, "Annual Energy Review, 1999," www.eia.doe (accessed June 3, 2006); Caplow et al., *The First Measured Century*, 255.

15. Amory B. Lovins, "Energy Strategy: The Road Not Taken?" Foreign Affairs 55, 1 (October 1976): 65–96; Shabecoff, *A Fierce Green Fire*, 113; Elizabeth Kolbert, "Mr. Green," *New Yorker*, January 22, 2007, p. 36; Gerald Ford, "Address before a Joint Session of Congress Addressing the State of the Union," January 15, 1975, http://www.fordlibrarymuseum.gov/library/speeches/750028.htm (accessed January 6, 2010); Phillips, *American Theocracy*, 55.

16. Painter, "International Oil and National Security," 197–99; McNeill, *Something New Under the Sun*, 301, 314; Meinig, *The Shaping of America*, 265–66.

17. Jackson, *Crabgrass Frontier*, 297–98.

18. Barbara Epstein, *Political Protest and Cultural Revolution: Nonviolent Direct Action in the 1970s and 1980s* (Berkeley: University of California Press, 1991), 64–65, 86–87, 96–97, 100–105; *New York Times*, April 24, 2001, p. C1; Bonnie A. Osif, Anthony J. Baratta, and Thomas W. Conkling, *TMI 25 Years Later: The Three Mile Island Nuclear Power Plant Accident and Its Impact* (University Park: Pennsylvania State University Press, 2004)..

19. Adam Rome, "'Give Earth a Chance': The Environmental Movement and the Sixties," *Journal of American History* 90, 2 (September 2003): 542; John Kenneth Galbraith, *The Affluent Society* (Boston: Houghton Mifflin, 1958), 258; Robert Poole, *Earthrise: How Man First Saw the Earth* (New Haven, CT: Yale University Press, 2008); Jeremy Black, *Altered States: America since the Sixties* (London: Reaktion, 2006), 26.

20. Riley E. Dunlap and Angela G. Mertig, *American Environmentalism: The U.S. Environmental Movement, 1970–1990* (Philadelphia: Taylor & Francis, 1992), 92; Mark Dowie, *Losing Ground: American Environmentalism at the Close of the Twentieth Century* (Cambridge, MA: MIT Press, 1995), 33–34; Rome, "'Give Earth a Chance'," 550–51 (quotation).

21. Annie Dillard, *Pilgrim at Tinker Creek* (New York: Harper's Magazine Press, 1974).

22. Dowie, *Losing Ground*, 33; Gottlieb, *Forcing the Spring*, 125, 128; James Morton Turner, "'The Specter of Environmentalism': Wilderness, Environmental Politics, and the Evolution of the New Right," *Journal of American History* 96, 1 (June 2009): 147; *New York Times*, July 6, 2008, p. BU6. A perceptive study of how regulatory reform efforts endured into the early 1970s is Gareth Davies, "The Great Society after Johnson: The Case of Bilingual Education," *Journal of American History* 88, 4 (March 2002): 1405–29. For background to the environmental laws of the 1970s, see Karl Boyd Brooks,

Before Earth Day: The Origins of American Environmental Law, 1945–1970 (Lawrence: University Press of Kansas, 2009).

23. Matthew L. Wald, "Automakers Use New Technology to Beef Up Muscle, Not Mileage," *New York Times*, March 30, 2006; Kolbert, "Mr. Green," 22.

24. Elizabeth Kolbert, "The River," *New Yorker*, December 4, 2000, p. 56; Mark Cargill, "The General Electric Superfraud," *Harper's*, December 2009, pp. 41–51; Eileen M. McGurty, *Transforming Environmentalism: Warren County, PCBs, and the Origins of Environmental Justice* (New Brunswick, NJ: Rutgers University Press, 2007), 1–4, 24–29.

25. Richard Newman, "From Love's Canal to Love Canal: Reckoning with the Environmental Legacy of an Industrial Dream," in *Beyond the Ruins: The Meanings of Deindustrialization*, ed. Jefferson Cowie and Joseph Heathcott (Ithaca, NY: Cornell University Press, 2003), 114–17; Dowie, *Losing Ground*, 129–30; McGurty, *Transforming Environmentalism*, 40–41.

26. Dashka Slater, "Moments of Truth," *Sierra*, July/August 2001, p. 54.

27. Gottlieb, *Forcing the Spring*, 187; Shabecoff, *A Fierce Green Fire*, 229 (Gibbs).

28. Donald Worster, *Under Western Skies: Nature and History in the American West* (New York: Oxford University Press, 1992), 188–208; "The Missing Chapter in the Bush Bio: A Modest Summer in Alaska," *New York Times*, November 4, 2009; Timothy Egan, "Alaska Changes View on Carter After 20 Years," *New York Times*, August 25, 2000, p. A14 (Udall).

29. Eichengreen, *The European Economy since 1945*, 296.

30. Osterhammel and Petersson, *Globalization*, 138–39; Andrew Gordon, *A Modern History of Japan: From Tokugawa Times to the Present* (New York: Oxford University Press, 2003), 287–88; Michael H. Brown and John May, *The Greenpeace Story* (New York: Dorling Kindersley, 1991), 10–12; McNeill, *Something New Under the Sun*, 97, 106–7, 145, 350.

31. Shabecoff, *A Fierce Green Fire*, xv (Leopold); Rik Scarce, *Eco-Warriors: Understanding the Radical Environmental Movement* (Chicago: Noble, 1990); Steven Shapin, "Paradise Sold," *New Yorker*, May 15, 2006, p. 84.

32. One of the best studies of the New Christian Right in this era is Lienesch, *Redeeming America*. One of the books most often read and cited by born-again Christians in the 1970s as a clear explanation of their faith was C. S. Lewis, *Mere Christianity* (1952; New York: Macmillan, 1960). The best articulation of the evangelical concern with secular humanism was Francis A. Schaeffer, *How Should We Then Live? The Rise and Decline of Western Thought and Culture* (Wheaton, IL: Crossway Books, 1976).

33. Joel A. Carpenter, *Revive Us Again: The Reawakening of American Fundamentalism* (New York: Oxford University Press, 1997); Armstrong, *The Battle for God*, 171.

34. Nancy T. Ammerman, "North American Protestant Fundamentalism," in *Fundamentalisms Observed*, ed. Marty and Appleby, 1; Lienesch, *Redeeming America*, 203 (Robertson), 219 (Falwell).

35. Susan Friend Harding, *The Book of Jerry Falwell: Fundamentalist Lan-*

guage and Politics (Princeton, NJ: Princeton University Press, 2000), 19; Lienesch, *Redeeming America*, 8; Putnam, *Bowling Alone*, 76–77.

36. Crespino, *In Search of Another Country*, 252–56, 265 (quotation).

37. Harding, The Book of Jerry Falwell, 21–22; D'Emilio, *Intimate Matters*, 349. On gospel music and Baptist faith as forms of liberation theology, see Nick Salvatore, *Singing in a Strange Land: C. L. Franklin, the Black Church, and the Transformation of America* (Boston: Little, Brown, 2005).

38. Schaeffer, *How Then Should We Live?* 217.

39. Robert McAfee Brown, *Theology in a New Key: Responding to Liberation Themes* (Philadelphia: Westminster Press, 1978); Jim Wallis, *God's Politics: Why the Right Gets It Wrong and the Left Doesn't Get It* (San Francisco: HarperSanFrancisco, 2005), 48; "The Move to Washington, D.C.," editorial, *Post American*, August/September 1975, p. 3 ("commitment"). The bimonthly *Post American* changed its name to *Sojourners* in September 1975. On public awareness of Sojourners, see "When Religion Blends with Social Activism," *U.S. News and World Report*, December 31, 1979/January 7, 1980, p. 81.

40. Laurie Goodstein, "How the Evangelicals and Catholics Joined Forces," *New York Times*, May 30, 2004, Sec. 4, p. 4; Patrick Allitt, *Catholic Intellectuals and Conservative Politics in America, 1950–1985* (Ithaca, NY: Cornell University Press, 1993), 7, 81, 123–24, 175; Will Herberg, *Protestant, Catholic, Jew: An Essay in American Religious Sociology* (Garden City, NY: Doubleday, 1955). See also Robert Wuthnow, *The Restructuring of American Religion: Society and Faith since World War I* (Princeton, NJ: Princeton University Press, 1988).

41. Lindsey, *The Age of Abundance*, 262 (Brown and Schaeffer); Moreton, *To Serve God and Wal-Mart*, 119–20; Gregory, *The Southern Diaspora*, 316–17; Collins, *Transforming America*, 175 (Falwell).

42. Peter J. Boyer, "A Hard Faith," *New Yorker*, May 16, 2005, 54–65; Philip Jenkins, *The Next Christendom: The Coming of Global Christianity* (New York: Oxford University Press, 2002), 145–47; María Cristina García, *Seeking Refuge: Central American Migration to Mexico, the United States, and Canada* (Berkeley: University of California Press, 2006), 21; Kepel, *The Revenge of God*, 48, 53; Tony Judt, "A 'Pope of Ideas'? John Paul II and the Modern World," in *Reappraisals*, 150–52.

43. "Columnist, Wordsmith James Kilpatrick Dies at 89," *New York Times*, August 16, 2010; Allitt, *Catholic Intellectuals and Conservative Politics in America*, ix, 2; Wallis, *God's Politics*, 340; Schaeffer, *How Should We Then Live?*, 205; Moreton, *To Serve God and Wal-Mart*, 86.

44. Critchlow, *Phyllis Schlafly and Grassroots Conservatism*, 221.

45. Joseph Crespino, "Civil Rights and the Religious Right," in *Rightward Bound*, ed. Schulman and Zelizer, 92; Bob Dylan, "Gotta Serve Somebody," *Slow Train Coming* (Columbia Records, 1979).

46. Phillips, *American Theocracy*, 184; Kepel, *The Revenge of God*, 133 (Falwell); Armstrong, *The Battle for God*, 309; Lienesch, *Redeeming America*, 11, 95; Moreton, *To Serve God and Wal-Mart*, 88, 93 (cashier), 126–27. See also Robert S. McElvaine, *Grand Theft Jesus: The Hijacking of Religion in America* (New York: Crown, 2008); and Jeff Sharlet, *The Family: The Secret*

Fundamentalism at the Heart of American Power (New York: HarperCollins, 2008).

47. Gershom Gorenberg, *The Accidental Empire: Israel and the Birth of the Settlements, 1967–1977* (New York: Times Books, 2006), 1–128, 250–62; Kepel, The Revenge of God, 154–60, 194–95.

48. Gideon Aran, "Jewish Zionist Fundamentalism: The Bloc of the Faithful in Israel (Gush Emunim)," in *Fundamentalisms Observed*, ed. Marty and Appleby, 265–67, 316 (quotation); Armstrong, *The Battle for God*, 280–83; Kepel, *The Revenge of God*, 140–42, 161. On the issue of whether Gush Emunim qualified for the category of fundamentalist, see Laurence J. Silberstein, ed., *Jewish Fundamentalism in Comparative Perspective* (New York: New York University Press, 1993).

49. Aron, "Jewish Zionist Fundamentalism," 280; Armstrong, *The Battle for God*, 285.

50. Samuel C. Heilman and Menachem Friedman, "Religious Fundamentalism and Religious Jews: The Case of the Haredim," in *Fundamentalisms Observed*, ed. Marty and Appleby, 197–264 (quotation at 213); Armstrong, *The Battle for God*, 207.

51. Suri, *Henry Kissinger and the American Century*, 61–62; Harding, *The Book of Falwell*, 238; Lienesch, *Redeeming America*, 229–31. On changing American perceptions of Israel, see Mart, *Eye on Israel*. On the U.S.-Israeli relationship, see Peter L. Hahn, *Caught in the Middle East: U.S. Policy toward the Arab-Israeli Conflict, 1945–1961* (Chapel Hill: University of North Carolina Press, 2004); and David Schoenbaum, *The United States and the State of Israel* (New York: Oxford University Press, 1993). On neoconservatives, see Ehrman, *The Rise of Neoconservatism*; Benjamin Balint, *Running Commentary: The Contentious Magazine that Transformed the Jewish Left into the Neoconservative Right* (New York: PublicAffairs, 2010).

52. Peter Novick, *The Holocaust in American Life* (Boston: Houghton Mifflin, 1999), 113. For an alternative perspective from Novick's, see Hasia R. Diner, *We Remember with Reverence and Love: American Jews and the Myth of Silence after the Holocaust, 1945–1962* (New York: New York University Press, 2009). The 1970s was also when some American universities pioneered the idea of privately endowed professorships in specific religions by establishing chairs in Judaic studies. Daniel Goldin, "In Religion Studies, Universities Bend to Views of Faithful," *Wall Street Journal*, April 6, 2006, p.1.

53. Marty and Appleby, eds., *Fundamentalisms Observed*, 405; Beverly Milton-Edwards, *Islamic Fundamentalism since 1945* (New York: Routledge, 2005), 19; Lawrence, *Defenders of God*, 101; Marty and Appleby, *The Glory and the Power*, 179; Vali Nasr, *Forces of Fortune: The Rise of the New Muslim Middle Class and What It Will Mean for Our World* (New York: Free Press, 2009), 85–115. On early twentieth-century precedents for transnational resistance to modernity, parallel to Protestant fundamentalism in the United States in the same era, see Adam K. Webb, "The Countermodern Moment: A World-Historical Perspective on the Thought of Rabindranath Tagore, Muhammad Iqbal, and Liang Shuming," *Journal of World History*, 19, 2 (June 2008): 189–212. On Islam's medieval prominence in world history, see Janet L. Abu-

Lughod, *Before European Hegemony: The World System A.D. 1250–1350* (New York: Oxford University Press, 1989).

54. John O. Voll, "Fundamentalism in Sunni Arab World: Egypt and the Sudan," in *Fundamentalisms Observed*, ed. Marty and Appleby, 360–61.

55. Milton-Edwards, *Islamic Fundamentalism since 1945*, 27; Armstrong, *The Battle for God*, 219–21.

56. David von Drehle, "A Lesson in Hate," *Smithsonian*, February 2006, http://www.smithsonianmag.com/history-archaeology/presence-feb06.html (accessed April 15, 2010) (Qutb); Lawrence Wright, *The Looming Tower: Al-Qaeda and the Road to 9/11* (New York: Knopf, 2006), 24.

57. Almond, Appleby, and Sivan, *Strong Religion*, 24–25; Voll, "Fundamentalism in the Sunni Arab World," 369–71.

58. Steve Coll, "Young Osama," *New Yorker*, December 12, 2005, pp. 48–61; Kepel, *The Revenge of God*, 19–20; Paul Chamberlin, "A World Restored: Religion, Counterrevolution, and the Search for Order in the Middle East," *Diplomatic History* 32, 3 (June 2008): 445–46; Ayesha Jalal, "An Uncertain Trajectory: Islam's Contemporary Globalization, 1971–1979," in *The Shock of the Global*, ed. Ferguson et al., 319–36; Milton-Edwards, *Islamic Fundamentalism since 1945*, 46; Voll, "Fundamentalism in the Sunni Arab World," 345, 376–78.

59. Nikki R. Keddie, *Modern Iran: Roots and Results of Revolution* (New Haven, CT: Yale University Press, 2003); Ryszard Kapuscinski, *Shah of Shahs* (San Diego: Harcourt Brace, Jovanovich, 1985). On the U.S. role in Iran, see James A. Bill, *The Eagle and the Lion: The Tragedy of American-Iranian Relations* (New Haven, CT: Yale University Press, 1988); Mark J. Gasiorowski, *U.S. Foreign Policy and the Shah: Building a Client State in Iran* (Ithaca, NY: Cornell University Press, 1991).

60. Nikki R. Keddie, "Iranian Revolutions in Comparative Perspective," *American Historical Review* 88, 3 (1983): 579; Margaret Talbot, "The Agitator," *New Yorker*, June 5, 2006, p. 60 (Fallaci); Armstrong, *The Battle for God*, 303 (Montazeri); Gary Sick, *All Fall Down: America's Tragic Encounter with Iran* (New York: Random House, 1985). For insightful perspectives on life in Iran under the revolutionary regime, see Keddie, *Modern Iran*; Nafisi, *Reading Lolita in Tehran*; Christopher de Bellaigue, *In the Rose Garden of the Martyrs: A Memoir of Iran* (New York: HarperCollins, 2005).

61. Steve Coll, *Ghost Wars: The Secret History of the CIA, Afghanistan, and Bin Laden, from the Soviet Invasion to September 10, 2001* (New York: Penguin, 2004), 46; Wright, *The Looming Tower*, 88–94; Yaroslav Trofimov, *The Siege of Mecca: The Forgotten Uprising in Islam's Holiest Shrine and the Birth of Al Qaeda* (New York: Doubleday, 2007).

62. Trofimov, *The Siege of Mecca*, 234–35, 241–45; Robert Dreyfuss, *Devil's Game: How the United States Helped Unleash Fundamentalist Islam* (New York: Metropolitan, 2005), 163, 264–66 (Brzezinski). On women in Afghanistan, see Asne Seierstad, *The Bookseller of Kabul* (Boston: Little, Brown, 2003). On the Taliban, see Ahmed Rashid, *Taliban: Militant Islam, Oil, and Fundamentalism in Central Asia* (New Haven, CT: Yale University Press, 2000).

63. Robert Entman and Bonnie Koenig, "The Conservative Myth," *Nation*, July 17, 1976, pp. 39–42; Betty Glad, *An Outsider in the White House: Jimmy Carter, His Advisors, and the Making of American Foreign Policy* (Ithaca, NY: Cornell University Press, 2009), 7 (Carter); Robert Scheer, "Jimmy, We Hardly Know Y'All," *Playboy*, November 1976, reprinted in *Thinking Tuna Fish, Talking Death: Essays on the Pornography of Power* (New York: Hill and Wang, 1988), 224–25.

64. Scheer, "Jimmy We Hardly Know Y'All," 226.

65. Ibid., 234–37; Burton I. Kaufman, *The Presidency of James Earl Carter* (Lawrence: University Press of Kansas, 1993), 14; Betty Glad, "The Real Jimmy Carter," *Foreign Policy*, February 3, 2010.

66. Scott Kaufman, *Rosalynn Carter: Equal Partner in the White House* (Lawrence: University Press of Kansas, 2007); Andrew J. DeRoche, *Andrew Young: Civil Rights Ambassador* (Wilmington, DE: Scholarly Resources, 2003); David F. Schmitz and Vanessa Walker, "Jimmy Carter and the Foreign Policy of Human Rights: The Development of a Post-Cold War Foreign Policy," *Diplomatic History* 28, 1 (January 2004): 113–43; David Skidmore, *Reversing Course: Carter's Foreign Policy, Domestic Politics, and the Failure of Reform* (Nashville: Vanderbilt University Press, 1996), 41–42, 65, 70, 88; Gary Scott Smith, *Faith and the Presidency: From George Washington to George W. Bush* (New York: Oxford University Press, 2006), 300 (quotation); Jerel A. Rosati, "Jimmy Carter, a Man Before His Time? The Emergence and Collapse of the First Post-Cold War Presidency," *Presidential Studies Quarterly* 22 (Summer 1993): 459–76; Douglas Brinkley, *The Unfinished Presidency: Jimmy Carter's Journey Beyond the White House* (New York: Penguin, 1998).

67. Jimmy Carter, State of the Union address, January 19, 1978, http://jim mycarterlibrary.org/documents/speeches/su78jec.phtml (accessed January 27, 2010); Jimmy Carter, *Keeping Faith: Memoirs of a President* (New York: Bantam, 1982), 69; Phillip J. Cooper, *The War against Regulation: From Jimmy Carter to George W. Bush* (Lawrence: University Press of Kansas, 2009), 14–28. His predecessors knew much less about running a business: Ford and Nixon were lawyers; Johnson, Kennedy, and Franklin Roosevelt worked almost exclusively in politics; Dwight Eisenhower was a life-long soldier; and Harry Truman famously failed in his early effort at managing a small men's clothing outfitter.

68. Jeffrey K. Stine, "Environmental Policy during the Carter Presidency," in *The Carter Presidency*, ed. Fink and Graham, 179–201; Shabecoff, *A Fierce Green Fire*, 199; Kaufman, *The Presidency of James Earl Carter*, 202.

69. Jimmy Carter, "Report to the American People," February 2, 1977, and "The Energy Problem: Address to the Nation," April 18, 1977, *Public Papers of the Presidents: Jimmy Carter, 1977–1981*, available at http://www.presidency .ucsb.edu/ws/index.php?pid=7455&st=&st1= and http://www.presidency.ucsb .edu/ws/index.php?pid=7369&st=&st1= (accessed January 27, 2010); Elizabeth Kolbert, "The Road Not Taken," *New Yorker*, March 27, 2000, pp. 33–34 (diary); Kaufman, *The Presidency of James Earl Carter*, 33, 148; Dorothy Wickenden, "Fuel Duel," *New Yorker*, May 22, 2006, pp. 27–28.

70. Bailey and Farber, "Introduction," in *America in the Seventies*, 7; Skidmore, *Reversing Course*, 43 (quotation).

71. Kevin Mattson, *"What The Heck Are You Up To, Mr. President?" Jimmy Carter, America's "Malaise," and the Speech That Should Have Changed the Country* (New York: Bloomsbury, 2009), 144, 185 (Reagan); Jimmy Carter, "Address to the Nation on Energy and National Goals," July 15, 1979, *Public Papers of the Presidents: Jimmy Carter, 1977–1981*, available at http://www.presidency.ucsb.edu/ws/index.php?pid=32596&st=&st1=   (accessed January 28, 2010). For a perceptive analysis of Carter's conservatism, see Andrew J. Bacevich, *The Limits of Power: The End of American Exceptionalism* (New York: Metropolitan, 2008), 30–43.

72. McNeill, *Something New Under the Sun*, 126 (headline), 305; Bill McKibben, *Eaarth: Making a Life on a Tough New Planet* (New York: Times Books, 2010).

73. Associated Press, "Religion Remains Important in U.S.," *Post-Standard* (Syracuse), December 20, 2002, p. A-6; Andrew Kohut and Bruce Stokes, *America against the World: How We Are Different and Why We Are Disliked* (New York: Times Books, 2006), 62–64; Dreyfuss, *Devil's Game*, 160–61; Howard Jones, "Liberty Is 'God's Gift to Humanity,'" *Reviews in American History*, 37, 4 (December 2009): 629 (quotation).

74. Ouimet, *The Rise and Fall of the Brezhnev Doctrine*, 113; *Wall Street Journal*, December 9, 2006, p. A5 (Hezbollah); *New York Times*, May 13, 2007 (Benedict XVI).

75. On the relationship between religious conservatives and the Republican Party, see Andrew Preston, "The Politics of Realism and Religion: Christian Responses to Bush's New World Order," *Diplomatic History* 34, 1 (January 2010): 99, and, more generally, Frank, *What's the Matter with Kansas?* and Sager, *The Elephant in the Room*.

CHAPTER 6. MORE AND LESS EQUAL SINCE THE 1970S

1. Richard W. Stevenson, "Race Not Factor in Aid, Bush Says," *New York Times*, December 13, 2005, p. A30.

2. Bill Carter, "Want Obama in a Punch Line?" *New York Times*, July 15, 2008 (quotation); David Remnick, *The Bridge: The Life and Rise of Barack Obama* (New York: Knopf, 2010).

3. Louis Uchitelle, "Volcker Pushes for Reform, Regretting Past Silence," *New York Times*, July 9, 2010; Public Broadcasting System, "The American Experience: Reagan," http://www.pbs.org/wgbh/amex/reagan/sfeature/quotes .html (accessed March 1, 2010); Ronald Brownstein, *The Second Civil War: How Extreme Partisanship Has Paralyzed Washington and Polarized America* (New York: Penguin, 2007).

4. Collins, *Transforming America*, 5; William Appleman Williams, *The Great Evasion: An Essay on the Contemporary Relevance of Karl Marx and on the Wisdom of Admitting the Heretic into the Dialogue about America's*

Future (Chicago: Quadrangle, 1964); Walter Benn Michaels, *The Trouble with Diversity: How We Learned to Love Identity and Ignore Inequality* (New York: Metropolitan, 2006), 6.

5. On women and domestic work, see Arlie Russell Hochschild with Anne Machung, *The Second Shift*, updated ed. (New York: Penguin, 2003); Sue Shellenbarger, "Giving Credit Where Credit Is Due," *Wall Street Journal*, May 19, 2005, p. D1. For a summary of research on unequal pay between the sexes, see Carl Bialik, "Not All Differences in Earnings Are Created Equal," *Wall Street Journal*, April 10–11, 2010, p. A2.

6. Thomas J. Sugrue, *Not Even Past: Barack Obama and the Burden of Race* (Princeton, NJ: Princeton University Press, 2010), 105; Associated Press, "Black Lawmakers Grow Impatient with White House," *New York Times*, December 10, 2009; Stephen L. Carter, "Affirmative Distraction," *New York Times*, July 6, 2008, p. WK10. For more on enduring black inequality, see Leon F. Litwack, *How Free Is Free? The Long Death of Jim Crow* (Cambridge, MA: Harvard University Press, 2009); Michelle Alexander, *The New Jim Crow: Mass Incarceration in the Age of Colorblindness* (New York: New Press, 2010); William Julius Wilson, *More Than Just Race: Being Black and Poor in the Inner City* (New York: Norton, 2009); Thomas J. Sugrue, *Sweet Land of Liberty: The Forgotten Struggle for Civil Rights in the North* (New York: Random House, 2008), especially the epilogue; Douglas S. Massey, *Categorically Unequal: The American Stratification System* (New York: Russell Sage Foundation, 2008); Harvard Sitkoff, *The Struggle for Black Equality*, rev. ed. (New York: Hill and Wang, 2008); Philip A. Klinkner with Rogers M. Smith, *The Unsteady March: The Rise and Decline of Racial Equality in America* (Chicago: University of Chicago Press, 1999); Andrew Hacker, *Two Nations: Black and White, Separate, Hostile, Unequal* (New York: Scribner, 1992).

7. Lou Cannon, *Official Negligence: How Rodney King and the Riots Changed Los Angeles and the LAPD* (New York: Crown, 1998); Dina Temple-Raston, *A Death in Texas: A Story of Race, Murder and a Small Town's Struggle for Redemption* (New York: Henry Holt, 2002); Dave Hall, Tym Burkey, and Katherine Ramsland, *Into The Devil's Den: How an FBI Informant Got into the Aryan Nations and a Special Agent Got Him Out Alive* (New York: Ballantine, 2008); Jeff Zeleny and Jim Rutenberg, "Officials Say They Saw a Spike in Threats Against Obama Early in His Term," *New York Times*, December 6, 2009, p. 27.

8. Thomas B. Edsall and Brian Faler, "Lott Remarks on Thurmond Echoed 1980 Words," *Washington Post*, December 11, 2002, p. A6; Crespino, *In Search of Another Country*, 274–75.

9. Kruse, *White Flight*; Kruse and Sugrue, eds., *The New Suburban History*; Peter Schrag, *Paradise Lost: California's Experience, America's Future*, paperback ed. (Berkeley: University of California Press, 1999), 10–11, 18, 21–22, 126; Eduardo Porter, "The Divisions That Tighten the Purse Strings," *New York Times*, April 29, 2007, Sec. 3, p. 4.

10. Jorn Madslein, "Military Spending Sets New Record," BBC News, June

8, 2009, http://news.bbc.co.uk/2/hi/business/8086117.stm (accessed March 9, 2010). For more on global military expenditures, see the website of the Stockholm International Peace Research Institute: http://www.sipri.org/.

11. Associated Press, "'You Lie!' on Yale List of Year's Memorable Quotes," *New York Times*, December 16, 2009; Hacker, *The Great Risk Shift*.

12. For an insightful analysis of the enduring importance in the Obama era of what political scientists sometimes call the "submerged state," along with its tendency to undercut its own legitimacy in the eyes of citizens, see Suzanne Mettler, "Reconstituting the Submerged State: The Challenges of Social Policy Reform in the Obama Era," paper delivered at conference on "Reconstituting the American State: The Promise and Dilemmas of Obama's First Year," Nuffield College, Oxford University, Oxford, England, March 10–12, 2010 (in author's possession). See also Julian E. Zelizer, "Rethinking the History of American Conservatism," *Reviews in American History* 38, 2 (June 2010): 374–80; Gareth Davies, *See Government Grow: Education Politics from Johnson to Reagan* (Lawrence: University Press of Kansas, 2007).

13. David Brooks, "Big-Spending Conservative," *New York Times*, April 20, 2009; David Leonhardt, blog, "Greenspan's Mea Culpa," *New York Times*, October 23, 2008, http://economix.blogs.nytimes.com/2008/10/23/greenspans-mea-culpa/ (accessed March 10, 2010); Neil Irwin and Amit R. Paley, "Greenspan Says He Was Wrong on Regulation," *Washington Post*, October 24, 2008; John Cassidy, "After the Blowup," *New Yorker*, January 11, 2010, p. 28 (Posner); Bob Davis et al., "Amid Turmoil, U.S. Turns Away from Decades of Deregulation," *Wall Street Journal*, July 25, 2008, p. 1; Bob Davis et al., "After the Bailouts, Washington's the Boss," *Wall Street Journal*, December 28, 2009, p. 1; Robert Skidelsky, *Keynes: The Return of the Master* (New York: Public Affairs, 2009). On the recession, see Joseph E. Stiglitz, *Freefall: America, Free Markets, and the Sinking of the World Economy* (New York: Norton, 2010); Paul Krugman, *The Return of Depression Economics and the Crisis of 2008* (New York: Norton, 2008); Richard A. Posner, *A Failure of Capitalism: The Crisis of '08 and the Descent into Depression* (Cambridge, MA: Harvard University Press, 2009); Roger Lowenstein, *The End of Wall Street* (New York: Penguin, 2010).

14. Eric Lipton, "With Obama, Regulations Are Back in Fashion," *New York Times*, May 12, 2010.

15. For a related argument focused on American intellectual life, see Daniel T. Rodgers, *Age of Fracture* (Cambridge, MA: Harvard University Press, 2011).

16. James Livingston, *The World Turned Inside Out: American Thought and Culture at the End of the 20th Century* (Lanham, MD: Rowman & Littlefield, 2010), 20; "Work Shift," *Wall Street Journal*, November 12, 2009, p. A21; Sam Roberts, "More Men Marrying Better Educated, Wealthier Wives," *New York Times*, January 19, 2010, p. A20; Nicholas D. Kristof, "Don't Write Off Men Just Yet," *New York Times*, July 21, 2010; Gail Collins, *When Everything Changed: The Amazing Journey of American Women from 1960 to the Present* (New York: Little, Brown, 2009), 291–405.

17. "Fact Sheet: Women in the U.S. Congress 2006," and "Fact Sheet: State-

wide Elective Executive Women: 1969–2004," Center for American Women and Politics, National Information Bank on Women in Public Office, Eagleton Institute of Politics, Rutgers University; Lizette Alvarez, "G.I. Jane Quietly Breaks the Combat Barrier," *New York Times*, August 16, 2009, p. 1.

18. *USA Today*, February 6, 2006, p. 3A; Sam Roberts, "Who Americans Are and What They Do," *New York Times*, December 15, 2006; Yilu Zhao, "Beyond 'Sweetie'," *New York Times*, November 7, 2004, Education Life, p. 20.

19. Katie Thomas, "A City Team's Struggle Shows Disparity in Girls' Sports," *New York Times*, June 14, 2009, p. 1; Ron Dicker, "After a Few Pioneering Steps, Women's Running Took Off," *New York Times*, November 3, 2004, p. C17; Carl Bialik, "Narrowing the Gender Gap," *Wall Street Journal*, March 15, 2004, p. R9; Cindy Lange-Kubick, "Long Road Traveled," *Lincoln Journal Star*, December 18, 2008, p. 1.

20. U.S. Supreme Court, *Meritor Savings Bank v. Vinson*, 477 U.S. 57 (1986); Samuel Walker, *The Rights Revolution: Rights and Community in Modern America* (New York: Oxford University Press, 1998), 44; Steven Lee Myers, "Another Peril in War Zones: Sexual Abuse by Fellow G.I.'s," *New York Times*, December 28, 2009, p. 1.

21. U.S. Supreme Court, *Planned Parenthood of Southeastern Pennsylvania v. Casey*, 505 U.S. 833 (1992).

22. Fukuyama, *The Great Disruption*, 4–6, 64, 103; "Over Half of Women in U.S. Not Married," *Omaha World-Herald*, January 16, 2007, p. 1. On the birth control pill, see Elaine Tyler May, *America and the Pill: A History of Promise, Peril, and Liberation* (New York: Basic Books, 2010).

23. Murphy, *Are We Rome?* 133; Renee C. Romano, *Race Mixing: Black-White Marriage in Postwar America* (Cambridge, MA: Harvard University Press, 2003), 3; Associated Press, "Interracial Marriage Still Rising, but Not as Fast," *New York Times*, May 26, 2010.

24. Dan Eggen and Shailagh Murray, "GOP Moves to Tone Down Criticism of Sotomayor," *Washington Post*, May 29, 2009; *New York Times*, April 12, 2009, p. 1; Timothy Egan, "The Asian Campus," *New York Times Magazine*, January 7, 2007; Kate Phillips, "New Voices in Congress," *New York Times*, January 6, 2009; Associated Press, "Minority Births on Track to Outnumber Whites'," *Lincoln Journal Star*, March 10, 2010, p. A3.

25. Yochi J. Dreazen, "Muslim Population in the Military Raises Difficult Issues," *Wall Street Journal*, November 7–8, 2009, p. A13.

26. Jeffrey Toobin, "Sex and the Supremes," *New Yorker*, August 1, 2005, p. 34.

27. Anderson, *The Pursuit of Fairness*, 223 (quotation); U.S. Supreme Court, *Bowers v. Hardwick*, 478 U.S. 186 (1986); U.S. Supreme Court, *Lawrence v. Texas*, 539 U.S. 558 (2003); David A. J. Richards, *The Sodomy Cases: Bowers v. Hardwick and Lawrence v. Texas* (Lawrence: University Press of Kansas, 2009); Charles M. Blow, "Gay? Whatever, Dude," *New York Times*, June 4, 2010; Andrew Gelman, Jeffrey Lax, and Justin Phillips, "Over Time, a Gay Marriage Groundswell," *New York Times*, August 22, 2010, p. WK3.

28. Ruy Teixeira, ed., *Red, Blue, and Purple America: The Future of Elec-*

tion Demographics (Washington, DC: Brookings Institution, 2008), p. 18; Margaret Talbot, "A Risky Proposal," *New Yorker*, January 18, 2010, p. 42; Catherine E. Rymph, "Phyllis Schlafly's Crusade," *Reviews in American History* 34, 4 (December 2006): 571; Yochi J. Dreazen, "Military Chief Says Gay Ban Should Go," *Wall Street Journal*, February 3, 2010, p. 1 (first Mullen); Frank Rich, "Smoke the Bigots Out of the Closet," *New York Times*, February 2, 2010 (second Mullen).

29. Akira Iriye, *Global Community: The Role of International Organizations in the Making of the Contemporary World* (Berkeley: University of California Press, 2002), 149–50; Johnson, *The Sorrows of Empire*, 161; William J. Bernstein, *A Splendid Exchange: How Trade Shaped the World* (New York: Atlantic Monthly Press, 2008), 360; Scott McCartney, "The Golden Age of Flight," *Wall Street Journal*, July 22, 2010, p. D1; Emma Rothschild, "Can We Transform the Auto-Industrial Society?" *New York Review of Books*, February 26, 2009, p. 8; Joseph Kahn, "Four Visionaries with Cloudy Visions," *New York Times*, February 28, 2007 (quotation); U.S.-China Business Council, http://www.uschina.org/statistics/tradetable.html (accessed March 15, 2010); U.S. Census Bureau, "Foreign Trade Statistics," http://www.census.gov/foreign-trade/statistics/highlights/top/top0810yr.html (accessed March 15, 2010).

30. Lindsey, *The Age of Abundance*, 273; *New York Times*, August 1, 2007; Murphy, *Are We Rome?* 151; Hodgson, *More Equal Than Others*, 20–21; U.S. Department of Labor, Bureau of Labor Statistics, "Union Members Summary," http://www.bls.gov/news.release/union2.nr0.htm (accessed March 15, 2010); Jefferson Cowie, "Solidarity Strikes Out," *American Prospect*, January 1, 2002, p. 41.

31. Ian Urbina, "States Face Drop in Gambling Revenues," *New York Times*, September 10, 2009; Diana B. Henriques, "Temptation Near for Military's Problem Gamblers," *New York Times*, October 19, 2005.

32. M. J. Stephey, "America's Quirky Alcohol Laws," *Time*, July 9, 2009; Eric Burns, *The Spirits of America: A Social History of Alcohol* (Philadelphia: Temple University Press, 2003).

33. Tax Foundation, "Federal Capital Gains Tax Collections, 1954–2006," http://www.taxfoundation.org/taxdata/show/2089.html (accessed March 16, 2010); "Easing the Impact of Higher Tax Rates," *New York Times*, October 29, 2009, p. 8.

34. Paul Krugman, "Reagan Did It," *New York Times*, June 1, 2009; Richard W. Stevenson, "For Bush, a Long Embrace of Social Security Plan," *New York Times*, February 27, 2005, p. 1.

35. Adam Liptak, "After 34 Years, A Plainspoken Justice Gets Louder," *New York Times*, January 25, 2010 (Stevens); Jeffrey Rosen, "Supreme Court Inc.," *New York Times Magazine*, March 16, 2008, p. 41; Ronald Dworkin, "The 'Devastating Decision'," *New York Review of Books*, February 25, 2010, p. 39; Ronald Dworkin, "The Decision That Threatens Democracy," *New York Review of Books*, May 13, 2010, pp. 63–67.

36. *Catch-22*, director Mike Nichols (1970); P.W. Singer, *Corporate Warriors: The Rise of the Privatized Military Industry* (Ithaca, NY: Cornell University Press, 2003); Robert Young Pelton, *Licensed to Kill: Hired Guns in the*

War on Terror (New York: Crown, 2006); Alexander Tabarrok, ed., *Changing the Guard: Private Prisons and the Control of Crime* (Oakland, CA: Independent Institute, 2003); Timothy Egan, "Paying on the Highway to Get Out of First Gear," *New York Times*, April 28, 2005, p. 1.

37. Louise Story, "Anywhere the Eye Can See," *New York Times*, January 14, 2007; Murray A. Sperber, *Beer and Circus: How Big-Time College Sports Is Crippling Undergraduate Education* (New York: Henry Holt, 2000), 34–35.

38. Drew Gilpin Faust, "The University's Crisis of Purpose," *New York Times Book Review*, September 6, 2009, p. 19; Louis Menand, *The Marketplace of Ideas: Reform and Resistance in the American University* (New York: Norton, 2010), 18, 145; *New York Times*, June 11, 2006; "Rising College Costs: A Federal Role?" *New York Times*, February 3, 2010; Levine, *The Price of Privilege*, 47; Sam Roberts, "Who Americans Are and What They Do," *New York Times*, December 15, 2006.

39. "Overweight by the Numbers," *Consumer Reports*, January 2004, p. 13; Michael Pollan, *Food Rules: An Eater's Manual* (New York: Penguin, 2009), 22, 123; Jane E. Brody, "Drink Your Milk: A Refrain for All Ages, Now More than Ever," *New York Times*, January 7, 2003, p. F5; "Life by the Numbers in America," *Omaha World-Herald*, December 9, 2004, p. 1; *Wall Street Journal*, December 12, 2006, p. D1; Amanda Hesser, "The Commander in Chef," *New York Times*, May 31, 2009, p. WK10; Daniel Gross, "Cigarettes, Taxes and Thin French Women," *New York Times*, July 24, 2005, p. BU5; Erica Goode, "The Gorge-Yourself Environment," *New York Times*, July 22, 2003, p. D1; Steven Gray, "For The Health-Unconscious, Era of Mammoth Burger Is Here," *Wall Street Journal*, January 27, 2005, p. B1 (quotation); Randolph E. Schmid, "America's Pets Are Getting Pudgier," *Lincoln Journal Star*, September 9, 2003, p. 6A; Greg Critser, *Fat Land: How Americans Became the Fattest People in the World* (Boston: Houghton Mifflin, 2003).

40. "Give Us Your Thin, Then About 10 Years," *Omaha World-Herald*, December 15, 2004, p. 4A (quotation); Alison Langley, "It's a Fat World, After All," *New York Times*, July 20, 2003, Sec. 3, p. 1; Elaine Sciolino, "France Battles a Problem That Grows and Grows: Fat," *New York Times*, January 25, 2006, p. 4; Deborah Ball, "Swedish Kids Show Difficulty of Fighting Fat," *Wall Street Journal*, December 2, 2003, p. 1; Gautam Naik, "New Obesity Boom in Arab Countries Has Old Ancestry," *Wall Street Journal*, December 29, 2004, p. 1; Larry Rohter, "Beaches for the Svelte, Where the Calories Are Showing," *New York Times*, January 13, 2005, p. A4.

41. D'Emilio and Freedman, *Intimate Matters*, 328–29; "New Network Will Showcase Greed, Lust, Sex," *Wall Street Journal*, February 23, 2006, p. B1; David Cay Johnston, "Is Live Sex On-Demand Coming to Hotel TVs?" *New York Times*, January 17, 2007.

42. Stephanie Coontz, "The Heterosexual Revolution," *New York Times*, July 5, 2005, p. A21; "Foot-Dragging on the Way to the Altar," *Omaha World-Herald*, December 2, 2004, p. 2; "Number of Births Out of Wedlock Slows," *Lincoln Journal Star*, November 26, 2004, p. 4A.

43. Jane Meyer and Jill Abramson, *Strange Justice: The Selling of Clarence*

Thomas (Boston: Houghton Mifflin, 1994); Janice M. Irvine, *Talk About Sex: The Battles over Sex Education in the United States* (Berkeley: University of California Press, 2002); Kenneth Starr, *The Starr Report: The Findings of Independent Counsel Kenneth W. Starr on President Clinton and the Lewinsky Affair* (New York: PublicAffairs, 1998).

44. Erik Monkkonen, "Homicide: Explaining America's Exceptionalism," *American Historical Review* 111, 1 (February 2006): 76; Michiko Kakutani, "That Bloody Shower and Its Violent Offspring," *New York Times*, December 18, 2009 (quotation). See also Franklin E. Zimring and Gordon Hawkins, *Crime Is Not the Problem: Lethal Violence in America* (New York: Oxford University Press, 1997).

45. Mark Atwood Lawrence, *The Vietnam War: A Concise International History* (New York: Oxford University Press, 2008), 177; Bernard Weintraub, "30 Years Later, Cake and Credit Cards in Saigon," *New York Times*, May 1, 2005, p. 3; James Hookway and Thu Nguyen, "For American-Style Movies, It's Good Morning Vietnam," *Wall Street Journal*, March 12, 2007.

46. Gottschalk, *The Prison and the Gallows*, 2–4; Joshua Guetzkow and Bruce Western, "The Political Consequences of Mass Imprisonment," in *Remaking America*, ed. Soss et al., 228–29; Adam Liptak, "Inmate Count in U.S. Dwarfs Other Nations," *New York Times*, April 23, 2008 (de Tocqueville); Roger N. Lancaster, "Preface," in *New Landscapes of Inequality: Neoliberalism and the Erosion of Democracy in America*, ed. Jane L. Collins, Micaela di Leonardo, and Brett Williams (Santa Fe: School for Advanced Research Press, 2008), xi.

47. Jason DeParle, "The American Prison Nightmare," *New York Review of Books*, April 12, 2007, pp. 33–36; Mark McDonald, "China Leads the World in Executions, Report Says," *New York Times*, March 30, 2010; Christopher Hayes, "Webb's Prison Crusade," *Nation*, April 15, 2009 (Webb).

48. Liptak, "Inmate Count in U.S. Dwarfs Other Nations"; Adam Liptak, "Lifers as Teenagers," *New York Times*, October 17, 2007; Adam Liptak, "Locked Away Forever after Crimes as Teenagers, *New York Times*, October 3, 2005, p. 1; DeParle, "The American Prison Nightmare"; Charles M. Blow, "Getting Smart on Crime," *New York Times*, August 15, 2009.

49. Bob Davis, "Lagging Behind the Wealthy, Many Use Debt to Catch Up," *Wall Street Journal*, May 17, 2005, p. 1; Hacker, *The Great Risk Shift*, 94.

50. "For Decades the Richest Pulled Away," *New York Times*, August 20, 2009; Bob David and Robert Frank, "Income Gap Shrinks in Slump at the Expense of the Wealthy," *Wall Street Journal*, September 10, 2009, p. 1; Catherine Rampell, "Income Inequality Reached High in 2009," *New York Times*, September 28, 2010; David Cay Johnston, "Tax Rates for Top 400 Earners Fall as Income Soars, IRS Data," http://tax.com/taxcom/features.nsf/Articles/0 DEC0EAA7E4D7A2B852576CD00714692?OpenDocument (accessed March 19, 2010); Robert B. Reich, *Aftershock: The Next Economy and America's Future* (New York: Knopf, 2010) 220–21; James Surowiecki, "Soak the Very, Very Rich," *New Yorker*, August 16 and 23, 2010, p. 33. For further discussion of this growing inequality and its direct link to the 1970s, see Jacob S. Hacker and Paul Pierson, *Winner-Take-All-Politics: How Washington Made the Rich*

Richer—and Turned Its Back on the Middle Class (New York: Simon & Schuster, 2010).

51. Teixeira, ed., *Red, Blue, and Purple America*, 110; "Minimum Wage Value Lowest since '40s," *Lincoln Journal Star*, July 23, 2006, p. 11A; "Easing the Impact of Higher Tax Rates," New York Times, October 29, 2009, p. 8. See also Nolan McCarty, Keith T. Poole, and Howard Rosenthal, *Polarized America: The Dance of Ideology and Unequal Riches* (Cambridge, MA: MIT Press, 2006).

52. Baker, *The United States since 1980*, 6–9; Lindsey, *The Age of Abundance*, 283; Helen Epstein, "America's Prisons: Is There Hope?" *New York Review of Books*, June 11, 2009, p. 31; Edward N. Wolff, "The Rich Get Richer: And Why the Poor Don't," *American Prospect*, February 12, 2001; Hacker, *The Great Risk Shift*, 14–15, 113; Peter Gottschalk, "Inequality, Income Growth, and Mobility: The Basic Facts," *Journal of Economic Perspectives*, 11, 2 (Spring 1997): 21–22, 34; U.S. Census Bureau, "Poverty: 2007 and 2008 American Community Surveys," http://www.census.gov/prod/2009pubs/acsbr08-1.pdf (accessed March 19, 2010); Bread for the World Institute, "Poverty in the United States," http://hungerreport.org/2009/chapters/us-poverty/62
-current-reform (accessed March 19, 2010); "The Return of the Millionaires," *Los Angeles Times*, June 10, 2010; Amy Glasmeier, *An Atlas of Poverty in America: One Nation, Pulling Apart, 1960–2003* (New York: Routledge, 2005). Japan also saw sharp increases in poverty during the past generation, reaching rates close to those of the United States. This was so potentially embarrassing for the Tokyo government that it kept the information secret for over a decade, admitting the scale of the problem only in the fall of 2009. Martin Fackler, "Japan Tries to Face up to Growing Poverty Problem," *New York Times*, April 22, 2010. On the correlation of economic inequality with a variety of social ills in industrialized societies, see Richard Wilkinson and Kate Pickett, *The Spirit Level: Why Greater Equality Makes Societies Stronger* (New York: Bloomsbury, 2009).

53. Edsall and Edsall, *Chain Reaction*, 131 (Reagan); G. William Domhoff, "Wealth, Income, and Power," http://sociology.ucsc.edu/whorulesamerica/power/wealth.html (accessed April 16, 2010); "Too Much" (online newsletter of the Institute for Policy Studies), January 5, 2009, www.toomuchonline.org (accessed January 6, 2009); Miriam Jordan, "California Dreams," *Wall Street Journal*, July 20, 2005, p.1.

54. Rosier, *Serving Their Country*, 25 (Gates, italics in original); Putnam, *Bowling Alone*, 260; Greg Winter, "Jacuzzi U.? A Battle of Perks to Lure Students," *New York Times*, October 5, 2003, p. 1; William Grimes, "Dead, Buried or Risen Again, Garbage Is Forever," *New York Times*, July 15, 2005, p. B32 (review of Elizabeth Royte, *Garbage Land: On the Secret Trail of Trash* [2005]); Bruce Mazlish, "Consumerism in the Context of the Global Ecumene," in *The Global History Reader*, ed. Mazlish and Akira Iriye (New York: Routledge, 2004), 126–27; George W. Bush, "Remarks to Airline Employees in Chicago, Illinois," September 27, 2001, The American Presidency Project, http://www.presidency.ucsb.edu/ws/index.php?pid=65084 (accessed March 22, 2010).

55. Center for Disease Control and Prevention, NCHS Data Brief, "Changing Patterns of Nonmarital Childbearing in the United States," May 2009, http://www.cdc.gov/nchs/data/databriefs/db18.htm (accessed May 18, 2009); Andrew J. Cherlin, *The Marriage-Go-Round: The State of Marriage and the Family in America Today* (New York: Knopf, 2009); Rothschild, "Can We Transform the Auto-Industrial Society?" 8; Sam Roberts, "Who Americans Are and What They Do," *New York Times*, December 15, 2006 (Putnam); Kruse, *White Flight*, 259.

Conclusion

1. Michaels, *The Trouble with Diversity*, 75; David Brooks, "The Sandra Bullock Trade," *New York Times*, March 30, 2010.

2. U.S. Supreme Court, *Regents of the University of California v. Bakke*, 438 U.S. 265 (1978); Howard Ball, *The* Bakke *Case: Race, Education, and Affirmative Action* (Lawrence: University Press of Kansas, 2000); Terry H. Anderson, *The Pursuit of Fairness: A History of Affirmative Action* (New York: Oxford University Press, 2004); Anthony T. Kronman, *Education's End: Why Our Colleges and Universities Have Given up on the Meaning of Life* (New Haven, CT: Yale University Press, 2007), 140–41.

3. Lyndon B. Johnson, commencement address at Howard University, June 4, 1965, *Public Papers of the Presidents, 1965, Book II*, available at "The American Presidency Project," http://www.presidency.ucsb.edu/ws/index .php?pid=27021&st=&st1= (accessed April 3, 2010); Frederickson, *Racism*, 143 (Blackmun).

4. Hugh Davis Graham, *Collision Course: The Strange Convergence of Affirmative Action and Immigration Policy in America* (New York: Oxford University Press, 2002); U.S. Supreme Court, *Grutter v. Bollinger*, 539 U.S. 306 (2003).

5. For an insightful analysis of how "market utopianism" often led, ironically, to an increase in the size and reach of government, see Lawrence D. Brown and Lawrence R. Jacobs, *The Private Abuse of the Public Interest: Market Myths and Policy Muddles* (Chicago: University of Chicago Press, 2008).

6. One final example of the trend toward self-celebration is emblematic. In 1950, pollsters asked thousands of teenagers if they thought of themselves as an "important person." Twelve percent said yes. In the late 1980s, the same question elicited agreement from 80 percent of girls and 77 percent of boys. David Brooks, "The Gospel of Mel Gibson," *New York Times*, July 15, 2010.

7. Tony Judt, *Ill Fares The Land* (New York: Penguin, 2010).